Samizdat and an Independent Society in Central and Eastern Europe

Samizdat and an Independent Society in Central and Eastern Europe

H. Gordon Skilling

Ohio State University Press
Columbus

First published in the U.S.A. by Ohio State University Press.
First published in Great Britain by The Macmillan Press Ltd.

Library of Congress Cataloging-in-Publication Data
Skilling, H. Gordon (Harold Gordon), 1912–
Samizdat and an independent society in Central and Eastern Europe
H. Gordon Skilling.
p.   cm.
Includes bibliographies and index.
ISBN 0–8142–0487–2
1. Communication—Political aspects—Europe, Eastern.   2. Freedom
of information—Europe, Eastern.   3. Underground literature—Europe,
Eastern—History and criticism.   4. Europe, Eastern—Politics and
government—1945–   I. Title.
P95.82.E852S55 1989   88–27443
001.51′0947—dc 19   CIP

Printed in Hong Kong

Václav Benda
    Václav Havel
        Miroslav Kusý
            Peter Pithart
                Vilém Prečan
            Jiřina Šiklová
        Milan Šimečka
     Ludvík Vaculík
Jiří Dienstbier

'The inner strength of a nation consists in its cultural development, its energy and zeal, its morality and good conduct. He who concerns himself with the enlargement of these qualities contributes most to future freedom. Let each of us do this at home and in our surroundings; no power can hinder us in doing this.'—Tomaš G. Masaryk, *Karel Havlíček*.

'The humanistic ideal requires us – ever, in everything and everywhere – systematically to resist evil and the inhumanity of society, both our own and foreign, and of its organs – cultural, political, national and church – all of them. Humanity is not a matter of sentiment, but of work, and again of work.'—Tomaš G. Masaryk, *Česká otázka*.

Those men form a moral government if they maintain in a subjugated nation a government over itself; if they repeat day and night, that the nation has in its own breast the will to act which nothing is able to suppress, that it need not descend to relying on foreign help, but can rely on its own strength alone; if they awaken in the nation, through its own act of generation, a feeling of strength and of its own divinity.'—Bronisław F. Trentowski, cited by Karel Havlíček, Masaryk, *Havlíček*.

Contents

List of Tables

Preface

Independent activity by individuals and groups within the 'totalitarian' societies of Central and Eastern Europe is a fascinating phenomenon, exciting the imagination and calling for study. These activities are said to constitute in modest form an 'independent society', or, in other words, a 'second culture', or an alternative or parallel community, and are regarded by some as constituting the embryonic elements of a 'civil society'. This was conceived as sharply distinguished from the 'first' or 'official' society, the party and the state, which sought to establish or retain total control of society as a whole. In writing this book my purpose was to analyse this phenomenon more deeply, to compare and contrast its scope and character in each of the countries of the region, and to estimate the degree to which it could properly be conceived of as a genuine independent society and as a precursor of a future civil society.

As I write these lines, extraordinary things are happening in the Soviet Union and in some parts of Central and Eastern Europe which may radically transform the social and political scene and place my study in a somewhat different light. During the time of the preparation of this book independent activities were severely condemned and persecuted with an intensity varying according to the country. Except for Poland, during Solidarity, and even afterwards, there seemed little prospect of the emergence in the near future of anything resembling a fully independent or civil society. The 'official' and 'unofficial' spheres seemed to be sharply divided one from the other, with little or no contact between life in each one. Only in Poland was the independent realm alive and vibrant, and the official structures permeated by freer tendencies, with frequent cross-cutting and interacting among the two spheres. Elsewhere the picture was much more black and white, with grey areas forming the exceptions.

At the present time, both in the Soviet Union and in several countries of Central Europe, there are more and more signs of autonomous actions within the official party and state institutions and there has been a veritable outburst of new forms of unofficial activity. The fusion of independent activities within and outside official life has led to a greater blurring of the line dividing the two cultures and the two societies. As a result the independent society, where it exists, *may* become even more independent and have a greater impact on the realm of authority. The first or official society *may* become more tolerant of its rivals and more receptive to their pressures. The second part of my title may become less appropriate as the independent society fuses more and more with the official and the whole of society increasingly escapes the thrall of the state. Even short of a pluralist or civil society this would mark a major shift in state–society relationships. All of this may, of course, prove to be wishful thinking. New repression may set the clock back and render the vestiges of an independent society less significant in the short run but still potentially important for the future.

In writing this book I was indebted, of course, to all the brave souls who provided me with its subject-matter and inspired me by their activities in culture, scholarship and politics. They served as a fount of information, and their writings, in *samizdat*, the principal documentary sources. Many of them, especially in Czechoslovakia, but also in other countries of the area, I came to know personally and to admire greatly. The book is dedicated to a few Czechs and Slovaks whose ideas have been of special value and whose friendship I have renewed, with my wife, Sally, during many trips, including the most recent ones in 1984 and 1987. Some of them joined with us in the latter year in celebrating the fiftieth anniversary of our first visit to Czechoslovakia and of our wedding in the Old Town Hall in Prague. I am thankful, too, to those Czechs, Hungarians and Poles who responded to my *anketa* (inquiry) on an independent society. I was also inspired by the writings of Thomas G. Masaryk, 'the perpetual dissenter' of the pre-1914 years, who has become an ever greater inspiration to many modern-day Czech and Slovak dissidents.

I owe a deep debt of gratitude to Dr Vilém Prečan, Czech historian, director of the Documentation Centre for the Promotion of Independent Czechoslovak Literature in Scheinfeld, West Germany. He has become a principal intermediary between the independent spirits at home and their friends and supporters abroad and has built up a most complete archive of *samizdat* materials. Thanks should also go to others who receive, distribute and translate these materials – Ivan Medek in Vienna, the Palach Press in London, and Radio Free Europe in Munich. I am grateful to the editors for permission to publish, in revised or partial form, articles which previously appeared in *Cross Currents* (Ann Arbor, Michigan), *Problems of Communism* (Washington, DC), *Canadian Slavonic Papers* (Toronto) and *International Journal of Politics* (White Plains, New York).

There are many other persons to whom I am obliged for contributing to this book. First and foremost is my wife, Sally, who gave me encouragement and advice and laboured long and hard to make the manuscript accurate and readable. Others deserving warm thanks are Archie Brown, of St Antony's College, Oxford, for his initial encouragement to seek its publication; Tim Farmiloe, publishing director, for his generous backing of the publication, and Susan Dickinson and Beverly Smith, editors, for their friendly cooperation; Keith Povey, of Bratton Clovelly, Devon, for supervising the editing, proof-reading and indexing of the book; Helena Wilson, of Toronto, for the photograph on the jacket, and Norman Davis, hardware merchant, and John Carter, Western Office Equipment, for loaning the typewriter, chain and padlock; Mildred Lewis, of the Department of Political Science, University of Toronto, for cheerfully performing administrative tasks. Special recognition should go to Luba Hussel, 'curator' of the Czechoslovak *samizdat* collections in the Thomas Fisher Rare Book Library at the University of Toronto; to Edith Klein, of the *Canadian Slavonic Papers*, for her splendid editing of the manuscript; and to Gen Kikkawa, of Hiroshima Shudo University, Hiroshima, Japan, for his research assistance during his study leave in Toronto. Finally I am under obligation to the Social Science and Humanities Research Council, Ottawa, and the Research Administration, University of Toronto, for grants which, although given for other historical research, enabled me to travel to Vienna, London and Prague, and to Scheinfeld, West Germany, and thus to produce this book as a by product.

Toronto, Canada H. GORDON SKILLING

Part I

Samizdat in the USSR, China and Central Europe

1 *Samizdat*: A Return to the Pre-Gutenberg Era?

On 22 December 1848, Dostoyevsky was sentenced to 'death' for having associated with a circle which met to talk of socialism and to criticize conditions in Russia, for having circulated a letter by the journalist Belinsky to Gogol which was extremely critical of the Orthodox Church, and for having attempted to circulate anti-government writings with the aid of a private press. Although the sentence was in fact eight years of penal servitude, this was later commuted to four years in jail and four as a private soldier. Dostoyevsky served his full sentence and dropped out of Russian literature for some nine years.[1]

This may be considered an early example in Russian history of what we would now call *samizdat*, the distribution of uncensored writings on one's own, without the medium of a publishing house and without permission of the authorities. Although this is not an entirely new phenomenon, and in varied forms has been the very stuff of revolutionary movements throughout history, in its modern form of *samizdat* it is a new medium of communication, emerging on a large scale in Soviet Russia in the mid-1960s and in Poland, Czechoslovakia, China, and other communist countries in the mid-1970s.

The action of Dostoyevsky in circulating illegally anti-government writings was not the first such case in Russian history. In 1790 a famous anti-serfdom book by Alexander Radishchev, *A Journey from Petersburg to Moscow*, after being confiscated by the police, was passed around in the few remaining copies, and in manuscript form, among educated circles – 'an 18th century example of *samizdat*,' writes the historian Isabel de Madariaga.[2] Before and after the Decembrist revolt in 1825, Pushkin and Griboyedov circulated manuscripts privately to avoid the censor. Alexander Herzen's journal, *Kolokol* (The Bell), was printed in London and copies were smuggled back into Russia. During later decades of the nineteenth century, many unpublished manifestos and tracts, usually produced on illegal printing presses or abroad, were distributed in Russia, despite severe punishment by the police. Lenin's Bolshevik party and other revolutionary movements depended on such underground publications to propagate their views and to advance the cause of revolution.[3]

This phenomenon did not disappear under communist rule. During the early 1920s the typewritten works of Osip Mandelshtam and other writers were passed around in what was then called 'Underwood', after the typewriter used. Mandelshtam was arrested, and eventually died in prison, his crime having been to write an anti-Stalin poem which circulated only by word of mouth and in a few manuscript copies.[4] The author Marina Tsvetayeva recalled that in the 1920s: 'I copy out poems sewn together in notebooks and sell them. We call this "overcoming Gutenberg".'[5] She also spoke of memorising her own work or that of others for eventual publication. During the years of Stalinist terror, small groups of intellectuals passed around typed literature which was forbidden or 'was not publishable'.[6] At this time, however, most literary works which could not be published were written 'for the desk drawer' (*v yashchik*), to take a phrase which had long been used in Russia.[7] In fact, however, such manuscripts had to be hidden in the safest possible place, somewhere far more secure than an ordinary drawer. Solzhenitsyn, for instance, reported the difficulties facing an 'underground writer', including the constant effort to conceal the very existence of his writings and to hide the actual manuscripts. He also wrote of memorising his writings, while imprisoned in a labour camp, where he committed many thousands of words to memory in the hope of eventually recording and even publishing them.[8] It was only after Stalin's death that manuscripts began to pass from hand to hand, and were copied, without permission of the author, by editors and by others anxious to read them. In the later 1950s and early 1960s this became increasingly the pattern of distribution of unpublished manuscripts, and several typewritten magazines, notably *Syntax*, *Phoenix*, and the *Sphinxes*, were issued and disseminated surreptitiously.[9] These were but 'timid shoots' of what later became the massive production of *samizdat*, as 'a self-contained and singularly original sphere for the realisation of society's spiritual and intellectual life'.[10]

THE MEANING OF *SAMIZDAT*

The term *samizdat* is said to have emerged in the late 1950s, when a Moscow poet described the bound, typewritten publication of his poems, 'Samsebyaizdat,' i.e., 'publishing house for oneself'.[11] This term was derived by analogy from the acronyms used for official publishing houses, such as *Gosizdat* (State Publishing House), *Politizdat*, *Voyenizdat*, or *Gosmedizdat* (publishing house for politics, military affairs, or medical writings). The same poet coined the term *samizdat*, with the same meaning. It was the latter word which came into general usage to refer to unofficial publications of all kinds (not limited to those by an author himself) and to the entire process of unofficial publication.[12] There is no English equivalent, other than the awkward 'self-publication'. In French and German, the Russian word is normally used, although there are the alternatives *auto-édition* and *Selbstverlag*.[13] *Samizdat* is a non-word in the official Soviet vocabulary (except for the occasional scornful reference to 'so-called *samizdat*' in Russian newspapers),[14] and does not appear in Soviet dictionaries.

For the sake of completeness in this etymological interlude, one might mention other Russian acronyms, none of which is officially recognised in Soviet dictionaries or reference books. Although at first most items of *samizdat* appeared separately, on an individual basis, and many still do, the practice of publishing a number of them together, in a typewritten journal or book, later developed and was soon nicknamed '*kolizdat*', i.e., publication in quantity.[15] Another term, '*radizdat*', referred to books and other materials, as well as music, which were broadcast by foreign radios and copied by listeners. Two other terms, '*magnitizdat*' and '*magnizdat*', were used to cover materials, especially music and verse, reproduced by tape recorder, either from foreign broadcasts or from reading and playing at home.[16] Finally the word '*tamizdat*' was coined to denote books published 'over there', i.e., abroad, which often found their way back to Russia in printed form or were reproduced in *samizdat*.

A turning point in the development of *samizdat* was the decision of Boris Pasternak in 1958 to publish his book, *Doctor Zhivago*, abroad, after he had failed to get it published at home through official channels.[17] Other authors had entertained some hope, after the death of Stalin, that their work would be published officially at home, for instance, in the magazine *Novy mir*, edited by Alexander Tvardovsky. Some, including Solzhenitsyn, had succeeded, to a limited extent, although always after great difficulty and with substantial emendation at the editors' request. As long as this hope existed, publication in *samizdat* or abroad was avoided lest it jeopardise the chance of publication at home. After the fall of Khrushchev, however, when such possibilities declined, the only alternative seemed to be *samizdat* or *tamizdat*.[18]

The term *samizdat* therefore does not have a precise and unambiguous meaning, having gradually expanded from its original meaning of an author's publication of his own works to encompass unofficial dissemination not only of any books in typewritten form within Russia, but also copies (typewritten or printed) of books published abroad by émigrés or by Russians still living in Russia.[19] It could also include books written earlier, which were either not published at the time or were later banned under Stalin, or even foreign literature which could not be translated and officially published in the USSR. *Samizdat* has been defined succinctly as 'typewritten copies, transferred by hand',[20] or, more fully, as 'unapproved material reproduced unofficially . . . by hand, typewriter, mimeograph or occasionally by Xerography'.[21]

DEVELOPMENT OF RUSSIAN *SAMIZDAT*

The evolving content of Russian *samizdat* has been fully analysed by the Russian émigré and former *samizdat* author Michael Meerson-Aksenov.[22] The first phase, already referred to, was mainly literary in character, beginning with Boris Pasternak's *Doctor Zhivago* and comprising eventually books by Solzhenitsyn, A. Sinyavsky, and Juri Daniel (who wrote abroad under the pseudonyms Abraham Tertz and Nicholas Arzhak); the memoirs of N. Mandelshtam; the novels of V. Maksimov; earlier works which had never been published by M. Bulgakov, O. Mandelshtam, and A. Akhmatova; and works of contemporary poets, such as Josef Brodsky, Bulat Okudzhava, and others. As another émigré wrote, there could be no doubt that 'the real "specific gravity" of Russian literature was now to be found jointly in *samizdat* and *tamizdat*'.[23]

This 'literary *samizdat*', which was in a sense removed from politics, was followed, and supplemented, by a second phase of 'social *samizdat*,' which was more political in content, and consisted of letters, appeals, declarations, and so on. It began to 'fulfill the function not only of a book but of a newspaper', especially with the publication of *The Chronicle of Current Events* from 1968 on. This bulletin, which appeared every two weeks or so, became the main organ of the human rights movement in the Soviet Union and reported on violations of human rights, house searches, arrests, trials, and imprisonments. The documents included were almost always signed, with addresses given, and represented therefore, it was said, 'the greatest internal freedom, a complete independence, not only from government, but from various groups which . . . determine limits of press accessibility in the West'.[24] Although interrupted by severe repression for a year and a half, the *Chronicle* reappeared in 1972, and came out so regularly that it was published abroad in English translation and could be ordered on subscription. Its circulation was estimated as running from 1000 to 10 000, and its readership as high as 10 000 to 100 000. The Chronicle was joined by other *samizdat* bulletins with national and religious emphasis, notably the Ukrainian Herald (*Ukrainsky Visnyk*),[25] the Zionist Herald of Exodus, the Chronicle of the Lithuanian Catholic Church, and the Herald of the Evangelical Christian Baptists, and the *Jews in the USSR*. An important journal, of Russian nationalist outlook, *Veche*, appeared from 1971 to 1974.

Finally, there emerged a third phase of *samizdat*, in which varied social programmes and expositions of independent social and political thought appeared, in Meerson-Aksenov's words, as 'the foundation of a growing independent consciousness in the intelligentsia as an emancipation from party-government ideology'.[26] Outstanding examples were the legal writings of A. Sakharov, V. Chalidze, and I. Shafarevich, the political works of Solzhenitsyn, and the historical studies of Roy Medvedev.

It could be said that by 1967 *samizdat* had started to become 'the mainstream of independent thought and opinion, of free uncensored Russian literature'. As the writer Georgii Vladimov wrote to the Writers Union in that year, 'creative freedom . . . is being realized . . . in the activity of the so-called *samizdat*'. He went on: 'There are now two kinds of art in the country. One is free and uninhibited . . . whose distribution and influence depend only on its genuinely artistic qualities. And the other one, commanded and paid for . . . is badly mutilated, suppressed and oppressed. It is not hard to predict which of these two arts will be victorious.'[27]

In 1947 Alexander Sinyavsky, in exile, wrote of 'a literature which had not long ago appeared in our country . . . modestly and simply called *samizdat* . . . the second literature'. 'It is difficult to think of a more precise and inoffensive name than *samizdat* which says only that a man has sat down to write everything he wants, as he sees fit

. . . we are already witnessing the planning of something great, fantastic and incomparable: the beginnings of Russian literature, which once before in the nineteenth century enriched mankind. Now once again it is going through its birth pangs.'[28]

Samizdat was not merely a voice for literature, but a vehicle for the expression of all forms of dissent and protest. It was, according to one of its exiled practitioners, Ludmilla Alexeyeva, 'the backbone of the human rights movement', its channels providing the 'connecting links essential for organizational work' and 'spreading out silently and invisibly . . . like mushroom spores'. *Samizdat* served as the medium of communication for the Moscow Helsinki Watch group (1976) and the other Helsinki groups formed in other Republics; for other organisations and groupings (see below, Chapter 8); for the movements of national protest among the Ukrainians, Lithuanians and others; for religious groups, such as the Catholics, Adventists, Pentecostalists and Baptists; and for the movement for emigration of Germans and Jews.

A detailed study of the content of *samizdat*, with the texts of important items, can be found in several places. F. J. M. Feldbrugge, in a book of over 250 pages, makes a thematic analysis of *samizdat* as a form of 'political dissent' or 'opposition'.[29] Meerson-Aksenov and Shragin, in a volume of more than 600 pages, give the texts of important items of political, social, and religious thought in Russian *samizdat*.[30]

Stephen F. Cohen examined in detail the content of A Political Diary (*Politichesky Dnevnik*) which was edited by Roy Medvedev between 1964 and 1971 and circulated among some forty to fifty people, mainly party members. This bulky journal, the very existence of which was not known until 1971, dealt with political questions, such as Stalinism, neo-Stalinism, and currents of dissent.[31] Later Medvedev edited the journal, *xx Century*, with essays expressing the views of the Socialist opposition.[32]

The rise of *samizdat* can also be roughly measured in terms of the quantitative growth of the material known in the West. According to estimates given by Feldbrugge, the various types of dissent documents began with a modest 47 items in 1965, doubled in number in 1966, and doubled again in 1968, when they reached 220 items. The total remained at that level until 1974 when it jumped to 362 items. The grand total over the first decade (1965–74) was about 2000.[33] It might be added that a complete archive of Russian *samizdat* (*Arkhiv Samizdata*), located at Radio Liberty in Munich, has been published under the title *Sobranie Dokumentov Samizdata* (Collected Samizdat Documents) (Munich, 1972–).

The process of producing *samizdat* has often been described and need not be repeated here in detail. The basic requirements are simple enough – a typewriter, thin paper, and carbon paper, together, of course, with an author eager to express his thoughts freely, without censorship, and willing to run the risk of putting them in writing. After this initial step the author types, or has typed, a number of copies, probably no more than five to fifteen, on onion-skin paper. The last copies are often almost illegible. The copying is usually done in single space and covers the entire page, with almost no margins and little space at the bottom, and often on both sides of the page. The typists are usually volunteers, or are paid for the work involved. Copies are given to those who supplied the item in the first place and are passed on to others who may make copies on their own. Since the original author soon loses touch with the process, as in a chain letter in the West, it is impossible to know how many copies are eventually made; they may amount to several hundred, or even a thousand or more. Occasionally photographic methods are used for reproduction, thus speeding it up, and eliminating variations and inaccuracies. Other methods, such as hectograph or mimeograph (sometimes on home-made machines), are rarely used in the Soviet Union, and still less frequently the printing press.

Dissemination of *samizdat* is equally difficult and fraught with danger. Most *samizdat* documents are signed by the author, with his address, although some are written under pseudonyms. Sometimes, for instance, in the case of novels or collections of essays or poems, or periodicals, the material is bound, but it is often disseminated unbound, which has the advantage that a group of people can read the work together, passing each page around separately. The copies are usually distributed by hand, not by mail, and are sent abroad through foreign correspondents, foreign embassies, travellers, or by more conspiratorial means. The process of diffusion is as spontaneous as the initial production, and has a number of disadvantages, such as the irregularity of the process, the difficulty of getting hold of specific items, lack of contact with readers, and hence an absence of follow-up and criticism. Moreover, since the materials are liable to confiscation by the police, there are problems of safekeeping and storage. A pseudonymous writer, S. Topolev, outlined some of these disadvantages in 1971 and urged a transition to *kolizdat*, i.e., the publication of journals, which would have the advantage of greater regularity of appearance, wider opportunity for contact with readers and the exchange of opinions, and more assurance of accessibility to back numbers. Moreover, the costs would be covered, through a kind of subscription. *Kolizdat* had its own problems, however, such as getting the journal started, raising the initial funds, distributing a bulkier product, and, if mimeographing or other machines were used, the problem of securing (or making) them and concealing them.[34]

It has sometimes been suggested that *samizdat* represented a return to the period before the invention of printing – a kind of pre-Gutenberg process of communication.[35] Certainly the mediaeval scholar, like the *samizdat* author, was his own polygrapher, editor, and publisher of the author he read or of his own work.[36] The *samizdat* copiers, too, resembled the mediaeval scribes, whether they were monks in a monastery or paid copiers in a lay stationery store.[37] The number of copies was strictly limited in both cases, although *samizdat* was perhaps more limited than the manuscript or even printed works (*incunabula*) in the first decades after Gutenberg. McLuhan writes of a handwritten book by Pliny which circulated in 1000 copies in the second century AD and argues that few *incunabula* before 1500 had such a large circulation.[38] A mediaeval historian, Eisenstein, while casting some doubts on McLuhan's estimates of the number of manuscripts, agreed that the number both of manuscripts and of *incunabula* was relatively small. She estimated that the average production of a printed book between the years 1450 and 1500 was between 200 and 1000 – a figure almost precisely equivalent to the estimates of the average *samizdat* product today.[39]

Although the analogy between the *samizdat* and the pre-Gutenberg manuscript is tempting, it should not be pressed too far. In a sense the typewriter is a form of printing, and not to be identified with, or even compared to, the handwritten process of 'scribal culture'. Like printing, the typewriter can reproduce a number of copies simultaneously, far more than the mediaeval scribe could by hand, although fewer than the developed printing press. With the more recent development of electronic forms of typesetting, printing has in fact come more than ever to resemble the typewriter. In other words, printing and typing may be conceived of as merely two types of reproduction in printed form, not essentially different from each other. The process of *samizdat* therefore is not a reversion to the pre-Gutenberg manuscript, a reversal of the revolution wrought by the invention of movable type, but more simply, a reversion to a less efficient form of printing.

It is nonetheless paradoxical that five hundred years after the invention of printing and at the beginning of the electronic revolution, *samizdat* writers have had to go back to less advanced methods of reproduction. This transformation in the media of communication has been due not to technological factors – the result of a new technology or the decline of an old – but to political factors: the attempt in totalitarian and authoritarian countries (communist and others) to control the written and spoken word by state and party management of publishing and by means of censorship. The only way to 'publish' a freely written and uncensored work is by *samizdat*, usually in typewritten form. Only if *samizdat* utilised xerox methods of reproduction (as to some degree has occurred in Poland) would there be, although on a small scale, a kind of 'miracle' equivalent to Gutenberg's invention.[40]

Although *samizdat* was Russian in origin, and in name, a similar phenomenon manifested itself in other communist countries, particularly in Czechoslovakia, Poland, and China. The Czechs, Poles, and Chinese had no doubt heard of Soviet *samizdat* through radio and other Western sources of information and were to some degree following the Soviet example. In large part, however, there was, in each country, a spontaneous development evoked by the same restrictions of censorship and state control, and expressing the same desire for freedom of expression. The means of reproduction used were similar, primarily the typewriter and carbon copies, although in Poland other methods, such as mimeographing and even xerox and photography, were employed, and in China the printed leaflet or booklet was supplemented by the unique medium of the wall poster. Uncensored material in each country had, too, its own distinctive origins and special features and should therefore be examined separately.

SAMIZDAT CZECH STYLE

'If the Russians invented *samizdat*,' wrote Pavel Tigrid, Czech émigré publicist and editor, 'it is undoubtedly the Czechs who perfected the system and made it an art.'[41] Tigrid had in mind the book series, *Petlice* (Padlock), which began to produce typewritten, bound books in 1973, under the general editorship of the novelist Ludvík Vaculík, and had issued almost 400 volumes by 1987. These included novels, short stories, poetry, plays, literary criticism, historical and philosophical essays, and, more rarely, political essays or studies. Strictly speaking, these books were not regarded as *samizdat* since the author signed each of a few copies personally for distribution to friends and expressly forbade, on the title page, further duplication. The volumes were prepared by typists who were usually compensated for their work, and produced several carbon copies, most of which were quite legible. The books were professionally bound, sometimes simply, in cardboard covers, but occasionally with more elaborate linen covers and with illustrations and photographs, and were often quite hand-some in appearance. The readership has been variously estimated at several hundred or even several thousand, but cannot be accurately measured because of unofficial copying and unknown circulation. The authors were the cream of the Czech literary profession – including many outstanding authors who were unable to publish in the normal way, as well as some younger writers who chose to be published, without censorship, in a series such as this.[42]

Other series began to appear in the late 1970s and published several hundred more books. There can be little doubt that this 'second' or underground literature was of much higher quality than the output of the official publishing houses, and many individual works were published abroad, in Czech or in foreign languages.[43]

Also noteworthy was the proliferation of feuilletons and of periodicals or journals. The feuilleton, a traditional form of Czech journalism, was initially stimulated by Vaculík, who wrote, and encouraged others to write, these light, somewhat humorous essays on serious subjects. He was able to publish an entire volume of them each year in *Petlice*, and these were in turn published abroad in German. Periodicals included journals in the fields of history, economics, foreign affairs, religion, Polish affairs, and music as well as several devoted to philosophy and literature. One of the latter was republished abroad, in printed form, by Index on Censorship in London under the title *Spektrum*, and smuggled back into Czechoslovakia.

In 1977 the founding of Charter 77, the human rights movement, gave birth to a substantial diffusion of typewritten materials, including 'authorised' documents signed by the Charter spokesmen, but also a great volume of uncensored materials written by individuals and groups, both of which will be discussed more fully in Chapters 3 and 4 below.[44]

This political *samizdat*, wrote the anonymous Josef Strach – the name means 'fear' in Czech – is 'a medium of communication which looks poor and miserable beside the fantastic rotary press and colour television, but which in fact is an unusually powerful and indestructible force . . . . It is written only by someone who has something to say . . . . When I take it in my hand, I know that it cost someone a good deal to write it – without an honorarium and at no little risk . . . . And it cost someone to devote his time and energy to copying it. this is something I cannot say of any newspaper, any journal, or any broadcast.'[45]

Petr Pithart, one of these 'pre-Gutenberg scribes', as he called them, spoke in similar terms: 'When the work is finished it is copied by others, once again in their spare time, and with no assistance from either the mail or the telephone; it is passed on to a few friends and acquaintances, and thus ultimately to hundreds and perhaps even thousands of readers. All of them share the additional worry of being possibly summoned to confess whether they have read it, from whom they received it and to whom they lent it, who talked them into doing it and who paid them for doing it, and how much . . . . Thus, entirely through the dedicated effort and expense of the people addressed, a work is published which cannot possibly lie idle, unwanted and superfluous. Are these circumstances really abnormal, when the extent to which the written words get circulated depends upon nothing more than the urgency of its message, moderated, let us admit, by the author's fear of trouble? How difficult and exhausting it all is!'[46]

Another prolific *samizdat* author, Milan Šimečka has written of these 'home-made books': 'Concealed in attics and in various absurd hiding places, they are passed secretly from hand to hand. Some of them are in safes, secured with ridiculous bits of string and plasticine. Some of them have been paid for dearly, by imprisonment, humiliation and anxiety. But one thing is certain: whatever the future may bring, it will be those home-made books which will provide a testimony of the time in which we live, for the language which sounds like falling gravel will not interest anyone.'[47]

A POLISH VERSION

In Poland it was the formation of the committee for the Defence of the Workers (KOR) in 1976, its transformation in 1977 into the Committee for Social Self-defence (KOR), and the founding in the same year of the Movement for the Defence of Human and Civil Rights (ROPCiO) which produced a veritable flood of *samizdat* materials, mightier than in Czechoslovakia or Soviet Russia. Beginning in September 1976 KOR issued a bulky bi-monthly, *Biuletyn Informacyjny*, and also *Kommunikat*, which also contained communiqués on cases of persecution. KOR also published *Robotnik* (The Worker), based on material from worker correspondents, which appeared in offset form in some 40 000 copies and was read by four to five times as many. Other important KOR publications were the *Black Book* on censorship, based on secret official documents and instructions, and *Document on Lawlessness* (April 1978).

The two organisations, KOR and ROPCiO, together with other associations, produced some thirty or more newspapers or periodicals, ranging from one or two sheets to voluminous texts, usually produced in large quantities with the use of mimeographing machines, and by more advanced techniques of duplication, including even printing. Among the papers produced by KOR were *Głos* (The Voice) and *Krytyka*; by ROPCiO, *Opinia*, its official organ; *Gospodarz* (The Farmer); *Droga* (The Way); *Gazeta Polska*; and *Bratniak* (a student paper produced in Gdańsk). Catholics relied mainly on long established, legally published newspapers such as *Tygodnik Powszechny*, a weekly, and *Więź*, a quarterly, both of which were subject to censorship. In addition there was a *samizdat* journal for young Catholics, published in Lublin, under the name *Spotkania* (Encounters).

Polish literary and scholarly publications were not as numerous as the Czech counterparts, or as handsomely turned out. There were, however, several *samizdat* publishing houses, notably NOWa, in Warsaw. There were literary journals, such as *Zapis* (Record) and *Puls*, in Lodz, and political journals, such as *Res Publica*, *Merkuryusz* (Cracow), *Postep* (Progress), *Indeks* and *Sygnal* (both student papers in Cracow), *Przegląd* (Review) which published western articles, and *Wiadomości Naukowe* (Scientific News).[48] In the words of one writer, literature was enriched by a new circuit entirely independent of party-state licence and the eye of the censor – 'a publishing network which attempts to be a conscious, consistent, and permanent alternative to the official, monopolised, and state-controlled circuit of literary publications', and which has among its authors and editors 'writers who constitute the forefront of contemporary Polish culture'.[49]

UNIQUELY CHINESE FORMS

In China after the death of Mao and the fall of the Gang of Four there emerged a democratic movement and an equivalent of Soviet *samizdat* in the form of many uncensored journals and of the uniquely Chinese *datzepao*, which literally means 'paper of big letters or bold characters'. A *datzepao* was simply a large sheet of cheap paper (or even old newspaper) on which large Chinese characters, more than an inch high, were painted with a brush, and which was then posted, in a prominent place, usually on the walls within an institution or on outside walls within a city. It had no fixed format, length, or style, and might consist of slogans, satirical prose, comic strips, cartoons, letters, reports, tables, graphs or songs, or long essays. It could be written on any kind of surface, including floors and sidewalks, or even hung on clothes-lines in offices or institutions. Because of its character it was inexpensive and could be produced by anyone.[50]

The origins of the *datzepao* can be traced back to the pre-communist era, when imperial edicts were posted on city walls. Mao Zedong posted his first *datzepao* at the age of seventeen, and wall newspapers were used in Red Army camps during the years prior to the communist take-over. Once established, the communist regime borrowed and extended the established Soviet institution of the wall newspaper in factory, farm, and institution and used it as a medium of offical propaganda but also of limited public criticism of persons and practices. During the period of the Hundred Flowers and the subsequent anti-rightist campaign in 1956–7, and again during the Cultural Revolution in 1966, millions of *datzepao* appeared in major cities throughout China, serving as a massive medium for the diffusion of both official and unofficial views and also as an instrument of factional struggle, as many posters were directed at individuals.[51]

A dramatic use of *datzepao* as a medium of authentic democratic protest occurred in November 1974 in Canton when a series of huge wall posters, 20 000 Chinese characters long and extending 100 yards, appeared under the title, 'On Socialist Democracy and the Legal System,' signed Li-Yi-Zhe. This was a pen-name for three authors who were at once arrested.[52] A new wave of democratic expression and protest posters began in 1976 after the suppression of the 5 April demonstration in support of the deceased Zhou Enlai, and crested for a few months after November 1978.[53] This was tolerated, and indeed for a time encouraged, by the vice-premier, Deng Xiaoping, who saw in it a source of support for his more pragmatic course. The movement was largely spontaneous and led to a spate of *datzepao* throughout China, in almost every town and city. In Beijing, the Xidan or Democracy Wall, on Changan Avenue, in the centre of the city, became the focal point of this extraordinary outpouring of free expression. On 27 and 29 November, thousands of people (no fewer than 10 000 on the latter day) gathered at Xidan Wall to read posters and to listen to speakers.[54] For several months the Wall remained a centre of poster activity and of heated debate and mass meetings. As the Human Rights League stated, in January 1979, 'Putting up big-character posters in itself is not only legal but glorious. It shows that we are exercising a right to which we are entitled as citizens. It also indicates . . . that putting up big-character posters is fulfilling a citizen's glorious obligations – such as showing real courage in being concerned over the future of the motherland and the destiny of the nation and over the unhappiness or happiness of the whole body of citizens.'[55]

The posters had, in fact, the endorsement of the constitution of 1975 which, in article 13, established the right of citizens to use big-character posters.[56] By March 1979, however, the authorities began to consider it a dangerous phenomenon going beyond the limited purposes envisaged officially and threatening the established order. The authorities in Beijing and elsewhere started to crack down on the entire *datzepao* movement, as well as the uncensored journals, arresting some of the leading figures and imprisoning them for long terms. At the end of the year the Beijing authorities issued a decree banning the use of the Xidan Wall entirely and limiting the *datzepao* to a more remote wall, where each one had to receive official permission from a special office. In 1980 the constitution was amended to remove the right of citizens to issue big-character posters.

Another element of the democratic movement, closely connected with the *datzepao*, were the uncensored journals which began to appear, often with the same editors. Many organisations were formed to defend civil freedom and to press complaints on the authorities. Although the most visible medium was the wall poster, most of these organisations issued their own publications, sometimes in mimeographed form, prepared from handwritten stencils, and in some cases even in printed form.[57] No fewer than eighty-two organis-ations and journals have been identified.[58] The journals were often affixed to the Xidan Wall, or were sold by vendors in the neighbour-hood. The *Masses' Reference News*, for instance, was published in 20 000 copies; others in more limited runs. The most militant was

Exploration, published by Wei Jingsheng, an electrician by trade, who was eventually (29 March 1979) sentenced to fifteen years in prison. The most broadly based organisation was the Chinese Human Rights League, led by a woman, Fu Yuehau, who was also later given a long prison term. More moderate journals were the *Beijing Spring*, published in 10 000 copies, *The April 5th Forum*, *Enlightenment*, and the aforementioned *Reference News*, as well as *Today*, a literary review, and student journals such as *Voice of the People* (Canton). By the end of 1979 most of these journals had been forced to suspend publication, and several of their editors received severe prison sentences.

SIGNIFICANCE OF *SAMIZDAT*

Samizdat emerged in some form or other, and in varying extent, in almost all countries of the communist world, and in other authoritarian lands, such as Chile and Iran. Only in those discussed above, where an organised dissent or human rights movement had come into being, did *samizdat* assume substantial dimensions.

In its simplest form it was a means of expressing one's thoughts and feelings openly and honestly, and of communicating these to others. It offered a way in which the individual could maintain his intellectual integrity and achieve a certain degree of freedom under repressive conditions. No less important, *samizdat* served as a vehicle of expression which assured the continuity of national culture at a time when it was threatened by repression and censorship. *Samizdat* joined independent activity in other spheres – painting, music, and drama – in helping to protect and develop a second or independent culture, and contributed to the preservation and extension of free and unrestrained scholarship. Finally, it served as a channel for the expression of political dissent and opposition and pointed a way for a possible transition to a freer and more humane society and polity. In addition, *samizdat* provided an important source of information at home and abroad, about the real conditions within a country, countering domestic propaganda and misinformation. It thus aided foreign governments, international organisations, and individual scholars and journalists in their efforts to understand and interpret the society concerned.

Needless to say, *samizdat* was seen as a dangerous threat to the authoritarian regimes whose control of information and culture was challenged by this competing force and whose very nature had given rise to this challenge. The ruling powers used every provision of the criminal code and every means of police harassment – house searches, interrogations, detentions, imprisonment and forced exile – to discourage people from writing *samizdat* and from copying and passing it on, or even from storing it in their dwellings.[59]

In varying degrees the communist regimes were successful in curbing or eliminating most of the media of free expression described above. In the Soviet Union, by 1982, voices of free dissent had been more or less completely stifled. In China the crackdown in late 1979 had achieved similar results even earlier. During 1980 there were still vestiges of the Democracy Movement during the elections and in an attempt to form a national reform newspaper. In a speech in December 1980, Deng Xiaoping, complained of 'counter-revolutionary leaflets', 'illegal organisations' and 'illegal journals'. By 1981 the democracy movement had to all intents and purposes ceased to exist.[60] In Czechoslovakia repressive measures made the continuance of independent communications more painful and difficult, but they did not succeed in eliminating it. Only in Poland, where repression had been less severe prior to the Solidarity period and *samizdat* was much more widespread, did free dissent and its media of communications help to create an atmosphere of civic freedom and to prepare the ground for a genuine movement of social and political reform in 1980–1. Even under military rule and afterwards, independent communications continued to flourish in spite of harsh measures of control and of punishment (see Chapter 2).

2 Independent Communications in Central Europe

'Everyone shall have the right to freedom of expression; this right shall include the freedom to seek, receive, and impart information and ideas of all kinds regardless of borders, either orally, in writing or in print, in the form of art, or through any other media of his choice.' – International Covenant on Civil and Political Rights, Article 19

Charter 77, in document no. 20 (1 December 1984), cited the above article of the covenant and observed that in Czechoslovakia 'all sources of information are controlled by a single political party and its apparatus since 1948 and have become the instrument of ideological propaganda'. As a result, not only is the citizen denied access to 'basic, truthful and complete information' on current events, domestic and foreign, but is subjected to a massive wave of disinformation in all fields of communication. This includes not only the distortion of news, but the suppression of major events or situations, such as the existence of famine in Ethiopia, or serious ecological problems in Czechoslovakia, and direct interference in the arts. For instance, in reporting the Nobel Prize in literature awarded to Jaroslav Seifert, the media within the country did so tersely, not mentioning the fact that Seifert's recent works remained on the publication index for a long time and appeared first in *samizdat* editions and abroad. All of this resulted from 'the government's exclusive power to decide the nature of information given. The party dictates what can be published and what cannot.'[1]

Although the Charter 77 document related only to Czechoslovakia and dealt mainly with information in its narrower aspect of news and public affairs, its critique of official media and their content clearly applied to other countries of Eastern Europe and to the entire realm of communication, including publication of ideas in books, journals, and other forms. In all these fields freedom of expression was restricted not merely by censorship, although this was a powerful instrument of constraint, but even more by the monopoly of control

19

possessed by party and state, enabling all forms of publication to be moulded in the shape desired through direct management of the media and of publishing, the constant purge of personnel, manipulation of the ideology, and enforced conformity with officially determined criteria.[2]

As a result it is not surprising that those who dissented from established policies and attitudes sought alternative forms of communication. György Konrád, Hungarian author, has written of 'the craving for communication' which was 'haunting Europe'.[3] Vilém Prečan, Czech historian, now in exile, referred to 'a parallel information system' in his homeland, a 'free journalism', 'born of the will for free expression' and publishing what 'the official information monopoly of a totalitarian regime conceals and keeps secret'.[4] In similar vein, a Polish journalist, Tomasz Mianowicz, also in exile, referred to 'the breaking of the Communist state monopoly of information' as 'one of the chief causes of the Polish workers' success in August 1980' and described the uncensored press and publications as 'an essential element of life in Poland,' even under military rule.[5]

These East Europeans were referring to the remarkable phenomenon of 'independent communications', well known in its Soviet form under the Russian acronym, *samizdat*. Although there was no equivalent term in the languages of Eastern Europe, the same phenomenon, which manifested itself in varying forms and degrees in the countries of the area, was, *faute de mieux*, called by this term.[6] High points of development occurred in Poland, not only in the four years preceding the rise of Solidarity and during the years of 'renewal' in 1980 and 1981, but even later, under martial law and its successor, the highly repressive authoritarian system of 'normalised' Poland. In Czechoslovakia, Charter 77 served as a catalyst for the substantial expansion of independent communications which already existed on a small scale before 1977. More recently, Hungarians, spurred on at first by Charter 77, and then by events in Poland, developed more restricted forms of free expression. Elsewhere in Eastern Europe the independent dissemination of information and ideas was limited largely to actions by individuals and did not assume the more institutionalised form of the other three countries.[7]

This chapter will discuss independent communications in Poland, Czechoslovakia, and Hungary and three main types of their content and transmission. The first, 'independent information', may be roughly equated with an independent press, and includes a great variety of publications, such as regular 'newspapers' or news bulletins (typewritten, duplicated, or printed) issued by dissident organisations such as KOR (Committee for the Defence of the Workers) or Charter 77, as well as a host of materials (letters, appeals, declarations, reports, articles, etc.) written and circulated by individuals or groups. The second, 'independent publishing', embraces the 'publication,' in typewritten, duplicated, and sometimes printed forms, of books of all kinds, both literary and scholarly, and challenges the official publishing houses in the quality of the works produced. The third form, 'independent organs of opinion, creative writing and scholarship', consists of journals or periodicals, which are edited by individuals or editorial teams, and appear at fairly regular intervals. These three kinds of independent communication overlap with each other and serve similar purposes in their specific fields. Moreover the boundary between official and unofficial communications, although usually sharply defined, is not impassable and is sometimes smudged, as will be shown later.

BEYOND *SAMIZDAT* – POLAND

The phenomenon of independent communications in Poland was unequalled elsewhere in the communist world, both in quantity and variety of form and content, but experienced significant changes in character in the successive periods before, during, and after Solidarity.[8]

The first great wave, in the five years prior to the rise of Solidarity, has been briefly described in Chapter 1. The striking feature of these dissident writings, wrote Joanna Preibisz in an introduction to her bibliography of these materials, was 'their sheer quantity, their variety, the length of the individual publications, the openness with which the editors and contributors to those publishing enterprises carried out their activities', as well as 'the multiplicity of views' expressed, providing 'a political pluralism otherwise totally absent in the Polish system'.[9] Tomasz Mianowicz, one-time participant in this activity, wrote: 'This was no longer samizdat. A whole network of independent publications was created, a readers' market, a distribution system for works of literature, journalism and academic works unhampered by censorship.' These uncensored publications were only a part, but the most important part, of a general 'self-defence of society against the totalitarian apparatus of a state whose goal was the control of all human activity, whether political, cultural or economic.' The result, he wrote, was 'the breaking of the Communist state monopoly of information'.[10]

The journals and newspapers which appeared in those dramatic years before Solidarity were estimated to number at least twenty-two; a full listing was given in a bibliography published abroad, which included a general analysis and a summary of their contents.[11]

Parallel with this proliferation of newspapers was the establishment of a 'publishing house', appropriately entitled NOWa (Niecenzurowana Oficyna Wydawnicza or Uncensored Publishing). It was headed by Mirosław Chojecki, a KOR member, a chemist who was dismissed from his job for his publishing activities. NOWa began with the publication of *Zapis* (The Record), which became a quarterly journal. It appeared at first in barely legible printed form; then by photocopy of the typed manuscript; eventually it was reproduced in England in printed form from the original and sent back to Poland. By the spring of 1980 NOWa had produced fifty-five books, as well as a number of regularly appearing journals, its editions running from several hundred to two thousand copies.[12]

Although the emergence of free and uncensored news, information, and publication was, it has been said, 'one of the foundations of Solidarity',[13] the rise of the latter diminished the need for the kind of independent media which had preceded it. In fact the line between 'official' and 'unofficial' culture became 'blurred', and the very concept of 'independent communications', as a separate category, became less appropriate.[14] For one thing, the 'official media', freed from the worst form of censorship and imbued in varying degrees with the spirit of 'renewal', became more objective and uninhibited, especially for instance in Cracow (*Gazeta Krakowska*) and in Gdańsk (*Głos Wybrzeża*), and even the central press, such as *Trybuna Ludu*, and the national radio (but not Polish television, the official press agency, and the army newspaper) changed their tone and content.

A host of Solidarity publications, some 350 in number, published by regional and factory branches throughout the country, and designated 'For internal Union use only', paid no attention to censorship or official guidelines. These were usually in duplicated, stencilled, or photostat form, and gained a very substantial readership. Solidarity's own national newspaper, *Tygodnik Solidarność* (Solidarity Weekly), which appeared in the spring of 1981, had a print-run of half a million copies, but was read by far more people. There were also five regional Solidarity newspapers, with runs of 10 000 in

Białystok and up to 70 000 in Katowice and Gdańsk. Two Warsaw dailies, *Niezależność* and *Wiadomości dnia*, came out in 25 000 and 10 000–12 000 copies respectively.[15] Other licensed newspapers, such as the Catholic weekly *Tygodnik Powszechny* (which had been appearing legally, with interruptions, since 1946), were subject to censorship, but constituted a kind of 'half-way house between the unofficial and the official cultures'.[16] Solidarity had its own regional press offices, especially *AS* (Agencja Solidarność) in Warsaw and *BIPS* (Solidarity Press Information Bureau) in Gdańsk. In addition, Solidarity Radio, which was not a radio station, prepared programmes for reproduction on loud-speaker systems in factories. Solidarity also negotiated a series of agreements concerning access to the official radio and television, but none was implemented before December 1981.

In this climate the need for media of the pre-Solidarity type declined, but did not entirely disappear. Some notable 'underground' newspapers, for instance *Robotnik*, ceased publication, but others, such as *Krytyka*, *Głos*, *Res Publica* or *Spotkania*, continued to appear. New ones came out, bringing the total of titles to around 200.[17] Since they were not registered they were still 'illegal', and occupied a kind of 'grey zone of the Not-Permitted but also rarely Forbidden'.[18] Although precise information is not available, it is estimated that their combined output amounted to some half a million copies. A new 'publishing house', Krąg (Region), in Warsaw began to reprint great historical works from the nineteenth and twentieth centuries. To make up for the inadequate supply and circulation of such volumes, Solidarity set up a network of libraries, numbering more than one thousand. As a result of these developments, the independent media offered severe competition to the official media and undermined the latter's monopoly of information.

When military rule was proclaimed in December 1981, all this changed. Solidarity and its publications were forcibly closed down; strict censorship was restored; and the official media reverted to their traditional practices of falsification and conformity. One might have expected that the voice of the general public and its various interest groups would have been totally silenced. On the contrary, anonymous publications began immediately to appear in the form of simple fliers during the first few days of military rule, and later as local information bulletins, often single-paged, typed, or even handwritten.[19] Gradually the underground press became more and more institutionalised, and regional and national in scope. By April 1982 some 149 separate titles could be identified, and by December 1982, 535. In fact it was estimated that at least 700 titles were appearing. Slowly techniques were improved; xerox, screen-process printing, and offset methods created higher quality products. A unique phenomenon appeared in the internment camps: clandestine news letters and papers, many handwritten and drawn on scraps of paper; at least twenty titles of this kind reached the West. Two news services were established, IS (Informacja Solidarnośći), giving information on union activities, and NAI (Niezależna Agencja Informacyjna), providing foreign and domestic news.

Many of the independent media were sponsored and directed by Solidarity's Interim Co-ordinating Commission (ICC) and its regional organisations. There were clandestine 'shopfloor bulletins', produced in factories and in individual departments, as well as inter-factory and inter-district publications. There were professional publications, put out, for instance, by teachers, students, the medical profession, educational institutions, private farmers, the youth, and even by the police (*Godność* – Dignity) and the soldiers (*Reduta* – Redoubt). Literary periodicals appeared, including once again *Zapis*, entitled *Nowy Zapis*, and a new one, from April 1982, *Wezwanie* (Challenge).[20] There were also satirical publications, with names such as Vulture, Scarecrow, Earthworm, etc., and even comic books, one portraying the history of Solidarity, another based on Orwell's *Animal Farm*.

New publishing houses, numbering at least eight or ten, joined the older ones, NOWa and Krąg, and produced some 600 volumes by January 1985. During that year another 500 were estimated to have come out.

It is impossible to describe the almost infinite variety of subject matter of these books, including, for instance, the writings of Czesław Miłosz and the outstanding contemporary novelist, Tadeusz Konwicki; the diary and a biography of Cardinal Wyszyński, and the sermons of Father Popiełuszko, issued only weeks after his murder. NOWa began to produce and circulate tape recordings, containing music, lectures for study circles, and even a newspaper, *Gazeta Dźwiękowa* (Sound Newspaper). More recently NOWa produced and distributed video cassettes to meet the needs of the boom in video use. This made it possible to view banned Polish films and Western productions, as well as specially prepared news reports or historical films, and to listen to prohibited music. It was estimated that there were already some 300 000 recorders in private hands;

cassettes could be rented in private shops as well as from underground sources. The Catholic Church also employed videography to show for instance, films of the Pope's visit to Poland and Father Popieɫuszko's funeral. Alarmed by these threats to its centralised control over information, the state initiated an official video network, including lending libraries for cassettes. The opposition regarded video tapes as their most useful weapon in the future.[21]

A unique development was the proliferation of newspapers and journals of organisations which were overtly political and opposi-tional. These included Wolnosc-Sprawiedliwość-Niepodlegɫość, (Freedom-Justice-Independence – WSN), Kongres Solidarności Narodu (Congress of the Solidarity of the Nation – KSN), Gɫos (Voice), Polityka Polska (Polish Politics), Sɫowo Podzięmne (Under-ground Word), Niepodlegɫość (Independence), Wyzwolenie (Liber-ation), Solidarność Walcząca (Fighting Solidarity), Wola (Will), and Group 13. Each had its own publications, usually one bearing the same name as the group, which set forth programmes which were liberal and democratic, social democratic or Christian in tendency, but almost always had a common denominator of Polish indepen-dence and parliamentary democracy.[22] Less overtly political was the Committee for Social Resistance (KOS), with an organ of the same name (KOS), a movement made up of small independent local circles which professed nonviolent resistance in small-scale daily work.[23]

The developments described above were but part of what a Western journalist called 'a vast underground counter-culture',[24] embracing other forms of independent activity, such as underground theatre, private adult educational activities in homes, music and lectures in churches, unofficial art exhibits, rock music concerts, human rights organisations, and even intermittent broadcasting by Solidarity radio. This was supplemented by widespread circulation of Western works and journals and extensive listening to foreign radio, and, in some areas, foreign television. As Stanisɫaw Barańczak described it, in the period before Solidarity, culture in Poland had become 'dualist as a result of the profound difference between the official – artificial and uniform, and the unofficial – authentic and intrinsically variegated'. There was, he then wrote (and there is even more now) an alternative to the dilemma of compromise with the official media of communication – 'Instead of "compromise or silence" today we say "compromise or independence," "compromise or authenticity," "compromise or freedom"!'[25]

A TYPEWRITER CULTURE – CZECHOSLOVAKIA

Charter 77, the human rights declaration issued in January 1977, stimulated a veritable explosion of typewritten materials, far surpassing in quantity and quality the individual items of protest which had circulated somewhat haphazardly previously.[26] This 'typewriter culture', as one of the Charter 77 spokesmen, Zdena Tomin, later termed it, was 'the only creative spiritually free and freedom-seeking literature there is, and also the only forum for independent, alternative political thinking in Czechoslovakia'.[27] Jan Vladislav, editor of one of the several independent publishing houses, wrote that the 'Parallel culture' provided 'the most eloquent evidence of the nation's desire for freedom of expression' and offered 'one way of preventing the Czech nation from being robbed of its identity and having an alien identity substituted instead'.[28]

This 'parallel communications system' continued without serious interruption for some ten years and produced a proliferation of materials. In the 'informational' category there were two main types. First, there was the authorised Charter 77 material, issued in the name of the Charter by the three persons acting as its spokesmen at the time. Some of these documents contained substantial analyses of specific problems, such as discrimination in employment, the suppression of literature, breaches of economic and social rights, environmental problems, health care, peace and human rights, the Belgrade and Madrid conferences, and the right to history and information. There was an even larger number of communiqués, declarations, open letters, and letters addressed by Charter spokesmen to governmental authorities, international organisations, or figures of world importance. Second, materials typed and circulated by individuals or groups on their own were even more numerous. Much of this was also informational in character, but a great deal was literary or scholarly in content, including essays – historical, philosophical, or literary – and feuilletons, or books – novels, collections of poetry, etc.[29] One can only roughly estimate that in the years since 1977 some hundreds of Charter 77 documents and several thousands of items from individuals were circulated.

Even during years of heightened repression there was no significant subsidence of this spontaneous outpouring, and no change in the method of preparation – typewritten production of carbon copies. Unlike the Poles, who employed many methods of duplication,

Czechs and Slovaks confined themselves to the typewriter in the belief that this method was permissible under the law and hence would not lead to the severe penalties given for other forms of production, but this limited the distribution to the number of copies which could be made in several typings. In any case, as one prominent Chartist argued in a private letter, the main purpose was not the widespread conspiratorial distribution of these materials to the public, but rather their transmission (particularly in the case of protests and appeals) to appropriate authorities, whether domestic or international, as well as to the official mass media, including the Czechoslovak Press Office (ČTK) or foreign news agencies. If some were copied by individuals, well and good, but 'circulation', regarded by the authorities as a criminal offence, was not the crucial objective. Indeed the citation or reading of the text of documents by Radio Europe (RFE) or the Voice of America (VOA) was worth far more than any amount of duplication. Modern telecommunications made it possible to transmit reports from the homeland for instantaneous reproduction, so that a trial or house-search taking place one morning could be reported by Western broadcasts the same evening.

Charter 77 did not have its own publications, but from January 1978 a bulletin, *Informace o Chartě 77* (Information on Charter 77) was virtually a Charter newspaper comparable to the *Chronicle of Current Events* in the Soviet Union or the KOR *Biuletyn* in Poland. It was not a forum for discussion or for literary or political essays, but it published all Charter 77 documents and other important *samizdat* material.

Parallel with Charter 77 there was formed, in May 1978, another organisation, the Committee for the Defence of the Unjustly Persecuted (VONS), whose members were all Charter 77 signatories. Its sole purpose was to issue regular communiqués (*sdělení*), usually half a page or a page long, on specific cases of injustice, such as arrests, searches, trials, beatings, etc. Even when a number of leading figures in VONS were tried and sentenced in 1979, there was no interruption in this series of reports. They constituted a full record of illegal actions by the regime and the police, including the names of the presiding judges, lawyers, witnesses, etc.

There are other features of independent publications in Czechoslovakia which are noteworthy and somewhat distinctive. In the first place there was a substantial quantity of religious materials, much of it issued by non-Chartists. These were not Church publications, but were the work of dissenting Catholics, sometimes priests or those whose permission to serve as priests had been withdrawn by the regime. Many of these documents, issued by individuals or groups of persons, as protests or appeals, were concerned with the same kind of questions as those of Chartists and other dissidents. The most important periodical was *Informace o církvi* (Information on the Church) which was issued regularly every month from early 1980 to the present. This bulletin reported news about Catholics and Catholic happenings throughout the world, as well as details of trials, house searches, and other persecution of Catholics in Czechoslovakia. Notable was the detailed reporting of the trips by the Pope to foreign countries, including full texts of his addresses in Rome and abroad. Two other journals were primarily religious and theological in content: *Vzkříšení* (Resurrection), from 1979 to the present, and *Teologický sborník* (from 1977 to 1979), which was succeeded by *Teologické texty* from 1980 to the present. From 1983 *Una Sancta Catholica*, an annual, was issued each year. In early 1986 a new religious periodical, *Velehrad*, began to appear. All of these were Czech publications. A Slovak religious journal, *Náboženstvo a súčasnost* (Religion and the Contemporary World) came out regularly from 1983 on.

In addition a number of 'underground' publishing houses of Catholic orientation existed, e.g. one in Olomouc, without a name, which issued eighty books before its organisers were arrested and imprisoned. Others, such as *Duch a zivot* (Spirit and Life), *Přátele* (Friends) and *Cesty Myšlení* (Paths of Thought) published volumes primarily religious, theological or philosophical in character. Since 1981, *Orientace* issued smaller booklets on themes of Catholic interest. An unusual feature of these publishing enterprises was that their editors abandoned the typewriter and, challenging the authorities more directly, used various forms of duplications, or offset techniques, thus producing quantities many times greater than Charter 77 materials.[30]

Another feature of Czech *samizdat* was the large number of periodicals which appeared regularly in the years from 1977 on.[31] These were issued in typewritten form, in Prague or Brno, or in smaller regional centres, and were of the most varied content. In addition to the Catholic journals mentioned, there were literary and cultural journals, such as *Spektrum*; journals published by groups of young people who belonged to the 'underground culture'; political journals of discussion such as *Dialogy*; several in the social sciences, such as *Ekonomická revue* (The Economic Review), and *Čtverec*

(The Square), devoted to foreign affairs; and the most enduring, the historical journal, *Historické studie* (Historical Studies) and its successors (each number with a different title). Two periodicals in philosophy began to appear in 1985: PARAF (*PARalelní Akta Filozofie*) edited by the Catholic, Václav Benda, and *Reflexe*, edited by the Protestant, L. Hejdánek. In 1986 a theatre journal, *O divadle* began to come out. In 1987 a sociological journal, *Sociologické Obzory* (Horizons) appeared. At present the most important journal is *Kritický sborník* (Critical Symposium), containing essays by well-known writers in many fields, which from 1981 has come out three times yearly. Another, entitled *Vyběr z Čs. čtenářské samoobsluhy* (A Selection from Czechoslovak Readers Self-Service) began to appear in 1982, as did *Prostor* (Space). The editors, noting that most of its predecessors had not been able to survive, wrote: 'Our living space is ever more and more restricted. It is surrounded by an alienated world, by a dehumanised state. Our inner self remains free, however.' (Uvnítř však zástává svobodný).[32] An important publication from 1981 on, which was not regarded strictly speaking as a periodical, was simply called *Obsah* (Contents) and contained literary and political writings.

Periodicals which appeared more recently were *Střední Evropa* (Central Europe) which dealt with the history and culture of this region, in 1984, and *Komentáře* (Commentaries) devoted to questions of peace and the peace movement, in 1985. *Vokno* (The Window) called itself 'a magazine for the second and other culture'. Another publication for the 'cultural underground' was *Druhá strana* (The Other Side). In 1986 a satirical magazine, provisionally entitled *XXX* (?), was described as the organ of the Society for Wearers of Stockings. More political were *Solidarnoćź*, a quarterly dealing with events in Poland; *Za zásuvky i z bloku* (From the Drawer and Notebook), concerned with the Soviet bloc countries; and *Alternace*, representing the 'non-socialist opposition'. In 1987 a journal entitled *Pokus* (literally 'an attempt', but based on the first letters of its subtitle), *Politika Kultura, Společnost* (Politics, Culture and Society), began to appear.

A host of other magazines came out, some of them no longer in existence. Among those known to the author were *Váhy* (Balance or Scales), handsomely illustrated; *Kde domov můj* (Where is my land, the Czech national anthem); *Slova* (The Word); *Nový brak* (New Rubbish), *Nový Petřín* (New Petřín), *Horizont* (Horizon), *Moravská čítanka* (Moravian Reader), *Čtení na dovolenou* (*Výběr*)

(Holiday Reading, A Selection), *Host* (Guest), *Diskuse, Mene Tékel Fares, KIFU* (Magazine of the Society for the Distribution of Information); *Salisburský výběr* (Salisbury Review: Selections), *Pražské komunikace* (Prague Communications); and most recently, *Jednou nohou* (On One Leg), later called *Revolver Revue*, with photographs on its cover and in the text. In Slovakia only a few were known to have appeared; one without a name, identified only by an X on its cover; a second entitled *Kontakt*; and in 1987, one devoted to culture and politics, with a meaningless title, *Mar.3-1K*.

The publication of journals was fraught with difficulties and with some danger. Most journals emerged as a kind of 'self-service', when several friends put together their own or others' articles, and then continued with further issues. Almost all were typewritten, or occasionally cyclostyled, and were usually unbound, or bound in the simplest paper covers. Some had a decorative format limited, however, by what a typewriter or camera could produce. Some appeared without even a title (for example, one nicknamed *Zebra* because of its striped cover). Many of these magazines soon perished, due to differences of opinion among the editors, or the high cost of production, or because the editors were jailed or forced into emigration. Others, such as the religious journals and scholarly periodicals, especially the historical ones, and journals of high repute, such as *Kritický sborník*, were more stable and appeared for many years. Some, published in other parts of Bohemia and Moravia, were not even known in Prague. No one was familiar with all of them or could read more than a few.[33]

One should include in this roster journals published abroad, which were shipped into Czechoslovakia by various channels and circulated widely among dissident intellectuals. *Svědectví*, for example, published in Paris, contained many articles written at home, and sometimes a whole issue was prepared in Czechoslovakia, e.g. no. 59 (xv, 1979), and no. 62 (xvi, 1980). Similarly, *Listy*, published in Rome, included many such contributions and a part of each issue was edited in Prague. Another journal circulating widely was *150 000 Slov: Texty Odjinud* (150 000 words; Texts from Elsewhere), containing articles translated from foreign periodicals.

Czechoslovak communications also excelled in the realm of 'publishing,' i.e. in issuing, in typewritten bound form, a large number of books.[34] The most famous of these 'publishing houses' (*edice*) was *Petlice* (Padlock), launched as early as 1972 by the noted author, Luvík Vaculík.[35] Nor was *Petlice* alone. *Expedice* (Dispatch), edited by Václav Havel, the playwright, issued 250 titles by the middle of 1987.[36] *Edice Kvart* (Quarto), published by the writer, Jan Vladislav, brought out 120 items before he went into exile. Another long-standing series was *Česká Expedice* (Czech Dispatch), issued by the author, Jaromír Hořec. *Edice Popelnice* (Ashcan), edited by Jiří Gruntorad, until his imprisonment, and then again after his release, could be credited with more than 120 titles. Still another series, *Krtek a Datel* (The Mole and the Woodpecker), issued by the 'revolutionary socialists', Dagmar Suková and Jaroslav Suk, between 1977 and 1981 (when both went into exile), produced some thirty books, including authors such as Seifert, Hrabal, Patočka, Egon Bondy, and studies of criminal argot by Suk and others.[37] From 1980 *Edice Jungiana* published 18 volumes of the works of C. G. Jung and his followers. From time to time *Sborník, výtvarníci* (Artists' Collection) appeared, including articles on the graphic and plastic arts in each volume.

One should not forget the contribution made by Czech publishing houses in the West, such as Index, in Cologne, or Sixty-Eight Publishers in Toronto, which published many *samizdat* works as well as books by exiles, and shipped copies to Czechoslovakia where they became 'salads' as they disintegrated from constant reading by many readers.

Finally, space should be found to mention publications in what has been called the 'grey zone,' i.e. on the borders of legality and illegality, not properly speaking *samizdat*. In particular, the Jazz Section of the Union of Musicians, legally existing for the promotion of jazz and rock, issued a bulletin for its members, several paperback series devoted to painting, poetry, music, and photography, and a library of books on these subjects.[38]

As in Poland, the independent communications described above form part of what has been called a 'second' or 'underground' culture or society, including the 'living-room theatre', art exhibits, rock music concerts, philosophical seminars, and an underground church. This was long ago defined by Ivan Jirous, musicologist and organiser of rock music, as 'a culture which will not be dependent on official channels of communications, social recognition and the hierarchy of values laid down by the establishment'.[39] Whether such activities were called 'a second culture', or termed 'independent', 'parallel', or 'unofficial', they existed, in the words of another writer, 'outside, rather than within, the sphere of state supervision and control'; they formed 'a culture that is independent of the state and not controllable by the state'.[40] Although not as widespread or as accessible to the public as in Poland, this 'typewriter culture, perhaps the strongest part of the entire resistance-culture . . . helps to keep the Czech soul alive. Small in numbers but big in courage and quality, it prevents the nation being reduced to a subculture within the Soviet empire. . . . Or perhaps even – once again – to be robbed of its rich, spirited language, the inner substance of independence.'[41]

HUNGARY – CHANGING CIRCUITS OF INFORMATION

The emergence of a new opposition in Hungary, and the development of a more substantial *samizdat*, were stimulated at least in part by events in Czechoslovakia.[42] The first step was a letter of solidarity with Charter 77 by thirty-four Hungarians representing a broad spectrum of the intelligentsia, including not only members of the so-called 'Budapest school' (neo-Marxist dissenters), but also some established literary figures, and even more significantly some younger intellectuals who had had no previous political involvement. The latter proceeded to publish several important *samizdat* volumes in 1977–8. The first of these, *Marx in the Fourth Decade*, contained the replies from twenty-one persons to a questionnaire concerning their attitudes to Marxism, which revealed on the whole a negative stance and a radical reformist approach. The second volume, entitled *Profile*, consisted of essays by thirty-four non-Marxist authors, all of whom had submitted their works to official journals, which had rejected them as not 'fitting our profile'. Since all had been intended for publication officially, none of them challenged the system as such. *Profile* thus represented a step toward crossing the line between official and unofficial publication, being self-censored and moderate in content, but issued in *samizdat* form.[43]

These initiatives can best be understood against the background of Hungarian communications prior to 1977. In the absence of legal censorship, it had been possible to express nonconformist or dissenting ideas in a few official publications, especially those which appeared in the provinces, or were intended for a restricted scholarly audience. Authors and editors had themselves to decide on the limits to which they could go. Hence critical views could be expressed in the social sciences, but less so in literature, provided there was 'no overt questioning of the fundamental legitimacy of the system'.[44] George Schöpflin termed this 'para-opposition' in the sense of 'opposition that does not overtly question the ideological bases of the system but does accept the leeway for a semi-autonomous political role'.[45] The 'circuits of information', as he called them, included not only official specialist or provincial journals, but also semi-public publications circulated within institutes and universities, and restricted materials issued 'for internal use only', usually in duplicated or typewritten form, or as draft manuscripts passed around among colleagues. Those who wrote for *samizdat* were at that time few in number, and were mainly older Marxists of the Budapest School or members of the New Left, whose writings were circulated among about 1000 people. These authors had been led to express dissent by the invasion of Czechoslovakia in 1968, and eventually suffered various forms of repression, including dismissals from their posts or enforced emigration. The resort to *samizdat* was not frequent, partly because other limited channels of communication were available, partly because authors and editors feared to risk such open dissent. Some critics of the system were opposed to *samizdat* as threatening to deprive them of the opportunity to voice their views in official media. The attraction of *Profile* lay in its offering an alternative form of publication without breaking with the official system entirely.[46]

The harassment of the bolder critics, and the proclamation of Charter 77, led, as noted above, to an expansion of *samizdat*, at first in the moderate form mentioned above, and then during 1978 and 1979, in the appearance of many other books, including translations of foreign authors and the works of blacklisted Hungarian writers. In 1980 a major project was the 1000 page *In Memoriam István Bibó*, consisting of essays by seventy-six contributors, written in honour of Bibó, former minister in the Nagy government in 1956, who had been imprisoned for some years.

Continued repression in Czechoslovakia, exemplified by the VONS trials in 1979, and the birth of the reform movement in Poland, followed by the establishment of military rule, inspired the further development of Hungarian *samizdat*, notably in the publication, on the Polish and Czech pattern, of typewritten journals. In March 1980, *Keleteurópai Figyelö* (East European Observer), appeared containing eye-witness reports of the 1956 revolution, and in subsequent issues, documents on opposition movements and trials in other East European countries, and materials relating to the 'Polish summer'. Another journal, *Szféra Magyar Figyelö* (Sphere, Hungarian Observer) literary in character, came out in September 1980 as a forum for younger writers.

In the following years there were other notable events in *samizdat* publishing. The first broke new ground in Eastern Europe, the establishment of a bookstore for the sale of *samizdat* literature, located in the apartment of László Rajk (son of the former Foreign Minister, who was executed in 1949). In 1981 two new journals appeared. One, in 1000 copies and containing 120 pages, entitled *Beszélö* (News from the Inside, or The Talker) which included many tendencies of opposition opinion,[47] and the other, *Kisúgó* (The Outformer), representing a more outspoken radical dissent. Of these publications, only *Beszélö* was able to continue, its issues dealing with a wide variety of taboo subjects such as the Polish solidarity movement, reform and democratic renewal in Hungary, and Hungarian national minorities.

Then in 1982 *Magyar Figyelö* (Hungarian Observer) came out with articles on similar subjects. In 1983 there appeared, in three issues only, *ABC Tájékoztató* (Information Bulletin).[48] In 1983 these were joined by another journal, *ABC Hírmondó* (The Courier) which established itself as a regular purveyor of information on human rights and democratic opposition in Hungary and Eastern Europe, and other themes not dealt with in the official press.[49]

In 1981 also, Hungarian dissidents, again following Polish and Czechoslovak examples, and modelling their work after NOWa, established an independent publishing house, under the name AB: Independent Publishers. It was directed by Gábor Demszky, a thirty-year old university graduate who had worked for several years on the magazine, *Világosság*, but had been dismissed after visiting Poland and lecturing on his experiences there. This enterprise launched a number of series on subjects such as Hungarian literature, Hungary in 1956, Hungarian minorities, and other countries of Eastern Europe.[50] Using a printing press instead of the hitherto customary typewriter, AB's purpose, according to Demszky, was to publish what could not otherwise be published, and thus to 'protect certain values'. He believed he could reach between 10 000 and 20 000 readers. AB reportedly later split into two sibling organisations, AB, continuing under Demszky's management, and ABC, established by AB's co-founder, Jenö Nagy, the latter apparently to specialise in publishing works by banned foreign and Hungarian authors, such as George Orwell, Arthur Koestler, Václav Havel, Adam Michnik, etc.[51] Other publishing houses also came into existence, and issued, for instance, a series of Peace Notebooks, booklets of photographs of the 1956 events, and a cassette of radio broadcasts from 1956.[52]

Beginning in late 1982, the Hungarian regime, abandoning its hitherto lenient attitude toward *samizdat* publications, began a crackdown, which continued in 1983 and after. The police raided the Rajk bookstore, confiscating large quantities of *samizdat*, and although Rajk continued selling in another flat, he soon had to suspend operations. Meanwhile the police conducted a series of raids on those associated with the publishing enterprises, kept them under constant surveillance in the streets, and imposed severe fines on some of them. Demszky was beaten up on the street outside Rajk's apartment, and later, in December 1983, convicted of assault, and given a six-month suspended sentence. This did not daunt the dissidents, who continued to publish *Beszélö* and AB *Hírmondó* regularly. A collection of documents of Polish Solidarity, in several volumes, began to appear in 1983.[53]

In comparison with the Polish, or even the Czechoslovak independent communication movement, the Hungarian was small and weak, numbering no more than fifty to sixty activists, about two hundred active supporters, and several thousand readers.[54] 'Centres of parallel culture' were few, including a modest flying university, an association for the support of the poor (SZETA), and several peace and environmental groups. This democratic opposition', as it called itself, was not organised even in an informal way comparable to Charter 77. Nonetheless Pierre Kende, Hungarian exile, saw in the 'defiance by the intellectuals' in the 1970s 'something entirely new', a decision, especially among the young, to 'break with the tactics of half-truths or concealment', and a refusal to 'accept the mutilation of free expression'. This 'active resistance', he believed had a durable result in that 'it has shifted the visible limits of official tolerance' and led those in charge of official culture to tackle head on the major problems of contemporary Hungary, or at least a large number of them.[55]

INDEPENDENT COMMUNICATIONS – COSTS AND BENEFITS

The description of the blossoming of independent communications must not obscure the fact that this process was attended by such difficulties that it could hardly be called 'free'. There was constant persecution of contributors, editors, typists and duplicators, and distributors, varying in intensity at different periods and in different countries, but especially serious in Poland under martial law. Arrests, house searches, interrogations, even violent beatings, and in some cases trials and imprisonment were among the prices paid. Even when the harassment did not lead to prosecution, it was designed to intimidate those involved and to discourage them from continuing their activities. Repression was also severe in Czechoslovakia, and, as noted, was stepped up in Hungary, but in no case were independent activities, including *samizdat* publishing, interrupted.

Independent activists in all three countries faced other practical obstacles in their work, such as the procurement of the necessary materials and equipment for publishing. Paper and carbon had to be of good quality, especially for books, and were not easily acquired in the open market. Some had to be purchased at high prices on the black market; some secured illegally from workers at paper factories. If the typewriter was the main instrument of reproduction, the process was not so difficult. 'All you need is a typewriter, paper and some carbons, and you're in business', wrote Jan Vladislav about Czech *samizdat*.[56] But for the production of books or journals, typists had to be found, some unskilled, on a voluntary basis, some more professional and requiring payment. The typewriters were usually old and were often confiscated by the police in house searches. Binding of books was a problem, according to Vladislav. At first he used young professionals, but he found this too dangerous and had to learn to do the job himself. Delivery was not easy, especially between towns and cities, but even within a large city, and had to be done by conspiratorial means. The books had to be moved from place to place for their safety. Prices had to be calculated so as to cover costs if possible, and payments had to be collected, in the form of subscriptions or donations.

The use of machines for xeroxing, duplicating, or printing had obvious advantages but also its own peculiar difficulties. Demszky, for instance, said that two people, in three days, could print 1000 copies of a fifty-page magazine and the distributing network could sell up to 2000 copies at 40 forints per copy.[57] Machines could be constructed relatively easily on a homemade basis, or in some cases smuggled in from abroad. Their use however, required time and effort, as they had to be assembled and re-assembled, kept in various locations, and shifted from place to place. The operators were often untrained and also had to be rotated. The resulting product was sometimes of poor quality, perhaps almost illegible, even in printed or xeroxed form, and next to impossible to copy abroad. If skilled or professional printers were used, the costs were greatly increased. In fact the financing of operations, whether typewritten, xeroxed, or printed, was not easy, since costs were high, requiring inordinately high prices. Contributions of equipment and funds from sympathetic organisations abroad were vitally necessary. In Poland a special insurance fund, to which publishing enterprises contributed regular fees, was set up to support independent publications and to cover financial losses resulting from police confiscation of supplies and equipment.

The head of one of the Polish publishing houses, *Przedświt* (Before the Dawn), which published more books monthly than *NOWa* or *Krąg*, admitted the problem: 'Working under extremely tough conditions, hiding from the police, changing our venue all the time, using inconvenient equipment that keeps breaking down, buying paper on the black market, putting books together in private apartments . . . . All these things take up to ten times more time than the actual printing.'[58] No wonder that publishing efforts were often short-lived. The results achieved, however, represented a veritable triumph of courage, persistance, and idealism, and a phenomenon of communications unique in history.

In the communist systems the ruling parties claimed, and enjoyed, a monopoly of power, with almost no limitations on its exercise. As George Schöpflin wrote in his study of censorship and political communication in Eastern Europe, 'information is as much a component of power as the police or armed forces'. The 'myth of unanimity' was a central source of the party's legitimacy and led to insistence on the maintenance of a monopoly of information through censorship and other means of control.[59] The official communications system, operating in a monopolistic and hierarchical manner, strove to socialise the population in the officially preferred values and to mould a public opinion in accord with official policy.[60]

The independent communications have, in varying degrees, challenged the myth of unanimity and weakened the monopoly of information on which communist power rests. Operating in a democratic and pluralistic way, these rival communications have rejected the party-line and its one-sided interpretations of reality; have articulated individual and group interests; and offered a channel for the flow of objective information about existing reality. They have acted as a watchdog on the government's actions and as an exposer of injustice and illegality. They have sought to create a more authentic public opinion capable of influencing the course of public affairs. They have provided a medium of intellectual expression and thus promoted a free and independent culture and scholarship in line with the country's traditions. They have given the individual a chance to voice his thoughts and feelings frankly and openly and thus to discover his personal identity. Above all, independent communications have stood for the truth – in history, in scholarship, in politics and economics, in creative expression and in personal relations. Without these independent media the citizen would have remained silenced and ill-informed. The world of 1984, with its Ministry of Truth, its Newspeak and doublethink, would have triumphed.

THE TWO CULTURES – DIVIDED OR NOT?

Independently minded East Europeans talk of a 'second' or 'under-ground' culture, distinct from the 'first' or 'official'; of 'parallel culture' or 'parallel society', challenging the official; of 'official' and 'non-official' information or communications, separate and opposed to each other. At the same time there is evidence that the line betwen the two cultures or two forms of communication is not always sharp and distinct, and varies according to the country or the period under consideration. Where everything is 'official', as in the 'perfect' totalitarian state, say Albania or Rumania, the term becomes almost meaningless, as the official media have a complete monopoly and there is no challenge to it. Where the official media are not in total control, or are flexible enough to permit the expression of some nonconformist ideas, there are autonomous elements within the official realm of culture, as in Czechoslovakia in the 1960s, or Poland in the 1970s and 1980s. When, however, a relatively free and genuine culture emerges in the form of *samizdat* and other self-directed kinds of activity, one can speak of a truly independent culture, and of an authentic system of communication, as described here.

A Czech participant in the process of cultural liberation emphasised the historic character of this achievement, but also admitted its limitations. 'For the first time in the history of totalism, there has been an actual breach in the official coat of mail (*krunýř*) in which culture, half-stifled, has hitherto vegetated: 'We are witnesses of the first effort of free culture to achieve once again a public sphere from which it was for so long a time exiled.' Yet there was something still lacking — 'a public space common to all and indivisible', without a separation into 'we' and 'they', and with some 'feeling of belonging together, i.e. solidarity.' In the absence of this, one could create only something apart, 'one's own cultural community, one's own spiritual space, in an "authentic" isolation of "kindred spirits"'.[61]

These words were written with culture as a whole in mind, but they applied equally, perhaps even more emphatically, to information or communications. As long as the latter function in a kind of ghetto, almost unknown to the general public (as, to a large degree, in Czechoslovakia) they are hampered in forming a genuine public opinion capable of challenging official indoctrination and acting independently in a free market of ideas.

Another Czech, Václav Havel, perceived the Czechoslovak scene in less black and white terms. In an interview given just after his release from over four years in prison, in early 1983, Havel described his impressions in tentative terms as follows: 'The once well-defined and impenetrable dividing line between the two cultures appears to be growing fuzzy, with more interesting things appearing within the boundaries of what is permitted – though usually only on the periphery – many of them inspired in one way or another by the "unofficial" culture, relating to it, competing with it, or in some cases almost indistinguishable from it where inner freedom is concerned.' This reminded him of the early 1960s, he said, 'when the process of self-realisation and spiritual liberation likewise began somewhere on the borders of the official and unofficial culture', and culminated in 1968.[62] One year later, Havel analysed the 'parallel culture', and the relationship of official and unofficial, somewhat more deeply, expressing some doubt as to the validity of the division, and noting 'good and important achievements' within the so-called 'first' culture. 'Even though the "second" or "parallel" culture represents an important fertile ground, a catalytic agent and often even the sole bearer of the spiritual continuity of our cultural life, like it or not, it is the first culture that remains the decisive sphere' for the 'future climate of our lives'. 'The "second" culture will stand in a relation to it analogous to that of a match to a glowing stove; without it, the fire might not have started at all, yet by itself it cannot heat the room.'[63]

In Hungary, in spite of its modest parallel culture and its limited *samizdat* communications, the nature of official culture, and the relationship of these two cultures, was markedly different than in Czechoslovakia, according to Pierre Kende.[64] As noted above, as a result of the 'active resistance' of Hungarian intellectuals in the 1970s, there has been 'a trend towards the recovery of the right to truth'. Breaking with 'the strategy of silence or circumlocution', they succeeded in their effort to 'widen the limits of official tolerance', in the cinema, in historiography, and in certain magazines such as two Budapest monthlies, *Valóság* or *Mozgó Világ*, several provincial papers, and an economic weekly. This 'relative permissiveness of the Hungarian authorities', extending also to the works of 'parallel culture,' was in part due to the attempt to compete with the latter and discourage intellectuals from joining it. It could be compared, he said, with the attitude of the Polish government and, as in Poland, was a 'tolerance' that 'did not drop from the sky; it had to be wrestled by massive resistance' (presumably in 1956).

Yet the Polish case was unique and passed through successive stages. Stanisław Barańczak, referring to the flourishing parallel culture prior to Solidarity, spoke of the 'dualist' nature of Polish culture at that time (above). Nonetheless the unofficial culture had a very large national audience and official culture was permeated with autonomous tendencies so that the dividing line between the two was not sharply defined. During the Solidarity period the line shifted still further, as the 'unofficial' exercised a dominant role in public opinion and cultural life, and the 'official' became freer. After Solidarity was crushed, cultural 'dualism' evaporated further, as the parallel culture, although illegal and repressed, remained a powerful influence and official culture lost much of its credibility.[65]

A leading Hungarian writer, György Konrád, emphasising the rebellion against censorship and the rise of parallel culture in Eastern Europe, notably in Poland, drew optimistic conclusions for Central Europe as a whole: 'The image of a civic society, based on a social contract, has ceased to be a Utopia in Central Europe. It has its roots in spontaneous solidarity, swelling up from below, valuing self-determination above everything else. This solidarity of autonomous individuals and groups transcends all politics. It is a lifelong venture, without end. Our societies have decided that they intend to replace, step by step, the closed culture of the state with their own open culture. . . . My guess is that censorship in Central Europe has now passed its zenith.' Censorship is 'in retreat'.[66]

Part II

Independent Tendencies in Czechoslovakia

3   Dissent and Charter 77

In the wake of the exciting movement for reform in Poland and the continued widespread resistance to the Jaruzelski regime, Czechoslovakia appeared in contrast to be a silent and stagnant land where 'dissent' had been more or less extinguished and had little or no potential for affecting the future. In a world rife with protest and opposition, often violent in form and massive in scope, the peaceful, non-violent activity of Czechs and Slovaks, modest in its dimensions and predominantly verbal, was ignored by the world public. Those who did act independently in Czechoslovakia did not enjoy widespread public support and did not aspire to be a political opposition, so that their efforts seemed to lack political significance. The repression of the few 'dissidents', draconic as it was for the victims and their associates, paled into insignificance in comparison to the severe repression practised in an Iran or Chile and awakened concern in limited circles.

To assess accurately the phenomenon of dissent in Czechoslovakia requires not only an updating of the work of Charter 77, but also a comprehension of the broader context of independent thinking, writing, and action within which this takes place. It is also necessary to clarify the somewhat misleading term 'dissent', which is commonly used to describe such activities in communists countries. The Czech playwright, Václav Havel, an outstanding exponent of independent action, analysed the nature of 'dissent' in a brilliant essay, 'The Power of the Powerless'.[1] Those who are called 'dissidents', he wrote, are not some kind of 'professionals', defending a 'group interest'; still less are they political persons presenting themselves as an alternative ruling group. On the contrary, they are '"ordinary people", living with their "ordinary" worries, and differing from others only in that they say aloud what others are unable to say or dare not say'. The so-called 'dissident' is simply someone 'who acts only as he feels he must act, and who has been led, simply by the inner logic of his thinking, behaviour and work . . . without consciously striving for this or even deriving any pleasure from it, to an open clash with those in power'.

Persons who thus contribute to 'the independent spiritual, social and political life of society' cover 'a wide spectrum', in Havel's view, including 'writers who write as they wish, without regard for censorship or official requirements and who publish their work in *samizdat* . . . ; philosophers, historians, sociologists and other scholars, who go their own way in independent scholarly research . . . and disseminate their work in *samizdat*, or arrange private discussions, lectures and seminars; teachers, who privately teach young people things concealed by the ordinary schools; clergymen who try, in their pastorate, or if they are deprived of their office, outside of it, to conduct a free religious life; painters, musicians and singers, who create independently of what official institutions think of their creations; all persons who share in this independent culture and disseminate it further; people who try . . . to express and defend the real social interests of the working people, to return real meaning to unions or to found independent unions; people who are not afraid constantly to draw the attention of the authorities to injustice and strive for the observance of the laws; various associations of young people who strive to free themselves from manipulation and to live their own lives, in the spirit of their own hierarchy of life's values; etc. etc. etc'.

The more organised 'dissident movement', Havel argued, is 'but one of the manifestations of the independent life of society . . . *the most visible*, at first glance *the most political*, and . . . *the most evidently articulated*, . . . but not necessarily the most mature or the most important', even from the viewpoint of their political impact. This is but 'the tip of an iceberg' and would be 'inconceivable without the whole background from which it grows, of which it is an integral part, and from which it derives all its vital strength'.

CHARTER 77

At the end of 1986, Charter 77 completed the tenth year of its activity.[2] When the original declaration, signed by 241 persons, was issued in January 1977, its sponsors had no idea that it would continue for more than a short time, and now regard its survival for so long as a kind of miracle. In an eighth anniversary document released in January 1985, its spokesmen declared that, in spite of persecution, 'Charter 77 is alive, is at work and wins recognition at home and abroad.'[3] The number of signatories had risen to 750 by mid-1977, and to over 1000 by June 1980. Very few, perhaps fifteen in all, had withdrawn their signatures. Perhaps eighty or so, unable to endure police harassment and job discrimination, had gone into exile. The losses caused by withdrawal or emigration and by a few deaths, which together totalled about 150 to 200, had been balanced numerically by additional signers, whose names were announced in groups once a year.[4] By 1987 the total number of signatories was over 1300, of whom some 1000 were still in Czechoslovakia. Although many had not been active since taking their original bold stance, a substantial minority, in spire of persecution and sometimes imprisonment, had assumed the heavy responsibilities and the substantial risks of sustained Chartist activity.

Charter 77 remained a relatively small 'community' of like-minded persons, united by a common resolve to work together for civic and human rights and was gradually forged into a kind of 'family' enjoying mutual confidence and intimacy. It had not aspired to be, nor did it become, a mass movement. Significance rested, it was said, not in the act of signature, but in the spirit of independence thereby demonstrated. Its diverse composition embodied a certain pluralism, with persons of different generations, occupations, religious persuasions, and political outlooks brought together by a concern for human rights. Although its leadership was primarily in the hands of intellectuals, it included people of many social backgrounds, including a substantial proportion of workers.[5] Young people were well represented, especially among later signatories, including many who were children at the start of Charter 77 and no more than babies at the time of the Prague Spring. It was at first, and still is, almost entirely a Czech movement, with very few Slovaks, and no more than one or two Hungarians, in its ranks.

Although Charter 77 deliberately eschewed organisation, it has been guided by a succession of 'spokesmen', numbering in all during the decade twenty-three.[6] The custom evolved of rotating these spokesmen, at the beginning of each year, with the outgoing trio nominating the new ones after consultation with others. All have been repeatedly harassed by the police; nine have been imprisoned for some years. The original spokesmen, Jan Patočka, eminent philosopher, Jiří Hájek, former diplomat and cabinet minister, and Václav Havel, playwright, were well known, as were some of their successors. More recent holders of the post were younger and less widely known. The older ones remained active and served as members of the 'collective of spokesmen' which was formed in early 1980, fifteen in number at that time. Even those in prison continued to be listed as spokesmen. Although they were not regarded as representing specific groupings, they usually included a former communist; a prominent non-communist; a religious person – priest, pastor, or layman; and a cultural figure (categories which frequently overlapped). There was almost always at least one women. As time went on persons willing and able to assume the risks and the responsibilities were not so easily identified but were always found. For 1987, those selected were Jan Litomiský (*b*. 1943), agronomist, active Evangelical, who had served three years in prison and described himself as a 'political conservative'; Libuše Šilhanová (*b*. 1929), mother of three, a former journalist and later instructor at the Higher School of Economics, whose speciality was the sociology of youth (expelled from the party in 1970); Josef Vohryzek (*b*. 1926), writer, translator, and literary scholar, who had spent the war years in Sweden, had been expelled from the party in the 1950s, and had thereafter broken with Marxism and politics.

A separate organisation, loosely associated with Charter 77, but acting independently, was The Committee for the Defence of the Unjustly Persecuted (known by its Czech acronym, VONS). It was formed in 1978, with seventeen persons named as members.[7] By late 1986 its membership had risen to thirty-five (of whom five were in exile). In late 1979 VONS became affiliated with the International Federation of Human Rights (FIDH) and added to its name a subtitle, the Czechoslovak League for Human Rights. In 1984, Ladislav Lis, a prominent Chartist, became a vice-chairman of FIDH, although he was unable to attend its meetings. By late 1987 VONS had issued some 700 numbered typewritten communiqués (*sdělení*) each of which contained a brief report of a case of persecution or prosecution. Noteworthy was the fact that credit was given to the courts when justice was done (e.g., nos 479, 502, 507). Moreover although cases of forced psychiatric treatment were sometimes criticised (e.g., the repeated harassment of Augustine Navratil), VONS went out of its way to reject the view that Czechoslovak psychiatry was comparable to its Soviet counterpart or was generally misused to liquidate political opposition (no. 495).

Each year VONS issued a comprehensive summary of cases outstanding. On 20 November 1986 (no. 591) VONS recorded 39 persons in prison, 4 under protective custody after release, and 32 under criminal investigation while not in detention. The report also noted that VONS had reported on 189 cases which were now closed, and 559 cases of extra-judicial repression (detention, house searches, surveillance, beatings, limits on freedom of movement, etc.).[8] After the amnesty of 8 May 1985, VONS reported that only a small proportion of those imprisoned for political reasons had been re-leased.[9] Rudolf Battěk, for instance, was not released until 30 October 1985, only six weeks before the completion of a five-and-a-half-year sentence.

Closely associated with Charter 77 was the bulletin, *Informace o Chartě 77* (Information on Charter 77), commonly known as *Infoch*, which was issued monthly without interruption from 1978 to the present. It was prepared by an 'independent editorial group of Charter signatories', under the names of Petr Uhl and his wife, Anna Šabatová (daughter of Jaroslav Šabata), who bore the brunt of editing it during the five years from 1979 to 1984 when Uhl was in prison. *Infoch*, usually from ten to thirty pages in length, contained Charter documents and VONS communiqués, other Charter materials, as well as individual protests and letters, information notes, reports from Poland and other countries, and lists of recent *samizdat*.

CHARTER DOCUMENTS

The principal activity of Charter 77, and the chief responsibility of its spokesmen, was the issuing of 'documents,' each bearing a number, as well as many other materials, unnumbered, called declarations, open letters, or communiqués. From early 1982, however, a new practice was adopted, namely to number all materials signed by the spokesmen, whatever their content or character. During its first decade Charter 77 issued a total of some 340 documents.[10]

The preparation of thematic documents was arduous and time-consuming, often taking months, and sometimes never completed. The drafts usually reflected the specialised knowledge of the authors, but were subject to modifications and amendments to satisfy the many persons drawn into the process, with the result that the final version was sometimes lacking in clarity and colour and not entirely satisfactory to any one. Collective consultation was hampered by police surveillance, confiscation of drafts and of typewriters, the absence of telephones, and the need for hand-to-hand distribution. All such materials were signed by the three spokesmen, who vouched for their authenticity.

During the first two years the numbered documents reflected the Charter's initial emphasis on human rights and dealt with violations of international agreements in areas such as education, the economy, literature and scholarship, or the treatment of prisoners. Others recorded details of individual cases of violation of rights and persecution. Criticism of this predominantly legal orientation, and of the failure to deal with matters of more direct concern to the population, led to a gradual change of emphasis. In May 1979 a document on consumers' problems appeared, followed by a supplement on this subject in November, and in May 1980, by a study of the problem of pensioners. After a lull in 1980 and 1981 the number of 'documents' greatly increased, but only a few dealt with specific themes in detail. During 1982 thirty-eight were published, including a review of the Charter's first five years (no. 3), and studies of price rises and the economy (no. 6); education (no. 20); prison conditions (no. 22); religion and the law (no. 23); and scientific research (no. 26). During 1983 forty-four documents were released, including studies of the economic situation (nos 4 and 36); literature (no. 14); environmental problems in northern Bohemia (no. 26); popular music (no. 31); drug abuse (no. 42); and the Madrid conference (no. 43). In 1984 twenty-two documents came out, including studies of the economic outlook (no. 6); the proposed school law (no. 7); discrimination in employment (no. 10); the right to information (no. 20); and religious orders in Czechoslovakia (no. 21). In 1985, Charter 77 issued twenty-eight documents, including one on the eighth anniversary of the Charter (no. 2); the Prague peace appeal (no. 5); proposed legislative reforms to implement the international human rights covenants (no. 7); a statement for the Budapest cultural forum (no. 24); an analysis of the economy (no. 28); and an ecological document prepared by the Danube Circle in Hungary (no. 22). During 1986 Charter 77 issued thirty-eight documents, of which four were thematic studies: 'Space for the young generation' (no. 4); tenth anniversary of the human rights covenants (no. 9); enterprise regulations limiting the rights of citizens (no. 21); and higher education (no. 32). Documents issued in 1987 included letters on the Charter's tenth anniversary addressed to citizens (no. 2) and to signatories (no. 3); housing for young people (no. 8); reconstruction of the legal order (no. 14); letters to Gorbachev and to the Czechoslovak authorities prior to Gorbachev's visit (no. 20 and no. 21); military service (no. 27); air pollution (no. 33); the right to travel (no. 36 and 38); the prison system (no. 48); the anniversary of T. G. Masaryk's death (no. 52); letter to the Vienna CSCE conference (no. 55); postal secrecy (no. 60); the anniversary of 28 October 1918 (no. 64); economic reform (nos 65 and 67).

INTERNAL CHARTER PROBLEMS

Although Charter 77 claimed not be an 'organisation,' it was a 'working human society', consisting of hundreds of signatories of differing views and backgrounds, and had to face the problem of enlisting their support and harmonising their attitudes on specific issues. Inevitably there was an active core of Chartists, who assumed most of the burden, and a 'passive majority', who had few contacts with each other or with the spokesmen and exerted little or no influence on Charter actions. Some of these problems had been dealt with satisfactorily by a kind of 'customary law' which developed, e.g., on the drafting of documents embodying a consensus and on the annual rotation of spokesmen. The 'collective of spokesmen' had brought together wider sectors of the community, and introduced younger persons to Charter work, but it had not elaborated a clear definition of its functions or of its composition. In one of the earliest documents issued in 1987,[11] at the beginning of the second decade of the Charter's existence, the new spokesmen, in a letter to signatories, advanced certain proposals for dealing more adequately with these questions. It was suggested that the 'collective of spokesmen' be re-named, or replaced by, a 'club of spokesmen', consisting of all former spokesmen, to serve as an advisory board for the current spokesmen and, in case of controversy, as a mediator. Side by side with the club would be a 'forum', open to all signatories and other interested persons, which would promote the exchange of ideas and give representation to all tendencies within the Charter ranks. It would, it was hoped, encourage the participation of younger people with new ideas and greater involvement in the Charter's work by less active signatories. The first meeting of this forum, in June, 1987, attended by some fifty persons, was devoted to ecological problems.

THE 'POLITICS' OF CHARTER 77

In its initial declaration Charter 77 denied that it was in any sense an opposition or that it offered a programme of political and social reform. In many expositions of its purposes by the spokesmen it was described not as a political movement, but as a moral challenge. Nonetheless it became, as a later document put it, '*via facti* a political force', both nationally and internationally. Václav Havel also later wrote of the 'political impact of what was seemingly a "non-political action" '.[12] In its later statements Charter 77 adopted a critical attitude toward economic or environmental policies which were not related with human rights as such and offered alternative courses in policy-making. In its appeals to its readers, the Charter also sought to win public support for its ideas. As might have been expected, its offer of a dialogue was rejected by the authorities who in fact treated it as an opposition force and by their attacks on it made it a highly visible political phenomenon.

Although there was a wide consensus among signatories on the nature and the purposes of the Charter, there were differences of view, and, during the early years, a good deal of controversy and open polemics among its leading figures.[13] Some, such as V. Havel and L. Hejdánek, conceived Charter 77, as Jan Patočka had done, as primarily a moral challenge, directed to individuals, and not requiring a high degree of organisation. At most they favoured a 'non-political politics', in Hejdánek's phrase, which would encourage, outside the framework of the Charter proper, various kinds of activity in the cultural and other fields. Václav Benda dubbed these 'parallel institutions' which might together constitute a kind of 'parallel polis'. Other Chartists, such as P. Uhl, J. Šabata, and J. Tesař, would have liked the Charter to be more avowedly political, challenging the regime directly, even at the risk of open confrontation; they also advocated a greater degree of organisation. Some of them engaged in a kind of 'surrogate' politics, informally grouping themselves on the basis of common ideas – 'reform communist', 'independent socialist', or 'revolutionary socialist' – and issuing occasional group statements. There were also heated debates among relatively non-partisan persons such as the writers Ludvík Vaculík and Václav Havel, who strongly disagreed on the nature of Charter 77 and its tactics. Vaculík preferred what he called small-scale work (*drobná práce*) by ordinary persons in their normal life. Havel defended more heroic and challenging actions, even at the risk of imprisonment.[14]

By 1984 these controversies largely faded away, and a consensus on tactics and methods seemed to have emerged. The spokesmen of more radical political views and advocates of a greater degree of organisation had been jailed for many years (Šabata and Uhl) or had gone into exile (Tesař and Julius Tomin). Some of their objectives had been achieved with the formation of VONS and the publication of *Infoch*. The long imprisonment of Havel and Vaculík's absorption in writing his long diary-novel, *Český snář* (Czech Dreambook)[15] which, without inhibition, described his personal activities and those of fellow Chartists, rendered obsolete the differences between the two writers.

During 1984 and 1985, however, undercurrents of conflict burst to the surface in sharp controversy focusing on the contents of Charter documents and the manner of their drafting. As noted above, most documents were the product of consultation and embodied a rough consensus. Some, however, expressing the views of a group of signatories, or even of non-Chartists, were issued by the spokesmen expressly to promote discussion. This was the case of the one on health (no. 14, 1984) drafted anonymously by persons working in the health system which stimulated two critical commentaries.[16] The Right to History (document no. 11, 1985) was issued by the spokesmen of the time (V. Benda, *et al.*) as if it embodied a consensus, although it had not been based on wide consultation. This prompted four Chartists who were formerly professional historians (M. Hájek, H. Mejdrová, J. Opat, and M. Otáhal) to circulate a critical commentary which complained that the document contained fundamental errors of fact and presented only the views of one group thereby violating the Charter's principle of respect for different viewpoints. There followed a prolonged and polemical debate in which a number of historians, as well as some others, expressed in written statements similar negative views both on the way the document had been issued and on its content.[17]

For the first time in Charter 77's history, the spokesmen had broken some 'unwritten rules' of procedure and touched off an open confrontation with a number of signatories. The new spokesmen who took over in January 1985 (J. Dienstbier, *et al.*) sought to smooth over the conflict by welcoming the discussion of both documents nos 11 and 14.[18] But they, in turn, stirred up new controversy at home and abroad by issuing the Prague Appeal with its contentious political proposals (see below) and other documents which evoked criticism. For instance, the one on the anniversary of the Soviet invasion in 1968 (no. 20, 20 August 1985), while condemning forcefully the consequences of that action in Czechoslovak life, referred to 21 August as 'a victory for the bloc mentality over the principles of detente' and expressed strong hopes in the possibility of reform in the USSR. Document no. 21 (3 September 1985), condemning apartheid in South Africa and expressing strong support for Bishop Tutu, produced rejoinders from Czechs and Slovaks in South Africa and in the United States.[19]

Even more provocative was the association of twelve Czechs,

including one of the spokesmen (Šabatová), as well as other prominent Chartists, such as Jiří Hájek, Šabata, Uhl, *et al.*, with a declaration published in *Le Monde* on 8 May 1985, signed by some 150 persons from many countries, condemning the United States' intervention in Nicaragua. One month later (5 June), a similar protest called for an end to the intervention, but, unlike the first statement, also for the end of Soviet intervention in Eastern Europe and Afghanistan. It was signed by more than one hundred persons, sixty of whom were Americans, but included were the names of others living in the USSR and Eastern Europe (East Germany, Hungary, Poland, and Czechoslovakia); eight of the ten Czechs had signed the earlier declaration. This was not published until 1 December in *The New York Times*.[20] On the same day, by chance, most of the Chartists who had signed one or other of the protests, sent a message to Daniel Ortega, Nicaraguan President, expressing concern over the denial of human rights in that country, which, they said, threatened the cause of liberation, as did American intervention.[21]

Meanwhile, on 15 September, the Council of Free Czechoslovakia in the United States addressed a letter to Charter spokesmen expressing their worry over the declaration on American intervention, noting that the developments in Nicaragua were similar to the process by which communist dictatorships had been established in Czechoslovakia and in Cuba. *Informace o Chartě 77* published this statement together with an answer from the spokesmen which noted that the pluralist character of Charter 77 gave each signatory the right to express his or her views. In reply, the Council, apparently unaware of the message to Ortega and confusing the two previous documents with each other, reiterated its solidarity with Charter 77 in its struggle for human rights in Czechoslovakia but warned against statements which might support Soviet policy.[22]

The exchanges described above generated misgivings, even among warm supporters of Charter 77 abroad, that the Chartist community was divided and, under successive spokesmen, was drifting first to the 'right', and then to the 'left', and adopting positions which were not in accord with the Charter's original mandate. Certainly some of the documents and statements by Chartists suggested there were significant differences which had to be reconciled. There were hints of a diversity of attitude toward the governments in East and West, with subtle gradations ranging from strong support to deep hostility toward Reagan's America, and from profound hostility to hopefulness toward Gorbachev's Russia. Some concern was awakened by a letter to Gorbachev (April 5 1987) prior to his visit to Prague in which eighteen leading Chartists welcomed his appeal for 'new thinking' and offered to support the reconstruction of Czechoslovak society. Another letter, addressed by fifty citizens, Chartists and non-Chartists, to each of the members of the Federal Assembly called in moderate tone for political reform, including the end of discrimination in 'cadre policy', greater freedom of information and more independence for oganisations, radical environmental measures, access to public life for all citizens and an amnesty for prisoners of conscience. The original proposal in early 1987 was not reported until October when another sixty-four signatures were added.

The miracle was indeed that Chartists, embodying a wide spectrum of opinion, managed to maintain a high degree of unity. As one Chartist wrote privately, Charter 77 was a veritable 'school of tolerance' and offered an umbrella beneath which persons of sharply differing views could work together in solidarity.

ROUND-TABLE ON CHARTER 77

The Council of Free Czechoslovakia had expressed a positive attitude toward Charter 77 and had suggested a 'dialogue' and a certain 'co-ordination of activities, without any kind of formal agreement'. The response of the spokesmen was to organise, under the auspices of *Informace o Chartě 77*, a round-table discussion in Prague among five well known Chartists representing a wide spectrum of Chartist opinion: Václav Benda, a Catholic, Ladislav Hejdánek, a Protestant, Jiří Hájek, former communist, Václav Havel, non-partisan cultural figure, and Petr Uhl, radical Marxist, who acted both as moderator and participant. The proceedings were taped and sent to the Czechoslovak Society for Arts and Sciences (SVU) as a contribution to its panel discussion at a conference in the autumn of 1986. The symposium was clearly designed to dispel misunderstandings of Charter 77 abroad and to respond, if only indirectly, to criticisms voiced.[23]

In an opening statement Václav Havel struck the familiar note that Charter 77 was not a political movement or opposition and asserted that the majority of the signatories had 'no concrete ideology nor political programme'. Hence political or ideological statements or activities by individual Chartists who *did* have a defined political position had 'nothing *de facto* in common with Charter 77'. Hejdánek also spoke of the Charter as 'a platform for people of different beliefs, different professions, different origins and different aims' and was convinced it would not have survived for ten years had it been an organisation or an opposition political party.

All agreed with Hejdánek that it was the responsibility of the spokesmen at a given time to decide how the Charter should 'live and act' and with Havel that the documents issued in their name could not 'go beyond the frame' (*ramec*) by which the Charter had 'limited itself and its mission'. This was difficult, the latter admitted, since there were 'no exact and precise boundaries' between what was and was not legitimate, and only 'a kind of free consensus and agreement'. Benda agreed with this view but noted the need for a 'compromise' between 'that which all signatories . . . were determined to respect in principle' and the 'practical steps which might deviate from the firmly established framework'.[24]

There was some discussion of the selection of spokesmen. Havel advanced the extreme view that it would be a matter of indifference to him if all three spokesmen were at a given time communists, or conversely, Catholics, as long as they observed the rules of Charter behaviour. Benda agreed that it was naïve to label (*kadrovat*) spokesmen as being of the 'left' or 'right' but argued that the composition of the group should take account of their political, religious, and other profiles. There must also be a certain balance between men and women, and of factors such as profession, age, education, and political experience.

Both Havel and Hejdánek stressed the value of 'initiatives' which might go beyond what the spokesmen themselves could do, but these should be undertaken 'on the basis of the Charter'. In Hejdánek's view Charter 77 was a 'catalyst' for such initiatives and thus opened up space for the encounter of different standpoints.

At the close of the symposium Havel referred to criticism of the Charter made abroad for not choosing to act as an opposition, which, it was said, thereby served the interests of the regime. On the contrary, he thought, Charter 77 had not prevented any one from acting as he saw fit and would support new initiatives provided they were non-violent. The Charter was indeed a standing 'appeal' to citizens to do something and had created a 'space' for developing independent culture and for greater religious self-confidence.

Jiří Hájek responded to specific criticisms of Charter 77, defending its support for human rights in other countries, such as South Africa, and positively evaluated the Charter's dialogue not only with other human rights movements, including the Polish, but also with Western peace movements. Although Charter 77 was primarily concerned with human rights at home, it should also concern itself with international commitments undertaken by governments and should take the latter at their word, thus striving to give real content to the Helsinki accord.

Václav Benda dealt with the notion advanced by some that the regime had eased up on its actions against Charter 77. He denied this, arguing that the methods, and the intensity, of repression, had varied greatly throughout the decade. Currently the brunt fell on young people and Catholics, who were being penalised severely not so much for their religious orientation as for their activities in defence of human rights and their participation in other forms of independent life. The severest penalties, however, had been meted out to those of a leftist persuasion, such as Uhl, Šabata, and Battěk, whom the regime considered to be 'heretics'.

All participants rejected what they called 'bi-polar' or 'black and white' thinking, which required loyalty to one side or the other of the world's 'left' or 'right' political alignments. This raised the question as to what 'authority' should be recognised as binding on Chartists. In Havel's view Charter 77 was entirely independent, not subject to any particular interest, nor obedient to any political tendency or structure; it did not belong to left or right, and did not favour either Husák (as some extreme critics suggested) or Reagan (as others argued). Chartists recognised no other authority than that of 'truth' and of 'conscience'. Benda suggested human rights as the source of authority but Hejdánek, questioned this as sufficient, since there were different concepts of human rights and no one of them could be regarded as binding on all.

THE INTERNATIONAL DIMENSION

Charter 77 derived much of its original inspiration from the United Nations convenants on human rights and the Helsinki Final Act, basing many of its appeals on these and other international agreements which the Czechoslovak government had endorsed.[25] When the CSCE review conference opened in Madrid in 1980, Charter 77 renewed its appeals to the Prague regime to honour its obligations under the Helsinki accord and to take the legal measures necessary to bring the country's laws into harmony with its commitments under international agreements.[26] It made a direct appeal to the delegates to strive for a concluding document which would not merely contribute to 'a truce among states', but also to 'a life within states which gave priority to values such as freedom, human dignity, responsibility, sacrifice for others and respect for truth'. It proposed the establishment of an international co-ordinating committee which would supervise the fulfilment of obligations and would work closely with 'civic initiatives' such as Charter 77.

The concluding statement adopted unanimously at Madrid was praised by Charter 77 for the inclusion of many provisions dealing with human rights; the document called for concrete measures to implement these principles, in particular the approval by Czechoslovakia of article 41 and of the optional clause of the covenant on political and civil rights. It also urged that the government guarantee the right of citizens to participate in monitoring human rights, demanded the release of prisoners, and protested police raids in November 1983 in connection with the stationing of missiles in Czechoslovakia. At the end of December, in a detailed evaluation of the Madrid meeting, Charter 77 declared that it had 'internationalised the whole problem of human rights' and had confirmed the legitimacy of groups such as Charter 77.[27]

Before the beginning of the Human Rights Experts Meeting in Ottawa, Canada, in May 1985, Charter 77 issued a long document calling again for legislative reforms in Czechoslovakia to bring the legal codes into harmony with the Madrid statement and the international covenants, including measures to guarantee the right to freedom and personal security and to travel; freedom of thought, conscience, and religion; freedom of speech, assembly, and association; and the right to form and join trade unions; as well steps to embody the state's duty to provide legal protection against violation of human rights.[28]

Prior to the opening of the CSCE Cultural Forum in Budapest in October 1985, Charter spokesmen issued, jointly with seven distinguished writers, including Jaroslav Seifert and Dominik Tatarka, a letter to the Czechoslovak government and to all delegates reminding them of the systematic suppression of culture since the Soviet invasion and the official assault on 'the spiritual integrity and the identity of two nations with long cultural traditions'.[29] In Budapest, several prominent Czech exiles, Pavel Kohout, playwright, Jiří Gruša, writer, and František Janouch, physicist and chairman of the Charta 77 Foundation in Stockholm, took part in an unofficial conference of writers from a number of countries, which had to meet in private apartments due to official banning of a public gathering. All delegates to the official session were presented with a copy of a specially prepared book. *A Besieged Culture*, which documented, in the words of statements by Czech and Slovak writers, the régime's 'total war against the very roots of Czech and Slovak spiritual life', and described the struggle of a large part of society 'for the nation's own culture, its own identity'.[30] At the official meeting speeches by Western delegates placed Czechoslovakia's delegates on the defensive on questions such as censorship, the treatment of Seifert, and the Jazz Section.

In May 1986 Charter 77 addressed a letter to the CSCE conference on human contacts in Berne, informing delegates of various Czechoslovak measures which hindered such contacts and created 'the atmosphere of a closed society'. State boundaries thus became barriers to the relations of family members with each other and to the free flow of information, thus contravening the provisions of the Helsinki agreement. Appended were other Charter documents which dealt with restrictions on travel and the flow of information.[31] At the meeting the official Czechoslovak delegates were subject to frequent criticism but denied any wrongdoing.

The following month Charter 77, noting the forthcoming meeting of the United Nations Committee on Human Rights at which Czechoslovakia's observance of the covenant on civil and political rights was scheduled to be discussed, called on the government and the National Assembly to take the necessary steps to bring its legislation and practice into harmony with the pact, and urged also that Czechoslovakia accept the provisions of article 41 and the optional protocol, which would make it possible for other state signatories and an individual citizen to appeal to the committee concerning Czechoslovakia's violations of the pact.[32]

At the opening of the CSCE review of conference in Vienna, Charter 77 addressed an open letter to the delegates in which it gave a strongly positive evaluation of the Helsinki process as a first step toward a really democratic and peaceful Europe – 'A Europe of free and independent nations'. They would welcome any strengthening of this dimension of Helsinki and the establishment of 'a real dialogue of nations, not a mere agreement of governments bound by a bloc mentality'. A year later, another letter to the Vienna conference, when it was trying to reach agreement on its concluding document, welcomed the open discussion of human rights initiatives and expressed a favourable opinion on the Soviet proposal of a human rights conference in Moscow. This would be a step forward if not only government delegations but also institutions and 'civic initiatives' were able to participate.[33]

Over the years Charter 77 spokesmen issued other documents relating to the international dimensions of the struggle for human rights. On every anniversary of the Soviet intervention in 1968 they released a statement condemning this use of armed force and calling for the withdrawal of Soviet forces in view of the improvement of relations with West Germany and the Soviet approval of the Helsinki Final Act. On 20 August 1985, for instance, Charter 77 noted that the policy of so-called 'normalisation' introduced after the occupation had resulted in stagnation and backwardness in all areas of life, and called for the withdrawal of troops and the adoption of reforms such as those introduced in some neighbouring states. In 1986, on the same date, the Charter document invoked the right of self-determination asserted for all people by article one of the International Covenant of Political and Civil Rights.[34]

Discrimination in employment was one of the worst consequences of post-1968 policy. This, and the later discrimination against Charter 77 supporters, were made the basis of repeated appeals to the government and to the International Labour Organisation. Although there was perhaps a slight change for the better after the ILO condemned Czechoslovak practices in 1978, the practice continued in the political requirements for employment under the party's *nomenklatura* system, and there was no reversal of the mass dismissals of 1969–70 and 1977. In document no. 11, 1985, Charter 77 provided evidence of the way the official policy flouted the ILO's principle of non-discrimination.[35]

SOLIDARITY IN CENTRAL AND EASTERN EUROPE

From the start Charter 77 considered itself a constituent part of a worldwide movement for human rights in both East and West, and sought particularly to achieve co-operation with fellow activists in Central and Eastern Europe. It felt a special affinity with the Committee for Social Defence (KOR) in Poland and in 1978 representatives of the two movements were even able to meet together on the common frontier. Charter 77 also declared its full support for Solidarity during 1980 and 1981, and after the declaration of military rule. The two communities of dissent expressed mutual solidarity and provided information about each other's activities in *samizdat* publications. In February 1984 Czechoslovak–Polish unity was expressed in a joint statement signed by Chartists, former KOR activists, and Solidarity leaders. This was later endorsed by nineteen Hungarian dissidents who had already been stimulated and influenced by the Polish and Czechoslovak human rights defenders in their own efforts in a similar direction. Solidarity transmitted to Charter 77 a number of messages from its independent commissions in the field of health, science, culture, and human rights, proposing closer collaboration in the pursuit of common aims. In July 1987 it was revealed that a Polish–Czechoslovak Solidarity group had existed since 1981. A new group, the Circle of Friends of Polish–Czechoslovak Solidarity was formed to exchange ideas and correlate activities. In August, on the anniversary of the invasion in August 1968, another meeting of Polish and Czechoslovak human rights activists was held on the frontier and affirmed their common ideas on human rights and freedom. They stressed the need for cooperation of independent citizens' groups in the Soviet European bloc countries in pursuit of such demands as a shortening of military service, alternative military service, free travel and radical environmental measures.

It was more difficult to achieve co-operation within the Soviet bloc as a whole, and in particular with the human rights advocates in the USSR. Charter 77 voiced strong protests about the treatment of Sakharov, Shcharansky, and other victims of repression in the Soviet Union, and an exchange of messages between Sakharov and his colleagues and the Polish and Czechoslovak activists took place in August 1979.

All the more worthy of note was the broadening of the links of co-operation with other dissidents in Eastern Europe, as well as with Western Europe in 1986. The first manifestation of this was a proclamation on the anniversary of the Hungarian uprising in 1956, signed by 122 persons from four countries of the Soviet bloc – 54 Hungarians, 28 Poles, 24 Czechs and Slovaks, and 16 East Germans. It was later endorsed by three Rumanians. This statement praised the aims of the revolution and lamented that these, and the similar objectives of the uprising in East Germany, the Prague Spring, and Polish Solidarity were not fulfilled. More boldly, the signatories pledged mutual support in the struggle for political democracy, pluralism based on self-government, the reunification of Europe and its democratic integration, and the rights of minorities.[37]

Even more remarkable was the joint document submitted to the

Vienna CSCE review conference the following month, to be discussed more fully below, which was signed by more than 400 persons and ten independent groups from fifteen European countries.

HUMAN RIGHTS AND PEACE

The rise of peace movements in Western Europe required Charter 77 to formulate its position on their aims and methods, usually in response to invitations to attend conferences or as messages to such meetings.[38] Charter 77, it was stressed, was a human rights movement, not a peace movement, but it had always regarded 'peace' or 'the right to life' as one of the fundamental human rights without which others could not be assured. Conversely, peace, as the Helsinki Final Act had stated, was inseparably linked with the observance of human rights.

Space prevents anything but a brief, almost telegraphic summary of the salient principles of the Charter's position.

1. Peace (the right to life) is but 'one of the fundamental rights' and enjoys no special priority. There are other values for which life may have to be sacrificed (document no. 13, 1982).[39]
2. 'Peace at any price' does not guarantee an enduring absence of war as the crisis of 1938 in Czechoslovakia demonstrated (document no. 29, 1982).
3. It is not enough to have 'any kind of peace', but it should be a peace of justice and of dignity, in which 'internal peace' between state and citizen promotes 'external peace' (document no. 20, 1983).
4. 'There is no peace without freedom' (document no. 20, 1983). Only freedom guarantees a genuine public opinion and thereby 'effective control' of governments and of international negotiations (document no. 29, 1983).
5. Peace is also directly linked with the relationship of the poorer and the richer nations, and with the danger of ecological catastrophes and the devastation of nature (document no. 9, 1983, and no. 20, 1983).
6. Arms reduction creates a favourable environment for peace, but the military threat is not the main danger for peace and is but 'one of the dimensions of that danger' (document no. 20, 1983; 25, 1982).

The world peace assembly held in Prague in the summer of 1983 was a high-point in Charter 77's impact on Western public opinion. When its request to participate in the proceedings was denied, Charter 77 submitted a long statement to the conference, supplemented by a collection of *samizdat* writings by Chartists on peace. The document advanced the original proposal that negotiations on arms control and peace should be opened to public examination by the publication in each country of the proposals, arguments, and statistical data of both sides.

Although Chartists were barred from the assembly their statement was read to the gathering by some Western delegates. An address by Cardinal Tomášek proclaimed the inseparability of peace and freedom in a manner greatly resembling the Charter's approach. Some Chartists held meetings with Western delegates, one of which was broken up by the police, and they were able to issue several joint statements on the link between peace and human rights.[40] Some three hundred young people, acting courageously, on their own, were able to carry out a short march in Prague under the banner of 'peace and freedom' but were soon dispersed by the police.[41] Although the domestic press gave no reports of these events, they received much attention in the European media, especially on British television, and became known in Czechoslovakia through Western broadcasts. As a result the official manipulation of the world assembly for propaganda purposes was counterbalanced, and the Chartist argument that lack of freedom was an obstacle in the way of peace was tellingly demonstrated.

At the end of 1983 came the deployment of Soviet missiles on Czechoslovak and East German soil – an event which profoundly touched the emotions of many citizens in both countries and aroused deep fears for the future. *Rudé právo* (5 November 1983) acknowledged receiving many letters expressing alarm, and anti-missile posters appeared in the streets. During police interrogations leading Chartists were warned against any expression of opposition, under penalty of criminal charges, but they managed to convey their views in a document which quoted an official declaration that the stationing of US missiles in Western Europe did not promote security.[42] A petition against the stationing of missiles 'anywhere in the world', initiated by two or three young people in Brno, was signed by several thousand persons.[43] On 22 November 1984, a joint declaration by citizens of Czechoslovakia (including fifteen Chartists, but not the three spokesmen) and of the German Democratic Republic condemned the deployment of missiles in both their countries and also in the West and called for a missile-free Europe from the Atlantic to the Urals.[44] Several months later an open letter from women of East and West – signed by ten Czechoslovak women (all of them Chartists), five from the German Democratic Republic, and others from Italy, the German Federal Republic, and Great Britain – expressed their fears of the consequences of the placing of nuclear weapons on their soil and appealed to the citizens of the whole of Europe to reject the militarisation of society and war preparations of any kind.[45]

During 1984 Charter 77 continued to stress the necessity of a dialogue with kindred movements of 'civic responsibility' in Western Europe, 'across the frontiers of the blocs, of ideological schemata and different experiences'. The two main documents issued (nos 9 and 13) were, however, critical of certain tendencies within Western peace movements which were described in the former as 'foolish and dangerous'. Both statements rejected 'unilateral disarmament', 'appeasement', or 'peace at any price' (citing the experience of Czechoslovakia in 1938), and 'one-sided' or 'myopic' pacifism which confined its attention to armaments, especially nuclear, and neglected other policies which threatened peace. The message to the British peace movements (no. 9) seemed to endorse Western armaments and favoured 'a firm stance in spite of its risks' in preference to appeasement, and was sharply criticised by some Chartists. The fact that it was cited by President Reagan in a speech in Dublin in June added fuel to the fire.[46]

THE PERUGIA CONFERENCE

The document prepared for a peace movement conference in Perugia (no. 13) required long discussion before a consensus was achieved, and was eventually signed by the three spokesmen, V. Benda, J. Ruml, and J. Sternová, and by ten others, including former spokesmen such as J. Hájek, J. Dienstbier, V. Havel, L. Hejdánek, V. Malý and J. Šabata, and two persons from Slovakia, Miroslav Kusý and Milan Šimečka. Although it was more positive to Western peace movements, it objected to the view advanced by some that 'dissidents' were 'enemies of peace'. The letter was vigorous in its criticism of the division of Europe, the conflict of military blocs, and 'the politics of armed strength' (without distinguishing between the superpowers), and called for the withdrawal of *both* Soviet and American forces from Europe. This would prepare the way, it was argued, for the end of the division of Europe and the establishment of democracy throughout the continent. The world peace movement must build up 'a mighty democratic coalition' which would seek 'allies "below" and "above", in the East and West, in Europe and overseas'.[47]

The proceedings at Perugia represented a substantial success for the Chartists. None of them was present, of course, but their concepts were widely discussed and some were embodied in a concluding declaration. Among the 1000 persons present were delegates of the official peace movements of the Soviet Union and other bloc countries (although not from Czechoslovakia or the GDR) and repesentatives of most of the disarmament and peace movements of Western Europe, as well as some East European exiles, including Jíří Pelikan, a Czech who represented the Italian Socialists in the European parliament. There were fifty-nine empty chairs symbolising the absence of unofficial East European delegates, including Chartists. In the discussions the Soviet delegates often found themselves isolated and the target of censure. At the conclusion a European Peace Declaration was endorsed by eight Chartists (not including the spokesmen), five unofficial Hungarian delegates, and fifty-seven representatives of peace movements from six West European countries, including France, Italy, and West Germany, but this was not acceptable to the Soviet and East European official delegates. The declaration emphasised the 'indivisibility' of peace and human rights, thus confirming the long-standing Chartist viewpoint. It condemned the arms race and the deployment of missiles in East and West, and called for the withdrawal of foreign troops from all countries, the creation of an atom-free zone in Europe from Portugal to the Urals, the dissolution of the two blocs, and the ending of the partition of Europe.[48]

THE PRAGUE APPEAL AND AMSTERDAM

At Perugia Charter 77 had moved a long way from its original non-political position to one which aimed at complex political goals of European unity and disarmament. This more 'political' tendency was even more evident in the Prague Appeal, a brief letter to the fourth conference on disarmament in Amsterdam, issued by Charter 77 as document no. 5, on 11 March 1985.[49]

It described the partition of Europe as the chief source of the danger of a new war and contended that the condition of a secure peace was the reunification of Europe and its transformation into a community of free and independent nations. This could be attained, it was argued, through the dissolution of the military organisations of NATO and the Warsaw pact, the removal of all nuclear weapons located in Europe or aimed at Europe, and the withdrawal of Soviet and American troops from all European countries. The Appeal raised the even more delicate issue of the division of Germany and urged reunification within present boundaries, in a form to be chosen by the Germans themselves. It was also asserted that the Helsinki Final Act, as well as the Madrid concluding document, did not merely guarantee the status quo but offered a programme of European co-operation in which all participants could act as independent partners.

Controversial ideas such as these, advanced earlier by reform communists Jaroslav Šabata and Jíří Dienstbier, were endorsed in the Prague Appeal by persons belonging to all major tendencies in Chartist ranks. The forty-five signatories included not only the three spokesmen (one of whom was Dienstbier) but other reform communists – J. Hájek, L. Lis, Šabata, V. Kadlec, and L. Dobrovsky; the revolutionary Marxist, Petr Uhl; the democratic socialist, J. Mezník; Catholics – V. Benda, V. Malý, and Father Zvěřina; Protestants – L. Hejdánek, M. Rejchrt, and B. Komárková; the independent, V. Havel; several historians – M. Hájek and R. Palous; and three Slovaks – M. Kusý, J. Čarnogursky, and J. Jablonický. The elaboration of a common position on such highly debatable issues was a remarkable achievement.

The Charter was also successful, for the first time, in stimulating a general dialogue among Chartists and non-Chartists at home, and individuals in East and West. Responding to the invitation to discuss the ideas in the Prague Appeal, Dutch, British, Danish, Norwegian, French, West German, and American peace groups reacted favourably. Some critical voices were raised both at home (Václav Slavík) and abroad (Ota Filip, Erazim Kohák, and the anonymous J.W.B.), expressing, for instance, strong opposition to German reunification and scepticism about the Helsinki process. Also censured was the Appeal's equation of the two superpowers and the assignment of blame for the danger of war to the partition of Europe, without considering the reasons, or the Soviet responsibility, for this division. Czechoslovak social democrats in exile endorsed the basic thesis and many points of the Appeal, but expressed reservations on its failure to distinguish among the 'peace movements' and its proposals for the withdrawal of troops and the unification of Germany.[50]

The Amsterdam meeting on disarmament was attended by some 1000 delegates, but none from the Eastern countries. The ideas of the Prague Appeal were presented by Czech exiles, such as Jiří Pelikan and Zdena Tominová, former Charter spokeswoman, and according to the latter were the subject of much discussion in the twenty-five workshops. Although no resolutions were adopted, the Prague Appeal, it was said, left an indelible mark on the thinking of Western peace activists.[51]

YOUTH, PEACE, AND FREEDOM

On 8 December 1985, the fifth anniversary of the death of John Lennon, an extraordinary event occurred in Prague – a demonstration for 'freedom and peace'. This started with an assembly of about two hundred people, in the traditional gathering place for such events, Na Kampě, where flowers, candles and signs reading 'When will there be peace, John?' were placed. An enlarged crowd, numbering some six hundred, then marched across the Charles Bridge and through the streets of the Old Town, singing and chanting 'We want freedom, we want peace', and even more provocative slogans, 'No rocket is peaceful!' 'Flowers, not weapons,' and 'Abolish the army'. By this time more than 1000 strong, the marchers crossed the river again and went up to the Castle, where a petition was signed by about 300 persons, protesting, in the name of young people, against 'the stationing of any number of nuclear weapons in either part of Europe'. The marchers dispersed peacefully about 9 pm.[52]

In its next document the Charter spokesmen described this spontaneous peace demonstration as 'a unique event in the past fifteen years' and linked it with the desire of young people to 'live their own life' and the denial to them of their 'right to look at the world through their own eyes.' Their only opportunity to break the silence imposed upon them was to listen to rock and pop music, so that the songwriter became for them 'a poet, a preacher and a spokesman'. The document, entitled 'Space for the Young Generation', called on the regime to abolish its 'pretty tutelage' of music and to 'let the bands play and the singers sing'. It also urged the authorities to let young people travel and proposed summer holiday camps where youth from both parts of Europe could become acquainted. It also suggested that compulsory military service be reduced to one-and-a-half years and that an alternative labour service be provided for those whose conscience or faith forbade military training.[53]

COPENHAGEN PEACE CONFERENCE

Events surrounding the World Peace Congress in Copenhagen in September 1986 offered further evidence of the growing influence of Charter 77 among West European peace activists. Although this meeting was organized, like the Prague Peace Assembly, by the pro-Soviet World Council of Peace, Charter 77 indicated a willingness to attend provided that the Czechoslovak authorities guaranteed that delegates would be allowed to return home. A Danish peace group – 'Not by Atomic Weapons' – was ready to participate but sought to secure participation by East European exiles and unofficial groups in Poland and Czechoslovakia. They persuaded the local preparatory committee to seek official Czechoslovak approval of Charter 77 participation and assurance of the return of the delegates to Prague. This was to no avail, but it indicated that some circles in the peace movement in the West were becoming aware of the need for co-operation with the advocates of peace and human rights in the East.

Charter 77 had to confine its participation to a message to Copenhagen, which restated its views concerning the link between human rights and peace and repeated its proposal to the Prague Assembly for openness of negotiations for arms limitation. It also said that official peace movements should have no monopoly on the discussion of such matters and asserted the necessity of including independent initiatives in both East and West. It recounted recent independent manifestations of the desire for peace in Czechoslovakia such as the Velehrad pilgrimage, the demonstration of young people, and the actions of the Jazz Section, and cited its own document on the younger generation and its participation in the Milan discussions of a joint submission to Vienna (see below). The conference was dominated by official delegations from the East and pro-Soviet Western groups, but two exiled Chartists, who were included in Danish delegations, were able, in spite of obstacles, to present the Charter's viewpoint.[54]

MILAN AND THE VIENNA FOLLOW-UP

As the next CSCE follow-up in Vienna drew near, the European

Network for East–West Dialogue, which had been established at the Perugia peace conference, scheduled a gathering of Eastern and Western peace and human rights initiatives in Milan to prepare for this event and circulated a draft memorandum entitled 'How to bring the Helsinki agreement into life'.[55] Charter 77 transmitted to the organizers its document on the younger generation and drew attention to its proposal for summer camps, under the slogan, 'Let young Europe become acquainted,' and its position concerning military service. The spokesmen also sent a more detailed exposition of views on peace and the European situation signed by forty-three Charter signatories, drawn from all tendencies in Chartist ranks.[56] This was a thoughtful analysis of the causes of tension in Europe and the need to strive for a 'democratic peace', which would guarantee the right of each nation to choose its own path and form of development. It recognised that the withdrawal of foreign troops from all parts of Europe, the dissolution of the military blocs, and the reduction of armaments depended on the establishment of confidence. The goal should be a democratic evolution of the whole of Europe, including the democratic transformation of the Soviet bloc. The Helsinki process was not merely a guarantee of the Yalta status quo but could be a point of departure for curbing the hegemonistic tendencies of the two superpowers and for working toward a pluralistic Europe. The arguments advanced in the document met some of the objections of previous critics and represented a more balanced appraisal of the conditions for ending the partition of Europe.

In mid-May a gathering of peace and human rights groups elaborated a new version of the document, which, after further revisions, was submitted to the CSCE follow-up in Vienna in November 1986. This remarkable document, the product of a year of discussion, embodied a consensus reached among Western peace groups and Eastern human rights movements, and was ultimately signed by more than 400 persons, including 10 Hungarians, 39 Poles, at least 40 East Germans, 33 Czechs and Slovaks, one Hungarian from Czechoslovakia (M. Dúray), 33 Yugoslavs, a number of East European exiles, including one Russian, Leo Kopelev, and many other individuals from Western Europe and North America, as well as by ten organizations, including the Group to Establish Trust between the USSR and the USA (a Soviet unofficial organization). The Prague Appeal to Amsterdam was acknowledged to have been the initial stimulus to action, and the influence of Charter 77 was noticeable elsewhere in the document. This united front was a climax in the co-operation of peace and human rights movements and marked the first occasion on which they had made a common appeal to the CSCE conference.[57]

The final text of the appeal to Vienna adopted in Milan recognised that the Helsinki process was in crisis, and that many provisions of the Final Act were not being implemented, in East and West; it took the Helsinki agreement as its starting point and advanced many detailed proposals for giving it new life. It laid stress on the interdependence of all three baskets of the Final Act and on the inter-relatedness of human rights and security. 'Peace on our continent could only be secure if it were a really democratic peace' which guaranteed human rights and civil freedom and made possible an effective control of governments by public opinion. It also emphasised that the revival of the spirit of Helsinki required the action of all countries of Europe, not merely the superpowers, and the participation of groups and individuals, not merely of governments and official organisations. Intensified dialogue and co-operation of 'independent' groups across frontiers would contribute to overcoming the structures of 'cold war' and laying the foundations of a 'hot peace'. Such a 'detente from below' could be promoted by all forms of co-operation, and specifically by the creation of a fund to support summer youth camps for music, sport, ecology, and language study.

It is not easy to summarise the specific proposals of the document in its several thematic sections. Under the heading of *European Security*, a whole series of goals included removal of medium-range missiles, nuclear-free zones, reduction of arms expenditures and publication of military budgets, the reduction of military service to a maximum of one year and establishment of alternative civilian service. Under *human rights* were proposed the right to travel without visas and to emigrate without compulsory payments for education, the recognition of the status of political prisoners and the immediate release of those not advocating or using violence, the abolition of the death penalty, and the establishment of an all-European commission for human rights, to which all citizens could appeal. Under *economic and ecological co-operation* it was suggested that changes be made in the economies of both Eastern and Western countries, that conferences be convened for discussion of these questions (with independent experts included), and that an independent CSCE commission be established to study ecological damage and propose necessary measures. Under *cultural and scientific co-operation* in the spirit of the cultural unity of Europe, it was proposed that a European foundation be established to support cultural exchanges and that all forms of censorship be abolished.

The ultimate aim was to overcome the division of Europe and to establish 'a pluralistic, democratic and peaceful community of European states, acting as equal partners'. This would involve opposition to superpower policies which were in conflict with the right of self-determination and increased pressure on the superpowers, by movements in East and West, to abandon their hegemonic behaviour and to act as democratic partners. This would require the withdrawal of foreign troops from all European countries, the dissolution of NATO and the Warsaw Pact, and a European peace constitution based on the right of all nations to self-determination and endorsing the ten principles of the Final Act as part of international law.

CONCLUSION

As the eighth anniversary document issued in January 1985 stated more than once, Charter 77 continued to regard itself, not as a political opposition, but as 'a moral stance', based on principle, so that its work could not be 'measured by some immediately evident effect'. The chief gain, perhaps the only one, for the individual Chartist was 'the liberating awareness of being at one with himself, of having once more accepted responsibility for himself publicly, of having stood apart from the common indifference and of no longer participating by his silence in matters that are evidently immoral'. This attitude was based on the conviction that 'the truth, spoken aloud, is always in the public interest'.[58]

In spite of all its tribulations Charter 77 had survived for a full decade and constituted what seemed to be a more or less permanent political reality, exerting a certain impact at home and abroad. Shunning violence of any kind, and abstaining even from demonstrations, it confined itself to the written word. Its documents were, the Chartists believed, carefully studied by the authorities who were thereby 'forced to come to terms with problems which otherwise they would in all likelihood overlook or would not know about at all'. There were more than a few instances in which questions hitherto ignored were discussed in the media shortly after Charter 77 had focused attention on them. The documents were well known to large sections of the population, if only because of their transmission in

Western broadcasts, and thus contributed to the development of at least a limited public opinion. There were even 'some changes for the better', for example, a stronger respect for legality, at least formally; a greater consideration of international public opinion; increased fear of the publicising of injustice; and signs of greater autonomy in enterprises and organisations. People also realised that they could turn somewhere for help and that a person affected by injustice would not remain 'forgotten, lost and unknown'. Moreover, as noted above, Charter 77 had opened up a 'space' for others, especially in the realm of culture but also in religious life.[59]

There was an even more subtle impact, impossible to measure but more profound than its small number would suggest. Amidst a population characterised by widespread indifference and passivity toward public affairs, and by strong tendencies toward personal opportunism, Charter 77 served as a kind of gauge of honesty and courage against which people judged their own and others' behaviour. It suggested what they, too, might do if they had the courage and the sense of responsibility to follow the example of the Chartists and other independent spirits. Even though Charter 77 disavowed the role, it did in fact serve as a kind of 'conscience of the nation', nudging people to act more independently and decently. This was even true of some persons within the structure of power at every level. In the Charter's own words, it played a 'catalytic and encouraging role . . . thereby unwittingly forcing many others to come to terms with it in one way or another, to make their inner peace with it or at least to be aware of it in the background as an alternative'. It thus 'renewed civic pride, it showed people it was possible to speak the truth, and awakened hope'. In this way it was 'an attempt to rehabilitate the concrete person in his inalienable and irreplaceable individuality and to return him to the centre of social action as the measure of politics, law and system'.

Finally, the international impact of Charter 77 could not be minimised. Although neglected by the world media and hardly known to the general public, it was taken into account, and often defended, by governments at international conferences such as those of the CSCE or the ILO, thus creating considerable embarrassment for the Czechoslovak government. During formal visits to Prague by French, German, British, and American government officials, politicians and diplomats, and by Willy Brandt, of the Socialist International, delegation members made a point of meeting with Charter 77 spokesmen. The Charter documents served as a source of information for governments, international institutions, non-governmental organisations, scholars, and journalists. It enjoyed the sympathy of fellow dissidents in Poland, Hungary, and the German Democratic Republic and human rights organisations the world over. Most important, it conducted a fruitful dialogue with some of the Western peace movements, encouraging them to recognize the link between peace and human rights and to perceive the causes of war in the social and political realities of the contemporary world. A British scholar, Roger Scruton, described Charter 77 as having made 'the only real contribution to peace . . . since 1968, and as providing a lesson for the world as a whole'.[60]

Nevertheless after a decade Charter 77 remained, as one of its warmest supporters abroad, wrote, 'a small island of civic activity in the sea of the overwhelming majority of people who had adapted to the situation'.[61] Some of its own signatories still described it as a 'ghetto', isolated from the bulk of the population, not only by police repression, but also by the inability, even the lack of desire, to reach out to non-Chartists within the official institutions. A few signatories, disagreeing with the general tactics, or specific documents, stood somewhat aside but almost no one regarded the Charter as valueless. Certainly Charter 77 had not been able to win mass support or to generate a social movement comparable to the one which swept Poland in 1980 and 1981. Workers and farmers were aware of the Charter's reactions from foreign radio but took no active part. The independent activity described in this and the following chapters affected significant social groups, especially the intelligentsia, the youth, and believers, but in small numbers.

Conscious of the apathy and fear which had hitherto deterred people from action, Charter 77 struck a more self-confident and demanding note in its appeal 'To Fellow Citizens' issued 1 January 1987, the tenth anniversary of its original declaration.[62] Asserting that the decade had brought about many changes, both at home and at an international level, and had produced a widespread yearning for greater democracy, the document appealed to all to 'awaken from apathy' and to 'overcome fear' and to have 'the courage to become citizens in the full, creative and strongest sense of the word'. It depended not on governments, but on citizens, whether the rights guaranteed in international documents and in the constitution were implemented or not. Only this could avert a 'catastrophic' development and eventual 'explosion.'

In concrete terms, Charter 77 called on all 'to speak the truth', at home, in workplaces, and in meetings; to strive for free elections in trade unions and for full participation by the unions in policy-making; to speak openly of ecological dangers; to demand truthful information and use to the full the rights of assembly and expression; to demand the abolition of privileges given to rulers; as teachers, to teach the truth; as believers, not to conceal their faith; as writers, to create freely. The only perspective for a real 'national reconciliation' was to be found 'on a democratic basis' and by 'non-violent resistance to all evil, tolerance, decency, openness to truth and other views, and patient persistence'. All citizens should be conscious of their freedom and remember the meaningful slogan of the Czechoslovak state, *Pravda vítězí* (Truth Will Prevail)!

A second tenth anniversary document, A Letter to Signatories, addressed itself to the Charter's ever recurring 'search for its own identity' and to the definition of the nature and limitations of its concrete work. Charter 77 had become 'a definite political force' at home and 'a political partner' on the international stage but it could not become 'more political' and adopt a programme which went beyond the original 1977 declaration. The latter could, however, be interpreted in a broader sense than usually assumed, as was demonstrated by the fact that Charter 77 had already become an 'icebreaker' for independent initiatives of all kinds and a substitute for public opinion. It was not an organization, but a 'human community of work,' in which each individual signatory was responsible to his own conscience alone. It was recognized that its previous pattern of activity had produced difficulties and problems, notably the gap between the 'active minority' and the 'passive majority,' but it was hoped that specific reforms, such as the proposed Club of Spokesmen and the Forum would provide solutions. In its second decade the Charter could contribute more effectively to its initial purpose: 'that people in our land should live in greater freedom.'[63]

4 Other Independent Currents

It was not surprising that Charter 77 was unable to become a mass movement or to exert a wide influence among the people. The experience of 1968 and of its aftermath, 'normalisation', had produced feelings of frustration and hopelessness among the population, a scepticism about the possibility of change, and an unwillingness to take personal risks by supporting new movements of protest. The emergence of Charter 77, however, represented the recovery of at least limited circles from this mood of depression and the rebirth of a will to act independently. The Charter also acted as a stimulus, or catalyst, of independent thinking and acting, even though it was sometimes difficult to distinguish its own direct or indirect influence and the more spontaneous social forces which produced these results. Nonetheless, as the spokesmen noted in the anniversary statement of 6 January 1985, 'It would be hard to imagine that, without the rise and work of Charter 77, independent thought, literature and art would have grown so extensively as they have done in recent years.'[1]

Most of the independent activity was carried on by individuals outside the official structures from which they had been removed against their will, or from which they had voluntarily withdrawn. Some of it, however, was practised, within narrower limits, by persons still working within established institutions and organisations who sought to improve the quality of work done or to achieve a certain degree of autonomy of action. Some was conducted by Chartists; some by those having no connection with Charter 77. It was also conducted by individuals who, in their personal or family life, tried to safeguard their values and traditions and to transmit them to their children, or who strove to keep their self-respect as human beings. Whether acting alone, or with others, such people attempted to 'live in the truth', to use Václav Havel's term,[2] and thus to escape from the all-pervading controls of party and state.

Therein lay the significance of such independent activity, and the reason for the regime's hostility to it. It challenged the central principle, and the dominant feature, of the system of real socialism, namely 'the leading role of the party'. No matter how limited, or how personal, any manifestation of independence was, it was feared by the authorities as something which defied the ruling ideology and threatened their exercise of supreme power in every nook and cranny of life. However non-political it was, such activity at once became political, and was treated as such by official circles. Only if the cost of crushing it appeared too high, and the danger of its continuance slight, could it be reluctantly tolerated. If, however, it threatened to spread and to link up with other forms of independent action, it had to be destroyed without compunction and by any means. Hence the refusal of the Soviet Union and its East European followers to countenance a broad programme of independent reform launched by the party in Czechoslovakia in 1968, or one initiated outside the party by Solidarity in Poland in 1980–1, and their strenuous efforts to restrict or prevent even the more limited kinds of independent action by Czechs and Slovaks to be discussed in this chapter.

This independent activity often takes modest and unspectacular forms, personal in character, and not widely known, although usually ferreted out and hounded by the police as if harbouring the germs of a dangerous social movement. For instance, people grow their own vegetables and fruit at their chatas in the country and even sell some of their products. Others earn extra income by 'moonlighting' in the evenings or weekends, or even during working hours, or by speculating in foreign currency or Tuzex coupons. Someone may write freelance, under a pseudonym, or publish a book under someone else's name. An artist exhibits his work in his studio or cottage to a limited circle of friends and acquaintances. Groups of specialists in foreign affairs, or in economics, meet every month to discuss their subjects, or persons interested in literature gather to read poetry or the works of a favourite banned or exiled author. Several historians meet regularly over many years to prepare a large-scale study of Czechoslovak history. Seminars in Greek philosophy are held in private apartments every week, or an occasional play performed in living rooms. Writers or philosophers hold private congresses every year as in the old days. Young people, or old, get together to talk in one of the thousands of inns or wine-cellars, or go on excursions at the weekend, sometimes pursuing historical or environmental interests. Thousands of young people assemble outside the city to listen to rock bands. Tapes and cassettes containing popular music, or even lectures and articles, pass from hand to hand. Graffiti appear on the walls of Na Kampě in Prague, reminding people that 'Lennon is still with us', and, when painted over by the police, are replaced with other slogans.

Four examples of independent activity which are broader in scope and significance will be discussed below: independent forms of expression, especially in writing and publishing; non-conformism among youth, for instance in popular culture; the revival of religion and the growing independence of the Catholic hierarchy and of some Protestant pastors; and the stirring of independent thought among Slovaks and among Hungarians in Slovakia. Finally, independent thinking and independent civic and political activity of various forms will be examined on the basis of data provided by a public opinion poll conducted secretly in Czechoslovakia.

WRITING IN *SAMIZDAT*

The most common form of independent action, among intellectuals, was to express one's ideas and thoughts in uncensored written form and to circulate these in *samizdat* among small circles of friends and professional colleagues – in other words to create a kind of miniature world of culture and scholarship more genuine and truthful than the official one.[3] When the Nobel Prize for literature was awarded to Jaroslav Seifert, a signatory of Charter 77, several of whose works had appeared in *samizdat*, the honour was hailed by the Charter spokesmen as 'a just evaluation of a great poet but also an encouragement for the whole of Czech unofficial culture'.[4]

We have, in earlier chapters, given details of this veritable avalanche of materials of all kinds and have discussed some of the important functions served by this unofficial literature. Estimating the number of books and journals published was impossible since no one, not even those actively engaged in unofficial cultural activities, had seen the whole of this deluge of written materials. Some books were published in more than one series; some series, especially the religious or these for young people, were not even known to many. No one had a full collection, except perhaps the police, as a result of confiscations made during house searches. Nor was there a complete archive anywhere in the world, since a good deal of the material was not sent abroad or was sent irregularly.[5] Taking into account the religious *edice*, one might hazard an estimate that in the period since 1972, at least eight hundred, and perhaps more than 1000, books appeared, all (except the religious) typed on carbon paper, some plainly bound, others more handsomely presented and even illustrated.

Nor could one even calculate the number of copies of this *samizdat* production, since readers were sometimes inspired to reproduce on their own typewriters something they found of value, and the number of copies issued originally was not known. Distribution was difficult and dangerous since even the possession of such works was often made the basis of criminal charges. Hence much was not seen by the bulk of the population, although many would have been interested in it but had no way of getting hold of it. Even those 'on the circuit' could not afford to purchase more than a fraction, and some items were passed from hand to hand quickly, each person permitted only a day or two to read them before passing them on.

The technical difficulties of producing *samizdat* were discussed in an earlier chapter.[6] The duties of the editor were time-consuming, and a heavy burden. His tasks included the reading of many manuscripts and the selection of those to be issued; editing the original and correcting the final typed copies; having the books typed and bound; distributing them, by hand, all over Prague and finding ways to deliver them to other places. Often the editor found himself doing almost everything, taking up the time which he would have preferred to devote to his own writing.[7] Vladislav calculated that on average a book took ten days to produce, and that in publishing the 120 volumes of *Edice Kvart* he devoted 1200 working days, or more than three full years.[8] Editorial difficulties were enhanced by police harassment, frequent interrogations, and house searches; sometimes by the confiscation of manuscripts of finished books; and occasionally by imprisonment. Vaculík miraculously escaped the latter, but Havel was confined for many years, ostensibly for his work with VONS. Vladislav was eventually forced into exile, and Gruntorad jailed for several years. Even typists, binders, and distributors, or those who merely possessed *samizdat*, were often prosecuted.

Leading practitioners of this new form of writing and publishing described its value for the writer and for literature, but also recognised difficulties in the *samizdat* form. Ivan Klima, well-known Czech playwright and novelist, who was able to publish in his own country only in *samizdat*, believed that a writer, even in conditions of outward non-freedom, could live and write. 'The great Russian literature of the nineteenth century', he noted, 'arose in one of the least free Empires the world had ever known.' It can happen 'that a man begins to think through what freedom means for him only when he loses it, and it can also happen that, quite unexpectedly, he gains an inner freedom'. 'The more I was deprived of things which I used to enjoy' – e.g. editorial meetings, lectures, applause, prizes, and public recognition – 'the freer I felt. Gradually I became less vulnerable and more independent.'⁹

Another writer, poet, and critic, Miroslav Červenka, describing *samizdat* as 'one of the main expressions of contemporary culture.' rejected the term 'parallel culture' as inadequate to describe the conditions under which the typewritten *edice* represent 'the legitimate continuance of the traditions of Czech belles-lettres whereas printed literature squanders its typographical resources and apparatuses in the production of marginal products which hang in the air without tradition'. The authors, editors and copyists of *samizdat* had to take on themselves 'the task of maintaining and developing the heritage of Mácha, Neruda, Vančura, Čapek and Čep in the gloomy conditions of the millenium's closing years'.¹⁰

True, such authors, lacking a broad audience and any confrontation with critics, could not enjoy the genuine communication with a readership that was necessary if their writing was to become part of a 'living culture'. Some resigned themselves to the lack of a public; others turned to an international audience; others, most of them, wrote as if they had a normal public, but all were affected in their style of writing as a result. Still others sought a 'new definition of literature' under totalitarian conditions and were able to 'create an integrated artistic meaning . . . not only for the initiated but also for the layman.'

Samizdat created a practical question, which might appear marginal or even absurd, but was of great importance, namely the problem of editing this typewritten material. In the absence of the normal processes of publishing, with editors, proofs, and proof-readers, and in the necessary copying of the texts many times over, making errors inevitable, the tradition of preserving and developing the Czech language was not followed and the correct meaning was sometimes lost. The responsibility for accuracy and style rested first and foremost with the author, but also with the copyist and with an editor, the latter forming an indispensable link between the original and the finished text, and assuring an authentic copy which could, if necessary, be printed at once.¹¹

A similar point was made by an anonymous commentator who criticised the term *ineditní literatura* (literally, unpublished literature) which was sometimes used to describe unofficial writing; in fact *samizdat* was actually 'published.' Why should we not use 'the deep-rooted term, *samizdat*, which expresses the essence of the matter', namely that 'we simply publish by our own efforts (*svépomoc*) what it is not possible to publish in the institutions subordinated to state control'. Why object to the 'euphonious' Russian word which properly reminded us of the 'priority which deservedly belongs to the Russians in this sphere'? This 'extraordinary and abnormal means, forced upon us by extraordinary and abnormal conditions', offered us the chance to 'preserve for future generations, even in a limited degree, not only the theoretical postulate of what is called a free, autonomous cultural institution, but also its practical meaning'. This author also wrote of the importance of the *redaktor* or 'editor', whose role was as important as, if not more important than, that of a good literary critic.[12]

Space prevents more than the briefest mention of other forms of non-written expression, usually in the spoken word or visual image. Since 1978, for instance, seminars have been held in private apartments, so that dismissed professors and scholars could teach, and would-be students could learn. The most famous of these, in philosophy, was started by Julius Tomin, and, after his exile, continued by Ladislav Hejdánek. It met every Monday in spite of frequent police harassment and was often attended by scholars from abroad. Some twenty other seminars in different fields are said to take place.[13]

Then there was the self-styled Living Room Theatre, initiated by the celebrated actress, Vlasta Chramostová, who for several years gave readings in private apartments of Seifert's memoirs, performances of Macbeth, and a play about Božena Němcová. Forbidden to perform publicly for more than fifteen years, she chose, she said, not to compromise and to live 'an uncensored life', regardless of the cost involved.[14] Young artists, unable to exhibit under the auspices of the all-controlling Union of Artists, for more than ten years sought space elsewhere, usually on the periphery of Prague or in the country, in cottages or farm-houses, or in small towns or villages. One exhibit took place in the empty rooms of the former concentration camp in Terezín. Another, lasting two weeks, showed the works of eighteen artists in the courtyards of the historic palaces on the Malá strana in Prague. There was a flourishing of modern art, and the number of 'undesirable' exhibits grew.[15]

Finally, there were electronic media which were likely to become of decisive importance in weakening further the official monopoly of communications. Tapes were already widely used for listening to music, or to recorded lectures and articles from the foreign press. Video cassettes of foreign movies and news reports spread like wildfire, in spite of official efforts to prevent the distribution of unauthorised cassettes and to compete by issuing its own and building up a network of video machines. Many people listened to foreign radio or watched television (in those areas where reception was possible); some programmes were taped in the border regions and taken to Prague.

YOUNG PEOPLE AND THE MUSICAL UNDERGROUND

Other types of independent activity were exemplified in the efforts by young people to find new values, to live their own lives, and to express their feelings freely in poetry and music. The persecution of rock musicians, in particular members of the band, Plastic People of the Universe, had been an important factor in the emergence of Charter 77.[16] A number of young people, including some rock musicians, signed the Charter and took an active part in its work. During 1977, when Marta Kubišová, a popular folk singer of the 1960s, was a Charter spokeswoman, a document was issued which described the official system of control of popular music and the measures taken to inhibit or ban independent and nonconformist musical expression. Several years later, a fuller Charter statement referred to the 'mass discontent of youth as a result of the crisis of civilisation and its basic values', and described music as 'a revolt of conscience and spirit,' and 'almost the main guide, or medium, of this important spiritual and social confrontation' with 'the establishment and its scale of life values'.[17] Various forms of popular music – jazz, rock and roll, folk, rock, and punk rock – and the accompanying lyrics expressed the young people's distinctive values and approach to life, and were a challenge, explicit or implicit, to the consumer society and the totalitarian polity in which they had to live. The regime, however, found popular music a threat to the conformity which they demanded. Each style, in turn, became the target of denunciation and persecution. Many of the musicians were hounded by the police, sometimes jailed, and often driven into exile. Ivan Jirous, guiding spirit of the Plastic People of the Universe, was singled out for special treatment and was sentenced four times to prison terms.[18] Concerts were often cancelled, or broken up by the police, and those who had come to listen were sometimes beaten or arrested. Many fans were jailed for the mere sin of possessing musical tapes in their homes.

Until 1970 some five hundred rock bands were able to perform, having been granted official licences. Thereafter, however, although jazz, and jazz rock, once condemned and banned, were officially accepted, hard rock was taboo and almost entirely eliminated by 1973. The Plastic People of the Universe lost their licence, and could not even appear privately. They had to confine themselves to making clandestine recordings, such as *Hovězí porážka* (Beef Slaughter) and in an unusual collaboration with Marta Kůbišová, *Půlnoční myš* (Midnight Mouse). There were several hundred other rock bands, often called 'alternative bands' (*alternativní kapely*), including such groups as Stehlik, Extempore, Elektra, and FOK, and many amateur and semi-legal bands, who sometimes gave public concerts, often outside the cities. The 'new wave', initiated by punk rock, also took hold, and some fifty such bands were able to play in spite of constant harassment. They experienced changing fortunes, as many of the alternative bands, seeking to secure the right to perform through compromises with the authorities, fell victim to official wrath and were subjected to numerous restrictions and ultimately banned.[19]

Although many young people, anxious to protect their university studies and their careers, shunned open participation in rock concerts, many enthusiastic fans attended the semi-legal performances in the countryside week after week and listened to tapes and cassettes, often made from radio broadcasts, or to foreign recordings smuggled into the country. There was a flood of home-produced cassettes, which were even listed for sale in a *samizdat* catalogue from Brno.[20]

The fans of popular music, it has been said, developed from being an 'interest group' of the youth to a kind of 'social community', which included older as well as young people, and extended its interests to other forms of art and culture.[21] The principal mouthpiece of this community was the Jazz Section, founded in 1971, as a branch of the Union of Musicians, the official transmission belt in musical affairs. The Section had a membership limited to 4000 but had a following estimated at close to 100 000. The Jazz Section (JS) received no funds from its parent organization and depended on its members' fees (40 crowns *per annum* each), and income from its activities. Its volunteer staff was headed by Karel Srp, who was subjected to frequent harassment, including dismissal from his regular job and trumped-up charges of financial irregularity. Although the JS had no formal link with Charter 77, it was described by the police as 'a legal arm' of the Charter.

From 1981 it faced persistent efforts by the Ministry of Culture to make its life difficult and was able to survive due to wide popular support and to its affiliation with the International Jazz Federation under the Musical Council of UNESCO since 1979. Its continuance was also helped by what has been called the 'Grey Zone', i.e., those persons within the official structures who have sometimes hindered or blocked official actions.[22]

The Jazz Section's original purpose was to promote jazz, and later rock. It became famous for organising for nine years the successful annual festival, Prague Jazz Days. In 1981 the festival was cancelled by the authorities at the last minute and thenceforth the JS could organise only private concerts.

The Jazz Section then turned to publishing and, in spite of ever increasing persecution, produced for its members *Bulletin Jazz*, a substantial magazine which dealt with art, theatre, and literature as well as music. It became a veritable publishing house, producing several printed book series, such as *Edice Dokumenty*, which published the only Czech text of Seifert's Nobel Prize address; *Edice Situace*, fifteen paperbacks on painting, with reproductions; and *Edice Jazzpetit*, with books on subjects as varied as rock poetry, John Lennon, Dada and surrealism, music in the Terezín concentration camp, and Czech rock and roll. It was also able to publish a novel by Bohumil Hrabal, banned by official publishers, *Jak jsem obsluhoval anglického krále* (How I Served the English King) and produced, in three volumes, *Rock 2000*, probably the largest dictionary of rock music in the world.[23]

In the spring of 1983 the regime launched an all-out war against 'the new wave' of popular music which culminated in a savage attack in *Tribuna* endorsed by the party's daily.[24] The article condemned the musicians for 'spreading among the youth opinions unacceptable to our ideology, a philosophy of nihilism and marasmus, a cynical approach to life and all its values': lamented the fact that such musical events were often sponsored by trade union and youth organisations, local authorities, and cultural centres; and called for 'strict control of their (the last-named) activities' and for 'uncompromising measures' against individuals. This vicious and ill-informed diatribe produced a wave of letters of protest (most of which were not, of course, published) and a response by the Jazz Section in a booklet entitled *Rock na levém křídle* (Rock on Left Wing).[25] This was designed to correct the distorted portrayal of rock music and charged that the regime's attitude to this popular and socially conscious musical form had created distrust of the Communist Party among the youth.

Charter 77, in document no. 31 (1983), warned that if young people 'are constantly denied the music which they enjoy, this can only lead to a deepening of general frustration, feelings of hopelessness, powerlessness and the emptiness of life – or on the other hand, to the nourishment of latent social tensions'.[26]

By the middle of 1984, the regime had been unable to bring the JS to heel, partly due to its dogged resistance to the legal actions taken against it, partly due to the failure of the Union of Musicians to put an end to its existence, as ordered. In July the Ministry of the Interior suspended the Union for three months, and when the latter still failed to terminate the JS, dissolved it on 22 October 1984. The Jazz Section, in letter after letter, protested the illegality of the measures taken against it and managed to carry on some of its activities, such as its open house on Wednesday evenings, the lending of books, journals, and tapes from its library, and some publishing. It continued to issue an internal (hence uncensored) bulletin for its members which by then numbered 7000 – a mimeographed publication entitled *43/10/88* (the JS telephone number). It undertook an original action by planting trees and erecting a plaque outside its headquarters to celebrate the 40th anniversary of the end of the war and the founding of the United Nations (this with the official endorsement of a high-ranking UN official). Karel Srp and one of his associates managed to make their way to Budapest during the CSCE Cultural Forum and presented their case to Western delegations. On his return his passport was taken away and he was warned against 'unjustifiably interfering in the competence of the Ministries of Culture and Foreign Affairs'.[27]

Mention should be made of another branch of the Union of Czech Musicians, the section for young musicians (*Sekce mladé hudby*) which was also banned. This organization, with 12 000 members, had an active programme, which included publishing an information bulletin, a journal, and other materials, and holding seminars and video shows. It launched a plan to raise funds for famine victims in Ethiopia and produced a tape by Czech rock groups, but this project, too, was forbidden.[28]

The guerrilla war of the regime against young people and music continued. For instance, eight young workers, all from Ostrava, were given sentences ranging from seven to twelve months for participating in an evening of jazz in a small town and in demonstrations provoked by police intervention. The charges were hooliganism and their action was described as 'socially very dangerous'. In 1986 another six young persons, also workers from Ostrava, were convicted of incitement or hooliganism for actions as long ago as September 1983 and July 1984 and given sentences of 6, 8, and 20 months in three cases, and heavy fines and reduction of wages in others. Their crime was painting on the walls of a clinic slogans commemorating the Soviet intervention and Palach's death, and calling for 'an end to Russianism', and proclaiming 'SS-22 means death', and 'we want freedom'.[29]

The Jazz Section, with its mass following and its 'spiritual freedom', was, in Havel's words, 'a scandalous fissure in the system of general manipulation' and represented a challenge and a model of behaviour for others.[30] In September 1986 the regime, its patience exhausted, arrested seven of its members, including Karel Srp, charged them with unauthorised business activity, and in the case of Srp damage to socialist property. An action committee sent an open letter (24 October 1986) to the CSCE review conference in Vienna, urging the governments to use their influence to bring about the termination of the proceedings and the release of the imprisoned. When the trial finally took place (10 March 1987), the accused received relatively light sentences, the highest being 16 months for Karel Srp, with credit for time already spent in jail. In a Kafkaesque atmosphere, the judge praised the cultural work of the accused, but found them guilty.

The authorities tried to distract attention from the fate of the JS by holding several jazz festivals in Prague and other cities. But jazz in its unofficial and independent form was too deep-rooted for the regime to succeed in co-opting or liquidating it. A report of an enquiry by the JS among its members concluded that music was much more than an interest activity or a way of filling free time, and was, for the youth, 'a special expression of their stand toward life, a spectrum through which they perceived the fundamental values of the world'.[31]

RELIGION AND THE CHURCHES

Independent activity of another kind was to be seen in the resurgence of religious faith, the growth of active dissent among Catholics and Protestants, and a more independent, self-confident stand by the Catholic hierarchy, in particular by Cardinal Tomášek.[32]

These developments were all the more striking in view of the situation prevailing within the Catholic Church. In the frank words of an exile, most of the Church leaders, including at least two of the

Bishops, most of the 'vicars capitular', who temporarily occupied vacant bishoprics, and many of the priests had struck an accommodation with the regime, thereby evincing a lack of courage and of concern for their neighbours, and of any feeling of political responsibility.[33] Many priests joined Pacem in Terris, the pro-regime so-called 'peace movement', condemned by the Vatican. Some five hundred who refused to conform lost their licences to preach. *Katolické noviny* (Catholic News) was Catholic in name only and did not even publish statements by the Cardinal, or by the Pope, and supported Pacem in Terris. Most of the young people were 'dead souls', who had succumbed to 'total apathy', according to another report.[34]

Nonetheless, although religious belief became weaker during forty years of communist rule, it still remained strong and encompassed perhaps one-third of the entire population. According to official statistics, 80 per cent of funerals were held in churches in Slovakia, 50 per cent in the Czech lands; 53 per cent of weddings were solemnised in churches in Slovakia, 15 per cent in the Czech lands; and of babies born, 71 per cent and 31 per cent respectively were baptised. Religiosity was highest in Slovakia, relatively high in Moravia, and lowest in Bohemia, in Prague least of all.[35]

The revival of faith, according to Jiří Lederer, former communist journalist, did not coincide by chance with the birth of Charter 77 and represented 'a new spiritual impulse', of great significance from a historical point of view.[36] Young people, who found no appeal in Marxism-Leninism and lacked any belief in communism, sometimes sought a meaning in their lives and a sense of community in religion. They were attracted by non-institutional creeds or illegal sects, such as the Jehovah's Witnesses or Pentecostalism, and still more by the Catholic Church, with its colourful symbolism in the mass. They saw the latter as a symbol of resistance and found in it a sense of authority and order. They attended services, formed groups to study religion, and some even joined long-banned religious orders. Some were privately tutored in theology and unofficially ordained as priests. Clergymen expelled from their offices conducted services privately in what some called an 'unofficial' or 'underground' church (a term rejected by the priests and the Church itself), and were often prosecuted and imprisoned for 'obstructing state supervision of church affairs'.

As noted, a number of pastors, priests, and theological students, as well as Catholic and Protestant laymen, took an active part in the

Charter 77 movement or in religious protest and became the targets of police harassment. Some one hundred clergymen and religious activists, it was estimated, were in prison. Charter 77 issued a number of documents on religious persecution, including one on the tragic fate of the religious orders, banned in 1949, some of whose survivors, still loyal to their faith, were hounded repeatedly by the police.[37] Catholic *samizdat* was pouring out (see Chapter 2) and the courts sentenced those producing and disseminating it. For instance, three persons, two of whom were scientists or technicians, were given suspended sentences of six and eight months for distributing *samizdat* Catholic literature and materials from abroad, and these materials, including the reproducing machines (xerox, cyclostyle, etc.), were confiscated.[38]

This revival of faith and upsurge of activism among Catholics was reflected in a changed comportment of Cardinal Tomášek, the Czech primate, who celebrated his 85th birthday on 30 June 1984. Customarily avoiding public hostility to the regime, he had sought to rectify serious problems through private discussions. Largely as a result of the election of Cardinal Wotyła as Pope, and under his influence, it would seem, the Cardinal adopted a more and more independent stance.[39] As a result the Cardinal acquired great authority and influence within the Church, even among Slovak clergy and among believers, and earned the deep hostility of the regime and its 'Catholic' supporters.

The starting point of this shift in the Cardinal's behaviour was the Vatican edict in March 1982 banning political activities by the priesthood, which led to his firm condemnation of Pacem in Terris. He forthrightly denied the right of *Katolické noviny* to speak for Catholics. Reacting to a personal attack on the Pope in the newspaper *Tribuna*, the Cardinal defended John Paul II as 'a great humanist, indomitable defender of human rights, and one of the great Popes of all time'.

The attitude of the Cardinal *vis-à-vis* the régime hardened in subsequent years, not only in regard to the proposed visit of the Pope to Czechoslovakia (see below), but also to the position of the Church in general. In a letter of 2 November 1985 Tomášek severely censured an article in *Otázky miru a socialismu* (Problems of Peace and Socialism) for its criticism of the Vatican; he also condemned government measures against the Church and believers. On 12 November 1985, he again protested to the editor of *Katolické noviny* about its contents. A climax was reached in his memorandum to the

Minister of Culture on 30 April 1986 in which the Cardinal demanded a radical revision of obsolete laws relating to the Church and called for the separation of Church and state. He set forth the chief problems of church-state relations, including difficulties in teaching religion and the training of priests, the banning of monastic orders and of spiritual exercises by laymen, the dire situation of the religious press, discrimination against believers in social and economic life. He also denounced the control by the state of appointment of clergy, which resulted in vacancies in eight of the thirteen bishoprics.[40]

Cardinal Tomášek took a tough stand during the officially sponsored peace assembly in the summer of 1983 when he made a strong declaration on the indivisibility of peace and human rights. 'He who threatens truth in the interest of propaganda threatens peace; he who threatens respect for justice for all without exception threatens peace; he who threatens basic human liberties, including religious freedom, threatens peace'. 'There will be no peace on a large scale', he proclaimed, 'unless there is peace on a small scale. This means peace within every community as well as within each individual.'[41]

The Cardinal's attitude toward Charter 77 also underwent a change. Earlier when Catholics, such as the former priest Václav Malý, and laymen such as Václav Benda and Radim Palouš, had served as spokesmen, Tomášek had been unsympathetic to Charter activity, and had been sharply criticised by individual Catholic Chartists.[42] Later there was a gradual meeting of minds of Church and Charter, and an increasingly friendly attitude of each to the other.

The culmination was a petition for a visit by the Pope to Czechoslovakia which was circulated, no doubt with the knowledge of the Cardinal and with the aid of Chartists. Some 26 000 signatures were secured (of which 10 000 were confiscated by the police). The Cardinal thereupon invited the Pope to come to Czechoslovakia to join in the commemoration of the 1100th anniversary of the death of the Slav missionary, Saint Methodius, who was buried, it was believed, in Velehrad in Moravia. The Pope's reply (dated 1 May 1984), accepting the invitation and thanking the thousands of believers who had supported it, was circulated in *samizdat*. The Cardinal transmitted the Pope's acceptance to the authorities, who at once rejected such a visit.

As the anniversary celebrations approached, the views of Catholics, the Cardinal, and the Pope continued to be expressed in challenging ways. Two large groups of Catholics, 2000 in one case, 500 in another, reiterated their desire for the presence of the Pope at Velehrad. The

Cardinal, on 18 March 1985, addressed two letters, one to the newspaper *Tribuna*, protesting its interpretation of the significance of the work of Cyril and Methodius in purely political terms, and the other to the President, Husák, protesting official attempts to counteract the Church's ecclesiastic commemoration. Denying that the gathering had any political purpose, Tomášek invoked freedom of religion, citing the Universal Declaration of Human Rights.

In early July the Pope, in his encyclical on the two Slav saints, repeated his desire to be present in person in Velehrad. In his absence he was represented by Cardinal Casaroli, but other European cardinals, including Glemp of Poland, were denied permission to attend. Some 150 000 pilgrims made their way to Velehrad, perhaps most of them from Slovakia. During the proceedings there were jeers for government spokesmen and calls for 'freedom of the Church' and for the Pope. Václav Benda, Catholic Chartist, wrote of the 'historic significance' of the event and of the profound political implications of this 'resurrection' of 'civil society'.[43]

Evidence of the religious devotion of rank-and-file Catholics was demonstrated, year after year, by the pilgrimages of hundreds of thousands to Levoča and other shrines in Slovakia, estimated in 1987 to number more than half a million.

An extraordinary happening in August 1986 was a pilgrimage of 40 000 Greek Catholics (Uniates), banned since 1969, in a small village near Prešov in Eastern Slovakia.

Protestants represented a small minority of the population; the two largest churches were the Slovak Evangelical – with about 500 000 adherents – and the Evangelical Church of the Czech Brethren – about 300 000. In most cases the Protestant churches had reached a certain accommodation with the state and avoided criticism of discriminatory measures. As a result they were not so severely persecuted as the Catholics and were able to conduct activities among the youth in their local congregations. In the years after the communist takeover, the Brethren, in spite of a centuries-old tradition of protest, gave their support to the regime, as a result of the influence of the theologian, J. L. Hromádka. During the Prague Spring the Czech Evangelical Church endorsed reforms and condemned the Soviet invasion, but they later recanted and sought to avoid public criticism of the regime. The Hromádka tradition was weakened by his own renunciation of this long loyalty to the existing social order. It was also challenged by the thought of earlier philosophers, such as Emanuel Radl and T. G. Masaryk, and by the teaching of contemporary philosophers such as Božena Komárková and Jan Patočka.[44]

Significant acts of protests were taken only by some of the Czech Brethren, and usually on an individual basis. Among the early signatories of Charter 77 were eighteen pastors or former pastors, all of whom were censured by the synod council and lost their licences to preach, as well as some students or former students of theology, and twelve lay members of the Church (three of whom later served as Charter spokesmen). Most active in Charter affairs were the former pastors, M. Rejchrt, Jan Šimsa, Jakub Trojan, and Jan Dus; the lay philosophers, Ladislav Hejdánek and Božena Komárková; and other laymen, such as Jan Litomiský and M. Kocáb (both engineers by training). Many were imprisoned or harassed repeatedly by the police. The synod council was sharply criticised for its failure to offer even moral support to those who suffered persecution for human rights activity and for the endorsement of the official 'anti-Charter' declaration by V. Keyř, who was for many years Senior of the Synod.

Unlike the Catholics, however, the Brethren were organised democratically, in local *sbory*, regional synods, and a national synod, an elected body which met every two years and offered a forum in which lay persons could voice criticism. Protestant journals were also freer than the Catholic ones and occasionally opened their columns to well-known dissenters. Young believers were often dissatisfied with the synod's passive attitude and turned to Chartists for advice and help.

From time to time the synod or its council did take positive action on controversial issues. In 1983, for instance, the synod adopted a resolution which condemned the stationing of missiles (without making any distinction between East and West). Although it did not protest the imprisonment of Jan Litomiský, it sent a message of greeting to him in prison.[45] In February 1985 the synod council protested the trial of Jan Keller, who had been deprived of his licence as clergyman and was charged with holding weekly gatherings of youth for prayer and Bible reading. As a result of this, and of a petition signed by two thousand persons, the case was dropped by the Pilsen court although Keller was still not permitted to serve as a pastor. In November 1985 the synod criticised the cancellation of the licence of Václav Hurt, and also adopted a proposal to the Federal Assembly for civilian service as an alternative to military for those whose conscience forbade them to bear arms. The arrest of another defrocked pastor, Jan Dus, who had been active in defending those in trouble with the authorities, led to several petitions for his release, one signed by three hundred persons.[46]

Two other cases deserve mention. One was Zdeněk Bárta, pastor in a small country parish, who was denied permission to continue in 1980 because of his Charter 77 associations. The *sbor* refused to accept his removal and he continued some pastoral duties while working in industry. The synod at first acquiesced in his removal but in 1983 and 1984 demanded the return of his licence. Although he refused to withdraw his signature from Charter 77, he was given permission, six years later, to return to his pulpit. The other was Alfréd Kocáb, also a Charter signatory, who after years of work in industry, was allowed to serve as substitute pastor in Prague and later assumed the duties of the minister (deceased) in the largest Evangelical Church in the city.

Little is known of dissent among the other Protestant churches. An unusual event was the demand for official recognition as a separate church of a group in Brno, numbering some eighty persons, who called themselves 'the decisive Whitsun Christians'. They were subjected to immediate harassment and many were arrested.

STIRRINGS IN SLOVAKIA

Charter 77 was signed by only a handful of Slovaks and did not stimulate a significant movement of dissent or independent activity in Slovakia.[47] For some years the only vigorous dissident voices were those of Miroslav Kusý, philosopher and Charter signatory, and the Czech Milan Šimečka, a political theorist who had lived for many years in Bratislava, both of whom were prolific *samizdat* writers.[48] The eminent Slovak novelist, Dominik Tatarka, signed the Charter and published his works in *samizdat* and abroad, but was not overtly involved in dissident activity. These few were later reinforced by Jozef Jablonický, historian of the Slovak National Uprising whose books were condemned and withdrawn (he was dismissed from his position in the Academy of Sciences); by Pavel Čarnogurský, Catholic historian; and by his son, Ján, a lawyer who had defended Slovak religious dissidents. In the late 1980s several discussion groups met regularly, including one of young Catholics. Alexandr Dubček, after years of almost complete silence, wrote a brief rebuttal to statements made by Vasil Biľak (published in *L'Unita*, 21 November 1985). He later sent several letters to Gorbachev and Husák, defending his 1968 programme and comparing it with Soviet reform proposals.

Other independent activity in Slovakia was linked closely with religious faith. Slovak Catholicism, unlike the Czech branch, had been closely tied historically with nationalism, generated by long years of Magyar persecution. During the war years the Slovak Church enjoyed a privileged position in the Slovak state, but lost authority due to its association with German Nazism. After 1948 repression was severe, driving Slovaks together in a somewhat closed society and strengthening national feeling. Of the two Bishops, one was strongly pro-regime, and Church leaders did not support Charter 77. But some of the rank and file priests and believers manifested overt or hidden dissent. It was reported, for instance, that the Charter document on religious orders was prepared by Catholics in Bratislava. The many cases of persecution reported in VONS communiqués and in religious *samizdat* indicated that dissent was frequent among younger Catholics. For instance in 1983 eighty-five Slovak priests, sisters, and lay persons protested the police raids on Franciscans. There were also protests against favourable reports about Pacem in Terris in *Katolické noviny*, and the promotion of the pro-regime organization by Bishop Jozef Ferenc. Young people in Nitra censured the dismissal of a teacher for her 'idealistic views'. A Catholic priest in Rožnava was sentenced for possessing religious *samizdat*; two young Brethren were detained for the same offence. Three young Slovak Catholics were charged with smuggling religious materials from Poland into Czechoslovakia as were two young Brethren. Another letter was sent to the President by a number of young Slovak Catholics urging an end to religious repression, an improvement of the conditions of the Church, and the rehabilitation of priests and believers unjustly condemned by the courts.[49]

The sharpest protest came in response to the Slovak government's decision to amend the law on abortion, easing considerably the conditions under which women might be permitted to have the operation. This produced two letters of protest, one signed by 7518 people, addressed to the Slovak Prime Minister, Petr Colotka (3 March 1986) calling for the withdrawal of the measure or a referendum on the issue. A second letter (25 March), signed by fifty people in Banská Bystrica, condemned the proposed measure as well as the current legal provisions for abortion. In September similar views were expressed by 7880 citizens in the Czech lands. Cardinal Tomášek, in a letter dated 20 April 1986 to the government presidium in Prague, opposed abortion and defended the right of the petitioners to make such protests.[50]

Several more general criticisms of the regime and its policies appeared anonymously. A long rambling essay, dated 6 December 1983, spoke of the failure to solve urgent Slovak problems and described spontaneous tendencies toward what was called 'creeping counterrevolution'. Two more cogently argued letters were sent to the President by 'young people of the ČSSR,' one from Nitra, on 19 March 1984, and the other from Banská Bystrica, on 29 August 1984. The latter, written on the anniversary of the Slovak National Uprising, appealed to Husák to correct the distortion of that great event in historical writings, and to restore the traditional Slovak national emblem (a double-barred cross standing on three hills) to the Czechoslovak national coat of arms, replacing the partisan symbol of a bonfire on a mountain. The young people, reporting that many of them had been beaten when seeking signatures for a petition proposing a visit by the Pope, reiterated their hope that such an event would occur. They warned against the presence of the Moscow Patriarch at the Methodius celebration and opposed the creation of a separate national church under Moscow, a proposal which had been the subject of rumours. They urged the regime to concentrate on solving serious problems such as alcoholism, drug abuse, criminality, divorce, illiteracy, etc., and offered their own services in such actions.[51]

In 1978 Hungarians in Slovakia formed a Committee for the Legal Defence of the Hungarian Minority which issued a number of protests against national discrimination. Their chief spokesman, Miklós Dúray, a geologist, was detained for several months during the winter of 1982–3. In August 1983 Dúray signed Charter 77, publicly thanking it and VONS for their support during his imprisonment and declaring that his actions were based on a general belief in human rights, not on national interests exclusively. Official plans to extend the teaching of Slovak in schools produced widespread discontent among Hungarians and stimulated even the official ethnic organisation, Csemadok, to protest. Dúray was again imprisoned on 10 May 1984 for publishing abroad a book on the injustices done to the Hungarians. He was released in May 1985 and the charges against him were dropped.

During his detention several Slovaks (Kusý, Šimečka, Jablonický, and Ján Čarnogurský), without identifying themselves with the substance of Dúray's complaints of discrimination, protested his treatment in separate letters dated 28 June 1984. Several years later, violent anti-Hungarian incidents in Bratislava led Charter 77 to take a strong stand protesting against discrimination.[52] In December 1987 Charter 77 (document no. 74) presented a proposal on national minorities, prepared by the Hungarian Committee, to the Prague government and the Vienna CSCE conference.

Miroslav Kusý, in a penetrating study of the nationality question, based on official data, presented evidence of oppression of the Magyar minority, numbering 559 490, which was, he said, proportionally under-represented in Slovak governmental bodies and in schools at all levels. Paradoxically, the small minority of Ukrainians – 36 850 in all – enjoyed a preferential position, even relative to the Slovaks on some matters. He cited examples of discrimination against the Slovak minority in Bohemia and Moravia; against the Czech minority in Slovakia; and, most flagrantly, against the gypsies. This reflected, he argued, the general denial of rights inherent in a totalitarian system, in which the interests of all groups, including the nationality groups, were subordinated to the 'superior interests' of those in power, whether Czech or Slovak.[53]

CITIZENS ACTING AND THINKING INDEPENDENTLY

The extent of independent thought and behaviour was indicated by a remarkable public opinion poll conducted by independent sociologists and analyzed by a Czech sociologist, Zdeněk Strmiska, living in exile in France.[54] Without detection or interruption by the police, eighty-five questions were presented to 342 persons throughout the country, principally, however, in the major cities of Prague, Brno, and Bratislava. This was not a scientific poll in the strict sense. Although the distribution of respondents did roughly correspond to the actual population categories based on sex, age groupings, and occupation, the sample was disproportionately high in respect of middle and higher school education, and substantially lower in terms of party membership (8.2 per cent instead of the actual 15–16 per cent). Of those polled 89.4 per cent were non-party persons; 70 per cent had never been Communist Party members; and almost 20 per cent had left or been expelled from the party. Although the results were therefore biased somewhat in favour of the educated, the urban-dwellers, non-party persons, and Czechs, they presented a revealing picture of the extent of official or independent civic activity and of independent thinking.

For official activity, those questioned were asked whether they participated in meetings and other activities of the two Communist parties (Czechoslovak and Slovak), the League of Czechoslovak–Soviet Friendship, or other authorised political parties. The results indicated that 75 per cent did take part, although only 6.7 per cent as active members or functionaries, and only 6.4 per cent regularly attended meetings and took part in discussions. On the other hand 62.5 per cent admitted that they attended meetings only 'sometimes', or 'rarely'. Although the poll did not provide a full profile of party members, especially of the higher echelons or the most loyal rank and file, Strmiska drew the conclusion that the results indicated the lack of a positive attitude to the political system and to the ruling élite.

The data on independent civic activity were revealing, even taking into account a certain bias in the selection of respondents. The results indicated that a substantial proportion listened to foreign radio or television broadcasts, saw *samizdat* publications or books and journals printed abroad, or took part in unofficial activity of various kinds.

More than half of the respondents listened to foreign radio or television broadcasts, either regularly or frequently (51 per cent in all), or occasionally (38 per cent), giving a total of nearly 90 per cent. Only 9.6 per cent indicated that they never, or almost never, did so.

Those who read the unofficial press, books, and journals published abroad, or typewritten feuilletons and articles, formed a smaller proportion – more than half of the sample. Regular readers constituted 37.7 per cent; those who read *samizdat* only by chance and passed it on, 31.2 per cent; those who read it exceptionally and did not pass it on, 8.2 per cent. Taken together, these categories amounted to a surprising proportion of more than 77 per cent. Another 8.5 per cent would have liked to see it, but did not have the opportunity. Only 9.1 per cent had never had such material in their hands; 1.8 per cent condemned it; and 2.6 per cent feared to read it because it was 'illegal'. In other words, these made up only 13.5 per cent of those polled. More detailed figures indicated that the materials which were read included Charter 77 and VONS publications, *Edice Petlice, Infoch* and other *samizdat* series; *Listy* and *Svědectví*; and religious publications.

Those citizens who took part in activity which was not officially approved or was considered illegal, such as lectures, seminars, religious gatherings, etc., were fewer, but in general constituted an astonishing 28.4 per cent, with another 47.9 per cent participating occasionally, and 24.7 per cent not participating.[55] Responses to questions 21–27 are presented in Table 4.1

Table 4.1   Participation in independent activity in Czechoslovakia (percentage)

	Participation	Non-participation
Musical or dramatic groups	8.8	61.4
Lectures or seminars	13.7	62.8
Private film showings	6.7	67.5
Unofficial religious gatherings	10.2	70.8
Unofficial scouting, woodcraft, etc.	1.8	94.1
Sports, communes or hiking	2.6	83.0
Charter 77 or VONS	10.2	51.4

Source: Zdeněk Strmiska, 'Výsledky nezávislého průzkumu současného smýšlení v Československu', *Svědectví*, xx, no. 78 (1986), pp. 265–334.

If one considered all types of independent activity, most striking was the conclusion that almost two-thirds of the sample (64.6 per cent) joined in one or other of the three main types, sometimes in more than one. More than half listened to foreign radio; more than one-third read *samizdat* or imported literature; and more than one-quarter engaged in group activities such as those listed in the above table. Even conformists, i.e., those who participated in official activities, also took part in some that were unofficial; more than half of the two categories of regular or occasional official participants did so.

Other results indicated a relatively positive attitude towards independent actions. Those who personally knew people engaged in activity against the present regime and held them in high respect constituted 71.9 per cent of the sample, with an additional 19.5 per cent partly disposed in this direction; only 6.4 per cent expressed disapproval. More than half (54.3 per cent) agreed with, and were willing to aid financially, those who were politically engaged against the regime; 33.6 per cent had mixed feelings, and only 9.6 per cent disapproved.

Even more revealing were answers to questions as to the self-identification of the individuals polled which gave each respondent an opportunity to indicate his religious and political beliefs and, in one question, to indicate whether he or she rejected any such classification and simply felt as an individual or human being (*člověk*). Table 4.2 presents the results.

Table 4.2 Self-identification of Czechoslovak opinion poll respondents (percentage)

	Decidedly so	*Partially so, did not know*	*Decidedly not*
I am a believer, a religious person	16.9	19.2	62.2
I am a Marxist	4.4	11.1	82.7
I am a communist	4.4	2.9	91.7
I am a socialist, but non-Marxist	21.6	32.7	44.4
I consider myself a democrat	54.0	26.9	17.2
I am a liberal	11.6	24.2	61.4
I am a conservative	4.7	13.4	79.8
I reject such a self-designation, I am simply a human being	50.8	23.3	22.5

Source: see Table 4.1.

The table reveals that the strongest group were those who called themselves democrats (80 per cent decidedly or partly); the second largest were those who preferred to consider themselves simply as human beings (74 per cent); the third group were those who considered themselves non-Marxist socialists (54 per cent). An overwhelming 80 to 90 per cent rejected such identifications altogether. The percentages were somewhat similar among the younger generation (no ages given), revealing a smaller proportion of believers (14.5 per cent) and of non-Marxist socialists (12.8 per cent), and an almost unanimous rejection of Marxism or communism.

A similar repudiation of communism was reflected in the replies to a question on the maximum support which the Communist Party could win in a free elections. Only 2.9 per cent expected the party to get 45 per cent or more of the votes; 2.6 per cent between 35 and 44 per cent; 9.4 per cent between 25 and 34 per cent. Conversely, 7.8

per cent expected the party to get 24 per cent or less; 61.5 per cent less than 15 per cent; 31.5 per cent less than 10 per cent. In other words almost no one expected that the party which arbitrarily claimed the 'leading role' in politics could win a majority of votes. Most believed it could gain the support of only a small minority.

Answers to another set of questions indicated that official indoctrination, after years of effort, had been less than successful in moulding opinion. Despite the dogmas that the USA and Germany were imperialist and threatened peace and that the Soviet Union protected Czechoslovakia against the danger of war and served the country's interests, the responses in Table 4.3 are illuminatory.

Table 4.3   Czechoslovak attitudes to other nations (percentage)

Statement	Yes	No	Partial agreement
The USA is imperialist, striving for war.	8.8	43.5	45.6
The Soviet Union is imperialist, striving for war.	27.7	12.8	57.3
The USA threatens peace more than the USSR.	6.4	63.1	27.4
The Soviet Union protects us against the danger of war.	5.8	54.0	37.4
Both the USA and the USSR are imperialist states, and defence against them should be sought in a United Central European State.	30.7	28.3	36.2
The German Federal Republic threatens the existence of Czechoslovakia.	3.2	65.7	28.3
West Germans are enemies of Czechs and Slovaks.	1.7	69.5	26.3
East Germans are enemies of Czechs and Slovaks.	5.0	69.2	23.3
We did well to transfer the Germans.	15.2	42.6	39.7

Statement	Yes	No	Partial agreement
Things would be worse if we separated from the USSR and became an independent state once again.	3.5	80.7	11.9
The Western states are in deep crisis with unemployment and a difficult life.	6.7	32.1	58.4

Source: See Table 4.1.

CONCLUSIONS

After 1969 Czechoslovakia presented a picture of immobility and stagnation in all spheres of life. There were no significant changes in political leadership or in policy; no steps were taken toward economic reform; literature, the arts, and scholarship were stifled by censorship and party control. In this stultifying atmosphere those commonly known as 'dissidents', or more accurately, 'independent spirits', entertained little hope for basic change in the system or even serious partial reforms in the immediate future. They were therefore concerned with the 'here and now', and aimed at living as freely and honestly as possible under existing conditions. There was an aversion to planning or to speculating about the future, and a preference for concentrating on the present or a short-run perspective, and for working on a small scale and within narrow circles. Any thought of revolution, such as was advocated by a few individuals abroad, was regarded as quite out of touch with reality. Nonetheless the conviction persisted that currents at work beneath the surface would eventually lead to something new, although it was impossible to predict what might happen, or when, or how.

Whatever the outcome of Gorbachev's initiative in the Soviet Union, and its repercussions in Czechoslovakia, it was still necessary to prepare oneself and others for the time when change became possible so that one would then be ready to act. In the words of the Charter, lasting changes were conceivable only if the necessary conditions were created, namely 'a transformation in the hearts and minds of people, in their morality, their relation to society, their civic postures, that is, in all that is called social consciousness'.[56]

Viewed from this angle, as Vilém Prečan wrote, Charter 77 and the autonomous activity stimulated by it constituted 'a great work of preparing and recultivating the soil for future political changes.' If such an opportunity did arise, it would probably be the consequences of forces other than the work of Charter 77, but the quality of subsequent deeds would be influenced among other things by 'the endeavours of those who did not give up hope yesterday and today, who refused, as incompatible with their conscience, to "live in the lie" and who took the path of their civic right and duty, even though to the majority of their contemporaries this seemed to be the dangerous conduct of a handful of fools'.[57]

Václav Havel spoke in similar vein when he accepted *in absentia* the Erasmus award in Rotterdam in November 1986. Citing Erasmus's *In Praise of Folly*, he recommended 'the courage to be a fool' and declared that the award honoured 'the hundreds of other fools who did not hesitate to voice their lonely call for the change of the unchangeable and to set against the giant power of the state bureaucracy the miserable power of their typewriters. Everyone of us, however insignificant and powerless, has the power to change the world.'[58]

5 Independent Historiography Reborn

'History has stopped. Nothing exists except an endless present in which the Party is always right.

'The mutability of the past is the central tenet of Ingsoc . . . the past is whatever the Party chooses to make it.

'And yet he was in the right: They were wrong and he was right. The obvious, the silly, and the true had got to be defended . . . *Freedom is the freedom to say that two plus two make four. If that is granted, all else follows.*' – George Orwell, *Nineteen Eighty-Four* (London, 1954, pp. 127, 171, 68).

No one has analysed more brilliantly the moral and spiritual crisis of contemporary Czechoslavakia, and the fate of its history, than Václav Havel, in his now famous letter to Gustáv Husák in April 1975.[1] 'In a society which is really alive', he wrote, 'there is naturally always something happening. . . . Any society that is alive is a society with a history.' However, in an 'entropic' society, as Havel called it, in which 'the mechanical prevails over the vital' and 'order without life' exists, true history cannot exist. 'In our country, too, one has the impression that for some time there has been no history. Slowly, but surely, we are losing the sense of time. We begin to forget what happened when, what came earlier and what later, and the feeling that it really doesn't matter overwhelms us. As uniqueness disappears from the flow of events, so does continuity; everything merges into the single grey image of one and the same cycle and we say, "There is nothing happening".' In this situation the 'disorder of real history' is replaced by the 'orderliness of pseudo-history' which is determined not by 'the life of society' but by 'an official planner'.

Two other authors, writing in *samizdat*, discussed the theme of 'a-historicalness.' The Slovak philosopher, Miroslav Kusý, condemned the 'ignorant usurper' who sought to make of historic Bratislava 'a town pro-Russian and pro-Communist from time immemorial'.[2] Everywhere there are Lenin statues, Lenin squares, and Lenin streets, and fewer and fewer are the reminders of great Slovaks such as Štur, Kollár, or Hviezdoslav. Štefánik, the eminent Slovak leader, has twice lost the street named after him. Goethe has been replaced by Gorky; Liszt by Tchaikovsky; Masaryk by the mundane 'Main Street'. A central square which once bore the name of Stalin, before that of Hlinka, earlier still that of Archduke Frederick, and was once called The Republic, has become 'The Square of the National Uprising'. This is the only Slovak event designated as a national holiday (29 August). 'It is not true,' Kusý concluded, 'that there are two histories: the real (the actual, the really happening) and the interpreted (or disinterpreted). There is, alas, only one living history – and that is the interpreted one. Every usurper knows this very well; what he succeeds in wiping out of the consciousness of the nation, what he succeeds in instilling into that consciousness in altered form – all that ceases to be the living national history.'

The Czech political analyst, Milan Šimečka, developed the same theme further in an eloquent afterword to a Czech edition of Orwell's *1984*.[3] 'Our comrade, Winston Smith', as he called Orwell's tragic hero, was 'forced to live in a society without history; better said, without real history, with only a history instrumentally derived from the present' (p. 275). In Orwell's *1984*, 'a-historicalness was brought to perfection,' Šimecka observed. 'The mass of the proles knew practically nothing of history and the members of the inner party had to put up with doctored history' (p. 279). History was effectively wiped from the consciousness of most people. Poor Winston Smith could only find some fragments of truth here and there, especially in the forbidden book by Goldstein to which he secured access. Nonetheless he was determined to seek out more of the truth about the past.

Czech and Slovak scholars suffered a fate similar to that of Winston Smith and, like him, sought to extricate themselves from it. 'We all live in an artificial state of a-historicalness', wrote Šimečka. At the same time, like Smith, some of them engaged in a sustained effort to escape from this state. 'The re-thinking, to which Winston, and all of us, devoted ourselves', observed Šimečka, 'was not an obsession – it was a simple act of self-preservation, a defense against total disintegration and a striving for human dignity' (p. 276). It is to this 're-thinking' of history of Czechs and Slovaks that this chapter is devoted.

THE USES OF HISTORY

History, and its interpretation, has always been a critically important factor in Central and Eastern European culture and politics. Historians have often played a political role unusual in countries of the West which have a much less history-oriented perspective. Czechoslavakia has been no exception, and indeed has been noteworthy in this respect. Czechs, and Slovaks, too, have always had a remarkable interest in their own past and a highly developed historical consciousness. Historians and historical writing have exerted a strong influence on politics and even on the general public. There have often been sharp debates among historians, and public figures, over the 'meaning of Czech history' and its relationship to the present. Eminent scholars, such as Dobrovský, Palacký, and Masaryk, have searched for, and found, in the historical past justifications for contemporary cultural and political behaviour and even programmes for the future. Among historians there has been a kind of cycle of controversy over the question of 'history for history's sake' as opposed to 'history for the sake of life'.[4] Masaryk, who was not a historian by profession, sought to use history, as he interpreted it, as a support and encouragement for his struggle for a new national awakening in the late nineteenth century, and this generated opposition by professional historians, such as Josef Pekař, and by rival political leaders. Retrospectively his achievement in establishing Czechoslovak independence was sometimes interpreted as a triumph of his conception of Czech history. Nonetheless when he became President of the new Republic, Masaryk did not try to manipulate history as an instrument of his own rule or as a source of legitimacy, and historians, such as Pekař, and politicians and other public figures were free to question his 'history' and his politics.[5]

After the communist seizure of power in 1948 the role of history and historians became even more significant but in a manner quite different than in the past. The ruling Communists, having always interpreted history in Marxist terms in a way calculated to serve their own party's interests, applied this instrumental view of history in an extreme degree and through coercive means. The new 'official historiography' was the only one permitted and 'a central pillar' of the totalitarian system. In the spirit of George Orwell's dictum, 'Who controls the Past controls the present; who controls the present controls the future', the communist regime strove to make history a servant of its contemporary interests, to legitimise its own power, and a tool for manipulating public opinion. New canons of interpretation were imposed on the study of history and on its writing, and enjoyed a monopoly over historical research and publication. New institutions were established to conduct research in the spirit of the official historiography and to publish the accepted product. These bodies, together with the system of censorship, served as agencies of control over all historical writings, and made the expression of dissonant views difficult. Most of the older historians, who were not Marxists and were not willing to obey the official directives, were dismissed and were replaced by younger Marxist cadres, who willingly and enthusiastically served the cause or were forced into conformity by indoctrination and a system of rewards and penalties.[6]

As a result, wrote Andrew Rossos, 'Czech historiography lost its free and independent position and was transformed into an instrument of the Communist Party and its government. It was forcibly isolated from outside developments and influences; it was deprived of its right to free and unhindered investigation. In short it was "Stalinized".'[7] In the words of another scholar, Vladimir Kusin, 'history was understood through the prism of historical materialism which recognized the perennial superiority of the working class' – 'an approach which made absolute the social and class movements in society while neglecting the factor of national interest'.[8] 'No period in history could feel safe' from 'plain distortion,' including, for instance, those as remote from the present as the age of Charles iv, Jan Hus, Comenius, and the national revival. Certain periods, events, and persons were singled out for negative treatment so as to reduce their influence on the popular consciousness. This included, for example, the establishment of the First Republic in 1918, the years of the First Republic and the immediate postwar years 1945–8; the Slovak National Uprising and the Prague Uprising; and individuals such as Masaryk, Beneš, and Štefánik. The history of the Czechoslovak Communist Party, its relationship with the Soviet party and the Comintern, and its leaders were subjected to special distortions. The result, wrote Stanley Pech, was an image of the Czech and Slovak past which was 'an ideological construction which future research was expected merely to refine and fortify. In effect, the results of any future research were thus predetermined. Marxist historiography had become an historical science as well as a set of unhistorical beliefs, a comforting compound of faith and reason.'[9]

In the 1960s, and once again in the later 1970s, there were

historians, as well as other scholars, who had the courage, and the will, to stand up against the barrage of ideological dogma and to assume the burden of seeking out the truth. There were, of course, some who avoided the challenge, and others who were able to produce works of good quality in spite of all impediments. More and more, after 1956, history became a battlefield, with the more independent historians locked in struggle, sometimes veiled, often open, with the state and party, who were supported by more conservative 'official' historians. There were two main stages in this struggle, one during the 1960s, the other during the 1970s, stages which resembled each other in some respects, but differed profoundly in others.

FERMENT IN THE 1960s

The 'remarkable renascence in Czech historiography' in the 1960s has often been described and need not be discussed in detail here.[10] A central feature of the period was a 'critical revaluation of the past', in which the historians reassessed all major events, periods, and persons in order to produce 'a truthful picture of the nation's past'.[11] The first tremors of change, in 1956, were short-lived, and the crisis was overcome by repression. The ferment erupted again in succeeding years, at first beneath the surface, and then exploding in an avalanche of criticism from 1963 on which the party was not able to stifle. In Pech's words, this was 'an upheaval of intellect, of conscience, of outlook, of courage. In 1963 the Marxist historian would no longer accept the intellectual tutelage of the Party. He would continue to be a Marxist and a Party member, but on his own terms and without compromising his integrity as a scholar. The two shocks had matured him, had made him tolerant of opposing views, but had also filled him with a new pride in his profession as a custodian of the nation's collective memory. Until then, it was the Party that had moulded the historian; henceforth it would be the historian who would seek to mould the Party.'[12]

The process of change in the minds of the historians and in the content of their writings was slow and gradual, and subjected to frequent obstacles and repeated reversals by an intolerant regime. It was a kind of 'controlled rehabilitation', reluctantly permitted by the authorities, who had in some degree initiated the process but were frightened by its course. It was conducted by Marxist historians who were members of the academic establishment. Some continued to be the incarnation of official history; others were led by their professional standards to oppose the abuse of history. The latter could not challenge openly the ideology or the party line and had to act indirectly and cautiously. They were themselves often hampered by taboos and inhibitions in their own thinking, and were still subject to ideological controls and censorship restrictions. Some of those who stepped out of line on delicate issues, such as Milan Hübl and Jan Mlynárik, were the targets of blistering condemnation by party leaders.

Nonetheless, by the time of the Third Congress of Historians held in Brno in 1966, much had been accomplished. Josef Macek, director of the Historical Institute, delivered a major address which was in marked contrast to that given by him at the preceding congress in 1959. Although he still described Marxism-Leninism as the starting point and the basis of historical study, he declared that 'partisanry' involved 'the maximum of objective reality and truth'. Symbolic of the change of attitude was a resolution adopted by the congress which demanded that 28 and 30 October be proclaimed as days of the birth of the Czechoslovak Republic, thus rescuing this event from the oblivion to which it had been consigned.[13]

Space prevents an examination of the major questions which were subjected to re-examination and re-interpretation by the more independently-minded historians. Their works dealt with all periods of Czech and Slovak history, and touched on sensitive and controversial issues of more contemporary periods. There were studies of the place of Masaryk and Štefánik in Czech and Slovak history; of the First Republic and of Munich; of the role of Beneš before and during the Second World War; of a wartime resistance and the Prague Uprising in 1945; of Slovak history and the National Uprising in 1944; of the history of the Communist Party itself, including the notorious Fifth Congress, and its relationship with the Comintern; of the postwar years of New Democracy and the communist takeover in February 1948; of the great trials of the 1950s and other aspects of Stalinism; even of Soviet history and Czechoslovak–Soviet relations.[14]

This process culminated in 1968 when historians proclaimed, and in the majority accepted, the principles of historical science taken for granted in open societies: 'the right to scholarly pursuits without any restrictions on political grounds; the right to publish the results of their research freely; open competition of all historical schools of thought, whether Marxist or not; unrestricted contact with the science of the whole world: and the demand for the removal of all taboos'.[15]

This intellectual awakening at the time of the Prague Spring has been called, a little exaggeratedly, 'an historians' revolution'.[16] Certainly historical questions bulked large in the ferment of public discussion and historians played a prominent role. The period of freedom was too short to bring about a profound development in research but opened up the prospect of the emergence of a genuinely independent historiography. One could confidently expect, as did Stanley Pech, 'that Czech and Slovak historians were on the threshold of a new creative era in which the finest historiographical achievements of the past century would be fused into a new historiography'.[17]

NORMALISATION OF HISTORY

The sudden termination of the Prague Spring by Soviet military intervention did not at once reverse the truth-seeking tendencies of Czech and Slovak historians. In the immediate aftermath of the invasion, the Historical Institute sponsored and published a documentary record of this event in a book entitled 'Seven Days in Prague', unofficially called the 'Black Book'.[18] Its editors (whose names were not given) expressed pride in the fact that, 'as historians', they were able to 'fulfill their professional duty to our own people' (p. iv). V. Prečan and M. Otáhal, two of its editors, were later indicted on charges of 'instigation' (later changed to 'subversion') and were subjected to police investigation and dismissed from their work, but were in the end not tried or imprisoned. The book was condemned by the Soviet authorities as a 'gross falsification of the facts, having nothing in common with historical scholarship', and had to be 'withdrawn'.[19]

The Black Book was almost the last gasp of the independent work of the 1960s and at the same time was a precursor of the independent historical writing which was to emerge in the 1970s. For some months, during the Dubček interregnum, most of the historians retained their positions and continued their work, and some publications appeared in the old spirit. After the elevation of Gustáv Husák to supreme power in the spring of 1969, however, the regime embarked on a course designed to restore the pre-1968 official historiography and its mechanism of controls. Old dogmas of interpretation were revived; new ones, such as that of the 'counter-revolution' of 1968, were promulgated. Historical institutions were reorganised and in some cases abolished. An Institute of Czechoslovak and World History replaced, for instance the Historical Institute. A newly-named Czechoslovak–Soviet Institute was placed under Václav Král, one of the most conservative and dogmatic of the old-style historians, who was also given responsibility for supervising all the historical institutes of the Academy of Sciences.

Under Král's auspices a relentless purge was carried through in 1970 and after, the victims being for the most part the younger historians who had entered the profession in the 1950s and had been the principal spokesmen of the 'new history' of the 1960s. They were relegated to manual work, as stokers, window-washers, or factory workers, and prevented not only from publishing but even from using libraries and archives. The virtual destruction of the profession was documented in a booklet, *Acta Persecutionis*, which was prepared in Prague and distributed in printed form to the XIVth International Congress of Historical Sciences at San Francisco in 1975.[20] It listed 145 historians who had been deprived of their employment in the universities, research institutes, and archives. Several historians – including Milan Hübl, Jaroslav Mezník, and Jan Tesař – were in prison.

The spirit of the restored official historiography may be gleaned from a major article on the tasks of the profession by Dr Jaroslav Purš, who was later appointed director of the Institute of Czechoslovak and World History. Rejecting the notion of continuity of historical work, and enunciating the necessity of a 'class approach' to historical interpretation, he declared: 'We do not accept everything from history; we do not accept mud, slime and filth, such as some rightist historians proposed in 1968–9. Just as we do not drink water from impure sources, but carefully filter and purify it, so also we do not draw from the past everything we know about it. We take as our point of departure only the pure, progressive, revolutionary traditions and use them as the foundations of the creative development of the values of our socialist present and future.' The task of Marxist-Leninist historiography, he went on, was 'to give a correct interpretation, to strengthen the historical consciousness of people and to guide them to correct standpoints in life'.[21]

Concrete meaning of this selective and arbitrary approach was given in the review of a major historiographical work by a distinguished historian, František Kutnar. The reviewer identified the progressive tradition as being embodied in the work of the Marxist scholar Zdeněk Nejedlý; the conservative or reactionary tradition, in the work of the distinguished historian Josef Pekař. Also condemned was the 'ideological marasmus of Masarykism'. Only the 'party and class approach', he urged, was valid.[22] The withdrawal of Kutnar's book from use in the universities indicated how dangerous it was to ignore the injunction of the official historiography. It was only by the exercise of special skills and adroitness that some historians were able to escape the guidelines, at least in part, and produce works of some quality, which were usually published in local or specialised journals of limited availability.

AN INDEPENDENT HISTORIOGRAPHY

For several years the prospect of a revival of independent historical writing seemed slight. Some historians, who had still hoped against hope for a relaxation of drastic persecution by the Husák regime, began to lose heart and, in some cases, reluctantly chose the alternative of emigration.[23] Most of those who had been removed from official scholarly institutions found it hard to carry on intellectual work after a day of enervating and demoralising labour. A few articles and books were written and circulated in *samizdat* form. The new form of existential terror at least did not involve physical liquidation or, in most cases long-term imprisonment, so that survival, and some scholarly work, were possible. Charter 77 encouraged writers and scholars to seek to 'live in truth' as Havel put it,[24] and to defend, and extend, the sphere of freedom which they, as individuals, could stake out for themselves in spite of official restrictions and police harassment. The historians, some forty of whom had signed the Charter, caught 'a second breath', as it were, and began to show anew their determination, in spite of everything, to remain historians. Although their audience was small – a few of their fellow historians and some interested scholars at home and abroad – some of them undertook the difficult task of preparing scholarly articles dedicated, like Winston Smith's, 'to the future or to the past, to a time when thought is free, when men are different from one another and do not live alone – to a time when truth exists and what is done cannot be undone'.[25]

The rise of an independent historiography, was documented abroad by Vilém Prečan, who had gone into exile in West Germany in 1976. In *Acta Creationis*, which he prepared by his own efforts for presentation at the 15th International Congress of Historical Sciences in Bucharest in 1980, Prečan listed all historical works (books, articles, and briefer essays) which had appeared in *samizdat* between the late 1960s and 1980 – an amazing total of 182 items, by ninety authors.[26] The volume also contained, in German translation, ten articles (in whole or in part), which had appeared, or were shortly to do so, in a journal of historical studies (its first issue was called *Historické studie*) which came out in typewritten form from 1978 on.

The rebirth of historical writing, under the conditions of 'normalized' Czechoslovakia, is a remarkable phenomenon. In a certain sense, as Prečan acknowledged, there is only a single 'history', just as there is only one Czech (or Slovak) literature, whether produced within or outside the official structures, at home or abroad. Yet there are differences in the conditions under which history is written. The work which 'seeks to reflect the world and the inner self of the author in an authentic fashion' is 'silenced and oppressed, and threatened with liquidation'; it exists only in manuscript form, and is read by a small audience; its authors are subjected to various handicaps and restrictions, and are not permitted to belong to the historical profession at home or internationally. On the other hand such historians have certain advantages over their 'official' counterparts at home: they are not subject to censorship or other controls, and can therefore protect and maintain their personal and professional identity, without compromise (p. xxv).

After careful deliberation Prečan chose the term 'independent' to describe this segment of Czech and Slovak historical writing. He rejected other terms – 'unofficial', 'oppositional', 'free', or 'parallel' – as inaccurate or misleading. The historiography with which he was concerned was not properly speaking 'unofficial', as *some* historians did move between the two spheres, official and unofficial (as they did in the 1960s). It was not 'oppositional', since they did not necessarily concern themselves with politics at all, but concentrated on historical research. It was not 'free', in view of the 'unfree' conditions in which the historians worked and the hazards they faced in doing so. It was not 'parallel', since it dealt with different subjects and often reached different conclusions. The essence of this form of historical writing was its 'independence': 'independence from the utilitarian and instrumental conception of official historical writing, and independence of its research from the dogmas and schemata of the ruling ideology'. It is this feature that linked their work with the historiography of the Czech and Slovak past and of the free scientific world. It is this that conferred on these historians the worth and dignity of free scholars (pp. xxi–xxv).[27]

The content of eight issues of the journal of historical studies has been analysed by this author in detail elsewhere.[28] Those which dealt with Czech history in the nineteenth century, or in earlier periods, had no special political implications except for their scholarly objectivity and its implicit challenge to prevailing doctrine. Of those treating Czechoslovak history between the wars, only one, which surveyed the literature on Munich, dealt with politically controversial issues, and severely criticized the writings of Václav Král, the dominant figure of Czechoslovak historiography after 1969. He was condemned for his simplified anti-British and pro-Soviet positions, his hostility towards Beneš, and his black-and-white 'class approach', and censured for 'neglecting the elementary principles of historical criticism'.[29] Several articles on the German occupation period, analyzing resistance and collaboration, and the 'escape into the past' in literature, had contemporary implications in respect to the Soviet occupation, although these were not explicitly drawn.[30] An article on the Prague Uprising in 1945, in a manner entirely inconsistent with official historiography, described this event as largely unplanned and spontaneous, and as reflecting the weaknesses of the Czech wartime resistance movement. Several articles on Slovak modern history broke with prevailing official dogmas, one, for instance, dealing positively with the role of Slovak Social Democrats in the early years of the Republic, another praising the role of Štefánik in the establishment of the Republic. Another essay dealt with an uprising in Trnava in 1944, ascribing it in heretical fashion to the initiative of the military, and not of the Communist Party.[31] Several articles on international communism dealt objectively with the rise of the Italian Communist Party and its relationship with the Comintern in the 1920s, and another examined the decline of democracy within the Communist International.

Reviews and comments included in the historical journal treated Western literature fairly and often quite favourably, and gave no attention to Soviet publications. The treatment of contemporary official Czech and Slovak scholarship was negative, in the main, and often somewhat polemical. In addition to the criticism of Král mentioned above, there was sharp censure of a major study of the Czechoslovak 'revolution' between 1944 and 1948 published on the occasion of the 35th anniversary of liberation in 1945. The book was written 'strictly according to the propagandistic pattern of black and white description', and was an example of 'the degradation of historiography.' In its almost 400 pages, it was said, there was 'almost nothing new', no serious analysis of the period, and no contribution to historical knowledge.[32]

The articles were objective and balanced, usually dispassionte, and often based on a wide array of sources. They were free of the dogmas and biases of official historiography, and did not reflect a Marxist-Leninist, or even a Marxist, approach. This writing constituted therefore a much sharper break with official historiography than the 'revisionist' literature of the 1960s. It was not the product of authors working within the establishment, or within an ideological framework, and was not subject to any form of censorship. The independent historians could write with considerable freedom and treat their subjects according to the canons of objective scholarship.

Since my review of the historical journals issued from 1978 to January 1982, other numbers appeared at irregular intervals, each bearing a different title. Paradoxically in November 1982, two separate collections of historical essays appeared, under different titles, because the original editors were unable to agree on editorial policy and had parted company. After several years of separate activity, a common editorial board was re-established in 1986 and again published a joint issue (no. 21). The editors also agreed on a single numbered list of all their publications.[33]

Table 5.1   Czechoslovak historical journals and *sborníky* in *samizdat*

---

1. *Historické studie, Sborník* (Historical Studies, A Collection) (January 1978), 261 pp.
2. (no title) (June 1978), unpaginated, 180 pp. est.
3. *Sborník historických studií* (Collection of Historical Studies) (Spring 1979), 234 pp.
4. *Studie z československých dějin, Sborník* (Studies of Czechoslovak History, A Collection) (Fall 1979), 169 pp.; another version, 183 pp.
5. *Studie historické, Sborník* (Historical Studies, A Collection) (June 1980), unpaginated, 188 pp. est.
6. *Studie československých dějin, Sborník* (Studies of Czechoslovak History, A Collection) (December 1980), 226 pp.
7. *Ž dějin, Sborník studií* (From History, A Collection of Studies) (Prague 1981), unpaginated, 232 pp. est.
8. *Sborník historických studií k šedesátinám Miloše Hájka* (A Collection of Historical Studies for the Sixtieth Birthday of Miloš Hájek) (May 1981).

9. *Historické a sociologické studie, Sborník* (Historical and Sociological Studies, A Collection) (January 1982), 189 pp.
10. *Z českých a slovenských dějin, Sborník* (From Czech and Slovak History, A Collection) (November 1982), 201 pp.
11. *State historické, sociologické, kritiky a glosy, Sborník* (Historical and Sociological Essays, Critiques and Comments, A Collection) (November 1982), 279 pp.
12. *Studie z dějin přjin předmnichovské republiky* (Studies of the History of the Pre-Munich Republic) (November 1983), 243 pp.
13. *Sborník k 65. výročí vzniku Československé Republiky* (Collection, 65th Anniversary of the Rise of the Czechoslovak Republic) (Prague, 1983), 241 pp.
14. *České a světové dějiny, Sborník* (Czech and World History, A Collection) (January 1984), 132 pp.
15. *Historické studie a recenze* (Historical Studies and Reviews) (April 1984), 214 pp.
16. *Studie z moderních dějin* (Studies of Modern History) (Autumn 1984), 198 pp.
17. *Historické studie, Sborník* (Historical Studies, A Collection) (August 1984), 172 pp.
18. *Historický sborník* (Historical Collection) (May 1985).
19. *Historický sborník* (Historical Collection) (October 1985), 178 pp.
20. *Sborník historický* (Historical Collection) (January 1987), 174 pp.
21. *Historický sborník* (Historical Collection) (June 1987), 222 pp.

Deserving special mention were two other *sborníky*, consisting of articles by persons of varied viewpoints and diverse professions, including a good number of historians. One commemorated the two hundredth anniversary of the Toleration Patent of 1781 and was dedicated to 'the memory of Josef II, Roman Emperor, King of Bohemia and Hungary, Archduke of Austria, etc., foremost representative of the ideal of tolerance in our history'. Edited by the philosopher, Milan Machovec, it contained eighteen essays on questions of toleration at various stages of European and Czech history, and dealt with the theme of tolerance in India, China, and Iran, in philosophy generally and in the thought of John Paul II. None of the essays made explicit reference to contemporary Czechoslovakia. The editor, however, in his final essay on the philosophical bases of tolerance, defined it as 'a conscious cohabitation of people of one world outlook (religious or philosophical) or of one political belief with people of another set of conviction', and characterised 'intolerance' as a negation of this, typically manifesting itself as 'anti-reformationist, anti-revolutionary, anti-humanistic, or anti-progressive'. The relevance of his analysis, and of the entire symposium, to the contemporary situation in Czechoslovakia which, in terms of tolerance, was far worse than two centuries earlier, could hardly be missed.[34]

The second *sborník*, devoted to the life and work of Thomas G. Masaryk, was a massive symposium of more than 700 pages, with essays dealing with all stages and aspects of Masaryk's career.[35] Milan Otáhal, for instance, wrote a highly original interpretation of the famous 'manuscript' controversy of the 1880s, analysing its historical significance and the leading part taken by Masaryk in exposing the falsity of certain ancient manuscripts on which Czech nationalism of the time was based. The main aim of the struggle, for Masaryk, was to achieve 'a rebirth of Czech life', which would have great moral significance for all aspects of life, including politics. As Otáhal concluded, Masaryk and his colleagues won 'this fight for the right of science to freedom of research, for the recognition of truth', a struggle which 'in fact continues, in all its urgency, to the present day' (p. 96).[36]

Some of these authors were recognised by their colleagues abroad as belonging to a world community of historians, even though their work could not be published at home (except in *samizdat*). Although unable to attend international conferences in person, some of them presented papers, read for them by Western colleagues and sometimes published in foreign scholarly journals or in special collections prepared by their exiled colleagues. For instance, on the occasion of the 16th International Congress of Historical Sciences, in Stuttgart (25 August–1 September 1985), two volumes entitled *Independent historiography in Czechoslovakia* containing some of the articles mentioned above, were distributed.[37] Similarly, at the Third World Congress for Soviet and East European Studies, in Washington, DC (30 October–4 November 1985), a special double issue of *Kosmas* was circulated. It covered a broad thematic spectrum of articles on the 16th, 18th, and 19th centuries, and on the First Republic and the Second World War, all of which were given in full.[38]

The significance of this independent history can hardly be exaggerated. It restored to the discipline its cognitive and interpretative function, seeking to reassess important episodes of the Czech and Slovak past and to rescue these events from the distortions and falsifications due to manipulation by the regime and its 'court historians'. It replaced officially written history with objective, truth-seeking history, filling in blank spaces and 'black holes'. It helped to restore the links between past and present historical work, links that had been severed by dismissals, deaths, imprisonments, non-publication, or self-censorship. It thus re-established some degree of continuity with research conducted under the First Republic, and during the brief periods of relative freedom between 1945 and 1948, and in 1968 and 1969. It thus revived, among the historians and their small audience of readers, a sense of national identity and an awareness of the uniqueness of Czech and Slovak historical experiences. Circulation abroad, if only limited, created at least a tenuous bond with the international community of scholars. Independent history also provided a connecting link with future Czech and Slovak scholars, when normal conditions of free historical research and writing might once again be restored. Finally, in its search for truth, it fulfilled a broader humanistic mission in common with those struggling in other spheres for an independent scholarship and culture, and thus helped to create an atmosphere favourable to the eventual moral and spiritual renascence of Czech and Slovak society.

HISTORICAL SELF-CRITICISM

The articles which appeared in the scholarly journals and other *sborníky* discussed above did not constitute the entire product of independent historical writing. Other books and articles appeared in *samizdat* and were sometimes published later in typewritten journals or symposia. Many of these were written by persons who were not historians at all, including scholars who had specialised in other disciplines. Banned from work in their own professions, a number of people turned their attention to history in an effort to work out their own views on historical events which they themselves experienced, or to reassess sensitive and controversial questions. As one such author noted, historians and participants have been trying to 'seek out the truth of past events' and to find 'a drastic cure for the old sickness of the schizophrenia of our historical memory'.[39]

Many of these essays or studies were self-critical, condemning actions of the nation in the past and employing strict moral standards of judgement. Highly personal analyses of past events provoked equally personal, and often polemical, responses by others. Articles circulating in *samizdat* were sometimes published abroad and gave rise to heated discussion in exile journals, in which Czechs and Slovaks at home and abroad took part.[40]

One such article, for instance, written under the pseudonym Jan Příbram, dealt with the historic turning-point of February 1948, but subjected the entire course of events from 1938 to the present to severely critical re-assessment.[41] Condemning the capitulation at the time of Munich and the relative lack of resistance during the occupation, Příbram wrote: 'The years 1938–1945 were a time of testing – and the nation failed in it' (p. 383). As a result, he wrote, 'The Czech nation was deprived of its identity . . . it ceases to be a nation in the modern sense . . . it loses its patriotic feeling . . . .' (p. 380). Příbram was equally critical of the transfer of the Germans in 1945, the postwar alliance with the Soviet Union, the nation's lack of resistance to the 1948 seizure of power and to the horrors of the 1950s. As a result of this sequence of events, he concluded, 'Czech society is in a moral decline such as has never existed since its rise (i.e. from the time of the national renascence)' (p. 394).

An anonymous author, cited above,[42] probed deeply and critically into the events of 1968 and the historical roots of the failure of the Prague Spring. The central cause of defeat, in his opinion, was the 'derivative' character of the Communist Party, which, by accepting the Comintern's Twenty-One Conditions, had been dependent on foreign authority from its very inception. This led to 'servility' to Moscow after 1948, passivity during the crisis of 1956, and the failure to resist Soviet intervention in 1968. The train of events could be traced back to the Munich crisis and the failure to resist at that time and to the errors and weaknesses of Beneš and the non-Communists prior to 1948. This raised the question of 'the capitulationist complex of the Czech character'.

The other side of the coin was the party's lack of real concern for the society in which it existed. After the war the 'principle of exclusion', first adopted in the forced transfer of the Germans, was successively applied to other parties and groups, ultimately including leading party members in the purge and trials of the 1950s. The reform of the 1960s was conceived as a party affair only and 'the others', the non-Communist majority, were excluded from real participation.

The reform communist intellectuals in 1968, according to the author, bore a heavy responsibility for the tragic sequence of events.

Absorbed in criticism of the 'unmastered past,' and enthralled with faith in the power of words, they did not exhibit the self-discipline which the situation demanded.

In sharp contrast were the studies of 1968 by two former members of Dubček's cabinet, Jiří Hájek and Vladimír Kadlec. Hájek, foreign minister during the Prague Spring, in a book published abroad in French, defended the entire policy of reform and at the same time stressed the continuity of Czechoslovak foreign policy under his direction. Criticism was reserved for the Soviet Union and its partners and for the conservatives within the Czechoslovak party, and to a limited extent for the more radical reformers, the 'jusqu' au-boutistes' of democratisation. Condemning the invasion as a breach of international obligations and of bloc commitments, Hájek saw nothing to be gained by resistance on the part of Czechoslovakia or by the adoption of a neutralist policy (pp. 109–14 and 132–3). Hájek based his book mainly on the published record, and did not draw upon his personal experiences or cite his own views at the time.[43]

Kadlec, Dubček's Minister of Education, limited himself to the presentation of Dubček's views as expressed in speeches and other documents. Kadlec's purpose was to describe Dubček's efforts to carry through economic and political reforms as a 'specific Czecho-slovak path to socialism', and to note the limiting internal and external circumstances in which he had to act. Kadlec described Dubček as a man of openness in whom the people believed, and as the first Czechoslovak leader to bring Czechs and Slovaks together in united effort. Without wishing to make a 'legend' of him, Kadlec argued that it would be wrong to underestimate the historical significance of his attempt to achieve a synthesis of democracy and socialism in the specific conditions of Czechoslovakia.[44]

Two other former communists re-examined the events of 1968 by critically evaluating the interpretations of the Prague Spring by others, at home or in exile. Zdeněk Jičinský, a lawyer active in the formulation of a federal constitution, offered a balanced critique of the views of Pavel Tigrid and Ivan Sviták, and expressed his unhappiness with their abstract and somewhat contradictory conclusions. On the one hand, the reform of communism was said to be impossible due to Soviet opposition and to the nature of the system, and on the other hand the reform objectives were too limited, not extending to a full pluralist system or socialist democracy. Jičinský believed that the chief desire of the ordinary people in 1968 was to live better and that this could be attained by limited changes in the system.[45] Luboš

Kohout, historian and radical reformer in 1968, engaged in a more polemical review of eleven interpretations of the Prague Spring given in the writings of persons ranging from the conservative Rio Preisner, to radical critics such as Ivan Sviták and Josef Sladeček (Petr Pithart), as well as Dubček, Z. Mlynář, J. Hájek, and other reform communists.[46]

The events of 1968 also received some attention in the replies given by some ten to fifteen persons to a questionnaire sent by several anonymous 'young Christians' who asked their 'seniors' to describe and assess their standpoints in that year.[47] Most of the responses were limited to a report of their own personal roles, sometimes with self-criticism. One, by Jaroslav Šabata, deserves brief mention as a kind of memoir of his own views as an independent communist, a strong critic of the Moscow protocol and the tactics of the restored Dubček leadership after August 1968, and an advocate of a firm alternative policy. He believed that the Moscow protocol, and early statements of the Central Committee of the Czechoslovak Communist Party, did not rule out the continuance of the post-January reform policy, even though within restricted limits. The party, even at the Vysočany congress, had rejected neutralism, and had refused to adopt an anti-Soviet line or to propose the abolition of the Warsaw pact. The urgent need, thought Šabata, was to renew Moscow's confidence in the party and to secure the withdrawal of the Soviet forces. This required from the leadership an imaginative initiative and 'an honourable compromise'. Like many others, he saw no rationale in military resistance to the occupation although he praised the non-violent passive resistance of the post-occupation days.

THE TRANSFER OF THE GERMANS

One of the bitterest and most controversial debates was provoked by a *samizdat* article on the forced transfer (*odsun*) of the Germans from Czechoslovakia at the conclusion of the Second World War. Issued under the pseudonym Danubius, it was the work, it was later revealed, of the prominent Slovak historian Jan Mlynárik, who had been a leading protagonist of reform in the 1960s and an original signatory of Charter 77.[48] He had written the article, he later explained, 'as a historian . . . out of his own conviction that this nation disgraced itself before history, and committed a terrible crime which will sooner or later fall upon its head'. The use of violence against the Germans could not be excused, and was not 'the behaviour of the nation of Hus and Masaryk and Štefánik. An ancient cultured and civilised nation must find within itself the strength to re-evaluate the deeds of its politicians and draw a lesson from them.'[49]

The Danubius essay was not a historical study in the proper sense, but a personal and emotional attempt to come to terms with this great tragedy. This 'violation of the basic human right to one's homeland' had, he said, been avoided by Czech historians, including the 'non-regime' historians. Even in 1968 the problem received only limited attention in public discussion. Now scholars had 'the duty honestly and in a dignified manner to come to a reckoning with the problem of the expulsion of the Czechoslovak Germans, and thus to help the nation to absolve itself of its guilt, concealed in collective silence and tacit approval' (p. 107).

The Danubius Theses condemned in particular the assumption of the 'collective guilt' of all Sudeten Germans, arguing that only a relatively small number (300 000 to 500 000) actively participated in criminal activity during the war. Moreover the Bohemian Germans had lived for many centuries in peaceful coexistence with the Czechs and could not alone be blamed for the breakup of the Czechoslovak Republic. The Czechoslovak leaders shared this responsibility at the time of Munich and had also failed to resolve the German problem under the Republic. The transfer was an act of 'irrational vengeance', accompanied by violence and followed by forcible assimilation of the few Germans who remained.

President Beneš, according to Mlynárik, bore the 'historical responsibility' for the transfer, and also for its brutality, in spite of his later efforts to moderate 'excesses'. The Communists, moved by 'national chauvinism,' were the chief executors of the expulsion. Worst of all, not a single voice was raised at the time against the principle of the transfer, and only the Catholic weekly *Obzor* queried the methods employed. The forced migration represented 'a betrayal of the humanistic and national ideals which had helped the nation to exist' (p. 120). The transfer was 'a general training in mass terror', preparing the ground for the use of similar methods against other groups, including Communists (ms. pp. 19–20).

The Mlynárik Theses became widely known only a year later when a substantial portion appeared in *Svědectví*, the Czech journal published by Pavel Tigrid in Paris. This touched off a storm of controversy among both Czech and Slovak dissidents and exiles, and brought together on common ground some former communists at home and anti-communist exiles.[50] The assault on Danubius was initiated by two ex-communist historians, Milan Hübl, a specialist on the Slovak question, and Luboš Kohout.[51] Some prominent exiles, including Zdeněk Mlynář, reform communist in 1968, and Radomír Luža, anti-communist from 1948, joined in the fray, the former criticising, the latter defending the transfer of the Germans. A spokesman of Charter 77, Ladislav Hejdánek, writing in his personal capacity only, censured the *odsun*.

Milan Hübl condemned the Theses as 'a political pamphlet, not a scholarly work' and charged the author with 'not being faithful to scholarly methodology in his selective approach to the facts and his *a priorism*'. Hübl re-stated his long-held view that the transfer was 'a hard but necessary measure' and that there was no alternative. He charged Danubius with 'idealising' German behaviour in the 19th century and their 'loyalty' to the Republic, and with 'bagatellising' the harm done to the Czechs during the occupation. The responsibility lay not so much with Beneš as with the entire Czech nation who were 'sick to death and had had enough of the Germans'. He condemned Danubius for implicitly raising the demand for the revision of the frontiers and suggesting a shift of Czechoslovakia's foreign political orientation to West Germany.[52]

Luboš Kohout agreed with Hübl in denying that the Danubius essay was 'a qualified historical study' and in defending the transfer – 'an act of national and state self-defence' – 'a sad, but necessary solution for which there was no alternative'. The responsibility lay not with President Beneš but with Hitler's Nazism and the more than 90 per cent support given it by the Germans in Czechoslovakia. The initiative came not from Beneš, but from the spontaneous reaction of the Czech population and the resistance. The Danubius article, he argued, was a 'torpedo' against Germany's Ostpolitik and 'an attack on the Helsinki agreement'.[53]

A group calling itself Bohemus gave its support to the Theses, although in a less one-sided and emotional manner. A nation, it was argued, must examine 'the dark sides of its own past' and was entitled to make 'moral judgements' on historical events. Examining the history of Czech–German relations in Bohemia in some detail, the authors of Bohemus concluded that the Czech linguistic concept of nationalism had impeded a settlement of the Czech–German question and that the Republic had not shown itself capable of resolving it. They condemned the notion of collective guilt as contrary to the traditional values of the Czech nation, and described the political and moral consequences of the forced transfer, especially the resulting exclusively Eastern orientation of Czechoslovak foreign policy, and the application of the principle of exclusion to other large political and economic groups, including in the end communists themselves.

The controversy became a highly political episode, which the regime tried to exploit in its own interests. Karel Douděra, in *Rudé právo* (4 February 1979), ascribed the Danubius article to Charter 77, but spokesmen of the Charter denied that there had ever been consideration of issuing a document on this subject.[54] Meanwhile, the police, in early 1979, and again in 1981, conducted searches to uncover the identity of Danubius, interrogating many persons, including Mlynárik, who after persistent denials, finally admitted his action. After a year of imprisonment he was released without trial, and was ultimately given permission to emigrate.[55]

THE RIGHT TO HISTORY

The Charter 77 document on 'The Right to History' (no. 11, 1984), as noted in Chapter 3, stirred up a polemical debate which focused not only on an alleged breach of Charter procedure, but also on the assessment of official historiography and the interpretation of Czechoslovak history.[56] The discussion, which lasted a full year, revealed the wide chasm between the views held by the anonymous authors, who were identified only as 'historians of a younger generation', and a number of independent historians, and others.

The Charter document depicted the state of official historiography as 'catastrophic,' condemning in sweeping fashion the work of the archives and research institutes and most of the historians, and lamenting the distortion and falsification of history. This was accompanied by a severe indictment of the regime's use of history as 'an instrument of its rule', and the urgent need for 'the revival of historical memory' and 'the reconstruction of historical experience'. These charges were not entirely unacceptable to independent historians who had been victims of the official persecution. What was surprising, however, was that the four historians who first censured the document (all of whom were actively engaged in the publication of *samizdat* historical journals) objected to the 'wholesale condemnation of the so-called official historians', suggesting that many of them were honest scholars producing good work. They thus came to the defence of former colleagues and new scholars employed by the very institutions from which they themselves had been expelled. Expressly associating themselves with the efforts of writers not to divide literature between the official and the unofficial, the four stated that they 'felt they were a part of Czechoslovak historiography, to which . . . belonged historians who work outside official institutions and in emigration, as well as those who work in these institutions – as long as they do not falsify and consciously suppress historical reality'. Their defence of the positive achievements of many official historians, and their criticism of the fundamental errors and distortions in the Charter document, was fully supported in two detailed responses by another independent historian, Jaroslav Mezník, of Brno.

The rift between the historians in their interpretation of Czech history was even deeper. The authors of the Charter document, the critics charged, had indulged in a wide-ranging critique of much of the historical work done since 1948, in particular of the Marxist approach which, it was said, conceived of history as being characterised by '*a priori* regularities' and closed its eyes to the significance of 'culture, religion and free human historical subjectivity'. The authors rejected the idea of 'a history without man and without God', and deplored the 'anti-Christian and anti-Church stance' of most historians, who treated the Catholic Church in particular as 'a retarding element', playing a 'repressive role'. The authors also criticised the treatment of the Habsburg era as 'always negative, always reactionary'.

The 'four' expressed regret, in relatively moderate terms, that the 'Right to History' reflected the opinions of a single group, 'those defending the dominant role of Christian culture' in Czech history, thus disregarding the views of other Chartists. Others, however, notably the reform communists Milan Hübl and Luboš Kohout, aggressively attacked the 'integral Catholic view' of the document, linking this with the late Catholic editor Jaroslav Durych, and his associate Ladislav Jedlička, characterised by 'militant intolerance'. They blamed the spokesman, Václav Benda, a Catholic, for the 'conspiratorial' manner of its issuance.

These critics, and others, vigorously defended the positive contributions made by Marxist historiography, especially during the 1960s; one (Křen) thought that the balance of the work done was on the whole not negative. Jaroslav Mezník, who had never been a party member or a Marxist, and had suffered imprisonment in the 1970s, made a detailed critique of specific errors in the document and evaluated positively the achievements of many Czech historians. Only one contributor, Radomír Malý, defended it, although even he had reservations, and admitted the validity of some of the criticism by the 'four'.

The authors of 'The Right to History', who remained anonymous, countered with a long statement, bitterly censuring Mezník's argumentation, and condemning even more strongly the role of Marxism and of 'ideological' history. This produced sharp responses from Mezník, Kohout and others, who rejected the 'one-sidedness' of the authors' standpoint, and raised many issues of interpretation of certain historical periods and individual scholars.

This controversy reflected a healthy pluralism of views, marred, however, by the dogmatic tone and the sometimes vituperative language employed. It could be better conducted, some Chartists suggested, not by fervent declarations and mutual denunciations, but by dispassionate discussion and by further research on disputed questions.[57] It was impossible, it was said, to draw hard and fast conclusions on the relations of the 'two histories', but enough had been said to suggest the need for reassessing the black and white approach hitherto adopted (and in some measure reflected in this author's earlier versions of this chapter). The interpretation of Czechoslovak history as a whole, and all of its periods, would remain a permanent task to be fulfilled at present within the confines of *samizdat* and later in a freer scholarly environment which might some day emerge.[58] Even then a common, generally accepted interpretation of the meaning of Czech and Slovak history or of specific historical events, would, of course, never materialise, nor would it even be desirable.

CONCLUSION

It is appropriate, after this review of the sustained effort by some historians to 'rehabilitate' history, to return to George Orwell and to his Czech expositor. In Šimečka's words, 'the worst illnesses which can afflict a man in a dictatorship' of this kind are 'disagreement and memory. In a system in which the past is always in accord with the present, memory convicts the falsifier of lying. When a man has a memory, he can agree with a lie only at the cost of awareness of his own piteousness and cowardice.' 'Memory' therefore 'is the great provoker of disagreement.'[59]

Historians who remain true to their profession are the preservers and the restorers of memory. The independent Czech and Slovak historians, and those who, without being historians, sought to purify and restore the memory of past events, clouded and distorted by official historiography, were following the example of Winston's 'searching for the past and for truth' (p. 281). Fortunately, as Šimečka put it, 'The actual obstacles to the investigation of the past were not, in our time, so complete as in Winston's year 1984. One could get around them and cautiously tear at the curtains of lies. The knowledge which today's generation has is the result of this slow, long-lasting reconstruction of the past' (p. 277).[60]

This search for historical truth faced great difficulties and required special virtues. As Miroslav Kusý pointed out, in a *samizdat* tribute to one of these historians (Jablonický), they must have 'stubbornness, patience and an indomitable faith in the meangingfulness of their own activity' if they are to preserve 'the purity of their historical craft'. Whereas the 'court historians', as he called the official scholars, treated this craft as 'a matter purely of expediency', serving ideological and propagandistic ends, the independent historian sought 'the scholarly truth which must be sought out impartially and without prejudice in history alone, in scholarly work with historical facts and events. The only task which he recognises in this context is derived from a scientific approach to history; his only authority is historical truth.'[61]

As Václav Havel observed in the essay cited at the beginning of this chapter, history cannot 'be brought entirely to a halt. A secret streamlet trickles on beneath the heavy lid of inertia and pseudo-events, slowly and inconspicuously undercutting it. It may be a long process, but one day it must happen: the lid will no longer hold and will start to crack.'[62] Needless to say, historians merely write history, and do not enact it. When, however, 'genuine history' once more erupts, to use Havel's term, the independent historians will have contributed something to this happening. In the 1960s, and in 1968 in particular, the revival of history *was* a highly political event, having a substantial influence on the actual course of history. In the 1970s and 1980s the historical renaissance has so far not exercised great influence on events. Perhaps in time, as in Poland, this quest for historical truth will be seen to have been a forerunner of a general awakening of Czech and Slovak society.

6   Parallel Politics

In a 'post-totalitarian' society, as Václav Havel has called Czecho-slovakia, 'all politics in the traditional sense has been eliminated. People have no opportunity to express themselves politically in public, let alone to organise politically. The gap that results is filled by ideological ritual.' In this situation, he wrote, 'people's interest in political matters naturally dwindles and independent political thought and work, in so far as it exists at all, is seen by the majority as unrealistic, abstract, a kind of self-indulgent game, hopelessly distant from their everyday concerns; something admirable, but quite pointless, because on the one hand it is entirely utopian and on the other extraordinarily dangerous'.[1]

Yet even in such a society, Havel noted, there were 'individuals or groups who do not abandon politics as a mission in life and who, one way or another, strive to think independently, to express themselves and in some cases even to organise politically, because that is part of their attempt to live within the truth'. These 'generals without an army' are 'immensely important and worthwhile', since they 'maintain in the face of enormous difficulties the continuity of political thought' and can, at an appropriate time, 'if a genuine political impulse emerges enrich it with the fruits of their own thinking'. In this 'parallel political life', as he termed it, 'various groupings of a more or less political nature will continue to define themselves, to act and confront each other'.[2]

Apart from the brief interlude in 1968, politics in any genuine sense has indeed been dead in Czechoslovakia for more than thirty years.[3] Competing political forces have been suppressed, and alternative political ideas are banned from public expression. There is at present no chance of developing any kind of real alternative or parallel politics in the form of political parties, programmes, or an organised opposition. Beneath the surface of public life, however, a surrogate, narrow and circumscribed, has appeared in the crystallis-ation of embryonic political tendencies, the expression of diverse ideological or philosophical standpoints, and the conduct of debate among their advocates. This substitute for politics is carried on not by political scientists nor by professional politicians, but by persons of different occupational backgrounds – historians, philosophers, writers, and the like, compelled by the realities of their daily lives to

123

formulate their views on politics. The contributors to this dialogue, although differing in their viewpoints, have in common a deep aversion to the established political orthodoxy, and the practice based on it, and a personal commitment to alternative values challenging the official line. Their efforts to express distinctive points of view constitute at least the beginning of an escape from the communist doctrinal straitjacket and a revival of independent and pluralistic political thinking after three decades of silence.

There is a wide spectrum of opinion among Czech and Slovak dissidents, although it is not as broad as in the Soviet Union or even Poland. There are, for instance, no outspokenly conservative or reactionary standpoints expressed, nor any extreme nationalism or chauvinism, either among Slovaks or Czechs. There is a general consensus of moderate democratic views close to the traditions of pre-communist Czechoslovak political life. Former communists and Marxists are more numerous and significant than in Poland or Russia, but they differ so greatly from one another in their present stance as to render the term 'ex-communist' virtually meaningless. There are a few, such as Jiří Hájek, one-time foreign minister under Dubček, or the historians Miloš Hájek and Milan Hübl, who remain 'reform communists' and Marxists at heart; but their number and importance are declining. Other former communists, such as Miroslav Kusý or Milan Šimečka, have moved far from their original faith and express themselves with originality and independence. There is a small group of 'revolutionary socialists' or Trotskyists, such as Petr Uhl, and an emergent independent or democratic socialist tendency, represented by Rudolf Battěk, who was never a member of the Communist Party. Still others, not really 'political' at all, have a religious orientation, either Catholic (Václav Benda and Jiří Němec) or Protestant (Ladislav Hejdánek and Jakub Trojan); but they are ecumenical, not sectarian, and generally humanist in outlook.

In striking contrast to the Polish scene, before and after Solidarity, no organised political groupings or parties were formed, nor were there even journals with distinctive political hues. In the early stages of Charter 77, as we have described elsewhere,[4] several very loose groupings, sometimes no more than tendencies of thinking, could be identified. At present only vestiges of these continued to exist as marginal factors, each including a handful of persons and none regarding itself as even a potential party. After the emigration of Zdeněk Mlynář in 1977, the so-called 'reform communists' had no leader of stature, and as a result of the decline of Eurocommunism in Western Europe could not look abroad for firm support except on occasion from the Italian Communist Party. The independent socialists, their leading figure Rudolf Battěk in prison for many years, and one of their most militant spokesmen Jan Tesař in exile, were reduced to a tiny group (Jiří Mueller and Jaroslav Mezník, both in Brno) and were disappointed by the absence of recognition and support by the Socialist International. During the long imprisonment of Petr Uhl, and with the emigration of his chief associate, J. Suk, to Sweden, the revolutionary socialists or Trotskyists were hardly a force of significance. Jaroslav Šabata, who might be called an 'independent communist', in view of his detachment from the main ex-communist group, was an imaginative political thinker, but had no organised supporters. The religious groupings, Catholic and Protestant, were not, of course, explicitly political, and as far as is known, did not meet or work together. The Catholics, however, enjoying increasing sympathy from Cardinal Tomášek, and a certain indirect support from the Pope, did constitute a kind of political force. These small clusters of like-minded persons, did not constitute clearly delineated political tendencies and did not advance programmes of their own. Nor was any of these grouplets homogeneous in outlook, and their members often expressed highly individual standpoints.

As a result 'parallel politics' consisted primarily in the writing of essays and books on political themes.[5] Some of these concentrated on Charter 77, its purposes and methods, and human rights in general. Others dealt with the central issues of politics as seen from the perspective of each individual's experience and convictions. Few of them had ready answers to the problems facing them and their country, but wrestled with them in a search for understanding.

Two common topics have absorbed their attention.[6] On the one hand, the authors seek to analyse and criticise the existing political system, which they, unlike Western specialists, have no hesitation in calling 'totalitarian'. In penetrating fashion they examine its central features: the party's monopoly of power; the concentration of this power in the centre, often in the hands of a single individual; the striving for total control of all aspects of life; the refusal to recognise different interests and the denial of the right to express different opinions; and the absence of 'democratic structures' or any form of popular participation in public life. Above all, they stress the ubiquitous fear that pervades society and the complete apathy and surface conformity this engenders. Overwhelmed with a feeling of complete helplessness, most citizens try only to escape from 'politics' in any shape or form.

On the other hand, the authors think about the future and ponder the problem of how to 'revive' or 'restore' politics and eventually to find a way out of the totalitarian confine. They realise all too well how difficult it is for ordinary citizens, in their millions, to break out of the vicious circle of fear and apathy and accept the risks of seeking to 'live in truth'. The prime essential, they believe, is the willingness of the individual to assume 'responsibility' for public affairs, in short, to act as a citizen. He must overcome the all-pervading fear and show courage in defending his civic rights and fulfilling his civic duties. The immediate solution, then, is to be found in moral and spiritual strength, in truth, in the 'small-scale work' of the individual within the framework of his day-to-day life. Such actions by the individual should be accompanied by an open dialogue of differing opinions and by the forming of independent democratic associations of citizens seeking to live in freedom. These 'parallel structures' help to undermine and erode the totalitarian system in the 'here and now' and pave the way for its future disintegration. In the long run, hope is placed on the development of pluralism, together with free elections, freedom of expression, proper representation of diverse interests, and public participation; in other words, the reverse image of the evils of the present system. These objectives can be attained not by extremism of any kind, least of all by revolution or violence, but only through the individual's long, slow self-training in citizenship.

One can hardly exaggerate the difficulties under which these essays were written – usually in spare moments, after a day or week of exhausting manual labour or deadening bureaucratic routine and without access to libraries or other sources. The authors lacked both the leisure to revise and polish and the benefit of editorial criticism, so that style and precision sometimes suffered. They lacked, too, the normal feedback from a wide readership or regular criticism by their peers, and were often the victims of vicious and distorted condemnation in the official media. They lacked familiarity with current political thought in the outside world, except as gleaned through the occasional book, journal, or newspaper. Sometimes their work may not appear highly original and may even seem to be a statement of the obvious or well-known. Sometimes one is surprised at how well they express simple truths in a moderate and dispassionate tone. In evaluating their ideas one must place them in the perspective of the conditions under which they wrote and realise that their rediscovery of pluralism, ideological tolerance, and democratic principles represents a negation of the existing order and a point of departure for overcoming it. Above all, the essays breathe the air of freedom, the spirit of men anxious to understand the nature of the system that constricts them, to communicate their views to each other and to others at home and abroad, to preserve some links with past Czech and Slovak traditions, and to prepare the way, however modestly, for a more tolerable and meaningful future.

In contrast to *samizdat* in the field of history there was no proliferation of journals, symposia, and books devoted to politics and political thought. Political essays usually appeared as separate *samizdat* items and were sometimes re-published in journals such as *Dialogy*, and later *Kritický sborník*, *Střední evropa*, and others. Only one major symposium, *O svobodě a moci* (On Freedom and Power) appeared in *samizdat*, in 1979, and this focused not on politics in general, but on the meaning of dissent and on independent activities and the concept of a 'parallel' society. Originally conceived as a joint Czech–Polish enterprise, the symposium was planned at one of the rare meetings of Czech and Polish dissidents in August and September 1978.[7] It was to consist of some twenty essays from each side, with an introductory essay by Václav Havel circulated as a basis of discussion at a future seminar. Unfortunately a third joint meeting on the frontier was blocked by the police and was followed by the arrest of a group of Czech dissidents, including five of the contributors to the proposed volume. Some of the Czech essays, including Havel's 'Power of the Powerless', were published in Polish *samizdat*, and were said to have influenced the course of events in Poland in 1980 and 1981.[8] No Polish volume appeared, presumably because, to paraphrase Lenin, the Poles found it 'more pleasant to make a revolution than to write about it'. Due to the arrests and the subsequent trial, the Czech contributions were issued separately in August 1979, under the title noted above. Dedicated to the memory of Jan Patočka it contained nineteen essays by Chartists of widely different world outlook and political viewpoint.[9]

In 1986 a number of briefer comments on politics were written in response to a questionnaire by 'young Christians from Moravia' who confessed a desire to 'learn politics' and conduct a dialogue with their seniors. They asked the latter to describe their attitude towards the events of 1968 and to indicate clearly their views on politics in general – their 'political credo'. Some of the replies were published by the Charter 77 spokesmen under the title *O odpovědnost v politice a za politiku* (On responsibility in politics and for it) as 'a first step toward the renaissance of responsibile political thinking'.[10]

In the pages which follow, we shall briefly present the ideas of ten persons, which together provide a representative sample of nonconformist political thought of Czechs and Slovaks in the 1970s and 1980s. Some of these have been published in English in the two collections referred to above (*Power of the Powerless* and *Parallel Politics*), in my *Charter 77* or elsewhere.

JAN PATOČKA (1907–77)

The philosopher Jan Patočka, one of the first three spokesmen of Charter 77, personified more than anyone the purpose of the Charter and in particular its 'moral dimension'. He had never been politically engaged in any way, and was neither a Marxist nor a party member. In the words of his obituary, 'he always remained true to his field, to his "speciality", philosophy . . . He was not indifferent to matters of human society but his attitude toward these matters was not that of a politician, but rather that of someone who respects them as fundamental philosophical problems.' During most of his life he was excluded from academic life, but continued to teach privately, in his own apartment, and published either abroad, some 125 items, or in *samizdat*. His writings related almost exclusively to philosophy – Hegel, Kant, Descartes, or phenomenology, or to Masaryk and Czech history. Few of these related directly to politics and the state; but most of them had an indirect bearing on the political realm, in particular the role of the individual in society.[11]

During 1968 he played a role limited exclusively to the intellectual sphere, taking actions in defence of freedom of science and scholarship. One of the first signatories of Charter 77, he was at first reluctant to accept the role of spokesman in 1977, but once having accepted, he threw himself into its work wholeheartedly and, as it turned out, sacrificed his life to it.[12]

During the few months before his death Patočka had time to give only brief expositions of the meaning and purpose of Charter 77, but revealed in them his fundamental ideas about politics and the state. In his earliest statement, he wrote:

> The concept of *human rights* is nothing but the conviction that states and society as a whole consider themselves to be subject to

the sovereignty of moral sentiment, that they recognise something unqualified above them, something that is bindingly sacred and inviolable even for them, and that they intend to contribute to this end with the power by which they create and ensure *legal* norms.

The Czechoslovak government, by signing the human rights covenants, 'avows the supreme moral foundation of all things political'. Individuals who signed the Charter 'accept the rule that politics are indeed subject to law and that law is not subject to politics'. In another memorable phrase, Patočka declared 'there are things which are worth suffering for' and 'the things for which one might suffer are the ones that are worth living for'.[13]

In important *samizdat* works before 1977, Patočka expressed ideas about the 'responsible courage' of the individual which were directly relevant to Charter 77 and his own role in it.[14] His 'Heretical Essays on the Philosophy of History,' written in 1975, was a profound study of the meaning of European history from Greek times to the present in which he described the transition from 'pre-history' to 'history', when truth, freedom, and justice replaced fear and the struggle for survival, thus giving life meaning. In the final chapter, 'Wars of the Twentieth Century and the Twentieth Century as War', he described this as 'the century of night, war and death', and depicted the collapse of modern European society in the two world wars, which led to the 'sending of millions into fiery Gehenna'. Beginning as a war against the status quo unleashed by Germany, it became a new war in 1917 when the Russian revolution fought the status quo on both sides. Victory was a figment, creating the 'illusion of a victorious peace', in which war continued, at full speed, in the country of revolution, where it turned inward against its own people. The war flared up again in 1945, leading to the fall of Europe, and was followed by 'a cold war or a smouldering one', based on constant mobilisation, with the 'perspective of infinite conflict.'

Patočka found a grain of hope in the front-line experience of the combatants, which gave them a sense of 'absolute freedom' and created 'a solidarity of the shattered' (on both sides of the front). This offered a path leading to 'real peace', if the resistance of the individual to force could be overcome by the *solidarity of the shattered* – 'the solidarity of those who can grasp the meaning of life and death – and thus of history; who can grasp that history *amounts* to the conflict between *mere life*, life that is bare and shackled in fears, and *life at the apex* which does not plan but which clearly sees there is a limit to the everyday and its life and "peace"' (p. 125). 'The solidarity of the shattered can say "No" to mobilisations which eternalise the state of war' and 'become a spiritual power that will impose certain limitations on the warring world'. That he is thinking of the domestic front, too, is clear when he writes of 'persecution and uncertainty' of the 'shattered' and of the common 'discomfort' of many social groups with the 'ruthlessness of Force' (*ibid.*). In an uncanny premonition of Charter 77 and his own death, Patočka, quoting Heraclitus, spoke of 'the will freely to take risks in *aristea*, in proving oneself to be good at the limits of human capacities, the will which "the best men choose" when they elect "everlasting fame among mortal men" instead of the ephemeral extension of a comfortable life'. Some may rise above a free human life and '"become gods"', thus touching on 'divinity, i.e. upon that which forms the ultimate unity and mystery of life' (p. 126).

In a brief article written in 1976, on the responsibility of the individual in an age of masses, Patočka referred not to the role of great men, or the cult of personality, but to the hidden 'heroes of our time', individuals such as Sartre, Oppenheimer and Sakharov, Solzhenitsyn and Heidegger, who recognized the categorical imperatives of freedom and truth. As a result each of them was 'a power, an entity, a talent, a "genius"', in which everything necessary for change is contained, as flower and fruit are contained in the seed.'[15]

Another essay, entitled 'An Attempt at a Czech Philosophy and its Failure,' paid tribute to T. G. Masaryk, who had made an effort to understand the crisis of modern civilisation and to elaborate a Czech national philosophy (although the latter contained contradictions and ultimately failed, in theory and in practice). For Masaryk, politics was 'life from freedom and for freedom'. Democracy was not only a state form but 'that theistic metaphysics which responds to the moral nature of human reality'. Masaryk's entire life, wrote Patočka, 'was a struggle against majority opinion, against insidiously and forcefully imposed moods of society, against fashionable, uncritical acceptance of views, and against traditions and collective myths' (p. 12). He restated this thought in other words: 'For a society which wants to live freely there is no other way except to participate as much as it can and with all its power, in the effort to discover meaning in the presence of the massive absurdity of the chaos which generates the paralysing feeling of the uncontrollability of the planetary situation'.[16]

During the First World War, Masaryk, taking America as his

example, recognised that 'the growth of democracy means a restoration of Czech freedom and independence'. Among political thinkers Masaryk thus became unique in building a state, not merely in his mind, but in 'concrete political action'. The national rebirth was, for him, 'by its nature a democracy – a disciplined humanism and a moral basis of humanity which is also capable of organising mankind politically and *must* bring, together with that organisation and an understanding of its meaning as liberation, a new entry of the nation into history' (p. 8).

In another essay Patočka returned to these twin themes: the greatness of Masaryk as a thinker who founded a state, and the responsibility of the individual to act in this spirit. His was 'an act of responsible courage' and for others, an 'appeal to their own responsibility'. Masaryk's great achievement ended in tragedy because those who followed him, and the Czech people, did not rise to his level and failed to become 'real, i.e. acting subjects of history' (p. 501). In words that unconsciously forecast the aims of Charter 77, Patočka declared that the 'appeal' remained today – 'to try to act freely under all circumstances, favourable and unfavourable, insignificant and great' (p. 498).[17]

VÁCLAV HAVEL (*b.* 1936)

Václav Havel, one of the founders and most active protagonists of Charter 77, resembled Patočka in never having taken part in politics nor having had a defined political standpoint. He himself denied that he was a 'politician' or even wanted to be one.[18] During the Prague Spring Havel, as a non-party person, confined his activities largely to the reform of the Union of Writers and the work of the Circle of Independent Writers, an association of non-communists. Nonetheless he was intensely interested in politics and even called himself on one occasion a '*zoon politikon*'.[19] During the 1960s, and again during the 1970s and 1980s, Havel engaged actively in the 'politics' of dissent and showed himself to be one of the most lucid and eloquent analysts of the crisis produced by 'normalisation' and of the phenonenom of 'dissent.'[20] In his first major political essay, his well-known letter to President Husák in 1975, he made a brilliant analysis of the political *anomie* and the moral crisis into which Czechs and Slovaks had been plunged since 1969. He placed the blame for this on fear, a fear produced, however, not by physical violence alone or even mainly, but by 'existential pressures' which led most people to concentrate on their material existence and to adapt outwardly to the new order of real socialism.[21]

Although not trained in philosophy, Havel acknowledged the profound influence Patočka had had on him since his youth.[22] While he never considered himself a philosopher, his writings became increasingly philosophical as he explored the nature of the global crisis, the meaning of dissent, and the effect of this on the individual human being. It was this theme of the 'crisis of human identity', he admitted, to which he returned in all of his plays.[23] During his years in prison in the 1980s he often discussed this topic in his letters to his wife, the writing of which, he said, offered him 'the opportunity for a new kind of search for himself, and for his standpoint to the basic issues of life'.[24]

His philosophical and deeply moral approach to life and politics was evident in his remarkable essay, 'The Power of the Powerless', in which he analysed the existing 'post-totalitarian system', as he chose to call it, and the broader crisis of contemporary technological society. The system under which Czechs and Slovaks, and others in Eastern Europe, lived, was, he believed, 'a kind of warning to the West, revealing to it its own latent tendencies'.[25] Moreover the 'independent citizens' initiatives' which challenged the system might be considered as a kind of 'model of those more meaningful "post-democratic" political structures which might become the foundation of a better society' (p. 95).

Since this essay has been published elsewhere in full, one need only summarise its content briefly. In a highly original manner Havel contrasted the post-totalitarian system with the traditional dictatorship, and, contrary to prevalent views of the decline of ideology, emphasized the vital importance of ideology as an active component of the system of power. This offered the citizen a way of showing his loyalty by 'living within a lie', that is, while not believing in the system's lies, behaving as if he did (p. 31).

The bulk of the essay is devoted to 'dissent' (always placed within quotation marks), i.e., the revolt of the citizen who refused to live in the lie and thus broke the rules of the game and became a threat to the regime. 'Living within the truth' (p. 39 *passim*), Havel argued, was a new form of 'politics,' difficult for those accustomed to the traditional forms to understand. 'Dissent' did not offer alternative political models and programmes or establish opposition parties, but performed actions which did not seem overtly political and resembled the 'small-scale work' (*drobná práce*) advocated by T. G. Masaryk in the late nineteenth century (pp. 51, 61). It was an 'attempt to create and support the "independent life of society" as an articulated expression of "living within the truth"' (p. 67). It was 'a real everyday struggle for a better life "here and now"' (p. 88). This 'existential revolution', as he called it, and the 'independent structures' which it generated, offered a recipe for solving the universal crisis of a technological society by returning to the human dimension of life, to the individual and his responsibility to others and to the human community, and to 'the rehabilitation of old values such as trust, openness, solidarity and love' (pp. 92–3).[26]

In an address, Politics and Conscience, delivered at the University of Toulouse, on receiving, *in absentia*, an honorary doctorate, Havel highlighted this theme of universal crisis and the place of 'dissent' as 'a warning, a challenge, a danger or a lesson for those who visit us (in Czechoslovakia)'.[27] The crisis of modern civilisation, he believed, was caused by the triumph of science and technology over the 'natural world' which he conceived of as 'a world of personal responsibility', in which values such as justice, honour, treason, friendship, infidelity, courage, etc. had 'a tangible content'. But there was also 'something beyond its horizon . . . the hidden source of all the rules, customs, commandments, prohibitions and norms that hold within it', an 'Absolute which grounds, delimits, animates and directs it' and which 'we can only quietly respect' (p. 31). The modern political realm expressed itself in the 'anonymisation and depersonalisation of power' and 'its reduction to a mere technology of rule and manipulation'. Rulers and leaders were no longer 'personalities in their own right, with a concrete human face', but had become managers, bureaucrats, *aparatchiki*, who were mere cogs in the machinery of the state (p. 33).

The most complete expression of this 'impersonal power' had been achieved in the totalitarian systems but they were but 'a mirror of all modern civilisation', 'a grossly magnified image of its own deep tendencies' (p. 34). The 'dissidents' in this context offered an alternative not well understood in the West, but one which was meaningful for the latter, too – that is, 'resisting vigilantly, thoughtfully and attentively, but . . . with total dedication . . . . the irrational momentum of anonymous, impersonal and inhuman power – the power of ideologies, systems, *aparat*, bureaucracy, artificial languages and political slogans' (pp. 36, 37). They pose the real question, relevant to all: 'whether we shall . . . succeed in reconstituting the natural world as the true terrain of politics, rehabilitating the personal experience of human beings as the initial measure of things, placing morality above politics and responsibility above our desires, in making human community meaningful . . . in reconstituting, as the focus of all social doing, the autonomous, integral and dignified human I, responsible for himself because he is bound to something higher' (p. 35).

This, argued Havel, was 'anti-political politics', that is, politics not as 'the technology of power and manipulation, of cybernetic rule over humans', but politics as 'practical morality, as service to the truth, as essentially human and humanly measured care for our fellow humans' (p. 37). The onus of responsibility rested with the individual. Experience has shown 'that a single seemingly powerless person who dares to cry out the word of truth and to stand behind it with all his person and all his life, has, surprisingly, greater power, though formally disfranchised, than do thousands of anonymous voters' (pp. 37–8). Using Patočka's term, Havel called for 'an international community of the shattered, which, ignoring state boundaries, political systems and power blocks (*sic*), standing outside the high game of traditional politics, aspiring to no titles and appointments, will seek to make a real political force out of a phenomenon so ridiculed by the technicians of power – the phenomenon of human conscience' (p. 38).

In two other statements Havel strove once again to explain the role of dissent as a unique kind of 'politics outside politics', 'politics outside the sphere of power'. In a message to the Amsterdam peace conference, 'Anatomy of Reticence', he wrote:

> The dissident does not operate in the realm of genuine power at all. He is not seeking power. He has no desire for office and does not gather votes. He does not attempt to charm the public; he offers nothing and promises nothing. He can offer, if anything, only his own skin – and he offers it solely because he has no other way of affirming the truth he stands for . . . The innermost foundation of his 'political' undertaking is moral and existential.

The dissident was 'more likely to describe and analyse the present than to project a future. He is far more the one who criticizes what is wrong here and now than the one who plans something better which is to be. He sees his mission more in defending man against the pressures of the system than in imagining better systems' (pp. 21–2).[28]

In his response to the questions of the 'young Christians,' Havel expanded on the idea that they were at present taking only the first step toward the restoration of politics in the real sense of the word. This was a stage of 'semi-politics (polo-politika)', when the first thing to do was to 'speak the truth, to articulate aloud our opinions, and the real needs and interests of society' which led to the forming of human rights movements. The second stage, that of 'programmatic and practical politics', was a long way off but, as the child of the first phase, it would have 'a moral dimension'. As a writer he felt at home in the first stage, but wished to avoid anything like a programme of political action. Others 'more competent' would have to take the leading part in 'real politics'. As for his role in 1968, he had mixed feelings at the time about the concept of 'reform communism', and as a writer and a non-communist did not have a role in leadership. He viewed with some reservations his own proposal of an opposition party at that time and was not sure that the creation of two or three large parties was the only guarantee of democracy in the future.[29]

Havel's most recent article, *Příběh a totalita*, had a title which is difficult to translate but which might be rendered as 'The Story in a Total Society'.[30] In it he analyzed the essence of the mature or late totalitarian society as being 'the destruction of events in their entirety', a process which eliminated the unusual, the accidental or the unexpected from life. Revolutionary ethos was replaced by a dull bureaucracy, alibi-istic caution, bureaucratic anonymity and lifeless stereotypes (p. 4). History was supplanted by pseudo-history; revolutionary fanatics by faceless bureaucrats; time and place were extinguished; political and economic plurality was superseded by 'absolute truth'. Hence nothing really 'happens' – there were no 'stories' or 'events'. The uniqueness of the individual was destroyed; life was standardised; any 'difference' became criminal; private life was merged with public. All of this was accomplished, not openly, as in the earlier stage of totalitarianism, but indirectly and was thus 'invisible', especially to the foreign observer. The only exception to this flatness, drabness and sameness of life was to be found in prison, where the inmates 'stick out, are unclassifiable and belong nowhere; they are peculiar and in many ways possessed'. Outside, 'life carried on a daily, hidden, inconspicuous war, without outward display and without pathos, against nothingness. The struggle of the event (story) and of history against their own non-existence was itself an event and a part of history'. One might add that Havel's own actions and those of his fellow-Chartists, which he analysed so powerfully in his earlier essays, also constituted exceptional and surprising 'events' in an otherwise unbroken conformity.

MILAN ŠIMEČKA (*b.* 1930)

Milan Šimečka, although not a Charter signatory, was an ardent supporter of the human rights movement and became well known for his feuilletons, essays, and books, many of which were published abroad in Czech or other languages. A resident of Bratislava for three decades, and a lecturer at Komenský University and at the Higher School of Music, he was the author of two books on socialist utopias and during 1968 contributed to the intellectual ferment through articles in Czech and Slovak journals and newspapers.[31] A party member for twenty years, he was expelled in 1970 and dismissed from his teaching post. After 1977 Šimečka was subjected to constant police harassment and vicious press attacks, and was held in custody for twelve months from May 1981, under investigation for the crime of subversion. In the end he was released without trial.

Šimečka became well known for his book, *Obnovení pořádku* (The Restoration of Order), a study of 'normalisation' in Czechoslovakia which was written during the years 1975 to 1977 and published abroad in Czech and several foreign languages, including English, in 1984.[32] One need do no more than indicate some salient features of this penetrating and often witty study of 'real socialism', an ideological term which was unfortunately translated by the awkward and inaccurate phrase, 'actually existing socialism'. Šimečka's work was not a philosophical or even highly theoretical study in the style of Havel, nor, as the author admits, a 'scientific treatise', replete with references, but rather a concrete description of the process of 'consolidation' after the Soviet occupation, in the light of the author's personal experiences and observations, a kind of 'worm's eye view' of the system, one might say. The author focused not on 'high politics' but on the mechanisms set in motion in all spheres of society to achieve 'the restoration of order', i.e., the re-establishment of the system existing prior to the so-called 'counter-revolution' of 1968. The work was, of course, not subject to censorship and showed no vestiges of the author's original Marxist standpoint.

Šimečka's chief aim was to describe and explain 'adaptation' to the new order by the overwhelming majority of the population, which he regarded as the key to the stability of real socialism. A chapter which bore this word as its title (Chapter 17) described 'the integration of their (the citizens') daily lives into the system, as well as their dependence, economically speaking, and indeed in complex human terms, on the all-embracing power of the State' (p. 139, English edn). Loyalty was secured, at least on the surface, by a kind of 'social contract', which assured to the loyal all the material rewards, even though limited, that were available under the system. This was supplemented by even more widespread benefits derived from corruption (bribery, the black market, etc.) and by the granting of education, not as a right, but as a privilege to those who conformed. Violence was sometimes used to assure obedience, but this was not the classical physical force known in the past, but 'civilised violence', employing 'refined methods' such as dismissals from work, screening and black-listing, interrogations, surveillance and house-searches, trials conducted in the spirit of Kafka and the use of children as hostages for their parents. These methods were used to punish nonconformists, but at the same time to intimidate the entire population. Such weapons were reinforced by the total control of information and the use of the 'State Lie'. This was the reality of 'real socialism', in Šimečka's view, a system designed to exalt the status quo, discourage any serious change, and exclude the very idea of a different model of socialism.

Šimečka discussed another feature of real socialism in a long, thoughtful essay on 'the community of fear'.[33] The process of growing used to fear had been going on for more than thirty years and was founded on 'one's defencelessness *vis-à-vis* a total and very real power concentrated into an anonymous pinnacle and then extending outward and downward like rays into the lower components of the social structure'. This caused political apathy, and apathy at work, too, which led to a systematic decline in the economy, and produced 'thought paralyzed by fear' and an all-pervasive cynicism. There were ways to escape this community of fear, but the most difficult was 'the path of truth', which required 'civic courage' and 'a victory, not so much over the community of fear as over themselves'.

Between 1981 and 1983, apart from an interruption during his term in prison, Šimečka prepared an epilogue for Orwell's *1984*, 'surely one of the most exciting books in world literature', in his words. This brilliant essay was eventually included in the first-ever Czech edition of Orwell's book, but did not appear in English or any other foreign language.[34] This 'anti-Utopia,' as Šimečka called it, had a general validity for the entire world and was a warning to all (pp. 283, 284). Nonetheless he felt a special bond of sympathy with 'Our Comrade, Winston Smith', as he entitled his essay, and concentrated his attention on the similarities between the existing system in Czecho-slovakia and the projected world of Oceania. We have already mentioned (Chapter 5) Šimečka's treatment of 'the crime of independent unpermitted thinking', and in particular the regime's constant efforts to control history. He went on to analyse the many similarities between real socialism and Angsocialism – 'newspeak' and 'the idea-police', brain-washing, mass mobilisation, surveillance, interrogation, and the imprisonment of 'thought criminals'.

Yet Šimečka was fascinated also by Winston Smith's 'search for truth', and found hope in his struggle, even under interrogation and torture, to 'strive for the meaning of his existence' (p. 307). During the ordeal of his own imprisonment he felt a special kinship with his comrade and found in *1984* much to assist and inspire him. He drew comfort from the fact that, unlike Winston, he could nourish himself with the belief that culture and the written word were indestructible and that he lived at a time when 'historical memory still functioned and the future didn't necessarily belong to those who governed the present' (p. 309). Šimečka was also encouraged by the fact that things would not be so 'perfect' in Czechoslovakia in 1984 as in Oceania but he warned that the world could be '"perfected" by 1994 or 2004 unless people took heed' (p. 311).

In 1982 Šimečka returned to his earlier interest in utopias in a brief contribution to the Colston symposium on this theme at the University of Bristol.[35]. He sought to explain the depressing fact that utopias always failed in the end; real socialism was one such 'stale, moribund utopia'. The failure, he believed, was inherent in the common attempt of all utopias to inculcate the ideas of a minority by force, which only produced utopias that were 'caricatures of themselves'. Why did such a system, so alienated from its original aims, seek to justify itself as a legitimate heir of the original ideas? The explanation, he thought, was quite evident to those who lived under real socialism: the motivation of those in power to protect, and to justify, the system from which they derived their material benefits, 'the golden egg of comfort and luxury'.[36] Nevertheless, Šimečka believed that a world without utopias, e.g., the end of pollution, peace and disarmament, would be 'a world without social hope'. Even the modest utopia of 1968, for instance, which aimed only at freedom and tolerance of different views, lived on – 'to live without it would be to live without human dignity'.

In a book published jointly with Miroslav Kusý, *Big Brother and Big Sister* (to be discussed in the next section), Šimečka turned his attention to Marxism, applied by Lenin and Stalin in the Soviet Union in a system which became the basis of real socialism: another example of the many utopias which offered salvation through a rational reconstruction of the social order and employed force to apply reason to human relations.[37] At each stage of development socialism and communism, in its Soviet form, became a new utopia, each serving as an apologetic of the existing order and as a model for other nations. The system, however, was characterised by the abandonment of reason and a total 'loss of reality'. The original ideas of liberty, equality, and the new socialist man were all abandoned in favour of power as the supreme goal. The East–West confrontation was, he believed, primarily a conflict of social systems and ideologies. The only hope of a solution was to be found in a revival of reason and an awakening from ideological stupidity.

MIROSLAV KUSÝ (*b.* 1931)

Miroslav Kusý, a Slovak, was for fifteen years a professor at Komenský University, during which time he published major works in philosophy, including *Marxist Philosophy*, *The Marxist Theory of Knowledge*, and *The Philosophy of Politics*. During the Prague Spring he wrote frequently on the democratic aspects of the reform movement, while supporting also the national aims of Gustáv Husák and others. A party member for twenty years, he served as head of the ideological department of the Slovak Communist Party for a few months after the occupation. Expelled from the party in 1970 and from his university post the year after, Kusý at first worked in the library, but after putting his signature to Charter 77 he was degraded to the rank of a manual construction worker and became the target of harsh attacks in the media and repeated police harassment. This did not discourage him from writing prolifically in *samizdat*, thus displaying the 'civic courage' of which his close friend, Šimečka, had written in *The Community of Fear*.[38]

One of Kusý's finest essays was his contribution, 'Chartism and "real socialism"', to the symposium *O svobodě a moci*.[39] Real socialism, in his view, was an 'étatist model of socialism of the Stalinist type', 'an ideal that had become a reality' and was deemed to require no further change. Instead of applying Marxist criticism to the given state of affairs, real socialism 'apotheosised' it. Any contradiction between the ideal and reality was simply ignored, or concealed by 'an ideology *als ob*, an ideology of *as if*', whose advocates behaved '*as if* the ideological kingdom of real socialism existed in "what we have here now"'. Charter 77, simply by calling things by their real names, destroyed 'the game of *as if*', and thus undermined the ideological foundations of real socialism. The specific human rights demands of Charter 77, although described as non-political, would strike at the essentials of the system and the personal power of the ruling clique and hence could not be granted.

Kusý openly avowed his continued belief in Marxism, calling it an 'instrument suitable for profound analysis . . . , by the use of which reality can be grasped in all its essential structure and relationships'. Marxism must, however, be tolerant toward every other method of thinking, Marxist or non-Marxist, each of which, although leading to different conclusions, was 'equally valid'. Marxisim, as an official creed, was 'dead' in Czechoslovakia, he believed, and was used primarily as a doctrine to silence creative thinkers. Those working in the official institutions professed it, not out of conviction, but for career considerations only.[40]

Kusý's own use of Marxism as an instrument of criticism was demonstrated in his long essay, 'Marxism and the Ecological Crisis', a detailed critique of the treatment of such problems in the writings of Soviet and Czechoslovak ideologues.[41] The latter ascribed the ecological crisis in the capitalist world to the objective factors in the system itself, which could be solved only by a social revolution. Ecological problems in the socialist countries, on the contrary, were due to subjective factors – non-socialist attitudes of people responsible, their lack of discipline, and their 'consumerist' relationship to nature. The solution was to be sought in changes in 'consciousness', which would be produced by ideological training. Kusý termed this a 'utopian approach', quite incorrect from a Marxist standpoint. He argued that ecological problems were global in scope, affecting both socialist and non-socialist systems, and should be dealt with primarily by technical measures to reduce or eliminate environmental damage.

In somewhat the same vein, in his essay, 'The Augean Stable of Real Socialism', Kusý condemned as 'utopian' and un-Marxist the regime's approach to the problems of theft of socialist property, corruption and bribery. These were not 'vestiges of the past', as officially argued, but in fact 'a new phenomenon' characteristic of socialist countries. Kusý's analysis went beyond the 'illegal' actions deplored by regime spokesmen to include privileges and advantages of the highest cadres, e.g. of enterprise directors and party leaders, which, although not necessarily illegal, were immoral and were usually concealed from the public view. These were the products of the very nature of real socialism and not of the failure of individuals to attain the virtues of the 'socialist man', as argued in orthodox theory. The solution was to be found, not in educative propaganda and legal penalties, as the regime believed, but in a thorough change in the conditions which produced these actions, including an economic reform which would reconcile individual, group, and societal interests.[42]

In 1980 Kusý and Šimečka pooled their ideas in a substantial *samizdat* publication originally entitled *Velký Brat a Velká Sestra: O strate skutočnost v ideológii reálneho socializmu* (Big Brother and Big Sister: On the Loss of Reality in the Ideology of Real Socialism), in which Czech and Slovak were used alternately. This book of essays began and ended with a dialogue between the authors, who responded to questions posed by someone speaking for 'the second generation'.[43] The authors described their book as an effort to reflect on their own experience 'after the fall' when they escaped from the 'intellectual smog' of their past life, characterised by the 'betrayal of their own reason' and 'a loss of reality', and enjoyed a relative freedom to think and to write as they pleased. In the essays, they delivered a severe and biting critique of real socialism, but, as the concluding dialogue revealed, remained skeptical of grandiose projects of reform, or even of political programmes, and were fearful of the chaos of radical change. They favoured a more or less conservative approach of gradual reforms aiming at the solution of concrete problems. Their relative optimism rested on the hope of the emergence of an 'open society', which would guarantee freedom of expression, the revival of a rational in place of an ideological stance, and the restoration of European standards in Czechoslovakia.

Kusý's major contribution to the joint volume was a hilarious satire, *Kozoturiáda*, a parody of the regime's effort to build and legitimise real socialism, using the metaphor of the *Kozotur*, a new animal combining the goat and the bison, to replace the 'obsolete' cow. In the spirit of Orwell's *Animal Farm* and adopting the term 'kozotur' invented by the Soviet science fiction writer, Fazil Iskander, Kusý described the struggle of 'the Guardians of the Sacred Kozotur Cause' to breed a perfect model of the new animal and to overcome both the beast's natural resistance and the hidden opposition of the breeders to the 'kozotur imperative'. A campaign to 'shoe' the kozotur crippled many of the animals and had to be abandoned. A campaign to shorten their tails was frustrated by the growth of new long tails. The efforts to produce more milk than the cow also failed, as did the endeavour to create a new 'kozotur man', making the breeder a kind of 'cowboy', imbued with the kozotur spirit. The goal of creating an ideal kozotur according to the model of the classics had to give way to a compromise which accepted the 'real kozotur' and sought to turn defeats into victories by changing the criteria of success.

In a final section, which bore the title, Big Brother and Big Sister, Kusý distinguished Stalinist socialism, the socialism of Orwell's Big Brother, from real socialism, the socialism of Orwell's Big Sister of Kesey's Cuckoo's Nest. Although both systems had a common aim, the maintenance of power, they differed greatly in how they sought to achieve it. Both Big Brother and Big Sister were dictators, but 'in one case it is a dictator in the name of a revolutionary change of the world, whereas in the second case it is a dictator in the name of the preservation of the existing order'. One needed revolutionary leaders and generalissimos; the other 'corporals' who 'did not have marshals' batons in their knapsacks'. The stability of the system was based on its capacity to reproduce Big Sisters to replace each other. The removal of an 'evil' Big Sister did not improve the situation, since the real problem was the system of real socialism, not 'good or evil Big Sisters.'[44]

JIŘÍ HÁJEK (*b*. 1913)

An active social democrat as a young man and a leading party figure in the postwar years, Jiří Hájek supported the merger of his party with the Communist Party in 1948 and served as a member of the united party's Central Committee until his removal in 1969; he was expelled from the party a year later. During the early 1950s Hájek was a professor and wrote several highly political works, including one on the 'traitorous' role of social democracy.[45] Under Novotný he held high positions in diplomacy but was nonetheless appointed Minister of Foreign Affairs during the Dubček reform period. Although he remained loyal to the alliance with the Soviet Union throughout the Prague Spring and even after the invasion, he condemned the latter in his appearance before the United Nations Security Council in 1968, and again in an open letter to L. Štrougal in 1975 and in his book on the Prague Spring.[46] One of the first three spokesmen of Charter 77, Hájek, after the death of Patočka and the arrest of Havel, served alone during the first difficult months. In subsequent years, he was a special target of police persecution but was never charged with criminal acts or imprisoned.[47]

His writings, both those written in his own name and in the name of Charter 77, concentrated on what he called 'The international of human rights' which had emerged since the Second World War.[48] He was an ardent defender of such documents as the international human rights covenants and the Helsinki Final Act. Hájek wrote as a 'convinced socialist', believing that 'socialism' was better able to assure both economic and social, and civil and political, rights than capitalism, but was highly critical of the failings of real socialism and its violations of human rights obligations. He found satisfaction that the Soviet Union and its partners, after initial resistance to the Declaration of Human Rights, had ratified the subsequent international covenants and other human rights agreements, and was ready to take them at their word, calling upon them to carry out the obligations of these pacts. He denied that socialism and human rights were in any way incompatible, noting that human rights had always been a primary aim of the socialist and working class movement and pointing to the endorsement of human rights by the Soviet Union, the conference of European Communist and Workers Parties in 1976, and the rise of Eurocommunism in Western Europe. He was confident that there were forces within the countries of real socialism which favoured democratic reforms and might be able to win out over the conservative forces in power.

Hájek recognised that no state could be forced from outside to carry out its human rights commitments but welcomed the recognition of the 'civil initiatives' in Eastern Europe by the Final Act and at the Belgrade and Madrid conferences. Charter 77, as one of these initiatives, was not anticommunist, he argued, but was ready to engage in a dialogue with the authorities on the implementation of the human rights commitments which had been incorporated in the country's legal code.

Although Hájek's writings were not expressly Marxist in formulation, they bore the marks of his communist and his diplomatic background in their phraseology. He couched his argument, for instance, in the language of peaceful coexistence and detente and deplored the return of a 'cold war' mentality. He criticized bipolarity in international affairs, in statements that did not sharply distinguish

East and West, and deplored the existence of both imperialist and hegemonic tendencies. The Helsinki Final Act, however, in his view was a retroactive condemnation of the Soviet invasion and of the Brezhnev doctrine, and in his book, a decade after the intervention, he called upon the Soviet leaders to reassess the events of 1968 in this light.

Hájek was very positive toward the Helsinki process, which, he felt, offered 'a conception of a pluralistic society of sovereign European states, differing in size and strength, but equal in rights, and acting in accord with agreed rules of behaviour'. After the CSCE conference on human rights in Ottawa, however, Hájek feared that 'the insitutionalisation of dialogue was endangered by the ideology of the cold war and the growing influence of the military–industrial complexes' and that the CSCE process might degenerate into 'a kind of routine diplomatic exercise . . . with rhetorical performances but with weak results'. He called for a movement from below, in the peace movements, which would give the Helsinki process new life and dynamism and thus support forces within the establishments which were capable of breaking down the walls of ideology and power.[49]

RUDOLF BATTĚK (*b*. 1924)

A sociologist at the Academy of Sciences between 1965 and 1969, and the author of books and essays in this field, Rudolf Battěk was dismissed from his position in 1969 as a result of his active participation in the Prague Spring, as a co-founder and vice-president of KAN (Club of the Non-party Engagés) and as a deputy in the Czech National Council. Thereafter his time was spent either in manual labour or in prison, where he was detained for thirteen months in 1969–70 for opposing the invasion; for three and a half years in 1971 for his part in a leaflet campaign during the elections of that year; and for five and a half years in 1980 for his activities in Charter 77 and VONS.[50]

During his few years of freedom Battěk was the co-founder and leading spirit of an informal grouping of Independent Socialists, who proclaimed their adherence to the traditions of the Czechoslovak socialist and working class movement. In a declaration on the 100th anniversary of the Czechoslovak Social Democratic Party in 1978, they professed as their goal the fulfilment of the objectives proclaimed a century ago – a just distribution of the proceeds of labour, free elections, freedom of the press, independence of the courts, and the right of citizens to participate in public affairs.[51]

Battěk set forth 'twenty-one politicological theses' on political democracy, including a decentralisation of political power down to the lowest units of self-management (*samospráva*), effective control of the apparatuses of repression, legal measures to make possible the rise, functioning, and demise of political groupings, and respect by the political majority of the rights of minorities.[52] From these fundamental principles were derived others, such as institutionalised political pluralism, political dialogue and opposition, social control of every power structure, and the sovereignty and independence of the state.

Battěk gave a fuller exposition of his conception of political plurality in the journal *Dialogy*, of which he was a co-editor.[53] A plurality of political interests was not something artificially introduced but a 'natural' expression of differences in opinions, ideologies, and political conceptions in a given society, whether communist or not. He distinguished such pluralism of opinion from institutional political pluralism, i.e. the existence of organizations which gave expression to the variety of opinion. In the authoritarian or totalitarian states of Eastern Europe, he noted, the expression of different opinions and any attempt to constitute institutional pluralism were blocked by the leading role of the Communist Party, the impotence of other parties, and the subordination of all political structures to the Communist Party. Only a pluralistic democracy, with genuine elections, could permit the institutional expression of the plurality of opinion which actually existed.

In his contribution to the symposium, *O svobodě a moci*, Battěk defined the system in Czechoslovakia as 'totalitarian' (not 'post-totalitarian') which differed from earlier phases of this type of rule only in using instruments of indirect and gradual liquidation of nonconformist actions. Political opposition, in the form of 'independent citizens' initiatives', was of fundamental importance. We must seek out, he urged, every possible form of spontaneous civic activity: 'extra-governmental, extra-managerial, extra-organisational activity on the part of voluntary associations established for the widest possible variety of both short-term and long-term needs and purposes.[54]

During his years in prison Battěk wrote letters to his wife, excerpts from which were later published in *samizdat*.[55] Such letters, he said, in his 'Essays from an Island', during his second prison term, were bound to reflect the psychic state of a prisoner – his fears, his uncertainty, his despair and neuroses, and were a test of his firmness of character and of his convictions. Yet, as he stated in 'Anxiety over the Infinite', the artificial separation of the prisoner from his ordinary social bonds, his isolation, led to a need for introspective thinking, recapitulation and perspective. Such letters could not contain political analysis, but could seek 'to understand the fundamental significance of moral, creative and spiritual integrity'.

He described his first set of thoughts as seeking 'a path toward becoming aware of oneself'. The second set went beyond this to wrestle with 'anxiety about the infinite', to understand as much as possible the unknown and the absolute. As a tentative step toward this, he proposed 'conceptual humanism', a collection of ideas about the entire conception of individual life. Rational materialism was not enough, but had to be supplemented by the 'irrational' and the 'spiritual'. The main principle of 'conceptual humanism', he wrote, was 'life with people for people, in society for society, but at the same time life of oneself and for oneself' (p. 71).

During his third term in prison, Battěk wrote in a quite different vein, often in witty style, about a certain John Baker, an imagined Moreman (*sic*: not Mormon) minister, who uttered aphorisms on human character, life and death.[56]

PETR UHL (*b*. 1941)

A socialist of a very different brand, Petr Uhl was close to the Fourth International but did not regard himself as an orthodox Trotskyist and preferred to be known as a 'revolutionary Marxist'. As a teacher in the Technical College in Prague, he was active in 1968 in the student movement and after the occupation organized the Movement of Revolutionary Youth (HRM) and distributed leaflets against the Husák regime in the name of a so-called Revolutionary Socialist Party. In spite of his radical stance Uhl was a loyal Chartist and was prominent in the creation and activity of VONS and *Informace o Chartě*. He became the target of severe repression, spending a total of nine years in prison.

His ideas were set forth in a booklet, *Czechoslovakia and Socialism*, written in 1968–9, and more extensively, in *Programme of Social Self-Management*, prepared jointly with Jaroslav Suk and others, which was issued in *samizdat* just after Uhl's imprisonment in 1979. Both these essays were published abroad, first in French, then in German, and finally in Czech.[57] A briefer version of his views, drawn from the two essays, entitled 'The Alternative Community as a Revolutionary Avant-garde', was given in his contribution to the symposium, *O svobodě a moci*.[58] A modified version of part of this essay was included in his response to the young Christians, a long semi-autobiographical document, 'Human Rights and Political Revolution'.[59]

Peter Uhl described the existing system of communism as 'bureaucratic centralism', the product of a social revolution which had been distorted by Stalinism and which exploited and alienated the workers as under capitalism. The system had two main features, totalism (*totalita*) and centralism, but was not completely totalitarian *à la* Orwell. The Czechoslovak version, built on the Soviet model, was loyal to 'conservative neo-Stalinism', and was basically 'unreformable'.[60] It could only be removed by a political revolution, which would take some time and should use a minimum of violence. During the transitional phase the emphasis would be placed on legal and informal forms of opposition, such as the independent initiatives stimulated by Charter 77, combined with some illegal activity.[61] The revolution would be an international one, it was hoped, joining with similar anti-bureaucratic forces in other East European countries (perhaps even in the USSR) and with anti-capitalist forces in Western Europe.

In the course of the revolution other forms of resistance, such as organisations of self-management, would emerge, as happened in Poland and Hungary in 1956 and in Czechoslovakia in 1968, and would in the long run lay the foundations of a new organisation of society, based on direct democracy. Self-managing institutions, both industrial and territorial, and even international in scope, covering not only the economy but the whole of society, would combine legislative, executive, and judicial functions and would be vastly superior to parliamentarism. This highly utopian system of self-rule and indirect democracy would be accompanied by full pluralism of opinions, organisations, and political parties, although the latter would not form the ruling organisations of the self-managing society.[62]

VÁCLAV BENDA (*b.* 1946)

A devout Catholic layman, Václav Benda was a student during 1968 and acted as chairman of the students' council at Charles University. He then limited his political and civic activity to a minimum until 1977, when he became an active Chartist, twice serving as spokesman, and was a member of VONS. As a result, although trained in both philosophy and mathematics, Benda was permitted to work only in manual jobs and served four years in prison. His writings on mathematics, philosophy and politics, as well as poems and a novel, were published in *samizdat*.

During Charter discussions in 1979 Benda advanced the idea of developing independent civic initiatives, or, as he called them, 'parallel structures', and even a 'parallel *polis*', which would enhance the appeal of Charter 77 to a broader public. Examples of this already existed in the form of parallel culture and the parallel economy. Other similar structures should be formed, including some in politics, which would encourage discussion and even lend support to specific political groupings. Charter 77 would continue to exert a primarily moral appeal, but it would become somewhat more political in the sense of replacing official structures, or at the very least of 'humanising' those which existed.[63]

Benda's other contributions to political analysis focused on Catholicism and politics. In an essay published in *O svobodě a moci*, Benda described the weak position of the Catholic Church and of Catholics generally as a result of the severe repression in the 1950s and its lasting psychological effects. The top hierarchy, he said, was servile and collaborationist; the cadres of the Church were decimated by the terror suffered. Most Catholics, oppressed by feelings of guilt and of powerlessness, were outwardly loyal to the regime and retreated into a kind of ghetto; at best individuals conducted a personal search for truth. A tiny minority, in Charter 77, in a kind of defensive unity, waged a struggle against everything which made life unfree and undignified, but had given up on politics as 'a struggle for the fate of the polis'. At that time Benda dimly perceived the possibility of what he called 'a new politics', far removed from politics as a struggle for power but political in its concern for the welfare of the polis. Although he did not define this concept he thought it would be concerned with human rights, parliamentary rules, and social justice, and might be called 'radical conservatism'.[64]

The election of a new Pope, Polish in origin, raised Benda's hopes that the political potential of Catholicism would be realised by giving encouragement to individuals to break with their accustomed obedience to the authorities and to overcome their feelings of hopelessness.[65] Six years later, the Velehrad celebration of the Saint Methodius anniversary confirmed his hopes, as he indicated in another essay on Christianity and politics.[66] The 'confrontation' of Church and State at Velehrad demonstrated, in his mind, the failure of the state, despite efforts over decades, to achieve the 'total destruction and total mastery of society'. The mass pilgrimage of the devout represented 'the resurrection of a real community of faith, hope and love', 'a genuine human community' (*obec*). The Cardinal, it had been shown, was the head of 'a mighty social force', and of a Church which could not be divided or destroyed, and could therefore present its demands for the conduct of its religious life in a more 'ultimative manner', refusing concessions without fear of being driven underground.

In a broader political context the task of Catholics, and of all citizens, was fourfold:

1. to strive to restore a civil society or *polis*;
2. to accept a certain 'social' or 'civic' engagement and thus to act as allies of all those who sought to defend human rights and to reform political life;
3. to break down the barriers between Czechs and Slovaks;
4. to internationalise the struggle against totalitarian power.

Although the fourth task was hardly begun, the other three had been fulfilled in some degree at Velehrad. Future political activity, according to Benda, was bound to be influenced by the illegitimacy of the state power and by its totalist character, expressed in the fact that 'it appropriated absolute rule over every passing quiver of our body, over the most hidden corner of our spirit', and acted as 'lord over life and death'. This changed the meaning of the ancient saying, 'Render unto Caesar that which is Caesar's' (since this Caesar demanded everything) and placed on Christians the obligation to resist all claims of the totalitarian power and to conduct an uncompromising struggle against it.

In his response to the young Christians Benda restated familiar views that politics was unthinkable without morality, but was not merely 'a moral stance'. Paradoxically these 'civic stands', such as for instance the defence of the right of freedom of expression, in present circumstances, became political actions and in the politics of tomorrow, would form a basis for 'the variegated architecture of the community (*obec*)'.

Unfortunately politics had become exclusively a matter of gaining and holding on to power and had abandoned its essential purpose, 'service to something higher – the *obec*, the community, or the value of the individual'. Politics should certainly not interfere in the private sphere, still less try to 'make the individual good', but at the same time it should not be a mere 'powerless observer', blindly following the free play of forces. The very justification of the state was to introduce something good, and to resist various evils, in the sphere of social relations. Benda did not underestimate the crisis of politics in the entire contemporary world, but could only recommend as a solution traditional democratic forms, including parliamentary democracy and the separation of powers.[67]

LADISLAV HEJDÁNEK (*b*. 1927)

A member of the Evangelical Church of the Bohemian Brethren, Ladislav Hejdánek was an active Chartist and one of the early spokesmen. Educated in mathematics and philosophy, he worked in the early 1950s and the 1960s as a manual labourer and in documentation work, and was able to serve as a philosopher only between 1968 and 1970 in the Academy of Sciences. In the latter year he lost his position and, after brief imprisonment, was forced to work as a nightwatchman, stoker, or clerk. He was one of the three founders of the journal, *Dialogy*, and wrote widely in *samizdat*, including his well-known 'Letters to a Friend' between 1977 and 1979, in which he discussed Charter 77, human rights, Christianity, socialism, and questions of philosophy and politics.[68] He conducted a regular seminar in philosophy in his apartment which was visited by many foreign guests and was frequently harassed by the police.

Although Hejdánek was a non-Marxist, he considered himself a 'socialist' and wrote several essays on this theme. Socialism and democracy were in his mind inextricably intertwined. As he said in his contribution to *O svobodě a moci*, socialism was the offspring of liberal-democratic principles and was 'the extrapolation of democratic principles into social and economic realms and its practical implementation of them'.[69] As he demonstrated from the New Testament, Christianity was 'on the same boat' as socialism, as long as the latter respected truth as 'the supreme criterion of its thinking and its practice', but must distance itself from socialism if it abandoned its original motives.[70] The task ahead was to 'emancipate civil society from domination by the state and its machinery' and to effect a thoroughgoing democratisation by establishing self-managing bodies at every level and by separating all economic structures from the field of government.[71] Contemporary socialism, he wrote several years later, was in deep crisis, both in capitalist countries where the social question was only partially solved and necessary profound reforms were postponed, and in the countries of real socialism where the existing reality was in deep conflict with the ideas of Marx and Engels and with the official ideology.[72]

Hejdánek expressed his views on politics in general in a number of his letters to a friend as well as in *Dialogy*.[73] 'Everything is politics: how I work, what I write, how I philosophise, how I share in the life of society, etc. etc. In a narrow technical sense, however, politics had to do with expertness, and with the maintenance and reform of the institutions necessary for society's life, and should be conducted, not by professionals, but by politicians of character and by statesmen endowed with personal authority' (*Dopisy*, no. 3, 1978). The danger lay in the hypertrophy of this 'technical' politics which led to the 'absolute state, i.e., a state which is completely emancipated from society and its life, which does not feel itself subordinated or responsible to it, but which on the contrary tries to organise and guide it in a directive manner according to its own needs and criteria'. The consolidation after 1968 was designed to 'stifle and to liquidate all spontaneous "non-political political" civic initiatives and to restore and strengthen the central direction and control of all organisations permitted by the state'. The escape lay in a return to what he called 'a spontaneous non-political politicalness.' It was up to the individual citizen 'jealously to defend the sphere of his freedom' and to resist 'illegitimate state intervention into the personal domain of the individual human and social being' (*Dopisy*, no. 6).[74]

OTHER AUTHORS

One is tempted to go on with the presentation of other books and essays on politics but space forbids more than a brief reference to a few authors.

Petr Pithart (*b*. 1941), for instance, one-time teacher of law at Charles University and a party member, lost his post due to his activities in favour of political reform during 1968, and was limited to manual and clerical work after 1969. A Charter signatory, Pithart wrote several essays which were highly critical of certain aspects of Charter activity, and an equally censorious book on the reform policies of 1968. He devoted his spare time to historical studies and wrote several in which he found serious fault with certain Czech political traditions.[75]

Jiří Dienstbier (*b.* 1937), former party member and foreign correspondent in the Far East and the USA, was a prominent advocate of reforms during the 1960s and active in post-occupation free broadcasting. He was dismissed from his work and expelled from the party in 1969. A Charter spokesman and a member of VONS, he was imprisoned in 1979 for three years. His *samizdat* writings were devoted mainly to international politics and he edited the short-lived foreign affairs magazine, *Čtverec*. He was prominent in the dialogue with Western peace movements and published many articles on peace and human rights, and on European unity.[76]

Jaroslav Šabata (*b.* 1928) was a university lecturer in psychology, a former communist, regional secretary in Brno during the Prague Spring; he was expelled from the party in 1969 and later spent five years in prison. A signatory and twice spokesman of Charter 77, he spent two more years in prison. Before his confinement he participated actively in discussions of Charter reform and of opposition strategy, and after his release took a leading part in formulating statements on peace and on European unity, including the Prague Appeal.[77]

Zdeněk Mlynář (*b.* 1930) might also be briefly mentioned as one who, before going into exile in the summer of 1977, had been prominent in organizing the Charter movement and was active in its first few months. A Secretary of the party under Dubček, he resigned this post in 1969 and was expelled from the party the following year. Before leaving the country, Mlynář wrote an excellent essay on dissidents and their political role which was included in the *samizdat* symposium, *O svobodě a moci*, and in the Czech edition published abroad.[78]

Two persons of religious orientation should also be mentioned. *Jiří Němec* (*b.* 1932) was dismissed from his work as a psychologist for signing Charter 77 and was imprisoned in 1979 for his work in VONS. A Catholic, Němec edited a number of books on religion, and several essays on religion and politics, e.g. 'New Chances for Freedom'.[79] *Jakub S. Trojan* (*b.* 1927), former Evangelical minister, with a doctorate in theology and a degree in economics, was removed from his pastorate in 1971 and wrote a number of essays and feuilletons on religion and politics, including *In Defence of Politics*, to be discussed in the following section.[80]

THE REVIVAL OF POLITICS

It seems appropriate to conclude this chapter, not with a synthetic summary or a personal critique of the ideas set forth above, but instead with a statement of the conditions for a 'rebirth' or 'renaissance' of politics by Jakub Trojan in the essay just cited. The problem could best be observed, he argued, from the viewpoint of 'powerlessness', which afforded 'an opportunity to see the world of politics in the proper light' – 'in the light of the possibilities of the emergent future'. Due to the profound crisis in Europe as a whole and the failure of the European churches, his own included, this involved going back to the 'spiritual foundations of politics, with the idea of acting morally and in truth, regardless of the cost'. The renewal of politics, he believed, could take place only through 'a series of small and modest steps' and through an awareness that everyone shared responsibility both for the present situation and for the recovery of politics. This meant a 'revolution of heart and mind' (the words of Havlíček and Masaryk) and a reintegration of humanity in Europe. 'Total power was the culmination of the catastrophe, not a solution to it, and citizens recognised this only when they realized that they were creatures possessed of full rights, and as such, could become the focus of unalienated activity. This was the moment when a movement that would lead to possible salvation was born.'

Trojan concluded his article by stating 'ten theses in which I defend politics and express my faith in its renewal:

1. Responsibility for public life is a part of civic and human completeness. Indifference to public life is a sign of decadence. Apoliticalness is a profound dysfunction of the personality.
2. Participation in public life and the co-ordination of relationships between citizens in society requires more than routine technology and pragmatic experience. Politics as the administration of human affairs is a human problem in the full sense of the word.
3. Politics is a modest aspect of the life of the spirit. It stands on moral and spiritual principles that keep it from slipping into opportunistic behaviour that gives precedence to tactical and utilitarian considerations.

4. True politics starts from a situation of dialogue. Anything that concerns everyone can only be settled by everyone. Such a politics is aware that it cannot impose from above without respecting the rights of different groups and individuals. It allows them to articulate opinions and points of view that are different from the official ones.

5. We achieve this by small-scale and persistent work. True politics today, in this country, requires the ardent apostleship and the determined witness of all those who stand up for responsibility in public affairs.

6. The rejection of extremism goes hand in hand with the overcoming of aversions, resentments, and hatreds. Only a positive approach, even toward those who now hold power, is appropriate for knights of freedom. Civil and social liberation, which is the meaning of politics, must concern everyone.

7. The aim of a renewed politics is a strong society and a weak state. A strong society is marked by vigorous and varied activity from below and by democratic self-administration. Small is beautiful. Hybrid entities, whether they are the supernational societies of the West or the centralised states of the East, are monocratic and operate through monologue.

8. Decentralisation of power, democratically functioning public control from below, civil and human rights guaranteed by law and positively developed by responsible institutions, the defence of minorities, freedom of the press and creative freedom, a public opinion safeguarded by functioning organizations and living churches, independent scholarship and law-making, and an independent cultural life – all these are signs of a renewed politics.

9. Without moral integrity, discipline, and freedom from worldly goods, it is impossible to advance toward self-revival and the growth of political responsibility. It will not help us to change external conditions if change catches us in a state of intellectual decline and moral and spiritual exhaustion (Masaryk).

10. A free society is created by free people. The foundations of external freedom are laid in the inner being of each person. To create the external conditions and institutional framework for inner self-renewal is one of the primary tasks of politics. Only in this way can politics demonstrate that its source and culmination is something *nonpolitical*: it gives all honour to the renewed power of truth and thus saves itself.'[81]

Part III

Independent Society in Central and Eastern Europe

7 A Second Society: A Theoretical Framework

The crushing of the Prague Spring by military force was a turning point in Soviet and East European politics, and also in the efforts, both in the East and West, to interpret the nature of communist systems.[1] During the 1960s the concept of 'totalitariansim', which had dominated thinking in the 1940s and 1950s, gave way to alternative models of communist society. The term 'totalitarianism' was hardly used in Central and Eastern Europe itself, as intellectuals and political activists were encouraged by the decline of total control over the individual and society and were hopeful that a pluralistic system might emerge as a result of actions taken within the system. Simultaneously, in the West many scholars discarded the totalitarian concept and advanced a plethora of alternative paradigms better able, it was thought, to explain the change and diversity within the communist world since 1956. The violent interruption of what seemed almost a revolutionary change in Czechoslovakia produced a resurgence of the concept of totalitarianism in Eastern Europe and to some degree a backlash in Western political science by those who felt that their conception of the realities was vindicated by events.

In ensuing years, in Eastern Europe, oppositionists were more or less unanimous in once again defining the prevailing systems as totalitarian. This was conceived as the 'absorption of society by the state, through terror or other means of control, so as to forbid any subordinate spontaneity or institutionalised autonomy'.[2] Ironically, however, it was becoming increasingly clear, especially during the 1970s, that there was another side to the coin, namely the expression of various forms of individual and group dissent, sometimes assuming dimensions which challenged the exclusive control of society by the state. At the 'lowest' level individuals began to resist the state's claims on their lives and to act independently, even at some risk, to vindicate their own values and interests. At a higher level, organised defiance of the existing system took place in what came to be called 'dissidence'. This took varied forms and assumed differing degrees of organisation and of mutual support among the various groups formed. A host of alternative concepts emerged, both among the so-called 'dissidents', and among scholars in East and West, who were

157

trying to comprehend these phenomena. We shall mention at the outset (and discuss more fully later) terms such as 'independent civic initiatives','independent' or 'parallel' society, 'civil society', 'second economy', 'second culture', 'second public sphere', 'self-organisation of society', 'parallel politics', 'anti-politics' or 'non-political politics', a 'second polity', a 'contra-system', and, broadest of all, 'a second society'.

Both the reality of 'independent activities' and the concepts employed to describe and define them seemed to run counter to the notion of the total domination of society by the state and to negate the essence of a totalitarian system. Paradoxically, however, in the European Communist countries, the systems were still regarded as 'totalitarian', in spite of tendencies toward autonomous activity which were present, sometimes in considerable strength. This dialectic of opposites, it was sometimes said, was the product of the natural inclination of individuals to resist the artificial system of state control of their lives and of society, and the equally logical efforts by the state to eliminate any independent and spontaneous actions and to maintain, or to reimpose, rigid state domination of society and the individual.

CIVIL SOCIETY AND THE STATE

The concept of an independent society resembled a much more ancient interpretation of the relationship of the state and of civil society, expressed in manifold ways by Hobbes and Locke, Paine, Hegel, de Toqueville, and Marx. This was argued in some detail by John Keane, in his discussion of what he called 'a rediscovery of civil society' – 'an independent, pluralistic, self-organizing civil society' – in Western thought. The central point was the relationship of the state, as a network of political institutions (including the military, legal, administrative, economic, and cultural organizations) to civil society as 'the realm of social (i.e., privately owned or voluntarily organized) activities which are legally recognized and guaranteed'. This concept of the state versus civil society was being revived and re-thought as a relationship which was applicable to both Western and Eastern European states.[3]

The idea of 'civil society' was explicitly applied to Poland, for instance, by Jacques Rupnik, in his study of Polish 'dissent' between 1968 and 1978, which was subtitled 'the end of Revisionism and the rebirth of the Civil Society'.[4] In a more detailed study, 'Solidarity and the Re-Birth of Civil Society', a contribution to John Keane's book, Z. A. Pelczynski, drawing his inspiration largely from the writings of Hegel and Gramsci, argued that it was misleading to apply the concept of civil society to Poland before the rise of Solidarity, when a realm of independent social organisation, activity, and pressure on the state did not exist. The democratic opposition was only 'groping for ways to institutionalise itself and to become a civil society capable of confronting the party–state from a position of some strength'. The establishment of Solidarity, however, did mean, in his view, that 'political society became institutionalised and civil society became truly reborn . . . .' The ensuing period, up to the establishment of martial law, witnessed a struggle of 'civil society vs. the state', with Solidarity seeking to establish 'a self-governing republic' in which the democratically organised social forces would exert a predominant influence in civil society and the old state structure would be confined to the army, police and the courts, and to the conduct of foreign policy; the party would be relegated to a minimal and insignificant position. This ended with the restoration of the state power by military means and the suppression of the embryonic civil society.[5]

In a fuller analysis, Andrew Arato, in his 'Civil Society Against the State: Poland, 1980–81', presented the evidence for what he called 'the reconstitution of civil society' from 1968 on, but notably after 1980, through the rule of law and the guarantee of civil rights, a free public sphere and a plurality of independent associations.[6] He buttressed his argument with similar views expressed in the writings of leading Polish activists, Leszek Kołakowski, Adam Michnik, and Jacek Kuroń, as well as the Hungarians, András Hegedüs, János Kis, and György Bence, and the exiled Czech, Jiří Pelikan, all of whom used terms such as 'social self-defence', 'social self-management', 'social movements', etc. Although this was, as we know, terminated by the military seizure of power in December 1981, the sixteen months of 'detotalisation of a totalitarian system' and the 'emergence of a new type of civil society', as he put it in a second article, did invent 'a path for the social transformation of Eastern European societies': i.e., the restoration of civil society, characterised by legality, individual rights and freedoms, the revival of a public sphere and public opinion, plurality, and solidarity, of interest groups, and democratic participation.[7]

A similar exposition was given by Kasimierz Wojcicki, a Pole, who expressly noted that contrary to the stereotype of a totalitarian society as entirely atomised and centrally controlled, in Poland society had been able to retain 'a high degree of organisation and autonomy'. The 'reconstruction of society' was based on the foundations of that which had not been totally destroyed, 'the values of democracy and pluralism', and developed both 'a social movement', highly political in character, and 'independent social instititions,' such as trade unions, which ought to resist politicisation.[8]

Jan Tesař, a Czech now in exile, used the concept of civil society, in an essay written while still in Czechoslovakia, in which he explored the notion of totalitarian mass movements as seeking to control all spheres of social life totally, and thus to replace the rich structure of civil society, the democratic organisations and institutions which had been developed in the most advanced European and North American countries. The best way to ward off a totalitarian threat, or to overcome a totalitarian society once established, in his view, was to encourage the development of a civil society, adducing the example of Spain as a society in which such structures had been created in the form of the workers' committees. He was not sure that a fully developed totalitarian society such as that in Eastern Europe *could* be overcome but stressed the importance of the struggle for human and civil rights as 'an irrestistible trend to civic emancipation'.[9]

THE SECOND SOCIETY

A different perspective, parting company both with the totalitarian premise and with the counterposing of state and society, was advanced by the Hungarian scholar Elemér Hankiss, in his highly original thesis of the 'dual society', or the dichotomy of the 'first society' and the 'second society', set forth in an initial and a later revised version.[10] This approach could help to explain why so-called totalitarian societies – a term not entirely unjustified in the early 1950s – began later to 'behave in a strange way', and it was difficult to define whether they were changing, and, if so, what has changed and what has not, and in what direction they have evolved. How could the same society be seen as totalitarian and pluralistic, or as bureaucratic and participatory? The explanation of these apparent contradictions rested in the fact that these societies were characterised by the conflict between a 'first society' – 'the manifest, formal institutional sphere', and the 'second society' – 'the latent and informal sphere of social existence'. This formulation, which resembled the more ancient dichotomy of state and civil society, did not, however, divide society into two or more groups of people, but cut across these groups and cut across social structures and institutions as well (revised edition, p. 27).

The first and second societies were not two distinct groups of people (e.g., state bureaucrats, dominant classes, and society as a whole) but were two 'dimensions of social existence' of a given society, 'regulated by two different sets of organisational principles'. In a detailed analysis of the criteria of differentiation of the two paradigms Hankiss included the following sharply polarised dichotomies: (1) homogeneity and bureaucratic integration versus an interactive process of differentiation and integration; (2) vertical versus horizontal relationships; (3) downward versus the upward flow of power; (4) predominance of state ownership or non-state ownership; (5) centralisation versus moderate centralisation and the emergence of economic and social autonomies; (6) political domination versus spontaneous social and economic factors; (7) ideological versus non-ideological or alternative ideologies; (8) legitimacy versus ambiguous legitimacy or illegitimacy (revised edition, pp. 3–4; Table 1, pp. 19–21).

Although his analysis focused on Hungary, it was relevant to other societies. The second society was 'an important sphere, or dimension, of social existence'. It was not, however, 'a fully developed model of a new society' but it might contain 'some rudimentary proto-elements of such a paradigm' and might play a catalytic role in the transformation of the first society into a more efficient and democratic type of society' (I, pp. 1, 36–7).

This interpretation of communist societies (and it was not limited to them alone) was a highly complex one, which cannot easily be conveyed, in the abstract given in Hankiss's article, let alone in my brief effort at summarisation. The second society subsumed a series of sub-systems – the second economy, the second public, the second culture, the second consciousness, and the second sphere of social–political interactions, each of which will be discussed further in later sections of this chapter. The analysis was complicated even more, Hankiss admitted, by the fact that the relationships were not fixed but were constantly changing. The second society in particular was heterogeneous, and not easy to define. And the two societies were not sharply opposed to one another. They might not be 'situated at two opposite poles', as implied, but might 'reach deep into the middle field of the continuum and overlap, or even intertwine, with one another' (I, p. 7).

In the revised version of his essay Hankiss developed his *caveats* further, and although he did not abandon his scheme of categories of the second society, drew very different conclusions as to its nature and its relationship with the first society. Many of the processes which he had earlier assigned to the second society, e.g., corruption, did not properly belong to it, but formed 'a separate sphere within the first society, a sphere that is bordering on, and is partly intertwined with, the second society' (pp. 46–7). The second economy, for instance, was not an 'autonomous alternative economy', but rather a 'complementary' one. The 'second public', which remained secret and not really open, was but a distorted counterpart of the first (revised, p. 44).

Abandoning his former sharp dichotomisation of the two societies, Hankiss proposed a fourfold classification. The first society included two sectors: (i) a formal, manifest, and legitimate sphere, and (ii) an informal, latent, and non-legitimate sphere (clientelism, corruption, nepotism, informal bargainings, etc.). The second society was 'a kind of no man's land, a "zero-degree" of social existence', which 'has been unable to develop its own paradigm' and at most contained 'some incipient forms of a possible alternative paradigm' (p. 48). The fourth 'hypothetical alternative society' did not yet exist but if fully developed would be characterised by the criteria hitherto ascribed to the second society: a rich inner articulation and strong social integration; a rich network of horizontal interrelationships; influence and power aggregation from below; decentralisation and the co-operation of the autonomous economic and social actors, etc. (see pp. 47a, 48a, Tables V and VI).

Developing further his reconsidered view of the relationship of the second to the first society, Hankiss argued that the first society 'tacitly let a latent dimension of social and economic interactions develop within its own power framework', but 'hindered the emergence of "system-alien" organisational principles and, even more, their combination into a consistent configuration, into a second para-digm'. The emergence of a second society, in spite of its de-ficiencies, strengthened the power structure and helped the system work; it was an 'indispensable safety valve', a domain 'which com-pensated for the dysfunctions of the first society'; it developed human skills and qualities needed for social regeneration; and provided 'an experimental ground for testing new forms of social interactions, processes and organisational principles' (pp. 48–50).

DIVERSITY IN THE STATE–SOCIETY RELATIONSHIP

The application of these concepts, and other supplementary ones which will be considered, is not easy, as the concepts themselves, as well as the realities which they are deemed to interpret, are not well defined, and the boundaries between the social spheres represented are neither sharp nor static. The independent activities (with which we are concerned) vary greatly, ranging from the spontaneous actions of individuals, for example, on the black market, through varying degrees of group actions, such as encouraging and organising literary activity, to the higher level of more organised and broad-ranging tendencies, say, for the defence of human rights. Some actions may express personal rebellion, or deviations from official norms, for instance prostitution or alcoholism; others may be collective acts of self-defence, seeking to right wrongs, defend freedom, or pursue wider aims. In some individual activities the motives may be predominantly egotistical and self-serving, lacking moral purpose; others may be positive in a societal sense, defending moral values and striving for correction of abuses. Some tendencies will be quite public, above ground; others, intimately personal and private, or underground and conspiratorial. Some will be highly organised, others loosely structured or lacking any structure at all. In some cases *samizdat* would not play a part; in others, it would be a crucial, although not the only, medium of communication. In some cases the objectives would be specific, limited, and immediate, lacking any political implications. In others the aims would be more general and long-term, challenging official society, striving to develop an alternate, or parallel society, and aspiring eventually to replace the official, or at least to transform it into a more 'normal' state–society relationship. The actions involved vary therefore in the degree of their challenge to the regime, some pursuing entirely non-political aims, although often defying state authority; others, seeking to defend moral values of truth and justice, a 'non-political politics,' having profound political implications; still others, openly seeking political change of a radical or moderate kind. In some cases individuals and groups would act entirely on their own, unfamiliar with, or unsympathetic to, the efforts of others, and perhaps even moving in contradictory directions. Other types of independent activity would be elements in collective actions, linked together in various ways and giving each other mutual support.

Complicating our task even more, of course, is the diversity among the communist states in their state–society relations, and the latter's shifting over time, so that no common and unchanging pattern can be set forth. There are some states which seek to exercise, or to maintain, complete authority over society and to destroy all forms of autonomy. Other states, authoritarian in form, permit, or are forced to recognise, some degree of independence and autonomy. In the former case independent actions will remain highly individualistic in character, subject to severe repression; nonetheless there will be certain ubiquitous tendencies, say in the second economy, or in the profession of religious belief, which will persist in spite of everything. Only in a few cases will there be simultaneous efforts to win greater freedom and independence, linked together in a common endeavour. Even in the latter type the embryonic independent society may remain isolated and confined to a kind of ghetto, living its own life but unable to affect the life of society as a whole. Only rarely will an emerging parallel society aspire to share in the public life of the society as a whole, gradually to extend its own influence, and to rival or challenge the official state power. The state–society relations in all these cases will go through a ceaseless ebb and flow, moving sometimes to greater or almost complete state control, then experiencing a revival of greater independence of action, and later suffering a resurgence of state power, as, say, in the situation in Czechoslovakia after 1968 or in Poland after 1981. In the latter case – so far unique – the society remains alive and vibrant, frustrating the efforts to re-establish total control, and making that country anything but a totalitarian society.

In what follows, we shall endeavour to bring into some degree of order the complexities of European Communist politics, using in part the conceptual framework outlined by Hankiss, and supplementing it with other approaches. We shall examine what might be considered the ubiquitous forms of dissent or independent action, prevalent even in countries where state authority is extremely strict, but possessing distinctive characteristics in each one. We shall then examine more developed forms of independent action which are present in certain countries and in differing degrees. Finally (Chapter 8) we shall discuss the unique experience of each country of Central and Eastern Europe, including the Soviet Union.

THE SECOND ECONOMY

The 'second' or 'private' economy was a generally recognised phenomenon in communist systems and has for some years been the subject of intensive study by economists.[11] In Hankiss's words, this, and other similar terms, referred to 'the sum total of economic activities outside the state sector'; these were more or less 'informal' and 'invisible'.[12] Many economists regarded this hidden economy as a substantial element of the economy as a whole, perhaps most fully developed in Hungary at the present time. It might take legal or illegal forms, or even a 'grey' semi-legal character. It was an indispensable part of the economic system, and was reluctantly accepted, and even to some extent supported, by party and government.

The Hungarian economist, István Kemény, listed among legal activities the sale of produce by collective or private farmers, work in cottage industries, licensed transactions by craftsmen, contractors, dealers, repairmen, or professional persons, the renting of flats, or the floating of loans. Illegal or semi-legal activities included similar transactions as those above, but were unlicensed: illicit dealings 'under the counter,' transactions by directors or managers to facilitate the carrying out of their official tasks, giving and receiving tips and gratuities (the 'bakshish' culture), bribery, stealing, speculation on the black market, or the conduct of underground enterprises.[13] The distinction between the legal and illegal was by no means a sharp one, and they were often intertwined and mutually supporting. The line, too, was constantly shifting and varied from period to period. It was generally accepted by scholars that the second economy, although eroding the ideological foundations of a Marxist state and countering the leading role of the party, had positive effects, ensuring the functioning of the economy and also contributing to consumers' well-being (Kemény, p. 361).

Virtually all citizens, according to Kemény, were in one way or another involved in the second economy in their daily lives. In fact, he argued, the Hungarian worker lived only to a small extent from his formal wage or salary and to a far greater extent from other activities, leading thus 'a double life' (p. 357). The Hungarian economy was a dual or mixed economy in which 'small independent entrepreneurs played a role far greater than in the capitalist countries or in other socialist states' (p. 359). There was a constant struggle between the state, seeking to thwart private or collective enterprise of this kind, and the individual's counter-strategies based on the spirit of private enterprise (p. 364). The motivation was not merely material self-satisfaction, he believed, but also 'the desire for independence and personal liberty' (p. 362). The reward was 'the joy of experiencing existential freedom and the attainment at great cost of a certain independence' (p. 363). Kemény even argued that the private economy represents not just 'isolated, individual acts' but 'collective action by social groups or bodies' (pp. 365–4).

Closely related to the second economy, and overlapping it in many respects, was what has been called 'the informal sector', which 'thrives within the interstices of bureaucratic organisation'.[14] Steven Sampson, in his study of this phenomenon in Rumania, included not only economic activities of an informal nature but also 'distortions' of the plan, 'poor organisation' in the bureaucracy, information distribution, such as rumour, gossip, and *samizdat*, and, above all, interpersonal relations based on 'favors, neighborly exchanges of goods and services, and the constant use of friends and connections to obtain scarce resources' (pp. 44–5). This was a highly organised realm, in which family and kin, common ethnic or territorial origin, ties of friendship, and patrons, brokers, and clients served as 'alternative ways of allocating resources', and not merely in terms of money. As Kemény wrote of the second economy, Sampson referred to these 'informal channels and social networks' as being 'absolutely *vital* for the day to day existence of virtually all East Europeans' (p. 50; also p. 64). They might function 'benignly', helping the system 'to work', but also might have corruptive effects, contributing to stagnancy, and in extreme cases they might even threaten the system by promoting crisis or revolt (p. 64). Certainly there could be no doubt that these activities helped the citizen to satisfy personal needs which could not be met by the system itself, but also to realise values, such as autonomous achievement, friendship, and social connections, outside the formal structure of society.

The latter aspect was brought out forcefully by János Kenédi, a leading Hungarian dissident, in his witty little book, *Do it Yourself*, which described his tortuous effort to build a house privately. He managed to accomplish this objective mainly through personal connections, 'pulling strings', and bribery or corruption, sometimes breaking the law, thus circumventing or overcoming the obstacles placed in his way by the state authorities and official regulations.[15]

SOCIAL DEVIANCE

Another kind of nonconformist or aberrant activity which was closely related to the second economy, and in fact included certain aspects, has been termed 'social deviance,' i.e., all behaviour that was not approved or justified ideologically and was often treated as 'criminal' by the regime. In a symposium on this phenomenon in Eastern Europe specialists examined not only the private or hidden economy in Hungary and Poland, but also other types of activity, such as prostitution and alcoholism.[16] In spite of ideological taboos and official efforts to wipe it out, prostitution persisted in most if not all communist countries. While one cannot neglect the social and psychological causes of such unorthodox behaviour, or ignore the fact that it is sometimes officially sponsored, it seems justified to describe it as a special kind of independent activity by which the prostitute seeks higher earnings than in ordinary employment and the clients seek sexual gratification outside the established institutions of the family.

Alcoholism was not usually considered an illegal activity but various measures were taken by the state to curb it. It, too, constituted an unusual attempt by an individual to seek the satisfaction of his needs, and might express an alienation from established society and constitute an act of individual rebellion. Other types of social deviance, such as the ever-increasing use of drugs, and even robbery and violent crime, were actions taken in defiance of the law and of public disapproval and might be thought of as desperate efforts by individuals to escape the controls imposed by society or the state and choose their own life-style. No political aims were involved, nor did most of these activities pursue ethical goals. Most of them expressed selfish personal interests and made no positive contribution to societal ends.

Walter Connor, in his study of social deviance in the Soviet Union, dealt with crime, delinquency, and alcoholism. Excluding deviance of a directly political nature (dissent), Connor argued that these were entirely 'apolitical' although they might have indirect political relevance. Following Robert K. Merton, Connor treated these forms of social deviance as 'aberrant' as distinct from 'nonconformist'. Unlike political dissidents, the perpetrators, in breaking the rules of society, did not announce their offences but tried to conceal them; they did not question the legitimacy of norms prohibiting their acts but violated them; they did not draw upon ultimate values or present arguments for an alternative set of moral and legal priorities.[17] Although Connor did not explain such deviance as forms of social protest, he clearly illustrated the presence of this element by telling the story of a taxidriver who justified 'cheating' of customers: 'I cheat because everyone else does . . . . Cheating's the thing to do. The boss of my taxi park has made a fortune selling petrol and spare parts, and all the shift supervisors take their cuts too . . . . Why should I be a martyr?'[18]

Brief mention might be made of an interesting essay by Alfred Meyer on 'civil disobedience' in the USSR and Eastern Europe. He drew on Christian Bay's definition of civil disobedience as 'an act of public defiance of a law or policy enforced by established government authority'.[19] Meyer here referred to many types of 'deviant behaviour' or 'deviant thoughts' all of which were regarded with suspicion by the authorities as 'manifestations of spontaneity', ranging from resistance to collectivisation by the peasantry, taking of independent positions by scientists on specialised policy issues, or the violations of legal or other rules by administrators and managers, to religious practices, occasional strikes or demonstrations, revolts in prison camps, and even suicide. Meyer also included dissenting or protesting activists, a kind of 'loyal opposition', who acted in a legal manner and from deeply moral motives, seeking to widen the range of permissible activity and to insist on the exercise of rights formally granted by existing laws.

COMMUNICATIONS, CULTURE, AND IDEOLOGY

Let us turn to other spheres of the second society which are closer to the usual conception of 'dissidence' and an 'independent society', namely the 'second public', the 'second culture', and the 'second consciousness', to use Hankiss's terms.[20] Although functioning 'under the surface' and subjected to severe restrictions and penalties, these independent activities are more open and visible than the second economy or the informal sector; they are sometimes organised for collective action, and pursue ethical ends and social purposes. They are in a sense more 'political' than the black market or the social network, and sometimes are linked, even in the same persons, with the parallel politics to be discussed below. Although they are ubiquitous in communist societies, these actions vary greatly in scope and degree. In some countries, such as Czechoslovakia, Poland, and the USSR, they are highly developed; in other countries, such as Rumania and Bulgaria, due to severe repression, they are less developed. In Hungary and Yugoslavia, where the official networks of communications and culture are more open, the need for them is less acute.

The *second public* requires little more discussion since the phenomenon of unofficial communications has been dealt with at length in earlier chapters. The 'second system of communications' (Hankiss, p. 25) included not only *samizdat*, but also foreign radio and television, the spreading of rumours and gossip, as well as foreign news (sometimes transmitted in written form), and sincere and frank conversations among close friends and relations. Within this system genuine information was circulated, and public issues were discussed more openly. As noted earlier, in some countries this was a highly organised and widespread phenomenon, but in others it was rare and sporadic. A broader 'second public' or public opinion, which is beyond the scope of this essay, consisted of the personal opinions of individuals on public policy questions and official ideology, expressed mainly in private, but revealed in a limited way by public opinion polling.[21]

The *second culture* – i.e. independent creative culture – needs limited treatment in view of earlier chapters. Strangely enough, Hankiss uses this term to refer only to subcultures, counter-cultures, or alternative cultures, by which he refers to pre-war middle-class, peasant and working-class cultures; youth subcultures and counter-cultures; religious and the nationalistic-populistic subcultures, as opposed to the 'cosmopolitan' or urbanite, all of which were regarded by the régimes as dangerous 'alien elements' (revised, pp. 31–2). The term 'second culture' should properly be used to designate the entire realm of creative effort (strangely neglected by Hankiss): *samizdat* writing (scholarship, literature, and philosophy), independent painting, independent theatre, as well as, of course, underground music and poetry.

As a Czech observer, writing under a pseudonym, defined it, this activity was independent in that it was not subsidised and hence not subject to state control, but it remained in some degree dependent, since official repression led to 'self-censorship'. The practice of independent writing became 'a kind of game', a constant probing of the limits of the permissible. Entirely free of market considerations, independent creative persons reaped no financial reward, but might gain a high reputation among their readers and their peers and sometimes achieve publication abroad. As in the second economy, the line between official and unofficial culture was not a hard and fast one, as independence was sometimes sought, and achieved, by persons within the official structures. Its consequences included the attainment of a feeling of 'inner freedom', the enjoyment of mutual support among kindred spirits, the raising of the standards of culture in general, and, above all, the gradual breaking of the monopoly of official culture.[22]

The *second consciousness*, a somewhat ill-defined and inappropriate term, denoted the situation when the official or dominant ideology exerted a limited influence on people's thinking, and various counter-ideologies or belief-systems persisted from the past or were newly developed. Many people, according to Hankiss, developed a 'double' or 'split' consciousness: they had 'two minds or souls: one for their daylight and official lives and another . . . which got activated in the second society or in their family lives' (Hankiss, p. 34). Sometimes this led to apathy, a kind of 'negative' second consciousness, which was unable to develop a positive alternative; and sometimes it had a more positive effect in the crystallisation of 'latent or semi-latent world views' – religious, lay humanist, conservative (middle-class or 'leftist'), liberal, technocratic, Eurocommunist, social democratic and populistic–nationalistic. These world views played, he believed, an important part in contemporary Hungary, although their inter-play with each other and with the official world-view was a far cry from 'the open articulation of well-developed autonomous world views' (pp. 36, 45). In fact, as another Hungarian noted, the majority of citizens lacked any political conception or were politically nameless.[23]

Hankiss, it would seem, exaggerated the 'latent' character of these world views, and the difficulty of describing them. The more explicitly political views, which properly belong to what we may call 'parallel politics' or the 'second polity' (discussed above, Chapter 6, and below), were set forth explicitly in *samizdat*, where this existed. Religious world views, too, were openly articulated in official church utterances and sermons, in worship by believers, in pilgrimages of the faithful, and in the turn of youth toward religion.[24]

Quite surprising was Hankiss's omission from the list of independent views of national beliefs, which, like religious faiths, were omnipresent in communist countries. In fact the former were particularly pronounced in Hungary, where there was a general concern for Hungarians in neighbouring countries where the nationalism of a minority 'subculture' confronted the dominant nationalist culture of the ruling nation. They articulated national needs and interests in a struggle for greater equality and autonomy. In some cases they took the form of a developed national movement, with its own *samizdat* publications, but they were normally more anomic and unorganised.

THE MUSICAL UNDERGROUND AND ROCK CULTURE

Few can doubt the existence and the importance in Eastern Europe of what has been variously termed the cultural underground or the youth counter-culture, and sometimes, rather confusingly, the 'second culture'. Hankiss, for instance, treated this phenomenon as one of several types of 'subculture', or 'counter-culture'.[25] Similarly, Pedro Ramet, in his study of 'rock counter-culture' in the Soviet Union and Eastern Europe, treated it as an example of the generic term 'counter-culture', along with other counter-cultures such as dissent movements, religious alternatives, criminality and social deviance, and foreign culture importations.[26] Curiously, Ramet, like Hankiss, restricts the concept of culture to such limited sub-cultures and does not deal with the whole realm of creative culture (art, literature, theatre, etc.)

The classic definition of the cultural 'underground' in Czecho-slovakia was formulated by Ivan Jirous, musicologist and spiritual mentor of the Plastic People of the Universe, in an influential article published in *samizdat* in 1975. For him the underground was 'a mental attitude' of persons who 'consciously and critically determine their own stance towards the world in which they live' and declare war on the establishment (p. 27); at the same time it was 'a community of mutual support of people who want to live differently' (p. 25). Its aim, he wrote, was to create 'a second culture', in an oft-quoted phrase, 'a culture not dependent on official channels of communications, or on the hierarchy of values of the establishment'.[27] Later Jirous, under the pseudonym Magor, defended the underground against severe criticism by V. Černý. Its core, he said, were the workers who, living hitherto in 'slavery', found in it 'a sphere of freedom'. Far from being hippies or negating culture, they had 'a consciousness of co-responsibility and of the indivisibility of freedom' and 'a hunger for real culture'.[28]

Jirous's concept of the 'underground' was sharply challenged by Mikoláš Chadima in a study of Czech rock and roll in which he rejected the view that the underground consisted solely of bands such as the Plastic People of the Universe which were unable to perform publicly after 1973. An important part of the 'unofficial rock scene' in the 1970s were the so-called 'alternative' bands which continued to seek licences and, in spite of constant harassment, were able to perform publicly until at least 1981. The alternative bands formed 'a parallel current of independent groups', which 'sought to search for a way to express [their feelings] in a manner adapted to the existing environment, traditions and language. . . .'[29]

However we may interpret and classify it, rock culture was universal in the European communist world, affecting all countries in some degree, even including Albania,[30] but assuming diverse forms and dimensions in each country. It was most fully developed in Yugoslavia, in Czechoslovakia during the 1960s, and in Poland in the 1970s, and in the German Democratic Republic where it existed in a kind of 'grey zone' of qualified acceptance (p. 164). In the more relaxed atmosphere of Hungary it also developed on a large scale, including even an officially permitted rock opera, 'Stephen the King', in 1983. In Rumania and Bulgaria, the entry of rock, punk, and heavy metal was slower but was causing concern to the authorities by the mid-1980s. Even in Soviet Russia, in the wake of a decline of jazz, there was 'a rock inundation' between 1968 and 1980, 'a veritable second revolution', which represented, it was said, 'a return to the quest for an individually liberating and truly popular culture'.[31]

The media for performing and listening to rock music were many and varied, ranging from semi-underground performances in private homes, farms, and pubs, or sometimes in the homes of foreign diplomats, to concerts, officially approved, in concert halls in cities, and occasionally at huge festivals in the countryside, where many bands, including foreign ones, took part. In Poland, for instance, such a festival took place at Jarocin for fifteen years; in 1986, 14 000 young people were present and a hundred bands played.[32] Similar 'Woodstocks' were held in Hungary and the GDR, at one time in Czechoslovakia, and in the USSR at Yerevan and Tiflis. Rock music may also be heard in youth clubs and discotheques under official controls, on foreign radio and television (often taped by fans), on domestic radio and television, performed by carefully selected and approved bands, and on cassettes or audio-tapes, which are smuggled in or purchased on the black market.

In many ways the rock culture is a kind of 'counter-socialisation' process, nullifying the official efforts of regimes to socialise the youth in the values and ways of communist society and to create a new socialist man.[33] The regimes were worried, writes Ramet, by the exaltation of personal feelings, the adulation of cult figures, the glorification of Western culture, the encouragement of dissident views, and the introduction of cultural standards, fashions, and behaviour independent of party control.[34] Worst of all, rock music promoted a distinctive way of life among performers and their fans, including the wearing of jeans and Western tee-shirts, tight trousers and mini-skirts, long hair, etc., and was linked by the regimes with social deviance. Although the music was condemned as raucous and cacophonic, the lyrics were even more disturbing, containing open and often savage criticism of the consumer society, and sometimes of the system. In some countries the rock underground produced its own *samizdat* journals, and some of its members were associated with human rights movements such as Charter 77. Occasionally, too, as in the West, devotees sought to live in communal fashion, with several families sharing a house in the country.[35]

The arrival on the scene in certain countries of the more extreme 'punk rock' and 'heavy metal' brought with it the outlandish attire and hair styles familiar in the West and provocative symbols, such as the swastika or the crucifix, and 'offensive' behaviour, such as the tearing apart of a live chicken in a Budapest performance. Punk rock, with its deafening volume and its obscene lyrics, was more openly political. Abusive statements were made about the rulers, such as the text of a song by a Hungarian punk group: 'Rotten, stinking communist gang/Why has nobody hanged them yet?'[36] In Poland the songs were even more outspoken, containing protests against almost everything and expressing feelings of hopelessness and despair for the future. 'This is the world you've created for us; This is the world of captivity and coercion; This is the world in which I live: This is the world in which I do not want to live.'[37] Hard rock also found a following among young people who had dropped out of ordinary society, for example the 'sewer dwellers' (*csöves* in Hungarian), who had no permanent employment and no fixed abode, and who lived in refuges such as the pedestrian underpasses of Budapest. These antisocial groups, existing on the margins of society and leading a life of alcohol, drugs, and even crime, found life in normal society intolerable and saw no future for themselves.[38]

A portrayal of the 'lower depths' of Czech life was given in a novel by Jan Pelc, entitled . . . *a bud hůř* (It's gonna get worse). This depicts that section of the young people who dropped out of ordinary life – drifters, drunks, thieves, jailbirds, prostitutes, alcoholics and scavengers who found their only solace in the taverns, in obscene language, promiscuous sex, alcohol, drugs, violence and crime, and who avoided fixed employment or permanent habitation.[39]

The communist regimes responded to rock music, and later punk rock and heavy-metal, as they had once responded to jazz, treating each of them in turn as illustrating the disaffection and alienation of some of the youth and as justifying the strictest methods of control, but often retreating and seeking to harness it in a more moderate form. This may be illustrated by the changing policies toward jazz in the Soviet Union, which passed through alternating phases of tolerance, severe repression, and co-optation.[40]

Other communist parties followed similarly ambivalent and erratic courses. Yugoslavia, Poland, and Hungary took no severe actions against rock or even punk. Bulgarian leaders condemned the influx of Western popular music and introduced a 9 pm curfew for teenagers. Czechoslovakia, as always, was more aggressively hostile to jazz and even to folk singers, driving a number of them into exile, even banning the more moderate 'alternative' bands, and conducting a vendetta against the Jazz Section (see Chapter 4 above). In 1986, however, there were signs that even Czechoslovakia was moving toward the policy of co-optation pursued by the Soviet Union and the GDR, when the authorities permitted a huge rock festival in Prague and jazz festivals in other places.[41]

PARA-POLITICS – A SECOND POLITY

We turn finally to a realm of independent activity which comes closer to what is commonly called 'dissent' but which is difficult to define precisely. Its main expression was the informal, or organised, groupings or movements for the defence of human rights and resistance to injustice; for peace and opposition to nuclear weapons; for ecological protection; for the conduct of private education; for the support of the poor; for free trade unions; and for women's rights. Closely linked with this kind of activity, and in a sense a part of it, were the independent communications and culture described earlier in this book. This was, in Havel's words, 'the most visible and the most political' expression of 'dissent'. Here and there, there grew out of the anonymous independent activities of individuals 'a kind of more connected and visible initiative, passing beyond the boundaries of "mere" individual rebellion and changing into a definite, more conscious and more structured and self-conscious kind of *work*'.[42]

This new form of independent or alternative politics, he acknowledged, was not politics at all in the traditional sense, but a kind of 'pre-political' activity, or as he expressed it elsewhere, 'anti-political politics', 'politics outside the sphere of politics', or 'semi-politics' (*polo-politika*).[43]

In strikingly similar fashion György Konrád, a leading Hungarian dissident writer, in his book *Antipolitics*, wrote that politics in the normal sense had exceeded its proper scope, embracing spheres that should not be included at all. He wanted to 'keep the scope of government policy, especially the military, under the control of civil society' and to 'free our simple everyday affairs from considerations of politics'. Antipolitics was, he wrote, 'the political activity of those who don't want to be politicians and refuse to share in power'. The democratic opposition, in this sense, was not apolitical; it was an anti-political opposition, working toward the goal of 'destatification' of society. It was primarily a moral opposition, based on the 'ethos of personal moral responsibility'.[44]

Paradoxically, but perhaps in order to facilitate publication, Hankiss did not deal with these phenomena at all. His final category of the 'second society' dealt with 'the second sphere of social–political interactions,' a somewhat vague term which, in his first draft, referred to the discrepancies between policy inputs of the first society (for instance the bureaucratic administration of the country according to strict rules) and the development of informal networks of personal relations (pp. 30–1, Table I). What Hankiss discussed under this rubric seemed closer to the 'second polity' of Zvi Gitelman, who referred to the many informal relations between bureaucracy and citizens, which helped, like the 'second economy', to make life more tolerable.[45] In his revised draft Hankiss expanded this sector considerably to include a number of emerging elements: the regeneration of micro-networks, such as traditional local, professional, cultural and religious, and family social networks; more active and effective channels and institutions of interest mediation (Table 3); the slow regeneration of local communities; and the resocialisation of state and party institutions, which ceased to be mere transmission belts but began to fight for functional interests (pp. 36–41).

Hankiss's analysis did not adequately treat the more political forms of independent activity which I shall call, *faute de mieux*, a 'second polity'. This included, as noted above, actions seeking to defend human rights and to rectify social abuses and injustice; it also embraced independent forms of cultural life and independent political thinking (discussed above as 'parallel politics', Chapter 6). Although often termed 'non-political' by its practitioners, it was the closest approximation to, or surrogate of, normal political life.[46]

8 A Second Polity: Contrasting Patterns of Reality

We turn now to a study of the contrasting patterns of reality in respect of a 'second society' in Central and Eastern Europe. We shall deal briefly with Czechoslovakia and Poland, already analysed in detail in preceding chapters, and more extensively with other countries of the area, including Soviet Russia before the 1980s, and Poland after martial law. Our aim is to estimate the degree to which the germs of a second polity or a parallel or independent society, or what Hankiss in his revised article termed 'an alternative society' developed (or did not develop at all). We shall also examine the distinctive terms and concepts which were used to interpret such developments.[1]

CZECHOSLOVAKIA

In Czechoslovakia the various forms of independent activities – Charter 77, VONS and Infoch, *samizdat* production, independent communications and culture, independent currents among the youth and believers – have been fully described in preceding chapters. All of these, including Charter 77 itself, were initially described as 'independent citizens' initiatives,' using, in Czech, the word '*občansky*' which like the German word '*bürgerlich*' could equally well be translated as 'civic' or 'civil'. The term was widely used in Charter documents and became part of the vocabulary of Chartist discussions.[2] Joint Polish–Czechoslovak statements also referred to 'independent citizens' initiatives' in Eastern Europe and the Soviet Union, as did the projected volume on *Freedom and Power*.[3] Václav Havel, in his celebrated introduction, used the term to refer to actions by citizens who wished to 'live within the truth' and who thus contributed to 'what might be called the independent, spiritual, social and political life of society'.[4]

Another concept, that of 'parallel structures', which laid more emphasis on the organized character of such initiatives, was introduced by Václav Benda, in his essay on a 'parallel *polis*'. This

177

embraced, in his mind, the second culture, the information system, popular music, unofficial education and scholarship, the second economy, etc., and could be expanded further to form a genuine parallel community. This idea was widely discussed and generally accepted by many other Chartists during 1978 and 1979.[5] Havel, in his contribution, spoke warmly of 'these informal, non-bureaucratic, dynamic and open communities that comprise the "parallel" *polis*'. These resembled similar tendencies during the Prague Spring, which were 'spontaneous attempts at freer forms of thinking, independent creation and political articulation'. They differed from them, however, in being entirely outside the 'official structures' and unrecognised by them. He welcomed this whole process as a genuine attempt of society to organise itself, that is, a tendency toward 'social self-organisation' (using the term common in Poland).[6]

POLAND

Independent currents in Poland in the mid-1970s, while sharing the Czechoslovak emphasis on an ethical approach, were far more political in their objectives and were openly described as an 'opposition'. In his important article on 'the new evolutionism', written in 1976, Adam Michnik called for gradual and piecemeal change of the system, for evolution, not revolution. Revisionism and Catholic 'neo-positivism', he believed, both of which had hoped for a change from above, within the party, had been defeated. His alternative 'strategy for the Polish opposition' turned to the 'independent public', in particular the working class, and advocated a programme of pressure from outside on the party to adopt reforms.[7] With the rise of the Committee for the Defence of the Workers (KOR) in 1976, and other human rights movements, the opposition became, wrote Jacques Rupnik, an independent social activity which virtually ignored official institutions and set as its main goal the 'self-organisation of the society *vis-à-vis* the state'. Drawing consciously on past Polish experience, it aspired to make a transition from totalitarianism to a pluralistic democracy.[8]

At the outset KOR had limited aims, namely to aid the victims of reprisals for their role in the strikes in Radom and Warsaw. While disavowing political aims, KOR asserted, however, that they had set in motion a 'process of organized opposition' and even expressed the desire for a liaison with dissidents in other Soviet-bloc countries.[9]

When KOR, in September 1977, renamed itself the Committee for Social Self-Defence (KOR), it outlined a broader programme for the defence of human and civil rights, opposition to violations of the rule of law, and assistance to the victims of injustice.[10] It stressed the significance of 'self-governing local, regional, cultural and social organisations', working 'independently of State organisations'.[11] A year later, in its appeal to the nation (dated 10 October 1978), the Committee presented a detailed indictment of the regime's policies and called for 'independent social action'.[12] Eventually such 'independent social initiatives' were to include, in addition to KOR itself (and its Intervention Bureau for recording violations of the law), the Initiative Committees for Free Trade Unions, already formed in Gdańsk and Slask, farmers' self-defence organisations, as in Lublin and Grojec, student solidarity committees, the Society for Academic Courses (TKN) (The Flying University), the independent press and publications, and later the Helsinki Committee, for reporting on violations of rights to the CSCE Conference in Madrid. As a result of the emergence of these oganisations, said Michnik later, 'we lived in a different Poland' and witnessed 'the beginning of a social organisation independent of the state'. A year earlier Michnik, in his book on the Church and the Left, had recognized that the Church was an important element of resistance to totalitarianism, and not a threat as the 'lay left' had once believed.[13]

Jan Lipski, the historian of KOR, described it as a social, not a political body, acting overtly and legally. Renouncing the use of force, KOR strove for its goals through respect for truth and ethical standards.[14] Another organisation, the Movement for the Defence of Human and Civil Rights in Poland (ROPCiO), was primarily dedicated to the defence of human rights, but its original statement appealed to everyone to 'take up and expand similar initiatives in all social, professional and regional milieux'.[15] It was, however, more openly political, urging repeatedly the need for Polish independence and the end of communist rule. It differed from KOR in its more nationalist and Catholic orientation, so that cooperation between the two was not easy and eventually broke down. ROPCiO itself was divided and later broke into two separate factions.[16] Another organization, the Polish League for Independence, in its 'alternative programme for the opposition', was even more radical and advocated a thorough-going reform of all aspects of the political system, complete Polish sovereignty, and the end of communist rule.[17]

Although the dissent movement was therefore not entirely unified, KOR remained the spearhead of independent activities such as the Flying University, many newspapers and journals, the trade union committees, etc. Two of its leading spokesmen, Jacek Kuroń and Adam Michnik, elaborated its purposes further. Kuroń, in his essay, 'A Unique Platform of Opposition', struck a militant note, advocating a programme of resistance to the totalitarian system, conducted through the social movements of workers, peasants, believers, and intellectuals, each of them seeking to restrain the power of the state and to work for an independent nation and state.[18] In an interview of the same date, Kuroń called for 'A Third Poland of Social Movements', which would bring together initiatives by individuals or small groups in wide-scale actions to press the authorities to carry out reforms.[19] By 1979, however, he was more cautious, expressing his fear of a nation-wide explosion and arguing the need for another type of organisation, within the official structures. Such a non-oppositional 'movement of demands', as he called it, would have to work out a programme for repairing the system as a means of averting the threatening national tragedy (namely, Soviet intervention).[20] Adam Michnik and Jan Józef Lipski questioned whether Kuroń was proposing an end to the creation of independent social movements in deference to activities within official institutions, and argued that there must be a continued struggle on both fronts.[21]

It was in the context of this emerging alliance of workers and intellectuals, as well as, of course, the Church and individual Catholics, and of the embryonic organisation of society, that Solidarity was born and raised both of these developments to a new height. In Michnik's words at the time, Gdańsk represented a compromise, 'the creation of institutionalised forms of dialogue between the rulers and the ruled'.[22] As Kuroń put it, this repesented the formation of a 'democratic pluralist society', based on many autonomous and self-governing social movements, with Solidarity, the independent labour union, as the most powerful component, striving gradually to dismantle totalitarianism. It was a curious hybrid system, combining both totalitarianism and democracy, wrote Michnik. Its immediate aims had to be limited due to the Soviet presence; it could not therefore involve a struggle for Polish independence and parliamentary democracy. Solidarity could not aspire to power but had to seek a compromise with a party that had no sympathy for its aims. It must seek minimalist goals and eschew the use of force (Kuroń, pp. 35–6). The chief objective must be to preserve the social movements, to curtail the sphere of action of the authorities, and to establish self-management in all spheres (p. 97).

As we know, this embryonic 'civil society' was crushed by force. Paradoxically, however, a similar symbiosis of party and society emerged again in a less comprehensive form during and after military rule (to be discussed below).

HUNGARY

Under Kádár, as noted in Chapter 2, a compromise had been struck between the majority of the Hungarian intelligentsia and the regime. As Mihály Vajda put it, 'the basic structure was not called into question by the intellectuals' and the party leadership introduced hitherto unthinkable reforms to make life easier for the population, 'always provided they renounced all claim to participation in decision-making'. Even the 'critical intelligentsia' drew some benefit, namely 'the right of criticism', although they were aware that 'criticism without organisation necessarily remains impotent'.[23] Although wider intellectual circles were not entirely satisfied, they were 'reluctant to engage in open protest because they wish to preserve the given margin of semi-freedom, or . . . their appointed privileges'.[24]

In these circumstances there was really little room left, and no urgent need, for independent or autonomous action such as developed in Czechoslovakia and Poland. The situation in Hungary was much better than elsewhere in the common bloc: there were few political prisoners, and individual human rights were not so flagrantly violated as to make a special human rights organisation seem necessary. Dissidents were seldom imprisoned, and some could travel freely abroad and return; they were, however, subjected to other penalties, such as dismissals from work, denial of the right to publish, occasional denial of passports, house searches, and heavy fines.

'Opposition' – or 'para-opposition' as Schöpflin called it – was thus confined to a small number of 'marginalised intelligentsia' who had a kind of unwritten pact with the authorities to carry on in relative freedom, provided they did not question the bases of the system.[25] Their job was to 'keep watch on political power, exerting pressure on the basis of their cultural and moral stature alone'.[26] This attitude was later criticized as representing a compromise with the regime, and thus in effect giving it some support.[27] János Kis, a founder of the democratic movement, lamented the lack of programme or strategy of action and called for a 'democratic opposition', with a defined set of ideals and demands which might improve the chances of a real compromise between government and people.[28]

The development of what was usually called 'a second public sphere', or, alternatively, 'a second public opinion', evolved only in the late 1970s and was derived, as János Kis put it, from the 'common fund of ideas in Eastern Europe at that time'.[29] Earlier critical writings had often been Marxist and had hoped for a reform of the existing system. The failure of the Prague Spring marked a turning point in their thinking, dissipating their belief in the feasibility of 'reform communism'.[30] The experience of Poland (prior to Solidarity) led them to see their function as being to 'create a public sphere, to subject the authorities to pressure from below, and perhaps even to abandon the previous compromise and to criticise the basic power structure as well'. Theirs was not to undertake political activity or even as yet to formulate a political programme.[31] Inspired by Michnik's 'new evolutionism', they gradually developed 'a loosely structured social milieu' which under the name of 'opposition' was 'a distinct entity in Hungarian cultural and political life'.[32] Missing entirely was a human rights movement, presumably for reasons already mentioned.[33]

The opposition was admittedly only a 'few small groups . . . acquiring a foothold outside the immense structure of the official establishment'.[34] It thus resembled the Czechoslovak rather than the Polish counterpart. They formed, wrote György Konrád in *Antipolitics*, 'a network of spiritual authority', which consisted of informal circles of friends and independent people, and constituted an 'intellectual community' or an elite, which would 'set limits to the state' and achieve for society 'the greatest autonomy, the freedom to express its own individuality'.[35] The task of the intellectual opposition was 'planning and monitoring our future course' and to do so by independent thinking and open expression (pp. 81–2, 161). There were in Hungary 'limits to openness, limits to freedom', but 'no tight totalitarian control' (p. 170). The second culture would strive for a slow expansion of these limits and thus 'stimulate and enliven the officially accepted culture' (p. 167).

The opposition intellectuals were vague and general in defining their goals, and had no specific political reforms in mind. In Konrád's view there could be no thought of revolution, but only of slow, gradual reform, carried out from the top down, within a framework of loyalty to the Soviet Union and the one-party system (pp. 81, 114, 122, 125). There could be no hope for 'radical, structural changes', but only for a change in the 'spirit and style in which power is exercised'. The best one could hope for, he admitted, was 'an enlightened paternalistic authoritarianism', 'a liberal conservative version of communism'. It was a Hungarian style of government – Kádárism – 'a limited pluralism within the confines of the Yalta system' (pp. 126–9, 163, 168).

Another opposition intellectual, András Hegedüs, former prime minister, was even more restrained. There could be no changes in the power structure itself, including the one-party system and the state bureaucracy. The structure was not monolithic, as commonly supposed, and manifested some degree of pluralisation. The objective must be to develop 'social control', by which he meant effective criticism of those wielding power by independent intellectual and social movements and by autonomous organizations independent of party control. He opposed a multi-party system.[36]

Smaller in scope and dimension than either the Polish or Czech counterparts, the 'newly emergent organised society' consisted of several components: *samizdat* and independent publishing, a small-scale Flying Kindergarten (seminars and lectures), discussion groups, occasional collective protests, private art groups, small theatres, rock groups and the use of video machines, and the Foundation for the Support of the Poor (SZETA), which gave money and other assistance to those in dire poverty.

Later informal 'movements' on peace and the environment developed, but both sought to keep their distance from the so-called 'political opposition' and to seek some degree of official recognition while preserving their independence from governmental control. Their numbers were small, and they had neither organizational structure, nor extensive *samizdat* communications.[37]

The peace movement developed spontaneously among university and high school students in 1981 and 1982; an anti-nuclear campaign was carried on through private meetings, the distribution of leaflets, and an attempted peace march. Several of the 'political opposition', notably György Konrád, Miklos Haraszti, and Laszlo Rajk, took an active part, and A. Hegedüs lent support. *Samizdat* publications publicised its activities, and a series of *Peace Notebooks* were issued. Quite separately, as a result of a number of jail sentences meted out to conscientious objectors, there developed within the Roman Catholic Church a movement in the hundreds of so-called 'base groups' which adhered to a policy of non-violence and advocated an alternative to military service. This led to the formation of a Committee for Human Dignity in January 1982, which issued a statement condemning nuclear deployment in East and West. These groups and their activities were sharply condemned by the church hierarchy which enjoyed good relations with the state and did not oppose compulsory military service. Priests active in the movement were defrocked by the authorities.

On 2 September 1982 a Peace Group for Dialogue was founded, under the leadership of Ferenc Köszegi, who rejected any form of opposition to the government and sought both official recognition and independence. The movement spread rapidly in Budapest and the provinces, and held a national conference in Visegrad in April 1983. Although its aims were moderate, chiefly a proposal for an alternative to military service, and its tactics were non-oppositional, the powers that be harassed their leaders and blocked their efforts to achieve official status within the National Front. As a result, on 6 July, Dialogue, under the influence of its moderate wing, dissolved. The younger, more radical adherents continued to act under the name Dialogue and circulated a petition for an alternative to military service. Its earlier leader, Köszegi, withdrew from the movement, condemning it as illegal and oppositional, and became head of the Peace Club under the official Peace Movement. Dialogue, although weakened, mounted a campaign against the stationing of SS-20s in Eastern Europe, and started a newspaper, *Mir-Peace*, in March 1984.

The advocates of environmental protection went through similar experiences.[38] Their initial concern was the hydro-electric power station and dam (Gabcikovo-Nagymaros) to be constructed on the Danube jointly by the Hungarian and Czechoslovak governments. The Danube Circle, founded in May 1983, conducted a campaign against the project before and after its endorsement by a treaty between the two governments in May 1986. The Circle held several marches along the Danube and circulated a petition for a referendum, ultimately signed by some 6000 people. It also appealed to the Austrian public through an advertisement in *Die Presse* in April 1986, and a petition to the Austrian parliament in June. Although it tried to avoid 'politics' and for tactical reasons did not associate with the 'political opposition', it was severely restricted in its actions by the authorities. It established relations with the Greens in Germany and received a Swedish award, known as the 'alternate Nobel Prize'.

The more militant youth, who came to be called 'The Blues', were more openly opositional and conspiratorial, and criticised the Danube Circle for its alleged willingness to co-operate with the government. Continuing the campaign against the Danube dam, they conducted large-scale leaflet campaigns in late 1985, sent letters to the Austrian press in January 1986 and to the Austrian Chancellor in March, and issued a declaration against nuclear power in May. The Blues were interested in environmental questions in general and sought to promote 'independent thinking' in all spheres of life.

In June 1986 *Vizjel* (Watermark) 'a journal of environmental protection,' began to appear – the first independent environmental journal in Eastern Europe.

During 1985 and 1986 there were signs of an increasing politicisation of the Hungarian 'opposition'. In spite of their claims to being non-political, some of their actions were implicitly, or even expressly, political, as for example *samizdat* publications deploring the fate of the Hungarian minorities in Rumania and Czechoslovakia and expressing support of Polish Solidarity. In 1985 some opposition members and environmentalists took part in the nominating procedures under the new multi-candidate electoral system, although none was approved as a candidate. On 15 October 1985 a document on the lack of cultural freedom in Hungary was addressed to the delegates to the CSCE Cultural Forum held in Budapest. In spite of official disapproval a counter-conference was held in the homes of Hungarian dissidents, where they joined in discussion with Czech exiles and Western writers. Even more noteworthy was the statement on the thirtieth anniversary of the Hungarian Revolution in October 1986, issued jointly with Czechs, East Germans, and Poles, and bearing the signatures of fifty-four Hungarians. Several Hungarians also endorsed the Milan appeal directed to the Vienna CSCE conference in November.[39]

A striking manifestation of a more political stance was a meeting of the main opposition groupings held in Monor near Budapest in the summer of 1985. Present were 'representatives' of the several wings of Hungarian opposition – populist, nationalist, economic reformist, and radical; intellectuals associated with the democratic opposition and with *samizdat* publications, such as György Konrád, M. Haraszti, and J. Kenédi; some of the environmentalists and peace activists; and the chairman of the Budapest Workers Council in 1956. This unique gathering discussed such serious problems as the 'vacuum of culture', the fate of the Hungarian national minorities abroad and the weak official response to this problem, and the need for expansion of economic reform and for democracy. There was severe criticism of the depoliticisation of Hungarian intellectuals and their willingness to compromise with the regime, better called their 'capitulation', said one speaker. There was much common ground, including the theme of an 'independent self-developing life' and freedom. The challenge by Kis of the need for radical changes and for a defined strategy went unheeded, however, and the conference closed without any resolution or even a plan for elaborating a common programme.[40]

There was evidence of mounting opposition during late 1986 and early 1987. At the congress of the official Hungarian Writers Union in November, for instance, there were heated debates concerning freedom of culture and almost no communists were elected to the board of the Union. G. Konrád even spoke of 'two parties', the Union and the Hungarian United Workers Party. On 15 March 1987, the anniversary of the Hungarian declaration of independence in 1848, 1500 people marched through the centre of Budapest calling for freedom of speech and assembly, the withdrawal of Soviet troops, and for a memorial, some day, to Imre Nagy. Although such parades had been an annual affair, this one was marked by the absence of police intervention and by the participation of members of the democratic opposition. Another unusual event at the turn of the year 1986–7 was a protest made by all Hungarian churches over the treatment of fellow-nationals in Transylvania.[41]

During 1987, in an atmosphere of gathering crisis in Hungarian life, other events testified to the increasingly political character of opposition thinking. In January a monthly journal, *Demokrata*, began to appear and in its first five issues dealt with the democratisation of the system and political reforms, the 1956 anniversary, Hungarian minorities in Rumania and other sensitive subjects.

In June 1987 a far-reaching programme of economic and political reform – 'A Social Contract' – was published in *Beszelö*. This boldly asserted that economic reform could not be achieved without political reform and called for an ending of the party's monopoly of power. Although the one-party system would remain, the party's dictatorial prerogatives must be greatly reduced. The government, too, must be made accountable to a strengthened National Assembly. This should be accompanied by a broadening of regional competence and greater freedom of grass-roots initiatives. The programme proposed legal limits to censorship, legal protection of workers, fair social policies and legal guarantees of human rights.

This document was followed by an open letter to the National

Assembly, signed by 100 persons (including ten members of the democratic opposition) and transmitted on September 8 to all parliamentary deputies prior to the full session of the Assembly. It criticised the official economic programme but lamented in particular the absence of proposals for political reform. The signatories urged greater opportunity for interest-group activity, a democratisation of representative organisations, including the trade unions, greater liberty for setting up associations and founding periodicals, legal guarantees of freedom of speech and independence of cultural association.

Even the Patriotic People's Front, headed by Imre Poszgay, a Central Committee member, presented a sixty-page study, 'Change and Reform', prepared by leading economists and sociologists, which called for a market-based reform and a modification of the leading role of the party so that it would only guide the country's economic and political affairs.[42]

GERMAN DEMOCRATIC REPUBLIC

In the GDR there existed hardly anything which might be called 'a second polity,' still less a parallel or independent society. Yet widespread dissatisfaction, disaffection, and dissent were documented by Pedro Ramet.[43] According to him, 'dissatisfaction' involved discontent with the way the system or parts of it functioned, or with certain policies of the regime, without, however, calling the system into question. 'Disaffection', by contrast, embodied discontent with the system itself, expressed through social nonconformism or deviance, but with no belief in the possibility of changing it. 'Dissent', on the other hand, was an expression of discontent with the system, coupled with the belief that change, however slight or gradual, was possible.

In his wide-ranging analysis Ramet included in 'disaffection' many forms of social nonconformism and deviance, for instance, an alternative culture, either in rock music or the Christian faith; criticism of specific official policies, notably its economic failures; opposition to the militarisation of education and abuses of human rights; the raising of environmental issues and the women's question; national dissatisfaction among the Lusatian Sorbs; the spread of crime, alcoholism, and drug abuse; and, most important, a concern about nuclear weapons and peace. There was also a strong tendency toward individualism and an all-pervasive feeling of being Germans first, and only secondarily citizens of the GDR. These phenomena constituted, it has been said, a 'political counter-culture' or a 'counter public sphere', which consisted of values, beliefs, and groups not conforming to the dominant or official culture, and represented 'a new type of political thinking' and a 'redefinition of policy priorities'.[44]

In the 1940s and 1950s dissent had manifested itself among older persons, such as the noted Marxist scholars Wolfgang Harich and Robert Havemann. In 1977 the party functionary Rudolf Bahro presented a systematic critique of the social order, and thus struck at the heart of the system.[45] Dissent was also rife among writers and other cultural figures, including Stefan Heym. When the folk singer Wolf Bierman was jailed and then forced to leave the country, there was a storm of protest in literary circles, leading to banishments from the country, voluntary exile, and in some cases imprisonment.

No common or organised opposition emerged from this welter of dissent, which involved, in Sodaro's words, 'a small and politically fragmented fraction of the population'. In spite of widespread disaffection among young people, no organised dissident youth movement developed. The technical intelligentsia, according to him, was successfully co-opted and depoliticised. The workers did not create an opposition movement, and the Marxist dissidents were unable to establish a rapport with the working class. Consumerism dominated the thinking and behaviour of the masses and this, together with severe repression by the regime, discouraged open dissent.[46]

Until 1961 there was also an 'escape hatch', the wide-open border to the West, over which 3 000 000 East Germans (half of them young) passed. Even after the building of the wall many continued to manifest their dissatisfaction by emigration, and the regime forced others to leave. It is estimated that since 1961 some 268 000 have been allowed to emigrate, and still more had their freedom 'bought' by the West German authorities. Another 190 000 tried to leave without authorisation, some 38 000 crossing the border illegally; some failed and were shot or imprisoned. There were said to be about 400 000 to 500 000 applications for emigration pending in 1986. On the twenty-fifth anniversary of the building of the Berlin Wall (13 August 1986), four persons sent a petition to the People's Chamber requesting freer communications between East and West, including the right of citizens of both parts of Berlin to travel.[47] One year later a crowd of East Germans, at the Brandenburg Gate, chanted the slogan – 'The wall must go.'

In the 1960s and 1970s there arose a new and vigorous movement of protest fuelled by resentment of the Wall, by a rising tide of individualism and discontent with the general climate of life, by the signing of the Helsinki Final Act and by the example of the West German peace movement. Youthful opposition manifested itself in a lack of belief in socialist ideas, anger at enforced conformity, opposition to the increasing militarisation of education, and the fears generated by the prospective stationing of missiles on East German soil. Small *ad hoc* groupings emerged, expressing concern with the environment, the women's question, and peace, but did not constitute an organised opposition or even a movement in the real sense of the word.[48]

The strongest of these inchoate protests was an independent peace movement which sheltered under the wings of the Evangelical Church in which there had been peace activities for many years.[49] It was a congeries of various movements, often concerned with environmental and feminist issues, made up mainly of young people, women, and young clergymen, and with support from Robert Havemann, later by his widow, and by Stefan Heym. Informal groups were formed in Jena and other cities, and conferences were held in Berlin, Dresden, and Jena. Several special appeals were issued, for instance by Havemann, in September 1981, and by Pastor Eppelmann, in association with Havemann and others, in January 1982; German women, in a letter to Erich Honecker in October 1982, protested against a new law providing for military service for women. There developed from all these tendencies an 'independent peace movement' – known from its motto, 'Swords into Ploughshares' – 'a spontaneous, grass-roots movement without an organisational structure, officers or spokesmen'. It numbered some 2000 to 5000 activists, including Christians, secular pacifists, environmentalists, and dissident Marxists, and had perhaps 30 000 to 50 000 supporters. It was from this milieu that the initiatives came for a joint statement in 1984 with Czechoslovak dissenters against the stationing of missiles, a positive reply to the Prague Appeal in 1985 (see Chapter 3), and a proposal for closer relations with Charter 77. A remarkable petition, signed by 140 persons, after Chernobyl, in May 1986, called for a discontinuation of the nuclear power programme.

The institutional base for this amorphous movement was the Evangelical Church, the only large organisation with its own infrastructure which was not a part of the system.[50] With its regional and national synods and a massive membership, it provided a valuable medium for the actions of the peace movement. Of the total population of 17 million in the GDR, some 16 million were Evangelicals; the Church claimed 2.7 million believers. After years of persecution in the 1950s, the Church worked out a *modus vivendi* with the state in 1978; it proclaimed itself to be a church, not against or beside, but *in* socialism. The Church was determined, however, to adopt an independent course, not only on religious matters, but on political questions, especially to conduct its own peace policy. Thus in 1978 it protested the changes in education that would have 'militarised' the schools; it gave its support to conscientious objectors and demanded an alternative 'social peace service'; it insisted that international peace was inseparable from 'internal peace', in which human rights were respected.

Although it was subjected to increasingly strict limitations, the Church organised discussions, meetings, and special services in almost every town and village, and convoked an annual peace festival and other peace conferences. Its synod in Potsdam in 1983 unanimously adopted a resolution calling for a moratorium on the installation of new missiles, whether by the Soviet Union or by the United States, and proposed a nuclear freeze and a ban on nuclear weapons from the GDR. Although it had been separated from the Evangelical Church in West Germany since 1969, the Church in the East and West continued to conduct joint actions, for instance, adopting in August 1982 a common statement condemning military means for safeguarding of peace. The Evangelical Church in the GDR was also associated with the World Conference of Churches and other international bodies and had contacts with the Greens and with German pacifists. Such activities attracted support from Protestant, Catholic, agnostic, and atheist circles, and in the eyes of the youth, many of whom, regardless of their beliefs, attended church services, the Church became 'a symbol of freedom'.

Church leaders disavowed any political purpose or dissident role and could hardly be considered as more than a limited element in a kind of 'second polity'. There was continuing tension between the Church leaders' caution in dealing with the state and the more radical position of some groups of young people. This was clearly revealed at the congress of the Evangelical Church in June 1987 and again at the Synod in September. At the latter the more radical presented a petition calling for an end to the policy of delimitation which curtailed contacts between East Germany and both West Germany and Poland. Although this was not adopted, the final resolution called for more contact between East Germans and other Europeans and expressed support for 'dialogue and openness in society'. It criticized restrictions on information and repeated its demand for an alternative to compulsory military service. The Church's future role as an 'opposition' clearly depended on its maintaining a delicate balance between itself and government, and within its own ranks, between more radical and more moderate forces.[51]

The Roman Catholic Church, representing a minority of a little more than one million, unlike its Polish counterpart, sought to avoid conflict with the state and hardly ever took actions that were even implicitly political. Nonetheless in a pastoral letter issued on 2 January 1983 the Catholic bishops condemned the militarisation of East German life and declared their opposition to nuclear weapons; they also gave support to the idea of a 'social peace service' as an alternative to military service for women and pacifists. Some joint actions by youth groups of the two churches were also taken. At the first all-GDR convention in July 1987, with 80 000 Catholics present, discussion was avoided of specific social and political issues (except behind closed doors in committees). Under pressure from below by the young people, however, there were signs that a more assertive role was under serious consideration by some Church leaders.[52]

Until early 1985 no organisation emerged for the defence of human rights. In that year a group of students and others formed Menschenrechte DDR (Human Rights GDR), which addressed letters to the government and declarations to young people in East and West. By early 1987 preliminary steps were taken toward the organisation of a movement for Peace and Human Rights within the existing peace movement. This 'peace initiative', represented by three spokesmen and having some thirty signatories, addressed a greeting to Charter 77 on its tenth anniversary, as a 'source of inspiration'. In January 1987 the three spokesmen, with Pastor Eppelman, sent a letter to the party and state authorities, calling for freedom to travel, freedom of assembly, and the legalisation of conscientious objection.[53]

RUMANIA

Rumania presented a bleak scene of profound economic crisis in which no second polity, or even an independent society, was visible on the horizon.[54] Although 'unspoken dissent' was, in the opinion of Vlad Georgescu, 'deeply entrenched' in the minds of the people, open expression of independent views was almost completely excluded by the ruthless repression meted out by the regime and by a generally timid and submissive population.[55] Dissent was almost entirely limited to brave individuals acting alone and often took the form of emigration (or attempts to leave) which has been called 'the only large-scale independent activity' which the regime was unable to halt. Emigration was highest among Germans and Jews, but was hindered by many obstacles and long delays. Attempts to cross the frontiers illegally, if unsuccessful, led to imprisonment.

The first attempt to form a human rights committee, inspired by Charter 77 in Czechoslovakia, was undertaken by Paul Goma, the prominent writer, and several of his colleagues, who were arrested and eventually forced to leave the country. Shortly thereafter others presented a programme of a 'Movement for Democracy', seeking implementation of the rights embodied in the constitution.[56] More recently young people from Bucharest and certain towns in Transylvania complained of violations of the constitution, the Helsinki Final Act, and the UN human rights covenants, and sought to form a Rumanian Association for the Defence of Human Rights. The leading figure was Florian Russu, aged 31, a musician and high school teacher, who was detained for four months and then kept under close police supervision. All members of the group were ethnic Rumanians, and most were workers and had been associated with the National Peasant Party, the largest political party prior to the communist take-over.

An influential participant was Iona Puiu, a former leader of the party's youth movement, who had earlier defended the right of the Peasant Party to re-form and had served seventeen years in prison. He took the lead in drafting a message of support for the four-country statement in 1986 on the anniversary of the Hungarian Revolution, and as a result was subjected to repeated interrogations and even beatings. Within the old Liberal Party, Ion Bratianu, a descendant of party leaders and former prime ministers bearing the same name, wrote a series of essays which dealt in pragmatic fashion with economic and social problems, deplored uninformed decisions taken without consultation with specialists, and called for open discussion and critical inquiry.

At the time of Gorbachev's visit to Bucharest, letters by two individuals were sent to the Soviet Embassy and to the Rumanian authorities, both urging the need for consultation with professionals and the public, suggesting specific economic and political reforms, and calling for the observance of human rights in conformity with the Helsinki Final Act.[57] Iona Puiu was arrested when he attempted to present a similar letter at the Embassy. During 1986 there were reports of demonstrations by small groups against the Ceausescu régime and of individuals apprehended when trying to cross the frontier, all of whom received draconic prison sentences.

In the literary world there were noteworthy examples of independent writings among works officially published and even protests against censorship within the Writers Union, but as far as is known no literary work circulated in *samizdat*. During 1984, 1985, and 1986, however, there were a number of typewritten letters by distinguished professors, architects, cultural figures, and members of the clergy, deploring the demolition of historic buildings in downtown Bucharest, including some churches and a synagogue. A major statement critical of urban and rural development in general appeared in April 1984.[58]

The most vigorous dissent came from individual clergymen of various churches, often only revealed when they were imprisoned, defrocked, or penalised for importing religious materials – the so-called 'Bible smugglers'. In March 1977 six Evangelical Christians issued a 'Call for Truth'. By July 1978, a somewhat larger group of twenty-seven Christians, embracing both Orthodox and Protestants, set forth a Programme of Demands, composed of twenty-four articles, calling for 'a free church in a free state' and for human rights in accordance with international agreements. An even larger group, consisting primarily of Baptists, organised a Rumanian Committee for the Defence of Freedom of Religion and Conscience (ALRC), which sent a letter to the government demanding an end to state intervention in religion and to indoctrination of the population with atheism. In April 1981 five Orthodox priests issued a Testimony of Faith, in which they criticized the regime and called for the release of Father Gheorghe Calciu-Dumitreasa.[59]

Calciu-Dumitreasa, an Orthodox priest, was the most redoubtable dissident and spent almost half of his fifty-odd years in prison. He openly expressed sympathy for the ALRC and for the movement for independent trade unions (SLOMR) (see below), and was associated with the banned Army of God movement within the church. Although he was removed from his seminary in 1978, he delivered a series of public sermons in which he denounced atheism, materialism, and the demolition of churches. For this and his other 'sins' he was sentenced to ten years in prison, and after five years was permitted to emigrate.

More recently some of his followers made public appeals for freedom of religion and an end to the subservience of the Orthodox Church to the state.[60]

There were three attempts to form a free trade union movement, all without success. As early as 1971, Vasile Paraschiv, a worker in Ploesti, who had resigned from the party in 1968 and had been associated with Goma and the human rights movement, sent a letter to the Central Committee calling for the creation of free trade unions, independent of party control, to defend the workers' economic, social, and political rights and interests. Trade unions should have democratically elected leaders, and should be represented in all administrative bodies, with a right of veto. He also demanded the abolition of censorship in the trade union press and freedom of thought and expression. His proposals were ignored and he was forcibly detained in a psychiatric hospital and then forced to emigrate. In March 1979 an attempt to form a Free Trade Union of Rumanian Workers (SLOMR) was initiated by some forty persons, sixteen of them workers, and eventually gained the support of some 1500 to 2000 persons. Its Charter set forth a series of economic and also political demands, including calls for respect for the fundamental rights of man and the abolition of censorship. The leaders were arrested or forced to emigrate. A third attempt was made in February 1980, but this was swiftly blocked by repressive measures.[61]

From time to time there were strikes by Rumanian workers. The massive miners' strike in the Jiu valley in August 1977 was crushed with severe reprisals against the organisers. A number of strikes and workers' protests were reported in January and October 1981, and between 1983 and 1987 there were strikes against government legislation which replaced guaranteed wages and imposed restrictions on compensation.[62]

Among the Hungarian minority in Transylvania there were movements of protest against alleged national discrimination.[63] Between 1981 and 1983 a Hungarian-language *samizdat* journal, *Ellenpontok* (Counterpoints), appeared in ten issues; in 1982 it sent a memorandum to the CSCE conference in Madrid. Its editor, Geza Szocs, prepared a memorandum in February 1985 in which he proposed the forming of a UN-supervised international agency for the protection of national minorities. In October Szocs sent a message on the lack of freedom for writers to the Budapest Cultural Forum. The organizers of *Ellenpontok* were systematically harassed, arrested, and forced to emigrate. In May 1983 another *samizdat* publication appeared, the *Hungarian Press of Transylvania*, which was still functioning in 1986; it recorded not only the plight of the Hungarian minorities, but also the ills of Rumanian society in general, and reported a number of strikes throughout the country. Another prominent dissenter among the Hungarians, Károly Királyi, a leading figure in the official Hungarian National Workers Council in Rumania, sent a letter in 1977 to the party leadership protesting against the treatment of national minorities, and another letter criticising party policy in general. In 1979 another party member, Lajas Takacs, a vice-president of the Hungarian Workers Council, prepared a memorandum containing eighteen demands for minority rights. A small movement of young Swabian German writers protested against restrictions on German cultural life.

According to Georgescu, Rumanian dissent was on the whole individual and pragmatic, but there were those who dealt with the problem theoretically. One of the most prominent was Mihai Botez, distinguished mathematician and economist, who was removed from his positions in 1977 and resigned from the party in 1984. He was a severe critic of all aspects of Rumania's economic policy, especially the strategy of development, and called for a public debate on these issues and for personal courage by critics.[64] Botez and others described the system as a perversion of socialism and in some cases rejected socialism as such. These writers condemned the cult of personality of Ceauscescu and asserted that his policy of 'national independence' masked neo-Stalinism. Their main aim, however, was the reform not the overthrow of the system, but they were pessimistic about the possibility of this under totalitarian conditions.

BULGARIA

During the 1960s and 1970s Bulgarian authorities were alarmed by the penetration of 'alien' or 'bourgeois' influences among the youth and intellectuals, and sought to counteract this by rigid controls, extreme Marxist-Leninist orthodoxy, and the promotion of 'patriotism'.[65] Official spokesmen issued frequent warnings against these influences and the government and Komsomol took measures to discourage them. Some literary works were condemned or banned.

By the mid-1980s the authorities became increasingly worried by the emergence of many 'informal groups' of young people, including students at élite secondary schools and the universities, and by the importation of video films, rock albums, and Western-style clothing.

The regime deplored the fact that young people were politically apathetic, had withdrawn from society into their own private circles, and often seemed to show no signs of working for a living. The groups included 'rockers', 'heavy metal fans', punks, and disco fans, who flaunted dyed hair and unorthodox styles of dress. There was also frequent lamentation by those in power about the illegal economy and the spread of 'consumerism'. In 1986 a campaign was waged against 'negative phenomena', which ranged from massive embezzlement and bribe-taking by high officials, to petty offences such as soliciting tips in restaurants.[66]

There was a pronounced swing toward religion, especially among young people, who were sometimes attracted to Seventh Day Adventism, Pentecostalism, Hinduism, and Buddhism. There was also a revival of faith in certain traditional Bulgarian cults, in which worship was conducted in secrecy, such as the Danovist cult, or White Brotherhood, a kind of fusion of Hinduism and Orthodox Christianity, and Bogomilism, an ancient heresy which rejected all temporal authority and preached resistance. Another strange phenomenon was the revival of the practice of folk medicine, and the private treatment of patients by certain renowned and popular healers. It was also reported that there were frequent protests by workers in the form of *samizdat* leaflets or of slogans painted on walls and even several strikes. In late 1985 an oppositional leaflet was issued by the workers at a locomotive factory in Sofia. Signed with the illustrious name, Dimitrov, it contained a number of economic demands and condemned the privileges of party officials. According to a US State Department report, a human rights group operated clandestinely near the city of Mikhailovgrad, but was forced to disband in 1984, and two of its members were arrested. Three other individuals, one of whom was a professor of law at the University of Sofia, were given sentences of three to five years for appealing to foreign embassies or to the UN Commission on Human Rights, on violations of human rights. In January 1987 six dissidents appealed to the Vienna CSCE conference and proposed an intra-European commission to monitor the performance of governments.[67]

Little is known about religious discontent or protest. The regime was, of course, committed to atheism and propagated it through all media. There was no evidence of organized resistance by Orthodox or other Christians. The Turkish Moslems were seriously reduced in numbers, at first by deportations and by voluntary emigration, and later by massive official de-nationalisation, but no information was available as to whether or how Turks protested against this persecution. Some thousands were, however, incarcerated, and all were forcibly assimilated.[68]

From the limited knowledge that we have we must conclude that independent activities were few and severely repressed in Bulgaria, and not even the rudiments of a 'second polity' or an 'independent society' existed.

YUGOSLAVIA

Until recently Yugoslavia, for reasons quite unlike those present in Bulgaria and Romania, was regarded by many Western specialists as 'a study in non-dissent', in the words of Sharon Zukin.[69] The absence of dissent, in her opinion, was due to the strategy of the regime of 'creating space within the state rather than restricting it', a strategy which allowed wide, frank discussion in the institutions of government and society, permitted relatively free travel abroad, and tolerated strikes and even demonstrations. A notable example of this permitted dissent was the Praxis group, which published a journal, *Praxis*, from 1964, issued *International Praxis* abroad, and conducted summer conferences in Korčula, attended by distinguished Serbian and Croatian scholars, and many foreign Marxists. Although it regarded itself not as an oppositional political movement, but rather as an 'institution of social criticism,' for ten years *Praxis* served as a vibrant organ of Marxist critique of Yugoslav theory and practice.[70]

Yet, as Zukin noted, the authorities set definite limits to the free expression of dissident views and could, and did, 'push people outside the social space' of official institutions.[71] Intellectuals were not infrequently imprisoned for their writings; journals were censored or banned; demonstrations forbidden and participants jailed. The League of Communists of Yugoslavia (LCY) granted some 'social space' within its ranks but could narrow this at will, and either expel or, sometimes, absorb radical critics. For instance, eight prominent members of *Praxis*, professors at the University of Belgrade, were suspended in 1975 and dismissed five years later.[72] By 1978 *Praxis* had to cease publication as the result of denial of funds from Republic authorities.

After 1977, the year of Charter 77 and of the Belgrade CSCE conference, a number of Free Universities were set up in Belgrade and elsewhere, and there was a great increase in the number of petitions and appeals to the authorities concerning restrictions on freedom and imprisonment of nonconformist intellectuals. There was no organised and systematic *samizdat*, partly because the opportunities for publishing officially were much greater than in other communist countries. Moreover for two decades an Independent Publishing House in Belgrade had been able to issue controversial books.[73] In the institutes, too, many reports and memoranda circulated in xerox form, and were often published in specialised publications.

The death of Tito in 1980 led to some political relaxation and a deepening national crisis, and dissent became widespread throughout the whole country. Pedro Ramet provided a detailed picture of the 'apocalypse culture' which resulted; by this he meant the wave of social criticism, reflecting the profound crisis in which the country found itself, a widespread mood of despair, a crisis of confidence, and a prevalent sense of the end of an era or of the system in its present form. He wrote also of 'apocalypse politics', which reflected political paralysis and 'the failure of the elite to provide generally acceptable solutions for pressing problems'.[74] There ensued 'one of the liveliest political debates in post-war Eastern European history', in which the fundamental political and social values of society were questioned and new visions and formulas were offered. Almost no subject was left untouched: the economic disaster, the federal system and its far-reaching decentralization, self-management and workers' management, the national question, religious and environmental problems, the role of the press, the place of women, the electoral system, and Marxism, socialism, and the role of the party. Even advocates of a two-party or multi-party system and of political pluralism had a chance to speak. Paradoxically this controversial discussion was conducted, not in *samizdat*, but within the party and state institutions at all levels, as well as in books, the press, and other media. Although Schöpflin wrote of the 'political decay of the system', the debate was regarded by Ramet as a positive phenomenon which perhaps offered a way out of the impasse.[75]

Outside the system, too, there were open manifestations of oppositional moods: New Left currents of thought; tendencies toward crime and the use of drugs among youth; even a phenomenon known as 'Punk Nazism'; a decline of religious belief; an increase in the divorce rate; some refusals of military service; peace and ecological movements in Slovenia; the spread of parallel communications in *samizdat* and the flying universities; a wave of some 1200 unofficial strikes, in protest against a federal wage freeze; and in Croatia a long coal miners strike. National conflicts, although in some measures articulated within and by official party and government institutions, also burst the bounds of restraint in 1981 in spontaneous demonstrations and riots in Kosovo, and in friction between Serbs and Croats, and between Serbs and Albanians. There were also religious conflicts with the state, for instance, in the case of Catholics in Croatia and Moslem fundamentalists in Bosnia and Herzegovina.

A sequence of punitive actions against intellectuals, including dismissals from work and imprisonments for the expression of independent views, produced a massive wave of protest.[76] This was particularly intense in the case of the so-called 'conspiracy' trial in 1984 of seven scholars who had attended a meeting of the Belgrade Flying University at which Milovan Djilas, veteran dissident, spoke on the national question. The proceedings against the 'Belgrade six' and against V. Šešelj, who was tried separately, were notorious as actions taken to punish as seditious views expressed in articles and books, or even privately. During the trial twenty issues of a photocopied *Bulletin* were issued. Similar protests took place over the trial and imprisonment of G. Djogo, the poet, and of Professor D. Petrović, condemned because of an article on party history. The Serbian Writers Association set up a Committee for the Protection of Artistic Freedom (CPAF) in 1981. In 1986 the Association created a Committee for the Protection of Man and Environment. In the same year Serbian journalists met informally to protest against censorship. The Belgrade Action Committee against the Abuse of Psychiatry and Medicine for Political Purposes, founded in 1980, issued reports on specific cases of such abuse.[77]

A significant document of protest was a draft memorandum prepared by the Serbian Academy of Science in May 1985, which was either leaked or stolen, and circulated widely. This contained a severe critique of the political system, especially its 'confederationist' character, and demanded democratisation. It also dealt with the contentious issue of the mistreatment of Serbs in Kosovo. This had led many thousands of them to leave the region, and some individuals and groups to protest to the National Assembly against alleged Albanian persecution.[78]

In November 1984, the first human rights organisation on a nationwide scale was formed as a result of the trial of the six – the Committee for the Defence of Freedom of Thought and Expression (CDFTE).[79] This was made up of nineteen distinguished Belgrade intellectuals (twelve of them belonging to the Serbian Academy) and was headed by the celebrated writer, Dobrica Čosić. Somewhat later a Solidarity Fund (OCSF) was announced, in a statement signed by over two hundred, to provide financial help to those dismissed from their jobs. The OCSF declared that they were striving to mobilise Yugoslav public opinion in 'self-organised resistance' to bureaucratisation. There followed many protests by the Committee and by CPAF and OCSF against dismissals, trials, and the banning of books. In October 1986 the CDFTE addressed to the Federal Assembly 'A Proposal for Establishing the Rule of Law' which urged not only the independence of the courts and other legal reforms, but called for the abolition of the one-party state, free elections, the right of peaceful assembly, and the right to strike. In November some thirty-three Yugoslavs signed the joint East–West document submitted to the CSCE conference in Vienna (see Chapter 3 above).

Dissent was most openly and widely expressed in Slovenia, even in the official youth newspapers, the Communist League of Youth, and the Socialist Alliance, as well as in street demonstrations and petitions. Among young people there was an increasingly critical attitude toward the military and demands were raised for an alternative to compulsory service for conscientious objectors. The depth of feelings of dissent was clearly expressed in an interview with four Slovenians, all of whom were associated with official institutions in that Republic. They asserted that the fundamental cause of the crisis in Yugoslavia was political – the domination of the economy by the party and the mediocre character of the leadership in all the Republic parties. They regretted the lack of a democratic tradition or of a memory of 'a strong and independent civil society'. It was impossible to be a dissident, because there was no coherent system against which one could dissent; there was 'neither a coherent state nor an autonomous civil society'. But the single-issue campaigns (such as those mentioned above) were the beginning, for the first time in the history of socialist Yugoslavia, of 'genuinely independent social movements'. We are witnessing, they believed, 'the birth of an independent civil society in Yugoslavia', especially strong in Slovenia. The forming of a united opposition was still a fantasy; what was needed was 'a plurality of democratic alternatives in various geographical regions and areas of social life'.[80]

By late 1987 the ever deepening economic and political crisis and the failure of the authorities to find coherent and workable solutions had plunged Yugoslavia into an emergency of profound magnitude.

This was worsened by a financial scandal in Bosnia-Hercegovina when the *Agrokomerc* bank issued billions of dinars of false promissory notes. This shook the foundations of the political establishment in that Republic and also caused the resignation of the vice-president of Yugoslavia, who was a Bosnian. At the same time in Kosovo the virtual control of the autonomous province by Albanians produced massive discontent among Serbs and ethnic conflicts, often violent, in the region and produced sharp conflicts of opinion through Yugo-slavia, and in Belgrade ruling circles. This, and the goal of the radical nationalists of establishing an Albanian Republic which would embrace not only Kosovo but Albanian regions of Macedonia, Montenegro and Serbia, and perhaps even Albania itself, raised the spectre of the breakup of the federal state.

Slovenia, on the other hand, presented a diametrically opposed picture of a Republic, which, with the encouragement of party and government leaders, had moved in the direction of pluralism within a one-party state. The authorities allowed public opinion to have an increased voice in the political process and permitted a number of independent organisations to function. These included peace and environmental groups, a women's club, and movements advocating religious freedom and even equality for homosexuals. All of these endorsed the need for the rule of law, freedom of speech and a decentralisation of power. This constituted an embryonic 'second polity' which could be a model for reform in the entire multi-national system, but it remained uncertain whether an embattled ruling party in Belgrade would accept such widespread pluralism, even while retaining one-party rule.[81]

THE SOVIET UNION

The democratic movement, or the human rights movement, as it later became known, was born in the mid-1960s. Its 'birthday' was said to have been 5 December 1965, when a demonstration was held in Pushkin Square, Moscow, to observe the anniversary of the Universal Declaration of Human Rights. As it subsequently evolved, it encompassed 'various active civic communities that oppose official ideology or politics', wrote its participant-historian, Ludmilla Alexeyeva. Within a decade a multitude of 'organisations' and *samizdat* publications were born, seeking to defend the rights of specific groups or to promote the rule of law and human rights in general. None of them was an 'organisation' in the usual sense, since their structures were informal and did not involve membership, officers, or rules, and in some cases their leading figures remained anonymous. By 1984 this remarkable congeries of persons and groups was more or less completely liquidated by repressive measures. It might be considered, while it lasted, as at least the seedling from which a more developed parallel community might have evolved.[82]

Even at its height this was hardly a 'movement' at all, but rather a small number of individuals of democratic orientation, who, as one of their number, Andrei Amalrik, put it, 'in an unfree country, behaved like free men, thereby changing the moral atmosphere and the nation's governing traditions'. As another participant, Boris Shagrin, said, this was a 'movement' of moral protest, based on elementary humanitarian values – truth and kindness – and not on political doctrines or ideology.[83] At the most it involved a few hundred activists, and a larger group of signatories of various petitions and protests, estimated at about two to three thousand.[84] Consisting primarily of intellectuals, they had few contacts with the workers and peasants, except in the case of the national and religious movements. As for the intelligentsia, of which the dissenters were a small fraction, the majority were politically apathetic and fearful of endangering their positions; as two exiled historians wrote, they preferred the approach of Galileo, who renounced his views, to that of Giordano Bruno, who defended his convictions until his death.[85]

The human rights movement has been compared with the reform strivings of the Russian *intelligenty* in the nineteenth century, or with the American civil rights movement of the 1960s, but it differed profoundly from both.[86] It did not share with the former their radical, highly political and populist, sometimes terrorist, features, but was peaceful and evolutionary, shunning violence of any kind. Nor was it comparable to its Bolshevik predecessors, who had worked primarily underground, in disciplined, conspiratorial organisations, but instead acted openly and publicly, without demanding unanimity of views, and its participants were often identified by name. How different, too, was the Soviet to the massive American movement, which enjoyed the sympathy of wide circles of both the black and white population, and could act, in spite of forceful measures against it, in a free and lawful society. The civil rights movement in the USSR was much closer in spirit, in tactics, and in aims to those of its *confrères* in Eastern Europe, and it had to function under conditions even more repressive.

In spite of its numerical smallness and the severe restrictions on its activities, the achievements of the democratic movement in the few years of its life were remarkable. Although it has received ample treatment in Western literature, it deserves at least a brief summation here. At the outset, to avoid confusion, one should note that the democratic movement (often referred to as the Democratic Movement) was not to be confused with a single secret group bearing the same name, the Democratic Movement of the Soviet Union, which, in October 1969, issued an extensive programme in the name of Democrats of Russia, the Ukraine and the Baltic area. The identity of its leading figures was later revealed, in the trial in 1975 of Sergei Soldatov and four others, all of whom belonged to the intelligentsia and were born in Estonia. Its programme therefore could not be regarded as expressing the viewpoint of the broader democratic movement which began to emerge at the same time.[87]

The principal human rights groups included the following:[88]

1. Initiative Group for the Defence of Human Rights in the USSR, started by V. Chalidze in May 1969.
2. Committee for Human Rights, founded in November 1970 by fifteen scholars and scientists (the 'Sakharov committee') which was affiliated in 1971 with the International League for Human Rights (New York City), an organisation with consultative status at the United Nations.
3. Russian Social Fund for Aid to Political Prisoners and Their Families (the 'Solzhenitsyn Fund') (April 1974).
4. Amnesty International – Soviet Section, based on an earlier group of scientists, Group '73, which affiliated with AI in 1974.
5. Helsinki Watch Group, properly the Public Group to Assist the Implementation of the Helsinki Accords in the USSR (May 1976), followed by similar groups in the Ukraine, Armenia, Georgia, and Lithuania (1976–7).
6. Working Committee to Investigate the Use of Psychiatry for Political Purposes (January 1977).
7. Action Group to Defend the Rights of Invalids (March 1978).
8. Association of Free Workers Trade Unions in the USSR (November 1977).
9. Working Group for the Defence of Labour and of Social and Economics Rights (April 1978).
10. Free Inter-professional Association of Workers (SMOT) (October 1978).

11. Elections 1979, established to nominate candidates in the elections of that year.
12. Group to Establish Trust Between the USSR and the USA (June 1982).

The last-named 'peace' group claimed not to be dissident, and did not openly attack Soviet foreign and defence policy. It called for a dialogue of the two governments and their general publics, a dissolution of the two blocs, and an end to the development of MX missiles. It spawned similar groups in other Soviet cities.

There were also groups devoted to the cause of emigration, including the Public Committee for the Right to Emigrate from the USSR (1979), Committees for Emigration of the Association of Citizens of German Nationality (mid-1970s), the Pentecostal Emigration Committee, and a number of informal Jewish groups dedicated to the same purpose.

Too numerous to list completely were religious and national groups, some of which antedated the more general human rights groupings. The former included the All-Union Church of the Faithful of the Seventh Day Adventists (1928) and its subsidiary group to investigate persecution (May 1978); the Council of Churches of Evangelical Christians and Baptists (1965), with its own publishing house, Khristyanin; the Christian Committee for the Defence of Believers, founded by Rev. Gleb Yakunin, Orthodox priest; the Lithuanian Catholic Committee to Defend the Rights of Believers (November 1978); the Council of Christians of Evangelical Pentecostal Faith (September 1979); and the Initiative Group for Defence of Rights of Believers and the Church (in the Ukraine) (September 1982).

The national groups included the Meshki committee for the return of their people to Georgia; a Crimean Tatar Group for the return to the Crimea; and Latvian, Lithuanian, and Estonian associations. A unique example of international co-operation was a joint letter issued by six Baltic underground organisations in September 1975.[89] In the Ukraine, although dissent by individuals was vigorous and sustained, severe repression made it difficult to form any organization other than the Ukrainian Helsinki monitoring group which was soon liquidated.

Almost all of these groups issued their own documents, typewritten bulletins, and newsletters. This swelled the volume of *samizdat*, which produced many books and journals of philosophical, economic, literary, political, or religious orientation.[90] Noteworthy for their durability were Baptist publishing house, Khristyanin, founded in 1966 and surviving to the present in spite of severe persecution, and *The Chronicle of the Catholic Church in Lithuania*, established in 1972 and publishing its seventy-second issue in 1986. It was unique in being bilingual (Russian and Lithuanian).[91] Another Lithuanian organ, of nationalist outlook, *Ausra* (The Dawn), lasted from October 1975 to the present, when its 51st issue appeared. *The Ukrainian Herald* appeared intermittently between 1970 and 1980. In 1984 *The Chronicle of the Catholic Church in the Ukraine* appeared, changing its name in 1986 to *The Chronicle of the Ukrainian Catholic Church in the Catacombs*.

The most important journal of general scope for the whole of the USSR was *The Chronicle of Current Events,* which antedated most of the groups, and stimulated their development. Initiated in April 1968, it continued, except for a brief interruption, until 1982, publishing sixty-four numbers. Each issue became more and more substantial, some containing two hundred pages of closely-typed materials. It had no programme and did not define its aims. Each issue, however, carried a subtitle, which, although changed slightly from time to time, expressed the continued purpose of defending, or struggling for, human rights. It also bore a banner heading, as a kind of motto, the text of article 19 of the Universal Declaration of Human Rights. It became a common organ of the many strands of the democratic movement, publicising materials brought to it by Russian Orthodox, Baptists, Catholics in the Ukraine and Lithuania, Georgian Orthodox, Pentacostalists and Adventists, as well as human rights questions in general. It was thus able to promote mutual knowledge of dissidents in different regions and with varied specific purposes, and to contribute to a sense of a community of interests. In effect it became a centre, perhaps even a kind of political centre, attracting like-minded people into a common enterprise.[92]

A similar coordinating function was performed by the Committee on Human Rights and, later, by the Moscow Helsinki Committee. The latter became known as a place where people from all parts of the Soviet Union could receive a sympathetic hearing and provide their latest information. Sakharov's apartment became the hub of the entire movement (I personally observed a visit from a young Pentacostal leader from Siberia). Information thus garnered was disseminated to foreign correspondents, and this, together with Sakharov's interviews with journalists and direct telephone conversations with people abroad, provided materials which were later broadcast to the USSR from foreign radio stations.

The chief purpose of the Moscow Helsinki Committee was to prepare reports on human rights violations and persecution throughout the country and to transmit them abroad, in particular to the meetings of the Conference on Security and Cooperation in Europe (CSCE). It transmitted twenty-six documents to the Belgrade meeting in 1977; by the time of the Madrid conference, convened two years later, it had prepared 138 reports. The sister organisations in the Ukraine, the Caucasus, and the Baltic states funnelled their reports to the Moscow committee which alone had direct and indirect contacts with the outside world.[93]

The democratic movement enjoyed a unique unity in the common defence of the rule of law and human rights, and of national and religious freedom. Nonetheless a wide variety of opinions was expressed in philosophical and political *samizdat*. This ranged from 'true Marxist-Leninist', to liberal, social democratic, and reform communist, and even a strong Russian nationalist trend which did not properly belong to the democratic movement. The lack of consensus on social and political issues produced a genuine philosophical dialogue among people of quite different outlook. This wide gamut of opinion was much more pronounced than in the more homogenous Czechoslovak and Polish counterparts.[94]

Strangely absent was what we might call 'self-analysis' of the movement and its purposes which was so characteristic of dissent in Poland and Czechoslovakia. Even though the Soviet dissidents had pioneered certain 'parallel institutions' they did not, like their Czechoslovak and Polish comrades, analyse their nature or articulate the idea of a 'second' or 'independent' society.[95] The only exception known to this author was a long article on the democratic movement published in the journal *Poisky*, probably in 1978, by Pyotr Abovin-Egides and Pinkhos Podrabinek.[96] They listed the groups of people with an oppositional mentality: intellectuals who had become workers, manual and white-collar workers and engineers, pensioners and war invalids, as well as some of the creative intelligentsia, religious believers, and national minorities. These divergent groups, they argued, should seek unity under the aegis of the Moscow Helsinki Group which *de facto* found itself at the head of the whole Democratic Movement. It had, however, hitherto devoted itself mainly to human rights as embodied in the Helsinki accord, and had little or no contact with the nascent free trade unions. The Helsinki Committee should interest itself more in social and economic rights, work for unity with the workers, provide a forum for all socio-political and ideological tendencies, and a centre for information, contact, and legal defence. As we have noted, this did eventually occur, although the link with the workers' movement, itself almost non-existent, was never a close one.

One should note also the search for greater freedom in the 'second' or 'unofficial' culture, as manifested in amateur theatre; film clubs; musical groups and song festivals; poetry readings; art shows; and later break-dancing, rock, punk, and heavy metal; worship in illegal sects such as Hare Krishna and Jehovah's Witnesses; informal youth associations and circles of friends or family. A most significant example of cultural freedom was found for several decades in guitar playing and 'mass song', with the compositions of such popular guitar singers as Bulat Okhudzava, Vladimir Vysotsky, and Aleksandr Galich, heard very widely on private tape recorders and, in some cases, published. Other types of protest were leaflets, wall graffiti, petitions and open letters, occasional strikes, marches, riots, and a rare act of self-immolation.[97]

Even more challenging to the authorities was the bourgeoning youth culture which did not limit itself to rock music or religion, but extended to the more negative activities of night bikers, drug and alcohol addicts, glue sniffers, soccer hooligans, muggers and vigilante gangs, such as the 'Lyubers', who took it on themselves to oppose, sometimes with violent means, punks, hippies, and metallists. These patterns of behaviour reflected disaffection and alienation of many young people and their yearning for a new style of life. This mood of rebellion was the product of job dissatisfaction; crowded and scarce housing; hatred of enforced conformity; contempt for the Komsomol; and the war-weariness of veterans from Afghanistan. Although this defiance of society was limited to a small minority, it expressed in extreme form a much broader, and for the regime, more dangerous phenomenon: widespread political apathy, ideological deviance, Western influence, anti-social behaviour, and juvenile delinquency.[98]

By the early 1980s the democratic and human rights movement was virtually destroyed by imprisonment and exile and the potentiality of a second polity or society shattered. From 1980 to 1986 Sakharov was in internal exile in Gorky. The members of the Helsinki committees were almost all in prison or had died or gone into exile; in September 1982 the remnants of the Moscow committee announced its dissolution. In the same year, in June, the *Chronicle* appeared in what was to be its final issue, no. 64. Only here and there did fragments of the movement survive, for instance, the *Lithuanian Chronicle*, and some of the national and religious groups. In spite of severe persecution, the Group to Establish Trust remained alive until 1987, and issued a monthly bulletin. Even some new associations emerged e.g. 'Helsinki-1986' in Latvia; a Lutheran group called Renaissance and Renewal, to defend the rights of believers, also in Latvia; environmental groups in Leningrad; and the Independent Christian Movement for Peace (1987). No doubt below the surface there was some spontaneous activity, on a personal basis, as frequent arrests and trials testified. Independent literary and scholarly *samizdat* seemed to have ceased although no doubt some materials circulated secretly. A striking exception were the Jews of Moscow and Leningrad, who continued to circulate materials, held study circles and discussion groups, continued their religious life and celebrated festivals, conducted a well-organised programme for the teaching of Hebrew, and held regular scientific and historical seminars, the proceedings of which were published abroad.[99] Nor did the second economy, religious worship, youth culture, and social deviance come to a stop.[100]

POLAND AFTER 1981

The crushing of Solidarity by military force in December 1981 ended the attempt to restore 'civil society', as Adam Michnik described its purpose during the movement's heyday. Yet four years later he was able to write of a 'veritable Miracle on the Vistula' – the structures of independent civil society functioning side by side with a totalitarian power which attempts to destroy all independent institutions. A non-violent struggle was in progress seeking not to take over power but to limit it, and to achieve a self-governing Republic. In this conflict the Church was a great asset, the only institution that is 'legal and authentic, independent of the totalitarian power structure and fully supported by the people'. This was, he believed, in his *Letters from Prison*, the 'barren twilight of the old world of totalitarian dictatorship'.[101]

In the immediate aftermath of the establishment of martial law those leaders who had not been jailed – some twenty-five in number – worked underground, in co-operation with the still surviving regional and enterprise organisations. They sought to restore Solidarity as a legal movement and to reach a compromise with the state by putting pressure on it, including the threat of a general strike. This tactic was endorsed by the Temporary Co-ordinating Commission (TKK) which was set up in April 1982 and consisted of the leaders of four underground regional organisations (later joined by others). The unity hitherto preserved had already begun to break down, however, and a debate over strategy ensued throughout 1982 and 1983. There were some, such as Jacek Kuroń, who wanted a tightly-knit and centralised conspiratorial organisation which would struggle against the state and seek to gain power, conducting mass resistance through a general strike and, if necessary, resorting to violence. Others favoured a long-term peaceful struggle, 'trench-warfare' in Z. Bujak's term, seeking to establish, through an informal decentralised movement of independent and loosely linked groups, not an 'Underground State', but an 'Underground Society'.[102]

This concept, introduced by Wiktor Kulerski, a former teacher who joined TKK in June 1982, was adopted as its principal strategy. In its statement of 28 July, TKK declared its aim to be 'a self-governing Republic', as defined by Solidarity's national programme of 1981, to be attained through an underground resistance movement which would gradually build up an 'underground society'. It later called on the people to create 'independent social institutions', such as a restored free trade union, independent farmers' and students' organisations, free scientific and creative associations, free education, press and publications, and a culture free from censorship.[103]

By November 1982 Solidarity was thrown into disarray and confusion by its de-legalisation by the government, the failure of the general strike on 10 November, the release of Wałęsa the day after, and some doubts about his intentions. The meeting of Cardinal Glemp and General Jaruzelski awakened suspicion of the former's attitude, and fear that the alliance of Church and Solidarity was breaking down. TKK, in its programme of 22 January 1983, called for resistance to the totalitarian dictatorship and for fundamental reforms, and urged the development of independent initiatives which would contribute to the independence of society.[104] Adam Michnik, from prison, expressed similar views, urging the need for a 'long march', a sustained peaceful struggle between 'organised civilian society and the power apparatus'; the objective was to develop a 'civil' or 'authentic' society as the basis for a future democratic state.[105]

In the building of the independent society the cornerstone was, of course, Solidarity, or at least those remnants of it which still existed underground in the form of TKK, about twenty regional and hundreds of clandestine enterprise organizations, and some one million dues-paying members. Lech Wałęsa, after his release from internment, remained above ground, as Chairman, recognized by TKK and by Solidarity generally, and acting as a symbol and spokesman of the once ten-million-strong movement. The underground was highly decentralised, the leadership shared by TKK and Wałęsa.[106]

Even after it was declared illegal by the government, Solidarity continued its resistance, co-ordinating publishing, raising financial aid for prisoners' families, mounting the occasional demonstration and local strike, and lending moral support to other independent associations and publications; it also organised passive resistance to the government-sponsored trade unions and the Patriotic Council, and conducted a massive boycott of the elections. From time to time TKK issued reports, for instance on proposed changes in labour laws, on the economy and economic reforms, and on living and working conditions. It submitted to the ILO session on 16 June 1986 a message from Wałęsa, in which he regretted that there was no genuine representation of Polish workers in the ILO and called for the state's recognition of Solidarity and of trade union pluralism.[107]

By mid-1986, in spite of widespread support, Solidarity was growing weaker. The number of strikes and protests declined; many leaders were in hiding or prison; all thought of a general strike or a nation-wide protest was abandoned. It was becoming clear that a new strategy was needed. In August a special *ad hoc* committee of TKK set forth a series of points for an updated programme; these were similar to the traditional Solidarity ideas but laid stress on clandestine work at the enterprise and regional levels. Nothing was said of the possibility of open activity.[108]

The general amnesty on 11 September 1986, and the release of some 225 persons, including top Solidarity leaders, presented the movement with a new set of circumstances. It responded almost immediately, although, as admitted later, without adequate discussion with the TKK or the rank and file, and in the face of sharp difference among the leaders. On 29 September Lech Wałęsa announced the formation of a Provisional Council of Solidarity (TR), made up of seven persons from the underground, which would work above ground for a dialogue with the authorities and for trade union pluralism. Wałęsa, who was not a member, continued to act as

Solidarity chairman. No reference was made to TKK and its underground work. The Council was at once branded as illegal by the authorities but no action was taken against it.

The move was welcomed, after the event, by some ten regional Solidarity underground organisations, most of which proclaimed their readiness to emerge to the surface. There was some opposition, e.g., in Lower Silesia, and some criticism of the lack of consultation and even of the wisdom of this step. TKK was not happy with the new strategy, as was clear from their statement of 12 October 1986 (issued jointly with Wałęsa!) which saw no cause for change in their own activity, restated the need for clandestine actions, and only briefly mentioned 'open struggle'. There was much confusion over the relations of the new Provisional Council with TKK and its regional and enterprise units, and over the future connection between underground and open work. In the ensuing debate many leading figures, e.g., Kuroń, Kulerski, Bujak, and Romaszewski, welcomed the new tactics but all argued for the continuation of both open and secret activity – in Kulerski's words for a flexible combination of the independent open movement and the clandestine civic structures, and a division of labour between TKK, responsible for the underground, and the Council, for public work.[109]

Solidarity continued to enjoy widespread moral support from the population at large. It received international recognition, not only from the ILO as noted above, but also from the International Confederation of Free Trade Unions and the World Confederation of Labour, as well as from Pope John Paul II, especially during his visits to Poland in 1984 and 1987.[110] Solidarity also received substantial financial aid from abroad, both through private donations and public appropriations, such as those of the US Congress.[111]

The revival of Rural Solidarity was more difficult. In May 1982 the All-Poland Committee of Farmers' Resistance (OKOR), headed by the seventy-year-old Josef Teliga, was formed and established some regional branches and two journals. It was more politically oriented than urban Solidarity, and sought to develop the political consciousness of farmers and to defend them against official policies and rural bureaucracy. It faced severe police persecution, including the arrest of Teliga in December 1983. Neither was it able to achieve a working understanding with TKK, which had little interest in or knowledge of rural problems. Another kind of rural organization, formed by members of the original Rzeszow–Ustrzyki agreement of 1981 (the counterpart of the Gdańsk agreement), was set up in February 1985 to monitor its fulfilment. In late November 1986 the farmers followed the tactics of urban Solidarity by setting up a Provisional National Farmers Council of Solidarity, composed of many veterans and victims of imprisonment, including Teliga.[112]

Other significant elements of an independent society which were sponsored and encouraged by Solidarity, but acted autonomously, were four independent committees on education, culture, science, and health, known collectively as OKN or OKNO.[113] The Committee for Independent Education (ZON), composed of teachers and academics, established in March 1982, gave support to the hundreds of self-educational circles throughout the country. Jointly with the Committee of Social Resistance (KOS) (see below) it established a publishing house and issued an educational journal, *Tu Teraz* (Here and Now), and a series of educational booklets on literature, history, economics, and philosophy. The Committee for Independent Culture (KKN), established early in 1983, represented writers, painters, musicians, actors, and journalists. They promoted creative work and popularised independent culture by sponsoring tours, exhibits, and performances, and by giving awards for outstanding achievement. An auxiliary organisation, the Council of National Education (REN), made up of outstanding academics, acted as an advisory board and prepared analyses of the situation in education.[114] The Social Committee for Scholarship (Science) (SKN), formed in April of 1983, had as members social scientists and university teachers; it supported scientific research through grants, undertook independent inquiries, and published works in history, economics, etc. The Social Commission for Health, set up in February 1984, published a significant journal of medical thought, and prepared reports on the health situation and on needed reforms.[115] This group, in co-operation with the Committee for Science, established a Working Group for Environmental Protection in April 1986; its first bulletin was devoted to the Chernobyl disaster. Three of the committees, together with the Helsinki Committee (below), addressed letters in September 1986 to Charter 77 and VONS in Czechoslovakia proposing co-operation in their respective spheres.[116]

The Polish Helsinki Committee, founded by KOR in 1979 and headed by Z. Romaszewski, was dissolved after his arrest in 1982. A new Helsinki Committee was formed in early 1983 (its members this time anonymous) to monitor human rights violations. It distributed comprehensive annual reports and special studies, sending them to the UN Commission on Human Rights, the ILO, and CSCE meetings. Following the murder of Father Popiełuszko in November 1984, Citizens' Committees Against Violence (KOPPs) were formed under different titles in a number of Polish cities; the names of their members were given. Their aims were domestic – to call for the investigation of unexplained deaths, such as that of Popiełuszko, to gather and publish information about rights violations, and to submit these to the state organs. The committees were at once declared illegal and constantly harassed by the police, but tried to continue their work of 'social self-defence'. A Polish Committee for Human Rights was formed in Szczeczin in October 1986, but was pronounced illegal by the authorities. In December 1986, Solidarity set up a Commission for Intervention and the Rule of Law, under Romaszewski. Its tasks were similar, on a national scale, to those of the committees: to defend human rights and to check on their observance, to provide legal support for victims of repression, and to exercise public control over the way state agencies applied the law.[117]

Independent publications, some as organs of Solidarity, others quite autonomous, were appearing in increasing numbers and with wide circulation.[118] As noted in Chapter 2, these included books, newspapers, journals, sound and video tapes, but also badges, stickers, calendars, and even Solidarity stamps and 'bank notes'. Although it was impossible to estimate the number of publications, it was said that some 500 had appeared each year since martial law was established. A most extraordinary event, in 1987 was the permission given to a clandestine journal, *Res publica*, to appear legally, subject, however, to censorship. A network of libraries and several central and regional archives of the Solidarity period were set up, and a multi-volume *samizdat* series of archival materials was begun. All of this was accomplished in spite of severe penalties for those involved, including heavy fines and confiscation of vehicles for those who were charged with the misdemeanour of editing, printing, and distributing these materials.

In late 1985 an Independent Publications fund was established to provide assistance and insurance for the major publishing houses. In October 1986 a Social Council for Independent Publishing was formed to oversee and advise on the Fund's activity, to mediate disputes, and to assess, and promote, the quality of publications.

Especially active in this field was the Committee of Social Resistance (KOS), established in December 1981, a decentralised movement with thousands of Circles of Social Resistance in many cities and towns. It gave aid to prisoners, had its own publishing house, and from January 1982 issued a journal, *KOS* (Blackbird) with a circulation of 10 000 to 15 000. Some of its circles, such as the one in the Maszowze region, had their own organs, aided others in printing and distribution, and prepared brief broadcasts for radio and even for television. It co-operated closely with Solidarity and with the OKNO committees. The KOS programme, in April–May 1982, set as its goal the building of an independent society. A special English issue of *KOS*, describing all aspects of such a society, was prepared for the officially organized Congress of Intellectuals held in Warsaw in January 1986. KOS also concerned itself with peace issues and co-operated with Western peace movements.[119]

A movement for peace, calling itself Wolność i Pokoj (WiP) (Freedom and Peace) was formed in the spring of 1985 in Cracow and other cities.[120] This was inspired, it was said, by the peace appeals of Pope John Paul II and followed the example of the peace movement in the GDR. More directly it resulted from the change of attitude among the youth towards the army and military service, exemplified by the refusal of some to take the military oath (which pledged allegiance not only to Poland, but also to the fraternal alliance with the Soviet Union) and the return of draft notices by others. Freedom and Peace activists launched protests against the imprisonment of these dissenters and appealed for an alternative to military service – for which they in turn were jailed.

From these relatively small beginnings Freedom and Peace developed into a broad movement, which, in its programme, adopted on 17 November 1985, took as its first priority the struggle for human rights, religious freedom, and national independence; warned against nuclear war and the militarisation of society; and proclaimed the tactic of non-violent resistance to evil. They declared their intention to seek a change in the military oath and to secure alternative service for draftees. They also expressed their concern over environmental damage; later they criticised official reactions to Chernobyl and opposed the construction of Poland's first nuclear plant.

A change of view toward the Western peace movements occurred in 1983. Until then there had been deep distrust of these and of the European left because they pursued a disarmament policy which seemed to coincide with that of the USSR and failed to recognize the crucial importance of human rights as a condition of peace. A dialogue with some of these movements produced closer co-operation, for instance at the Perugia and Amsterdam peace conferences, and at a gathering of representatives of nine countries in Budapest in August 1986; and in the drafting of the joint statement for the Vienna CSCE conference (see Chapter 3). This culminated in an international peace seminar held in several Warsaw churches in May 1987. On this extraordinary occasion Polish peace activists, and Solidarity leaders, conducted a wide-ranging discussion with some sixty persons from the USA and Western Europe; even one representative of Charter 77 succeeded in getting to Warsaw. Agreement was reached on several joint statements on human rights, military service, disarmament, ecological questions, and the phasing out of atomic energy establishments.[121]

In 1987 Experience and the Future, an ad hoc association of former communists, Catholics and independents, which had issued reports in the pre-Solidarity days, put out its first report in five years which dealt at length with the crisis in all its aspects and the major problems to be solved.

One can only mention other smaller groupings, such as local youth and students, punk rock groups, scouts, local farmers' organisation and pastoral communities, both sponsored by the Church, the Catholic Intellectual Clubs, economic societies to promote private enterprise and a market economy, independent teachers' committees, centres for documentation and analysis and for public opinion research, committees of pensioners and the disabled, and, most unusual, the Youth Movement for Combating Drug Abuse (MONAR) for the rehabilitation of addicts, and the associated Pure Hearts Campaign in the schools to warn of the dangers of drugs.[122]

There were a number of more expressly political groupings: some quite large in membership such as Fighting Solidarity (radical-liberal), Robotnik and Committee of Social Resistance (KOR) (both socialist); and others much smaller, such as Independence, Liberation, and the Polish Social Labour Party (all socialist), the Workers Opposition (left socialist), and Independence, Confederation for an Independent Poland, and Congress of Solidarity (all right-wing nationalist).[123]

The part played by the Church in the development of an independent society was crucial but difficult to summarise in a few words.[124] Throughout modern history it had performed a dual role, seeking, on the one hand, to reach a *modus vivendi* with the state, but at the same time to preserve its independence and support the aspirations of society – which required a combination of diplomacy and resistance developed to a fine art by Cardinal Vyshiński as Adam

Michnik noted in his *Letters from Prison* (pp. 94, 113–14). It could not, however, become a political actor or tie itself to a specific movement or party. Nonetheless, before Solidarity, it gradually developed an anti-totalitarian stance, became an ally of the democratic opposition, and supported the workers' movement for human rights (Michnik, pp. x–xi, 145).

During the Solidarity period, too, its role was a double one; many priests, and even the hierarchy, showed sympathy for Solidarity, but the latter sought to moderate the opposition's demands, to mediate between Solidarity and the regime, and to achieve a compromise (Michnik, pp. 34, 58, 126–7). After martial law the Church continued to pursue two goals. On the one hand, it sought the restoration of Solidarity and gave concrete aid to the victims of repression through a special committee, and churches became an asylum of independent culture (Michnik, p. 94). Later it established some 10 000 local chaplaincies to give moral and financial support to the farmers. Some priests, personified above all by Father Popiełuszko, were strong supporters of Solidarity.

Yet the Church continued to seek a compromise with the regime and after November 1982 was more conciliatory to it, for which it was criticised by some priests and the secular opposition. During the Pope's visits in 1984 and 1987, John Paul II seemed to be more pro-Solidarity than Cardinal Glemp and the bishops, so that many priests, Catholics generally, and even non-Catholics, welcomed the Pope's words as a boost to declining morale. True to its traditional mission, the hierarchy continued to negotiate with the regime, seeking concessions for itself and for the people. Its proposal of an independent Farmers Aid Fund, based on donations from abroad, was stalled by the unwillingness of the authorities to grant it the necessary autonomy. In October 1987, however, a fund for the more limited purpose of improving irrigation and the water supply was agreed upon.

Solidarity, the Church, and many other independent groups in Poland constituted the elements of at least a partial, although circumscribed, independent society, eclipsing what had been achieved in any other country in Eastern Europe. Some groups acted more or less openly, such as Freedom and Peace, and, of course, the Church. Even after the adoption of the new strategy of 'openness' in late 1986, however, the need for an 'underground society' persisted, in varying combinations of under- and above ground activity. Eventually some underground groupings might emerge into the open, but for the time being there had to be, in Kulerski's words, 'clandestine civilian structures, in deep hiding, whose members would not come out from the underground, so long as communism remains what it is'.[125] He referred expressly to the printing and publishing houses, editorial boards, all the technical and organisational structure, and the network of contacts abroad. Hampered as they were by the absence of constitutional and legal restraints on power and the lack of open means of articulating opinions and interests, these independent social initiatives could not constitute a fully developed civil society. It was recognised that 'no independent social institution can substitute for a well-organised, efficient, and competent state administration democratically controlled by society.[126] 'To live as if we were free', in Michnik's expressive phrase,[127] was not the same as to be free. But these 'enclaves of independence' advanced the prospects for eventual independence.[128]

Poland in 1987 had certainly long ceased to be a 'totalitarian society' but it was equally far from being a genuine civil society. What existed, through no conscious policy of the regime, was a rudimentary and fragmentary quasi-pluralism, or 'imperfect monism', in which two extremes confronted each other. On the one side the party, which had ceased to exercise the leading role over every sphere of society, vainly sought to restore total control of society and to deal with the worsening economic crisis without serious political reforms. It had perforce to accept the reality of opposition and to recognise some elements of pluralism, although subtly seeking to dismantle the opposition and refusing to have any dealings with Solidarity. The latter, on the other side, had achieved some elements of an 'independent' or 'parallel' society although distorted and weakened by state intervention and continued to enjoy substantial public support and to exercise influence on public opinion.

Yet in spite of this polarisation of two extremes there was no simple dichotomy of 'two nations' – of state and society – of the regime and Solidarity.[129] Within both the official structures and among its supporters, and within the oppositional movements and opponents of the system in general, there were substantial disagreements on basic issues of economic and political reforms. There was a strong realist tendency willing to work with Church and State (but not with Solidarity) and a substantial silent minority. The Church was the only fully independent force, but both clergy and believers differed strongly as to the proper course to follow. Solidarity still sought to win legitimacy for itself and to promote the growth of pluralism and the self-organization of society, but was plagued by continuing differences of opinion over strategy, by a lack of unified direction and by the absence of a close relationship between leaders and the rank and file.[130] Its ambivalence was shown in the announcement in April 1987 by Wałęsa, TR and TKK of a relatively moderate plan of economic reform (without radical political proposals) and the decision of the newly formed National Executive Committee (KKW) on 25 October, to boycott the forthcoming government referendum on reform.[131] Another source of disunity was Wałęsa's personal decision not to accept the offer of US funds for Solidarity but to assign the money to health and other social purposes. The KKW was designed to overcome the lack of co-ordination in the triumvirate of Wałęsa, TR and TKK, but was still hampered by deep divergences as to the proper strategy to adopt in relation to the party and government and their professed policies of democratisation and economic reform.

9 Towards an Independent Society?

The notion of an 'independent' or 'parallel' society caught the imagination of nonconformist circles in Central and Eastern Europe. It seemed to distil the essence of the independent activity undertaken within the framework of an otherwise totally controlled society and to demarcate it from the life of the official institutions. The 'parallel' structures which sometimes grew out of 'individual civic initiatives' represented ways of protesting against the marasmus of official society; substitutes for the inadequate or harmful performance of official structures (V. Benda); spheres where a different life – based on truth – could be lived (V. Havel); oases of values and intellectual orientations and of the life linked with them (Z. Mlynář); or elements of a revolutionary *avant-garde* (P. Uhl). These structures were capable of constant expansion into other spheres of life and offered a path toward a more developed independent society in future, even a model of it.[1]

The two principal terms used in Czechoslovak discussions, 'independent'[2] and 'parallel'[3] society, and the many synonyms or equivalents, were often used almost indiscriminately or interchangeably. Some persons distinguished carefully between them and expressed a preference for one or the other. Others chose different concepts such as civic society, alternative or parallel community or communities,[4] or self management.[5]

Whatever the term used, they all referred to the phenomena described in preceding chapters: (1) the ubiquitous informal acts of protest or self-expression by individuals in the economy, culture, and society, which could not be suppressed entirely even in the most totalitarian society; (2) the rarer, more developed and structured forms of dissent in Poland and Czechoslovakia, to a lesser extent in Hungary, the GDR, and Yugoslavia, and temporarily in the USSR. We have used the term 'second polity' to describe a more advanced system of parallel structures which implicitly, or overtly, constituted a kind of alternate political system challenging the official power structure.

The Hungarian scholar, Hankiss, as noted above, constructed a more sophisticated paradigm of what he called the 'second society' which did not, however, include anything resembling a 'second polity'. He later concluded that the various forms of a 'second society' were not really separate or independent of the first society, but were really only components of the latter, heavily dependent on and influenced by it. He coined a term 'alternative society' to describe a hypothetical future system which would be characterised by all the features he had ascribed to a second society, but in fully developed form, and would become therefore a new paradigm of society.[6]

The analysis of the theme of an independent or parallel society was initiated in Czechoslovakia in early 1978 by Václav Benda, in his essay entitled 'Parallel *polis*'.[7] To his surprise this became the subject of vigorous discussion, not only in his own country, but also in Poland, where it seemed to coincide with, or approximate, the more customary terms, 'social self-organisation' or 'social movements'. Elsewhere in Central and Eastern Europe there was no corresponding debate, no doubt because the actual course of events did not produce anything which could be said to resemble the *polis* as Benda conceived it.[8]

In retrospect, and in light of the empirical investigations of independent activities in the preceding chapters, what further conclusions may be drawn as to the validity of the term 'independent' or 'parallel' society? What precisely is its meaning and its essential features? Is there a difference between the two alternative words used? Is either of them relevant to present conditions in Czechoslovakia and elsewhere in the region? What are the immediate purposes of such a society? What are its long-term implications and possible consquences? How independent is it of the official context in which it may function? How independent *should* it be of the official structures and of society as a whole?

Some of these questions were posed in an inquiry conducted by the author by correspondence with active participants in the independent life of society in Czechoslovakia, and to a lesser extent in Hungary and Poland.[9] This *anketa* was not in any sense a systematic poll of dissident opinion. However, the responses to the questionnaire by some twenty Czechs, four Poles, and three Hungarians offered many insights and much food for thought. The ideas were integrated with my own conclusions in the following pages, sometimes with direct citation, more often without definite attribution. Since the bulk of the replies related to Czechoslovakia, they cannot be taken as reflecting accurately the situations in other countries but seemed often to be valid (*tous proportions gardées*) for the region as a whole.

VALIDITY OF CONCEPTS

With a few exceptions, there was a consensus that the concept of an independent or parallel society, or its several equivalents, was useful in interpreting the conflict between society and a totalitarian state. An anonymous respondent regarded the term 'independent society' as the fundamental concept for the political analysis of totalitarian systems. 'Whenever mobilised to demonstrate publicly the unity of the people with party and government, society displays, in its day-to-day life, a face that is turned the other way. Step by step, in a thousand ways, it strives for independence from party and government.' This was an 'inexorable conflict with state power of a civil society being reborn'. The term independent society, or others such as 'second culture', parallel structures, or *'samoorganizace* of society' 'characterised the conflict of thinking and behaviour independent of the state and the claims of the total state to control all of social life'. Ivan Jirous, the apostle of the 'second culture', considered the 'independent community (*společenství*)' 'the only meaningful construction which people can create if they do not want to remain passive appendices of the political and social structures created by the ruling power'. Others distinguished, as I have above, between what Benda called 'the natural resistance of life to totalitarianism and the more consciously expanding sphere of the parallel *polis*', or what Libuše Šilhanová described as the more spontaneous, centrifugal tendencies in the economy, society, and culture, or in nonconformist private life, and the more consciously independent and programmed protest movements.

As between alternative concepts, Václav Benda, a mathematician by training, expressed his preference for the one he had coined, *paralelní polis*, and seldom, if ever, used the words 'independent' or 'society'. He used the Greek noun as synonymous with 'community' (*obec* or *společenství*). Although the adjective, he admitted, confirmed the differences between the official and non-official, this did not signify the absolute independence of the latter. It did not assume that the parallels (*rovnoběžky*) 'cannot ever flow together or intersect; in geometry (this may occur) only at infinity, but in practical life far more frequently'. The theory did not involve, as some feared, a sectarian and élitist exclusiveness or a community of people who lived in the truth, but on the contrary took as its priority the revival of the national community (*společenství*) in the broadest sense of the word. Other terms, such as the underground, or second or alternative culture, were much more negative or narrow in their connotations.

AIMS: IMMEDIATE AND ULTIMATE

It was difficult to separate the short-term and long-run objectives of independent activities or of an independent society since they were interlaced in a dynamic process of development. It would perhaps be more accurate to distinguish between those that were more individual and personal, and those more general and societal.

The immediate or personal goals have been described at many points in this book and were restated, often eloquently, in the responses to the *anketa*, in ways that seemed applicable to all or most communist countries. Put most simply, people wanted to be themselves, to live according to their own lights; or in other words, 'to defend against *Gleichschaltung* the inner I and its right to authentic expression' (Eva Kantůrková). More specific aims were to promote genuine criticism, and to develop individual talents; to struggle for spiritual values such as the dignity of man, justice, love, and responsibility. Other objects were to promote civic courage and human solidarity, to increase the number of participants in the independent life of society, and to encourage criticism and independence in other than dissident circles and even in official structures (Šilhanová). Václav Benda best expressed the specific and ultimate goals: to resist the tendency of totalitarianism to atomise and destroy every individual community, and to break down the 'iron curtains' which it tried to create, not only between East and West, but between the individual nations of Communist Europe, between regions, towns, and municipalites within each country, and between factories, families, and individual members of families – and, one might add, between social, national, and religious groups.

The more general long-term goals grew naturally out of the more specific and immediate. One can agree with the formulations of these ends given in the responses to the *anketa*, which were:

1 not to seek power, but to criticize it, take it at its word, and to influence its exercise;

2 to promote civic conscience and an interest in the welfare of the community (*obec*) as a whole;

3 to broaden spiritual horizons and to restore national memory; to encourage independent thought, based on a sense of truth;

4 to promote the consciousness of individuality and ethical values (Václav Malý); in particular to re-establish the values and traditions common to Europe as a whole;

5 to break the monopoly of official culture, to influence and erode it, and to create a higher level of culture based on values common to the unofficial and official creative spheres;

6 to strive to transform the totalitarian system into an authoritarian one, in which there would be extensive zones of autonomous life;

7 to stimulate the revival of society, to broaden autonomous areas, and to restore a civil or self-organised society (Jiří Dienstbier); to prepare a living, pluralistic society based on brotherhood, human reciprocity, and international co-operation (Jan Šimsa);

8 to promote a democratic revival, and to offer a model of real democracy;

9 more practically, to combat the stagnation of society and to defend it against imminent catastrophe by gradual democratisation and reform (Dienstbier);

10 to prepare people for the next great crisis, so as not to repeat the 'missed opportunities' of 1938, 1948, and 1968; if there was once again a failure of 'the political (and military) representation', to replace the latter with people of authority and prepare the majority of the population to articulate its will clearly (Benda).

HOW SUCCESSFUL?

To what extent was the independent society able to vindicate its existence and to achieve some or all of its ambitious aims? Václav Havel warned that there were at present only the 'germs' of such a society in Czechoslovakia; Libuše Šilhanová observed that, in contrast with Poland, there were only 'tendencies, or the first manifestations of independence'. A pseudonymous respondent, George Moldau, asked whether the proponents were Don Quixotes, doing things which had no meaning and were not worth the risk and suffering involved? Yet even Quixote, it was argued, though not successful, remained an inspiration for people pursuing worthwhile causes at great cost and sometimes with little or no apparent success. Was the preservation, creation, and expansion of Czechoslovak culture not as worthy a goal as other unrewarding tasks, such as, say, searching for a vanished Troy, or striving to prevent the extinction of a rare species?

It was not easy to measure success or failure of independent activities. The criterion would not be concrete, tangible 'results', but rather the 'essence' of these actions in themselves (Jozef Zveřina). Moreover there was always a 'hidden influence' and a 'potential significance', not at once apparent, so that the social impact was difficult to estimate. Success could not be calculated in numerical or in absolute terms. Activities involving some hundreds of persons in Czechoslovakia, or many thousands in Poland, or even an isolated case of protest in Rumania could be evaluated only within the specific context.

Yet the results of independent activity might not be so small as seemed at first sight. Benda confessed that not even his boldest expectations in 1978 could have foreseen the degree to which the elements of a parallel *polis* would be formed in Czechoslovakia in the next ten years, and still more, in Poland. Such events demonstrated that a parallel *polis* was not only possible but could expand into new areas, including foreign policy, and gradually shift the boundaries of the permissible. There had been serious failures, as for instance, in Benda's view, in education, but elsewhere much had been achieved. There was no equivalent counterpart in the official sphere to the independent philosophy of *samizdat* (and the same could be said of history, literature, or rock music). Independent activities were not vegetating on the margins of society, as some opined, but were penetrating it and exerting a significant impact on the thinking and actions of others (Kantůrková). Charter 77, wrote Havel, was 'a small fire of relative independence' but 'its light shines far beyond its boundaries'. It was, agreed Dienstbier, not an 'islet in a sea of apathy', but the visible tip of the iceberg of general dissent; it exerted a wide influence on public opinion, even abroad, and served as a catalyst of other independent activities.[10] In Poland the picture was even more impressive. KOR, which in its small beginning seemed without influence or great potential, contributed to the development of the mighty Solidarity movement. Although the outburst of independent activity after 1981 was crushed by force, the seeds were planted and despite adverse conditions, germinated again in what was closer to an 'independent society' than anywhere else.

HOW INDEPENDENT?

How independent *was* the so-called independent society? Earlier chapters indicated that such activities were everywhere subject to strict controls and severe penalties, including jail and exile. In most countries independent structures were usually snuffed out as soon as they appeared. Even when they managed to come into existence and were reluctantly tolerated, they were hindered by restrictions of all kinds. The repression varied as between, say, Hungary and Rumania, the GDR and Bulgaria, or Czechoslovakia and Poland, but nowhere were the shoots of an independent society allowed to grow freely. In the unique case of Yugoslavia, where independent activities flourished within the official structures, those that were attempted outside were strictly limited.

The life and work of individuals who sought personal freedom or participated in more organised activities were, in varying degrees, circumscribed. Indeed no person could be completely independent. Limitations imposed by government restrictions or by societal restraints affected the form and the substance of independent culture. Writers were forced into a certain self-censorship, and had to choose their words, ideas, examples, and allegories with caution (Moldau). Václav Havel underlined the dependence of everyone on the society around them and the state system under which they lived and worked. Everyone was employed by the state or lived on state pensions; shopped in state stores; lived in state housing; enjoyed state health care; were subject to state laws and regulations. Yet everyone, even a state bureaucrat, could find some degree of independence and ought to seek to expand it. There were, he wrote, 'not two separate societies or two groups of persons, those who were independent, and those who were dependent'; all possessed, or claimed, some degree of independence, and all suffered a greater or lesser degree of dependence. There was not 'a small enclave of completely independent people in an ocean of the completely dependent', with no interactions between them.

AN INTERNATIONAL POLIS

There were some Czechs who envisaged an 'international *polis*', which would unite, according to Petr Uhl, independent communities in Eastern Europe. Radim Palouš, a historian, wrote of a *polis* which would emphasise the global as opposed to particular interests, not only of parties or social groups, but of nations, blocs, and continents, and would 'appeal to the whole of human society, in the country and in the world'. A Catholic writer, Iva Kotrla, thought of the independent community as 'the community of the persecuted', i.e., of the faithful who refused to collaborate as others had done. If they did not give in, she hoped that 'a single choir of freedom' would embrace not only Czechs and Slovaks, but Poles, Ukrainians, Hungarians, Croats and Slovenes, Austrians, Italians, and French.

The steps toward such an international community were hampered by difficulties of communication and the absence of organisational ties. In the early years an 'iron curtain' divided not only East and West but also the individual countries of Eastern Europe, and even more impenetrably these lands and the USSR. Direct contacts were the exceptions – the Polish–Czech meetings in 1978, the visit of Z. Romaszewski to Sakharov in Moscow in 1977–8, or the visits of Demszky and Rajk to Poland in 1980–1. In spite of this Sakharov thought it possible to speak of a 'unified human rights movement', based on the closeness of ideas and methods of the dissidents in Eastern Europe and the Soviet Union.[11] Certainly events in one country (as, for instance, the Prague Spring, Charter 77, and Polish Solidarity), gave mutual encouragement and inspiration, and helped them learn from each other's experience. There were mutual expressions of solidarity and widening knowledge through *samizdat* coverage of events in other countries, translation in *samizdat* of major articles and even books, widespread listening to Western radio and television, and telephone contacts between dissidents of each country and their exiled supporters abroad.[12]

In the mid-1980s there was an escalation of indirect communications and of joint actions. We have noted the influence of East European dissidents at peace movement conferences in Perugia and Amsterdam, of co-operation between East Germans and Czechs on nuclear weapons, the reaching outward by Hungarian environmentalists, by the German Evangelical Church and its grassroots groups, and by the Polish KOS and WiP, and the unusual meetings at the Cultural Forum in Budapest and the WiP seminar in Warsaw. Czech and Slovak dissidents as well as Hungarians made common cause with the Hungarian minority in Slovakia. The Hungarian oppositionists gave even stronger support to their national brethren in Rumania.

One could speak of the development of a kind of independent foreign policy conducted through such informal interactions and co-operation across frontiers.

The joint statement by Poles, Czechs, Hungarians, and Rumanians, on the anniversary of the 1956 Revolution, was a milestone. Ferenc Köszeg, who prepared the ground for this by visits to Czechoslovakia and Poland, described this as a 'symbolic act', in which the signers recognised the revolution as a 'common heritage and inspiration'. His colleague M. Haraszti, called it the opening of a new era, in which they recognized the 'need to internationalise our common problems' and thus prepare for the next great crisis. Even more significant was the joint statement on peace and human rights, which the Information Network for Dialogue between East and West prepared, after months of exchange across frontiers, and presented to the CSCE conference in Vienna. Another step forward was the international forum sponsored by the European Network in Budapest on 21–2 November 1987, at which 130 delegates from sixteen countries, both Eastern and Western, demanded troop withdrawals from Eastern and Western Europe.[13]

VOICES OF CRITICISM

How independent *should* the independent society be? There were some who thought that the effort to create such a society was dangerous; it encouraged a sectarian approach, glorified the separate community, and treated its members as 'people of special stamp', who were the exclusive possessors of truth and did not need to engage in self-criticism. Individual participants practised a kind of escapism, delighting in their narrow community and not showing real interest in establishing links with society. The idea of a parallel *polis* might be an 'inspiring exaggeration' but it ran the risk of becoming a 'dissident micro-world' or 'cloister of protest'. The very concepts of an independent or parallel society were barriers to understanding and helped to create a special atmosphere within the group and even a special vocabulary.[14]

Charter 77's strategy of verbal protests and confrontational tactics created a gulf with the state authorities and official circles, and alienated people within those structures as well as the mass of the population. Most people were relatively satisfied with their material lot, guaranteed under a kind of 'social contract' with the state, and did not want to jeopardise this by contact with Charter 77 and *samizdat* or by any form of overt action. The dissidents tended to adopt a black and white approach, seeing nothing good in the official realm, and exaggerated their own virtues and the value of their deeds. Yet there were good people in official circles, especially in the in-between areas, not fully official nor fully outside. Such persons were often, like the dissidents, 'dispossessed' and were potential allies, serving as bridges between the dissidents and the broader society.

The critics favoured what they called a 'constructive' approach which took account of reality and concentrated on society, not on the state. The Charter's programme of demanding full implementation of human rights on Western models and in accordance with international covenants was completely unrealistic in existing circumstances. They believed their own approach to be non-political, avoiding confrontation and trying to speak to, and with, the ordinary people, 'the silent majority'. Small-scale work (*drobná práce*) was preferable to 'the great truth'. The objective was to achieve 'national reconciliation', on the basis of Czech national traditions, especially those of T. G. Masaryk.

It was not easy to identify the precise differences between the protagonists of an independent society and their critics. The latters' analysis of the nature of the existing system and its crisis, and their ideas of reform (to the extent that they offered specific proposals) were not much different to those held by the Chartists. The latter seemed fully aware of the perils pungently set forth by their critics. In the 1978 discussions much attention had been paid to the danger of becoming a ghetto or sect, and to ways of expanding the Charter's influence in society at large as well as in official circles. In the tenth anniversary appeal Charter 77 had called upon all citizens to act on their rights, at home, in the work place, and in public milieux.[15] Moreover Chartists often called for *drobná práce* and invoked the example of Masaryk, never really expecting the authorities to respect the human rights acknowledged in law and statute.

The *anketa* replies reasserted such views vigorously, disavowing a desire to remain a ghetto and stressing the need to establish contacts with society and with those in official circles. Václav Benda in particular argued that the very concept of 'parallel *polis* implied the desire to work for the good of the whole community (*obec*) and opened the way for the merging of the two communities, with the community anchored in truth eventually dominating that based on mere manipulation and powers.' Charter 77 should be a pluralistic movement, open to all and tolerant of different views. Contacts with the public were desirable, although not always easy, especially for leading dissidents. Independent actions by people within the authority structures and in broader reaches of society should be encouraged and welcomed. Some people in official circles read *samizdat*, on a scale impossible to determine in view of the secrecy of distribution. Some contributed anonymously to *samizdat*. There were no unpassable walls between the official and parallel societies. The boundaries were not hard and fast, and every effort should be made to expand the space of free activity and autonomy.

The concept of a parallel culture met with bitter condemnation from another quarter. Rio Preisner, conservative Czech Catholic in exile, in a highly polemical article, denied that a genuine 'parallel culture' had ever existed in modern Czech history or at present. Basing his argument on a detailed historical analysis and on a definition of parallel culture as one which fundamentally challenged a dominant culture, he asserted that the present so-called parallel culture was not really nonconformist as its acceptance of socialism established a kinship with the dominant monoculture. This onslaught was challenged by Václav Benda, who argued that a parallel culture did not have to espouse certain specific values but was 'simply that culture which refutes the rules of *gleichschaltung* and liquidationist perspectives (of the official culture) and which realised itself and developed from free and self-governing efforts of responsible citizens'.[16]

INDEPENDENT SOCIETY IN POLAND AND HUNGARY

Polish and Hungarian thinking about an independent society, as reflected in responses to the *anketa*, paralleled to some extent that in Czechoslovakia, but with significant variations reflecting the uniqueness of the situation in the other two countries. As already noted (Chapter 8), Polish ideas of 'social self-organisation' and an 'independent society' were, as a result of the momentous happenings from 1976 on, more political and were closely tied up with the country's crisis and the problem of finding solutions through economic and political reform. The Hungarian concept of 'a second public sphere', in contrast, was more muted politically, did not directly challenge the official realm, and envisaged only small and gradual changes as the result of its activities.

Jacek Kuroń continued to use the term he had coined – social self-organization (*samoorganizacje*) – which in origin had been based on the experience of KOR, the self-defence efforts by farmers, workers, and creative professional people, and independent publishing. Even before Solidarity this had succeeded in breaking the party–government monopoly of information, organisation, and decision-making. After December 1981 three forms of independent activity developed: (1) illegal underground structures (trade unions, cultural, educational, and scientific activities, and publishing); (2) quasi-open activities which were not recognised by the authorities and might at any time be pronounced illegal (group actions in enterprises, self-education in private homes, the committees against violence, and actions by individuals); (3) activities within official institutions (pastoral councils, self-managing committees in some factories, co-operatives, etc.). All three were equally important and none could exist by itself. These experiences showed that people could solve their own problems by independent actions, which exerted pressure on state power, restored social ties destroyed by totalitarianism, and generated democratic structures.

Another respondent, Bronisław Geremek, historian, considered the term independent society ambiguous. After the Gdańsk agreement, it involved the widening of the sphere of independence in social life, in the economy, culture, and science, while recognising the supremacy of party rule. After martial law the intention was to create an independent society, based on self-organisation, ignoring rather than opposing the authorities, but this was shown to be utopian by subsequent experience.

In reality the most important transformations were taking place in society, not in the state. This demonstrated the possibility of creating a *société civile*, involving mass opposition against the authorities and the exercise of pressure by individuals, groups, and institutions acting in the name of society and aiming at its well-being. These phenomena, linked with the church and independent publishing, and supported by Polish broadcasts from abroad, created an independent circuit of opinion and information and nourished a feeling of independence. Whether this would continue depended on a government policy of liberalisation and an economic reform, which required a reform-oriented movement based on the idea of self-management (in work place, territories, etc.).

Jan Strzelecki, sociologist, regarded the concept of independent society as a 'counter-concept,' which rejected the leading role of the party. More positively it contained a social and moral appeal to citizens to exercise a responsibility to preserve and develop human values, such as truth, independence of mind, civil courage, democratic faith and human rights. It showed people an arena of action outside the official theatre. It also offered a 'counter-model of a good society,' characterised by independence, self-government, participation and unstructured decision-making. This moral appeal was not, however, in his view, a practical project of common living or a source of political strategy.

Tadeusz Kowalik, an economist, considered an independent society as a counter-reaction to the étatisation of social life and its subordination to the ruling party. It was widely recognized that the scope of state domination was far too great, but even pressures by some groups connected with the establishment left the party-state elephantiasis intact. The main social and institutional bases for society's independence were the Catholic Church and the private sector in agriculture, which had been strengthened rather than weakened by martial law, and the development of independent publications which broke the monopoly of information.

The Gdańsk agreement had striven to enlarge the sphere of independent social life through trade unions and workers' participation and in exchange had recognised the leading role of the party. Martial law ended this strategy and created in fact two independent societies, that of the apparatus and that of society; this made impossible co-operation or co-responsibility between the two and blocked the path to economic reform. The present degree of society's independence, and any extension of it, were dependent on recovery and economic reform, and this in turn required social pressure on the state power and a commitment of the latter to such reform.

Wiktor Kulerski, in a recent interview, continued to espouse 'a social movement organised in an independent, pluralistic, and decentralised society, consisting of various independent and self-governing structures, united by the common ideas of Solidarity and common goals of democracy and independence'. Solidarity, as an organisation, was an important element, but only one of many, and should encourage the social movements but recognize their independence. These were the main centres of action and should be created and managed by people who were not active in the underground. He admitted that there were still those who favoured a centralised, hierarchical, and monopolistic underground society which would control other social movements and that there were conflicts of decision-making between the TR, operating above ground, and the underground TKK. He recognised the value of the underground and urged a division of labour between the two spheres and consultation and co-operation between the TKK and the TR. The chief strategy should be to try to get the party to recognise, in its own interest, 'a margin of civil freedom', he argued, and the attainment of this goal would be furthered by the strength of the underground.[17]

The Hungarian responses reflected the weakness of the opposition and the absence of a significant independent society. Mihály Vajda distinguished the second society of E. Hankiss from an independent society. Like the latter he believed that the second society was not independent from the first or from the totalitarian society, but at best was an informal relationship inside the first society, which contributed to the functioning of the system. An independent society not only ignored the official prescriptions of the totalitarian state but made itself free by carving out for itself territories of action where the state had no rights at all. But such a society did not exist in Hungary. The democratic opposition consisted of small groups which could best fulfil the role of very restricted free media, but did not form any kind of society. The opposition was at most a group of intellectuals who tried to formulate their problems openly and thus contributed to the erosion of official culture. Individuals enjoyed a certain independence, but limited themselves to seeking solutions for their own personal problems and did not try to form interest groups or societal organisations.

György Bence, who had earlier espoused the Kuroń–Michnik conception, had become, after 1981, skeptical that an independent society could gradually reduce the first society to impotence. The second public sphere had achieved considerable success in *samizdat* publications, organised protests, and group actions, but did not really form an independent society since few participated in it and some of the protest groups refused to identify themselves with opposition. It was hard to see the opposition as the core of an independent society; unlike the Polish and Czechoslovak cases, it was a small and marginal group which had a catalytic effect but had to interact closely with the state-controlled sphere.

In like vein Peter Kende, in exile, did not think one could speak of an independent society in Hungary (or for that matter in

Czechoslovakia). There were political dissidents, groups of nonconformists, and individual young men and women seeking to find their own way, but they did not constitute an independent society, or even an ensemble of interconnected micro-groups. Each group (or *groupuscule*) challenged the rules in its own individual way but had no intention of working outside the system. The immediate purpose was a limited one: to provide a conscious example of civic courage and in the long run to encourage similar attitudes in larger segments of society.

Elemér Hankiss, a member of the academic establishment, in a recent interview described the opposition in Hungary as consisting of concentric circles: (1) the radical opposition (*samizdat*, etc.); (2) radical critics who seek to operate legally; (3) 'mediators' within established society; (4) advisers within this society, sometimes seeking reform; and (5) different circles within the core of power itself. He classified himself as belonging to the second category and described the difficulties he had experienced in publishing his articles and books. The second society was an invaluable stimulant, the sphere where social regeneration took place, where people met and established associations; where they expanded horizontal relations and were not just subordinated to the vertical and hierarchical networks. In the second economy or second culture people felt autonomous in the domain of personal existence. Most of the population did not even participate in the first society, let alone the second. The latter was twisted and distorted, and consisted of 'proto-institutions', and could not evolve into, or be taken as a model for, a new social system. Such an alternative society – a new paradigm – might eventually appear in the wake of a radical reform programme, which would help to transform the current authoritarian centralised system via the gradual democratisation of the power structure, the separation of powers, autonomy for parliament, and the divorce of state and economy.[18]

FUTURE PERSPECTIVES

The search for 'free social space', for autonomy and for personal independence within the framwork of society is not something unique to communist systems or in world history. Scholars have analyzed, for instance, the struggle for 'free spaces' in nineteenth-century America – black church life and black associations, women's groups, and early labour and farm organisations – and have described these, in terms strikingly similar to those used in this book, as 'settings between private lives and large-scale institutions where ordinary citizens can act with dignity, independence, and vision', in which 'people were able to learn a new self-respect, a deeper and more assertive group identity, and the values of cooperation and civic virtue'.[19] One can think at random of more radical efforts in relatively open societies such as the early American communes or the counter-culture of the sixties, and in more closed societies – the Jewish stettl or the ghetto in Eastern Europe, the Doukhobors in Tsarist Russia, or the Polish and Czech national movements in the nineteenth century. These groups sought to live their own lives and pursue their values and goals in a hostile environment. In communist Europe the search for similar objectives was carried on in more difficult circumstances than in open societies and was akin to the strivings within other autocratic states and institutions. A comparative study of the degrees of civil dependence or independence in disparate communities in history and in the contemporary world would be valuable but is beyond the scope of this book.

Our study has indicated that success or failure in these efforts depended on the extent of totalitarian controls and the strength of independent currents in different countries at different times. In Czechoslovakia, during the Prague Spring, or in Poland during the Solidarity period, at least an incipient and imperfect parallel society began to emerge. During the period of normalization which followed in the two countries, a system of more or less co-ordinated structures developed which, at least in embryo, represented a 'second polity' or independent society at a lower level of development. In Hungary and the German Democratic Republic independent activities were fewer, more informal and less co-ordinated. In Rumania and Bulgaria not even this measure of limited freedom could develop. In Yugoslavia a freer society made independent tendencies more feasible within official institutions and obviated the need for a broad infra-structure of parallel institutions. Dissent that overstepped strict boundaries, or genuinely independent activities, were condemned, or persecuted. Only in one Republic, Slovenia, did something approaching a 'second polity' materialize. In the Soviet Union some shoots of an 'independent polity' or 'society' did manifest themselves but they were extinguished by repression before they could mature.

If the reform course initiated by Gorbachev went ahead in the USSR and led to similar steps in Central and Eastern Europe, significant changes would most likely occur initially, not in the second or parallel society, but in the first, or official society. This was already manifested in the Soviet Union in the greater ease of publication and performance of creative works, vigorous discussion of economic and political measures, open debate over environmental problems, a reassessment of Soviet history, and greater 'openness' or 'publicity' (*glasnost*) in the communications media.[20] As ideas first raised in *samizdat* were broached in official media, wrote Ludmilla Alexeyeva, there would be a narrowing of the gap between dissident and heterodox opinion tolerated within the system.[21] What degree of independence of thought and action might be anticipated within and outside the official spheres in the period of 'new thinking' which opened up in the Soviet Union? The situation in both respects was fluid and unclear.[22] Reforms moved slowly in the USSR and at a snail's pace in other European communist countries. The official regimes reacted differently to the Gorbachev course, ranging from strong verbal approval by Poland, Czechoslovakia and Bulgaria, restrained approbation in the GDR and Hungary, and outright hostility in Rumania. Even where lip service to reform and to openness was given, this was not translated into concrete action.

The popular reaction was a mixture of hopes and doubts. Adam Michnik dubbed Gorbachev the 'Great Counter-reformer' who sought by modest change to preserve and improve the existing system.[23] Yet many were encouraged to expect change in their own countries in the style of Gorbachev and used his example as an argument against the caution of their own rulers. At the same time there was great uncertainty as to the durability of the Gorbachev course and skepticism as to the likelihood of their own authorities following suit. Nonetheless, if Gorbachev could carry through his proposed reforms, the impact on Central and Eastern Europe was bound to be great and would be accelerated by indigenous forces of change.

At the time of writing (May 1988) we can only point to various straws in the wind, but they blow in different directions. In the USSR, for instance, the permission given to Andrei Sakharov to return to Moscow and even to express his disagreement with official policies, an amnesty and the release of some hundreds of political prisoners, and the widening opening for Jewish emigration, might be swallows of a coming spring or mere gestures designed to win public support abroad. Actions taken by oppositionists themselves raised similar questions, especially the bold initiative of some former political prisoners to publish a magazine of critical opinion, provocatively titled *Glasnost*. The journal was not granted official registration as requested by the editors, but appeared in *samizdat* form, dealing with sensitive topics such as the law on public discussion, Jewish emigration and nationality problems.[24] Equally intriguing was the emergence of a large number of groups, including the conservative nationalist Pamyat, Democracy and Humanism, the Club of Socialist Initiatives, and the Federation of Socialist Clubs, and another called the Perestroika club, pressing the case for reform. There were also councils for the release of political prisoners in Armenia and Georgia; a Crimean Tatar movement; Friendship and Dialogue (an outgrowth of the Group to Establish Trust); a cultural and democratic movment, with its own journal, *Mercury*; Afghan veterans' clubs; and other informal discussion clubs dealing with peace, ecology or culture.[25] More challenging still were demonstrations by Jews and by students in Moscow and Leningrad and by ethnic groups in Kazakhstan, Azerbaizhan and Armenia and in the three Baltic republics.

Even more remarkable was the establishment of the Press Club *Glasnost* which, in a declaration on 4 August, demanded the release of all political prisoners and government measures to bring the criminal code into line with the international covenants and to guarantee the rights of information agencies and public organisations. Their most spectacular achievement was the holding of an international human rights seminar, without official sanction; it was attended by 400 delegates from the USSR and abroad, including a representative of Charter 77. The meeting welcomed the Soviet proposal of a human rights conference under CSCE auspices in Moscow, but urged the prior resolution of the issues raised in the August declaration.[26] Equally surprising was a conference of Socialist clubs in August 1987, with fifty groups represented, which urged a larger role for independent groups as a way to develop 'social self-management'.[27] There was also a proliferation of new magazines, and some twenty independent publications held a meeting in Leningrad in October.

Such developments confronted the authorities with a serious dilemma. *Pravda* (27 December 1987) welcomed this independent activity but warned that some might be breaking the law. In February 1988 the government issued a ban on the creation of independent publishing and printing co-operatives. Komsomol leaders declared that there was no intention of crushing independent groups but sought to co-opt them, as it had done in the case of the Afghan veterans.[28] The ultimate decisions on the future status of *Glasnost* and the groups, to be made by a special Central Committee commission and by Komsomol officials, would be a litmus test as to whether the regime was ready to legitimise dissent and tolerate genuine pluralism.

In other European communist countries the situation was even more ambiguous, as the case of Czechoslovakia illustrated. The Gorbachev reforms resembled in some ways the goals of the Prague Spring, as Dubček pointed out in an interview with *L'Unita* (10 January 1988). The mouthing of the ideas of *perestroika* and *glasnost* by leaders who had been fighting them tooth and nail for twenty years sounded hypocritical and insincere. Was *perestroika* really to become 'přestavba', as the term was usually translated in Czech, or was it more likely to be mere '*přestrojení*', a masquerade or disguise?

Portents of change in the treatment of independent activities and the toleration of freer expression were few and far between. Charter 77 was able to hold its first public meeting on the anniversary of the death of T.G. Masaryk, when some two hundred people gathered at the grave in Lány and heard a tribute delivered by Ladislav Hejdánek.[29] But there was no let-up in the harassment of leading Chartists or the criminal prosecution of Catholics and non-conformist youth, and political prisoners languished in jail. A request by some citizens in June 1987 to form a Society of Friends of the United States was turned down. Permission was not given for a Charter 77 manifestation on 10 December 1987, United Nations Day, and the gathering was prevented by police action. But more than 300 000 Catholics, in a petition endorsed by Cardinal Tomášek, called for separation of Church and state and made thirty other demands.

Annual conferences of the cultural unions were uneventful, with no criticism or debate, in striking contrast to similar conclaves in the Soviet Union and Hungary. Only at the Union of Theatre Arts was the stillness shattered by the actor, Miloš Kopecký, who in a daring and powerful indictment of the regime raised the question all were asking – was the Gorbachev revolution 'for real' in Czechoslovakia? 'The word Gorbachev is translated into Czech as hope,' he said. Leaders should possess 'the art of knowing when it was time to depart. Leave in time, that is at once, and you would still receive thanks.'[30]

Elsewhere the situation varied. In Hungary a Democratic Forum was created in late September 1987 to encourage social participation and public discussion of the serious crisis. Its founding statement urged a meaningful parliament and elections in which anyone with 5000 signatures could be a candidate. In the GDR the Evangelical Church became more assertive and youth groups multiplied.

Demonstrations in early 1988 met with firm police action and the expulsion of two leading figures to West Germany. In Rumania, in November 1987, a big demonstration in Brasov against wage cuts and food shortages was met with harsh reprisals. Protests were issued by groups calling themselves Rumanian Democratic Action and Free Rumania. In Bulgaria new clubs and organisations came into existence and were sharply condemned by the party. In Yugoslavia there were many strikes, including one in Ljubljana in December 1987, when the strike leader called for an end to the single-party system. In Poland the regime did not grant approval to new groups or clubs or to the restoration of the Polish Socialist Party.

Independent initiatives more and more often transcended national boundaries. For instance, after the Brasov riots Charter 77 called for a day of solidarity with the Rumanians. On 1 February demonstrations were held simultaneously outside Rumanian embassies in Prague, Budapest and Poland. An even broader movement of cooperation took place on 21 March when some 400 activists from six countries (Czechoslovakia, Hungary, the GDR, Poland, Yugoslavia and the USSR) signed a joint appeal to the Conference on European Security and Cooperation in Vienna, urging all states to introduce alternative civilian service. It is not yet clear how far such independent activities will be tolerated by the Soviet and East European regimes.

Even if independent activities were given greater leeway, this would be a far cry from the civil society envisaged by some authors in Eastern and Western Europe. As Iván Szelényi wrote some years ago, 'civil society, self-management, political self-determination, participatory management and decision-making without institutional guarantees' would remain but 'empty slogans', 'caricatures of democracy'.[31] The crucial question was whether existing autonomous spheres would be greatly broadened and legally guaranteed so as to constitute a genuine civil society. As a Czech critic noted, this did not require absolute independence of society from the state, but autonomy, a balanced and constantly self-correcting co-existence of state and society. The state must not intervene in the inner life of the autonomous spheres, but would regulate, by democratic process, the general conditions of social life, including the guaranteed, but still delimited spheres of autonomy.[32] More than that would be required; not a mere separation of society and state but the 'institutionalising of democratic control from below', in a new dialectic of society–state relations.[33] Then we could perhaps speak of a genuine civil or independent society.

Notes and References

1 Samizdat: A Return to the Pre-Gutenberg Era

Published originally in *Transactions of the Royal Society of Canada*, Series IV, XIX (1981), pp. 51–66; reprinted in *Cross Currents: A Yearbook of Central European Culture* (Ann Arbor, Mich., 1980), I, pp. 64–80.

1. D. S. Mirsky, *A History of Russian Literature, from Its Beginnings to 1900* (New York, 1958), pp. 182–3.
2. Isabel de Madariaga, *Russia in the Age of Catherine the Great* (London, New Haven, 1981), p. 545.
3. Gayle Durham Hollander, 'Political Communication and Dissent in the Soviet Union', in Rudolf L. Tökés, ed., *Dissent in the USSR: Politics, Ideology and People* (Baltimore, 1975), pp. 263–4. On the dissemination of 'secret' works by the young Pushkin and Ryleev, see also N. L. Stepanov, in *Ocherki po istorii russkoi zhurnalistiki i kritiki* (Leningrad, 1950), I, p. 194. Other writers refer to the letters of Prince Kurbskii to the tsar during the reign of Ivan the Terrible, unpublished letters of Chaadayev, and in the 1820s the dissemination among the peasants of a handwritten text of the New Testament in Russian (instead of the usual Church Slavonic); Michael Meerson-Aksenov and Boris Shragin, eds, *The Political, Social and Religious Thought of Russian 'Samizdat': An Anthology* (Belmont, MA, 1977), pp. 25, 439. Another example of early *'proto-samizdat'* was the encyclicals of Patriarch Tikhon which the government printing establishments refused to print; D. Pospielovsky, 'From *Gosizdat* to *Samizdat* and *Tamizdat*', *Canadian Slavonic Papers*, XX, no. 1 (March 1978), p. 46.
4. Cited by Hollander, 'Political Communication,' p. 264, from N. Mandelshtam, *Hope against Hope*.
5. This phrase she took apparently from G. K. Zaitsev; see Julius Telesin, 'Inside "Samizdat"', *Encounter*, February 1973, p. 25.
6. Meerson-Aksenov and Shragin, eds, *Russian 'Samizdat'*, p. 25.
7. F. J. M. Feldbrugge, *Samizdat and Political Dissent in the Soviet Union* (Leyden, 1975), p. 4.
8. A. Solzhenitsyn, 'The Writer Underground', in *The Oak and the Calf: A Memoir* (New York, 1979–80), pp. 3, 5.
9. Hollander, 'Political Communication', p. 264.
10. Meerson-Aksenov and Shragin, eds, *Russian 'Samizdat'*, p. 25–6.
11. Telesin, 'Inside "Samizdat"', p. 25.
12. Feldbrugge, *Samizdat*, pp. 3–4.
13. In Ukrainian *samvydav* is used. There is no Polish or Czech equivalent.
14. Feldbrugge, *Samizdat*, p. 4. In 1978 the Soviet Small Political Dictionary for the first time included the word 'dissidents', defined as 'those who

239

deviate from the doctrine of the church (heterodox)', and used, it was added, by imperialist propaganda to designate 'isolated renegades' who engaged in anti-Soviet activity. For this, see Mikhail Heller and Aleksandr Nekrich, *Utopia in Power* (New York, 1986), p. 662.

15. For a discussion of *kolizdat*, see Meerson-Aksenov and Shragin, eds, *Russian 'Samizdat'*, pp. 446*ff.*
16. Feldbrugge, *Samizdat*, p. 4. For a full discussion of musical *magnitizdat*, by Gene Sosin, see Tökés, ed., *Dissent*, pp. 276–309.
17. Pospielovsky, 'From *Gosizdat*', pp. 48, 50; Meerson-Aksenov and Shragin, eds, *Russian 'Samizdat'*, pp. 57–8.
18. For a full discussion, see Solzhenitsyn, 'Out of Hiding', *The Oak and the Calf*, pp. 18ff. On the relationship of *samizdat* and *tamizdat*, see Pospielovsky, 'From *Gosizdat*', pp. 44 *passim.*
19. Meerson-Aksenov and Shragin, eds, *Russian 'Samizdat'*, pp. 28–9n; Feldbrugge, *Samizdat*, pp. 3–4; Telesin, 'Inside "Samizdat"', p. 26.
20. Feldbrugge, *Samizdat*, p. 1.
21. Pospielovsky, 'From *Gosizdat*', p. 44. The Oxford Russian–English dictionary defines *samizdat* as 'unofficial reproduction of unpublished MSS'.
22. Meerson-Aksenov and Shragin, eds, *Russian 'Samizdat'*, Part I, Introduction, pp. 28–30, esp. n. 19.
23. Pospielovsky, 'From *Gosizdat*', p. 51.
24. Meerson-Aksenov and Shragin, eds, *Russian 'Samizdat'*, pp. 33–4, 228–9. For analysis of the Chronicle, see Peter Reddaway, ed., *Uncensored Russia: The Human Rights Movement in the Soviet Union* (London, 1972), Introduction, and pp. 350–1. This book is an analysis of the first eleven issues of the *Chronicle* in English. From no. 28 *A Chronicle of Current Events* (in Russian, *Khronika tekushchix sobytii*) was published in English by Amnesty International in London, England. A good history of the *Chronicle* is given in Mark Hopkins, *Russia's Underground Press: The Chronicle of Current Events* (New York, 1983).
25. For Ukrainian human rights documents, see L. Verba and B. Yasen, eds, *The Human Rights Movement in Ukraine: Documents of the Ukrainian Helsinki Group 1976–1980* (Baltimore, 1980).
26. Meerson-Aksenov and Shragin, eds, *Russian 'Samizdat'*, pp. 35–7.
27. Cited by Pospielovsky, 'From *Gosizdat*', pp. 58–9.
28. Abraham Tertz (pseudonym), 'Literarnii protsess v Rossii' (The Literary Process in Russia), *Kontinent*, I (1974), pp. 154–5, cited in English in Leonid Vladimirov, *Soviet Media and Their Message* (The American Bar Association, Washington DC, 1977), p. 37.
29. For an analysis of *samizdat* and of dissent in all aspects, see her book, *Soviet Dissent: Contemporary Movements for National, Religious and Human Rights* (Middletown, Ct, 1985), citation on p. 284.
30. Feldbrugge, *Samizdat*, with a summary of the main themes on pp. 7–10. For similar lists of categories see Tökés, ed., *Dissent*, p. 265; Telesin, 'Inside "Samizdat"', pp. 26–7; Meerson-Aksenov and Shragin, eds, *Russian 'Samizdat'*.
31. Stephen F. Cohen, *An End to Silence: Uncensored Opinion in the Soviet Union* (New York, 1982).

32. Published abroad in *The Samizdat Register*, edited by Roy Medvedev, vol. I–(1977–   ).

33. Feldbrugge, *Samizdat*, facing p. 12.

34. See S. Topolev (pseudonym), in Meerson-Aksenov and Shragin, eds, *Russian 'Samizdat'*, pp. 489–501; Feldbrugge, *Samizdat*, pp. 15–19; Tökés, ed., *Dissent*, pp. 266–8; Telesin, 'Inside "Samizdat"', pp. 30–3; Hopkins, *Russia's Underground Press*, Chapters 7 and 8.

35. Feldbrugge, *Samizdat*, p. 18.

36. Marshall McLuhan, *The Gutenberg Galaxy: The Making of Typographical Man* (Toronto, 1962), p. 95.

37. Elizabeth L. Eisenstein, *The Printing Press as an Agent of Change* (Cambridge, 1979), I, pp. 11, 37, 91n.

38. McLuhan, *Gutenberg*, p. 78.

39. Eisenstein, *Printing Press*, esp. pp. 37, 45.

40. Meerson-Aksenov and Shragin, eds, *Russian 'Samizdat'*, p. 40

41. 'Quinientos anos despues de Gutenberg . . .' (typescript).

42. H. Gordon Skilling, *Charter 77 and Human Rights in Czechoslovakia* (London, 1981), Chapter 6.

43. See Jiří Gruša's interesting discussion of this 'unpublishable literature', as he called it, as an integral part of Czech literature as a whole, including that which was published abroad (J. Gruša *et al.*, eds, *Stunde namens Hoffnung, Almanach tschechischer Literatur 1968–1978* (Lucerne, 1978), pp. 47–56). See also the essay by Jan Lopatka on the 'literature of the catacombs', *ibid.*, pp. 300–10.

44. Skilling, *Charter 77*, Chapter 5.

45. Typescript, April 1977, also in *Listy* (Rome), VII, no. 3–4 (July 1977), p. 26.

46. 'Onion-skin paper, white, 30 gr/m^2', typescript, Prague (n.d.), published in Czech in *Spektrum* (London, 1978), no. 1.

47. Typescript, Bratislava, 20 February 1979, published in English under the title 'Home-made books', *Index on Censorship*, VIII, no. 5 (September/October 1979), pp. 24–5.

48. For the above, see special issue on Poland, *Survey*, XXIV, no. 4 (109) (Autumn 1979), in particular Lidia Ciolkosz, 'The Uncensored Press', pp. 56–67, and *passim*, pp. 9–10, 18, 37, 46–7, 55. See also the regular summaries of 'Poland's Uncensored Publications', *Radio Free Europe, Research*, beginning with III, no. 16 (9–15 February 1978), and continuing in subsequent issues. See Chapter 2, below, pp. 13–14.

49. Stanislaw Barańczak, 'The Gag and the Word', *Survey*, special issue on Poland, XXV, no. 11 (110) (Winter 1980), pp. 66–7.

50. David Jim-tat Poon, '*Tatzepao*: Its History and Significance as a Communication Medium', Chapter 7 in Godwin C. Chu, ed., *Popular Media in China: Shaping New Cultural Patterns* (Honolulu, 1978), pp. 184, 187, 201. This chapter gives a full analysis of the role of *datzepao* (modern spelling) in communist China.

51. Poon, '*Tatzepao*', p. 189*ff.*, 193*ff.*, respectively. See also B. Michael Frolic, *Mao's People: Sixteen Portraits of Life in Revolutionary China* (Cambridge, Mass, 1980), pp. 169*ff.*

52. Roger Garside, *Coming Alive: China after Mao* (London, 1981), p. 102.

53. James D. Seymour, ed., *The Fifth Modernization: China's Human Rights Movement, 1978–79* (Stanfordville, NY, 1980), esp. the introduction by Mab Huang and Seymour. The volume contains the texts of many documents of the democratic movement.
54. *Ibid.*, pp. 12–13. For a vivid personal account of the events at the Xidan Wall, see John Fraser, *The Chinese: Portrait of a People* (Toronto, 1980), Chapter 12. See also Garside, *Coming Alive*, Chapter 10.
55. *US Joint Publications Research Service* (JPRS) 73421, 10 May 1979, p. 66.
56. Poon, '*Tatzepao*,' p. 221.
57. For a survey of these journals, see Seymour, *Fifth Modernization*, Introduction. Seymour lists thirty organizations and periodicals in an appendix, p. 291. See also Garside, *Coming Alive*, Chapters 11, 12.
58. *Freedom Appeals*, no. 9 (March–April 1981), pp. 21–4. This included seventeen in Beijing and eleven in Shanghai.
59. Peter Reddaway, 'Policy towards Dissent since Khrushchev', in T. H. Rigby, A. Brown, and P. Reddaway, eds, *Authority, Power and Policy in the USSR* (New York, 1980), pp. 158–92. See also Alexeyeva, *Soviet Dissent*, p. 452.
60. Andrew J. Nathan, *Chinese Democracy* (New York, 1985), pp. 230, 241–4. For discussion of the heyday of the democracy movement, see Nathan, Chapters 1 and 2; also David S. G. Goodman, *Beijing Street Voices: The Poetry and Politics of China's Democracy Movement* (London, Boston, 1981). For the events of 1980 and 1981, see Robin Munro, 'China's Democracy Movement: A Midwinter Spring', *Survey*, xxviii, no. 2 (121) (Summer 1984), pp. 70–98; Jeremy T. Paltiel, 'Recent Dissidence in China', *Studies in Comparative Communism*, xvi, nos 1 and 2 (Spring/Summer 1983), pp. 121–37.

2 Independent Communications in Central Europe

This chapter is based on a paper prepared for a conference at Indiana University, Bloomington, Indiana, 9–11 November 1983, and revised for publication in *Cross Currents: A Yearbook of Central European Culture* (Ann Arbor, Mich., 1985) v, pp. 53–75.

1. Document no. 20/84, 'The Right to Information,' typescript, *Informace o Chartě 77*, December 1984, pp. 1–5; in English, in *Summary of Available Documents*, no. 25, January 1985 (Palach Press Ltd, London), pp. 26–30. For the treatment of Seifert and his works, see Jan Vladislav, 'Poets and power: Jaroslav Seifert', *Index on Censorship*, 14, no. 2 (April 1985), pp. 8–12; *Moravius*, 'What the censors omitted', *Index on Censorship*, 14, no. 4 (August 1985), pp. 15–17.
2. For a collection of documents on censorship, see George Schöpflin, ed., *Censorship and Political Communication in Eastern Europe* (London, 1983). On Poland, see Jane L. Curry, *The Black Book on Polish Censorship* (New York, 1984).
3. György Konrád, 'Censorship in retreat', *Index on Censorship*, 12, no. 2 (April 1983), pp. 10–15.

4. Vilém Prečan, *Kniha Charty* (The Book of the Charter), (Cologne, 1977), pp. 13, 10.
5. Tomasz Mianowicz, 'Unofficial publishing lives on', *Index on Censorship*, 12, no. 2 (April 1983), pp. 24–25.
6. In Poland the independent books were called 'bibula', a term referring to the thin carbon paper originally used. The term 'second circuit' was used to describe the circulation of independent publications.
7. See booklet, *Samisdat, Unabhängige literatur in Osteuropa und der Sowjetunion* (Cologne, 1985), published by Stadtbibliothek Köln and Osteuropäisches Kultur- und Bildungs-Zentrum Ignis.
8. For all three periods, see Helga Hirsch, 'Unabhängiges Publikations-wesen in Polen, 1976–1983', *Osteuropa*, 7 (7 July 1984) (also in part in *Samisdat*, pp. 33–39). For the pre-Solidarity see Joanna M. Preibisz, ed., *Polish Dissident Publications: An Annotated Bibliography* (New York, 1982); also special issue of *Survey*, xxiv, no. 4 (109) (Autumn 1979), in particular Lidia Ciolkosz, 'The Uncensored Press', pp. 56–67; regular summaries of 'Poland's Uncensored Publications', *Radio Free Europe Research* (hereafter *RFE Research*), beginning with iii, no. 16 (9–15 February 1978) and continuing in subsequent issues in 1978, 1979, and 1980. For the Solidarity period, see Chris Pszenicki, 'Polish publishing, 1980–81', *Index on Censorship*, 11, no. 1 (February 1982), pp. 8–11, and *RFE Research, passim*, 1980–81. For post-Solidarity see Ann Sabbat-Swidlicka, 'Poland's Underground Press', *RAD Background Report*, 168 (Poland), *RFE Research* (18 July 1983); Mianowicz, 'Unofficial publishing'; Vincent Wolski, *Le Monde*, 12 December 1984. For briefer analysis, see Jacek Kalabinski, 'The Media War in Poland, the Government vs. the Underground', *Poland Watch*, no. 5 (1984), pp. 63–82. For a detailed study of pre-Solidarity independent activity, see Peter Raina, *Independent Social Movements* (London, 1981), espec. chap. 3, 'The Need for Uncensored Publications'. For more recent surveys of *samizdat* publishing and intellectual activity, see *Reinventing Civil Society: Poland's Quiet Revolution, 1981–1986* (New York: US Helsinki Watch Committee, 1986); Jakub Karpiński, 'Polish Intellectuals in Opposition,' *Problems of Communism*, xxxvi, no. 4 (July–August 1987), pp. 44–57.
9. Preibisz, ed., *Polish Dissident Publications*, p. xxiv.
10. Mianowicz, 'Unofficial publishing', pp. 24–5.
11. Preibisz, ed., *Polish Dissident Publications*. See also Chapter 1 above.
12. *Ibid.*, pp. xxviii–xxxi. For the origins and initial period of NOWa and a list of unofficial publications, see Jan Walc, 'Unofficial publishing', *Index on Censorship*, 8, no. 6 (November–December 1979), pp. 10–14.
13. Mianowicz, 'Unofficial publishing', p. 25.
14. Pszenicki, 'Polish publishing, 1980–81', for the following.
15. *Samisdat*, p. 36.
16. Pszenicki, 'Polish publishing, 1980–81', p. 10.
17. *Samisdat*, p. 37.
18. *Ibid.*, pp. 10, 34, 37–38.
19. For a detailed analysis see Sabbat-Swidlicka, 'Poland's Underground Press'; also Teresa Hanicka, 'Underground Publications in Poland',

RAD Background Report, 132 (Poland), *RFE Research* (26 July 1984). For a partial list (by region) of uncensored periodicals printed underground in Poland as of December 1983, see *Committee in Support of Solidarity Reports* (New York, 1 March 1984). For newspaper accounts, see Michael T. Kaufman, *The New York Times*, 7 February 1985, and Kaufman, 'Polish Writers: The Underground is on Top', *The New York Times, Book Review*, 4 August 1985, pp. 1*ff*.

20. Other periodicals included *Arka* (The Arc) in Cracow, *Obecność* (The Presence) in Wrocław, *Ziarno* (Grain) in Warsaw, *Obraz* (The Picture) in Szczecin, *Preglad Mysli Nieżaleznej* (Review of Independent Thought) in Wrocław; the monthly *Fakty* (Masowsze region); bi-monthly *Spectator*; and *Obóz* (The Camp) which dealt with the countries of the Soviet bloc; *Samisdat*, p. 39; Hanicka, 'Underground Publications in Poland'; Kalabinski, 'The Media War in Poland', pp. 70–3. Still other names are given in the underground newspaper, *Solidarność Gdańsk*, 20 August 1984, *RFE Research*, 10, no. 3, pt 1 (18 January 1985) and in *Tygodnik Mazowsze*, Warsaw, 16 January 1986, *East European Reporter*, 1, no. 4 (Winter 1986), p. 26. For Polish *samizdat* extracts see *RFE Research*, 6 June 1984, *passim*.

21. *RFE Research*, 10, no. 29, pt 2 (19 July 1985); *Index on Censorship*, 15, no. 6 (1986), pp. 24–6.

22. Article by Sejan, *Biuletyn Miedzywydawniczy*, no. 5–6 (1984), in *RFE Research*, 9, no. 39, pt. 3 (28 September 1984).

23. Julian Tynski, *KOS*, no. 54 (7 May 1984); given in *RFE Research* 9, no. 39, pt. 3

24. John Kifner, *The New York Times*, 3 April 1984.

25. *Samisdat*, pp. 28–32. A fuller version of this excellent statement, in English, was given by Raina, *Independent Social Movements*, pp. 48–54, but he replaced the word 'dualist' by what seemed to be the inappropriate 'two-faced'. The Polish original was not available.

26. For the following, Zdena Tomin, 'The typewriters hold the fort', *Index on Censorship*, 12, no. 2 (April 1983), pp. 28–30; Jan Vladislav, 'All you need is a typewriter', *ibid.*, pp. 33–35; H. Gordon Skilling, *Charter 77 and Human Rights in Czechoslovakia* (London, 1981), Chapters 5, 6.

27. Tomin, 'The typewriters hold the fort,' p. 30.

28. Vladislav, 'All you need is a typewriter', pp. 33, 35.

29. Skilling, *Charter 77*, pp. 97, 100, for a detailed classification of these materials.

30. See *Český katolický samizdat 1978–1985* (Czech Catholic *samizdat*, 1978–85), typescript, March 1986, summarized in *Informace o Chartě*, no. 5 (1986), pp. 10–11.

31. Skilling, *Charter 77*, pp. 113–14.

32. Leading article, *Prostor*, 1, no. 1 (June 1982). *Prostor* did not last beyond three issues.

33. George Moldau, 'Samizdatové časopisy v ČSSR' (*Samizdat* journals in ČSSR), *Listy*, XIII, no. 5 (October 1983), pp. 59–61. For summaries of the contents of some of the journals noted, see *Summary of Available Documents* (Palach Press Ltd), espec. no. 26 (May 1986).

34. Skilling, *Charter 77*, pp. 113–14.

35. The rise of *Petlice*, and the choice of name, were both somewhat accidental. When Ivan Klíma wanted to have a manuscript copied for his own use, Vaculík and he agreed to make several copies and to sell the extras, a decision from which developed the idea of a book series. The name *Petlice* (literally, hasp), sprang into Vaculík's mind when he happened to see an advertisement for the official Czechoslovak Writers publishing house, *Edice Klíč* (Key) (private communication, 8 February 1986). The duties of preparing *Petlice* books for publication were later performed by Jiří Gruša and eventually devolved more and more on the authors themselves. During years of intensified repression some sixty volumes appeared without the distinguishing *Petlice* features.

36. Unlike *Petlice, Expedice* books were selected by Havel and were signed by him. During his incarceration many items appeared under the rubric, *Edice Svíce* (Candle). After his release the old title was resumed, but without his signature.

37. A full list of the series is found in Dagmar Suková and Jaroslav Suk, *Naše zavádové psaní* (Our defective writing), *Svědectví*, XVII, no. 66 (1982), pp. 260, 262.

38. Fuller treatment below, Chapter 4.

39. Cited by Skilling, *Charter 77*, p. 116.

40. Petr Fidelius, 'Kultura oficiální a "neoficiální"' (Culture official and 'unofficial'), *Svědectví*, XVII, no. 68 (1983), pp. 685, 682 respectively.

41. Tomin, 'The typewriters hold the fort', p. 30.

42. For the following, see Bill Lomax, 'Hungary, The Rise of the Democratic Opposition', *Labour Focus on Eastern Europe*, 5, no. 3–4 (Summer 1982), pp. 2–7; Bill Lomax, 'Independent Publishing in Hungary', *Index on Censorship*, 12, no. 2 (April 1983), pp. 3–5; Konrád, 'Censorship in retreat'; Anon., 'AB: Hungary's independent publisher', an interview with leading persons of AB, *Index on Censorship*, 12, no. 2 (April 1983), pp. 5–7; Einer Odden, 'Gábor Demszky – interview with non-existent publisher', *Index on Censorship*, 13, no. 4 (August 1984), pp. 17–19; 'Samisdat und Opposition in Ungarn', in *Samisdat*, pp. 47–52.

43. See 'Hungary Profiles – An Interview with Miklos Haraszti', *Labour Focus on Eastern Europe*, 2, no. 6 (January–February 1979), pp. 15–19. Balázs Rab (pseudonym), 'New Hungarian samizdat', *Index on Censorship*, 7, no. 4 (July/August 1978), pp. 37–43, quotation on p. 40; excerpt from *Profile* given in George Schöpflin, ed., *Censorship and Political Communication in Eastern Europe: A Collection of Documents* (London, 1983), pp. 147–54. For summary of the volume on Marx, see Balász Rab, *Index on Censorship*, 7, no. 6 (November/December 1978), pp. 21–5. See also George Schöpflin, 'Opposition in Hungary: 1956 and Beyond', in Jane L. Curry, ed., *Dissent in Eastern Europe* (New York, 1983), Chapter 5.

44. George Schöpflin, 'Opposition and Para-Opposition: Critical Currents in Hungary, 1968–78', in Rudolf L. Tökés, ed., *Opposition in Eastern Europe* (London, 1979) Chapter 5, pp. 142–86, quotation on p. 180; excerpt given also in Schöpflin, ed., *Censorship and Political Communication*, pp. 143–7.

45. Schöpflin, 'Opposition and Para-Opposition', p. 142.

46. Rab, 'New Hungarian samizdat', p. 39.
47. Statement of purpose by Miklos Haraszti, *et al.*, *Index on Censorship*, 12, no. 2 (April 1983), pp. 8–9. The title literally means one who speaks, but is also used to refer to a prison visit.
48. For example, a long article on the future of Eastern Europe, by János Kis, one of the editors, *Beszélö*, May 1982 (*Labour Focus on Eastern Europe*, 5, no. 5–6 (Winter 1982–83), pp. 12–17).
49. *RFE Research*, 9, no. 16 (20 April 1984); *Index on Censorship*, 13, no. 4 (August 1984), pp. 18–19.
50. Anon., 'AB: Hungary's Independent Publisher'; Odden, 'Gábor Demszky'.
51. Elizabeth Heron, interview with György Konrád, *Index on Censorship*, 14, no. 2 (April 1985), pp. 15–16.
52. A poster prepared by L. Rajk and G. Demszky in Budapest in November 1985, entitled *5 Years of Hungarian Samizdat* (*A Magyar Szamizdat 5 Éve*), gave a full bibliography of Hungarian *samizdat* from December 1981 to November 1985.
53. Bill Lomax, 'Samizdat under seige', *Labour Focus on Eastern Europe*, 6, no. 1–2 (Summer 1983), pp. 29–31; Bill Lomax, 'Harassment of Opposition Intensifies', *Labour Focus on Eastern Europe*, 7, no. 1 (Winter 1984), pp. 26–8.
54. As estimated by János Kis: John Kifner, *The New York Times*, 20 November 1983.
55. Pierre Kende, 'Censorship in Hungary', in Zdeněk Mlynář, ed., *Crises in Soviet-Type Systems*, Study no. 9 (Cologne, 1985), pp. 52–3.
56. Vladislav, 'All you need is a typewriter', p. 33. On the difficulties, see Suková and Suk, *Naše zavádové psaní*, pp. 260–1.
57. Odden, 'Gábor Demszky'.
58. Preibisz, *Polish Dissident Publications*; also interview with an underground printer, *KOS*, no. 57 (June 1984), *RFE Research*, 10, no. 3, pt 1 (18 January 1985); interview with head of publishing house, Przedświt, in *Vacat*, no. 15 (March 1984), *RFE Research*, 10, no. 3, pt 1 (18 January 1985).
59. Schöpflin, ed., *Censorship and Political Communication*, pp. 1 *et seq.*, 150–1.
60. For an excellent discussion of official media in the Soviet Union, see Durham Hollander, 'Political Communication and Dissent in the Soviet Union', in Rudolf L. Tökés, ed., *Dissent in the USSR: Politics, Ideology, and People* (Baltimore, 1975), Chapter 7, esp. pp. 236–41.
61. Fidelius, 'Kultura oficiální a "neoficiální"', pp. 682–4.
62. Interview with *Le Monde*, 10–11 April 1983, p. 8; full text in English in *Index on Censorship*, 12, no. 6 (December 1983), pp. 3–6; Czech version, prepared by Havel, *Informace o Chartě 77* (April 1983), pp. 16–22 (also in *Listy*, no. 2 [April 1983], supplement, pp. i–vi).
63. Havel, 'Šest poznámek o kultuře', typescript, 11 August 1984 (also in *Listy*, 14, no. 5 (October 1984), p. 105); English translation, 'Six Asides about Culture', in joint issue of *Kosmas*, 3, no. 2 (Winter 1984), and 4, no. 1 (Summer 1985), pp. 39–48.
64. Kende, 'Censorship in Hungary', pp. 52–3.

65. Jacek Kalabinski, at a conference at Yale University (*The New York Times*, 27 May 1984).
66. Konrád, 'Censorship in retreat', p. 15.

3 Dissent and Charter 77

This Chapter and Chapter 4 are based on H. Gordon Skilling, 'Independent Currents in Czechoslovakia', *Problems of Communism*, XXXIV, no. 1 (January 1985), pp. 32–49.

1. Václav Havel, 'Moc bezmocných' (Power of the Powerless) (October 1978), included in a *samizdat* symposium, *O svobodě a moci* (On Freedom and Power), which was published abroad under the same title (Cologne: 1980). An English version, edited by John Keane, appeared later under the title, *The Power of the Powerless; Citizens Against the State in Central–Eastern Europe*, by Václav Havel *et al.* (London, 1985; Armonk, NY, 1985). For further details, see Chap. 6 below. Citations are from Keane, pp. 57–61, 64–7, modified from the Czech original, pp. 29–32, 35–8.
2. For the first five years, see H. Gordon Skilling, *Charter 77 and Human Rights in Czechoslovakia* (London, 1981). See also an essay by Vilém Prečan, in *Vývoj Charty, Záznam z konference ve Franken* (The Charter's Progress; Record of a Conference in Franken), (Cologne: Index, 1981). For the tenth anniversary, see Vilém Prečan, ed., *Ten Years of Charter 77* (Hanover, W. Germany, 1987); fuller Czech version in Prečan, ed. *Deset Let Charty 77* (Cologne, 1987). For events leading up to Charter 77, see V. Havel in his *Dálkový výslech* (Cross-Examination from Afar) (*Edice Expedice*, 1986), pp. 106–19. He did not reveal who drafted the declaration but ascribed the name Charter 77 to Pavel Kohout.
3. Charter document no. 2, 1 January 1985, to which was appended the text of the original Charter 77 declaration.
4. These lists, as well as letters of withdrawal, were published in the bulletin, *Informace o Chartě 77*, henceforth cited as *Infoch*.
5. Among the first one thousand signatories, the proportion of workers was about 40 per cent (Skilling, *Charter 77*, pp. 40–1). In later listings, signatories who called themselves workers numbered 30 (of a total of 44) (27 April 1981); 21 (of 36) (5 February 1982); 21 (of 37) (3 March 1983); 11 (of 25) (7 February 1984); 16 (of 27) (20 May 1985); 19 (of 25) (1 October 1986); 7 (of 13) (28 December 1986); 4 (of 10) (5 April 1987); 9 (of 18) (30 June 1987) 6 (of 15) (30 September). In these lists some were pensioners or did not identify themselves by type of work.
6. For biographical sketches of spokesmen up to 1987, see Prečan, ed., *Ten Years*, pp. 103–9; also *Radio Free Europe Research*, 12, no. 6 (February 13, 1987), pt. I.
7. Skilling, (*Charter 77*, pp. 118–20; Ann Ward, *East European Reporter* (London), 1, no. 1 (Spring 1985), pp. 22–4.
8. *Infoch*, 1986, no. 13; also VONS communiqué no. 713, *ibid.*, 1987, no. 18.

9. VONS communiqué no. 455, 11 June 1985. Of the sixty persons given in the VONS summary report, no. 400 (8 November 1984), the amnesty related to only twenty-nine.
10. Skilling, *Charter 77*, pp. 86–94, 331–6. For a full list of Charter documents to the end of 1986, see Prečan, ed., *Ten Years*, pp. 53–93; also *RFE Research*, 12, no. 31 (7 August, 1987, pt. I. English translations, in full or in summary form, are available in the *Bulletin* and the *Summary* of *Available Documents* (the title varies), published irregularly by the Palach Press Ltd., London. The documents are usually given in Czech in *Listy* (Rome). A rich collection of Charter 77 materials is located in the Thomas Fisher Rare Books Library, University of Toronto.
11. Charter 77 document no. 3, 6 January 1987.
12. *Ibid.*; also 'Doing without utopias; An interview with Václav Havel', *Times Literary Supplement*, 23 January 1987, p. 82.
13. Skilling, *Charter 77*, pp. 43–51, 66–77, 181–3. See Jan Kavan, 'Czechoslovak Opposition Since 1968'. *Poland Watch* (Washington DC), 1984, no. 5, and 1985, no. 2, especially the latter, pp. 123–8. For documents, see *Labour Focus on Eastern Europe*, 2, no. 3 (July–August 1978) pp. 9–18.
14. Skilling, *Charter 77*, pp. 77–80, n. 15; texts of statements, see *Svědectví*, xv, no. 58 (1979), pp. 257–76; *Labour Focus on Eastern Europe*, 3, no. 2 (May–June 1979), pp. 16–21.
15. Toronto: Sixty Eight Publishers, 1983.
16. Document no. 14, 1984; commentaries, *Infoch*, 1985, nos. 1 and 3; document no. 4, 1985.
17. See Charter document no. 11, 20 May 1984; a later statement by the authors (n.d.), *Infoch*, 1985, no. 3, pp. 9–17; criticism of the 'four', dated 25 June 1984, partial text given in Charter document no. 16, 26 September 1984; later statement by the four, 27 March, 1985; See below, chap. v, for further discussion and for the relevant contributions.
18. Document no. 4, 14 February 1985.
19. Criticism by Ota Ulč, *Infoch*, 1986, no. 2; statement of the Council of Czechs and Slovaks in South Africa, and Charter document no. 4, 1986, in reply (*ibid.*, 1986, no. 4).
20. Briefly reported in *Infoch*, 1986, no. 2, p. 9. Havel did not sign, but was reported to have associated himself with the declaration with some reservations.
21. Both letters of 1 December were published in the *New York Review of Books*, 23 January 1986 (*Infoch*, 1986, no. 2). The letter to Ortega was given in *Infoch*, 1985, no. 12, pp. 33–4; also in *Listy*, xvi, no. 1 (February 1986), pp. 11–12; *East European Reporter*, 1, no. 4, (Winter 1986), pp. 34–5.
22. The initial Council letter and Charter 77's reply were given in full in *Infoch*, 1985, no. 12. The final statement of the latter was contained in document no. 19, 16 June 1986. For the first three communications between the Council and Charter 77 see *Czechoslovak Newsletter* (New York), x, no. 12 (111) (December 1985), pp. 1–5. For the controversy, see also Jan Kavan, 'Chartists and Nicaragua', *East European Reporter*, 1, no. 4 (Winter 1986), pp. 34–5.

23. A full text of the discussion was given in *Informace o Chartě 77* (May 1986). Havel's contribution, 'Dvě poznámky o Chartě 77' (Two Comments on Charter 77), was published separately, *Listy*, XVI, no. 4 (July 1986), pp. 1–3.

24. In a reply to the Council of Free Czechoslovakia, the spokesmen had stated that Charter 77 was neither 'left' nor 'right' and no spokesman representing a 'clan' opinion could dominate the others; each spokesman had in effect a veto over decisions although each would respect the others. When someone accepted the office, he would not strive to effect the views of his own 'clan' but would feel bound by 'a more subtle authority' arising from his decision to serve. See document no. 19, 1986.

25. For the international aspects of Charter 77, see Skilling, *Charter 77*, Chapter 8.

26. Document no. 29, 22 October 1982. For other proposals along similar lines, see Skilling, *Charter 77*, pp. 153, 163, and Charter documents no. 14, 1982, no. 7, 1985, and no. 9, 1986.

27. Document no. 39, 14 November 1983; no. 43, 30 December 1983. For a full treatment of the Madrid conference, see H. Gordon Skilling, 'The Madrid Follow-up', in Robert Spencer, ed., *Canada and the Conference on Security and Cooperation in Europe* (Centre for International Studies, University of Toronto, 1984), Chapter 8.

28. Document no. 7, 20 March 1985.

29. Document no. 24, 25 September 1985; translation, *RFE Research*, 10, no. 42, pt 2 (18 October 1985).

30. *A Besieged Culture, Czechoslovakia Ten Years after Helsinki*, edited by A. Henka, F. Janouch, V. Prečan, and J. Vladislav (Stockholm and Vienna, 1985). On Budapest, see *Index on Censorship*, 15, no. 1 (January 1986), pp. 51–4; F. Janouch, 'Two Cultural Fora in Budapest,' *Listy*, XV, no. 6 (December 1985), pp. 48–51; *ibid.*, supplement, XVI, no. 5 (October 1986).

31. Document no. 14, 2 May 1986.

32. Document, no. 18, 19 June 1986.

33. Document no. 31, 30 October 1986; no. 55, 25 September 1987.

34. Document no. 20, 20 August 1985; also no. 47, 1 August 1987.

35. Document no. 11, 22 May 1985. For other documents on this theme, see Skilling, *Charter 77*, pp. 156–7; documents no. 19, 1982, no. 18, 1983, and no. 10, 1984.

36. *Infoch*, February 1984, pp. 2–3; *ibid.*, March 1984, pp. 14–15. For earlier co-operation with KOR, see Skilling, *Charter 77*, pp. 172–3, 277–9. See also Jan Józef Lipski, KOR, *A History of the Workers' Defense Committee in Poland, 1976–1981* (Berkeley, 1985, pp. 278–85). For the texts of the messages from Solidarity (n.d.), and from the commissions (May), see *Infoch*, 1986, no. 9, pp. 7–11; in English, Palach Press Ltd., *Bulletin*, no. 27, November 1986, pp. 70–9. On the circle, *RFE Research*, 12, no. 28 (17 July), pt 1. For the text of the August 1987 meeting, *ibid.*, 12, no. 35 (4 September 1987), pt 2.

37. Issued in Budapest, East Berlin, Prague, and Warsaw on 18 October 1986; full text in English, *East European Reporter* 2, no. 2 (n.d.). This

appeal was later endorsed by the European Parliament (23 October 1986), *Infoch*, 1986, No. 13, p. 25.

38. The most important Charter documents on peace were listed in the original version of this chapter in *Problems of Communism* (see above, p. 247), pp. 46–47. For an analysis of 'Charter 77' relationship to questions of peace and to the contemporary peace movement', see Vilém Prečan, in Czech, in Milan Schulz, ed., *Mír, mirové hnutí, křesťanská etika* (Peace, the Peace Movement and Christian Ethics) (Munich, 1984), pp. 75–100.

39. *Cf.* the phrase 'one of the important human rights' in document no. 25, 1982. This was wrongly translated as 'that most basic of human right' (*sic*) in Jan Kavan and Zdena Tomin, eds, *Voices from Prague, Czechoslovakia, Human Rights and the Peace Movement* (London: European Nuclear Disarmament and Palach Press Ltd., (1983), p. 26.

40. Document no. 20, 1983. See collection, *Sborník, Charta 77 o míru* (Symposium, Charter 77 on Peace) (Prague, 1983). Some of these documents were included in *Voices from Prague*. For the texts of joint statements, see document no. 24, 1983. See also report of an attempted rendezvous in Prague with representatives of French and Dutch peace movements, also interrupted by the police (Charter document no. 5, 1984).

41. *The Times* (London), 23 June 1983.

42. Charter documents, no. 38 and 39, 1983.

43. *Infoch*, January 1984, p. 14.

44. *Ibid.*, November 1984, p. 17.

45. *Ibid*, 1985, no. 5, pp. 10–11.

46. Document no. 9, 1 May 1984, and no. 13, 30 June 1984. For criticisim by Petr Uhl, see *Infoch*, October 1984.

47. Document no. 13, 30 June 1984. Partial text or summary given in *RFE Research*, 9, no. 33 (17 August 1984) and no. 36 (7 September 1984); Palach Press Ltd., *Bulletin*, no. 25 (December 1984), pp. 19–25.

48. Text given in *Infoch*, September 1984, pp. 15–17; proceedings described *ibid.*, October 1984, pp. 5–9; *The New York Times*, 20 July 1984; *RFE Research*, 9, no. 33 (17 August 1984).

49. *Infoch*, 1985, no. 4, pp. 1–2; English version, *East European Reporter*, 1, no. 1 (Spring 1985), pp. 27–8.

50. For comments on the Prague Appeal, see successive issues of *Infoch*, from 1985, no. 5, *et seq.*, and of *Komentáře*, 1985, no. 2, *et seq*. For Czechoslovak social democracy abroad, see *Právo lidu*, 1985, no. 2. For a sharp critique of the Appeal by a former party leader, Čestmír Císař, a non-Chartist, see Laureatus (pseudonym), 'To wish or not to wish?' *samizdat*, April 1985, and by Petr Valentík, of the Czechoslovak Socialist Party (*Infoch*, 1985, no. 5, pp. 3–4). For a defence of the Prague Appeal, see J. Šabata, 'A democratic and revolutionary identity for today's Left', *Diskuse*, July 1985; English summary, *SAD*, no. 26 (May 1986), pp. 27–34.

51. Letter by Tominová to friends at home, 6 August 1985, *Infoch*, 1985, no. 9, pp. 14–18; *Listy*, xv, no. 5 (October 1985), p. 13. For V. Havel's personal letter to Amsterdam, 'The Anatomy of Reticence', *ibid.*, xv, no. 2 (April 1985), supplement; full text in English in *Cross Currents:*

Yearbook of Central European Culture (Ann Arbor, Mich., 1986), v, pp. 1–23.

52. *Infoch*, 1986, no. 1, pp. 8–10. An outgrowth of the demonstration was Mladé umění pro mír (Young Art for Peace), an organisation which had the support of 500 and requested approval by the National Front, but gave up its efforts after police repression (*Infoch*, 1986, no. 8, p. 18).

53. Document, no. 7, 6 March 1986.

54. *Infoch*, 1986, no. 11, pp. 4–7; 1986, no. 13, pp. 24–5.

55. There is a brief summary of the Milan appeal in *ibid.*, 1986, no. 4, p. 10, together with an excerpt from a text by L. Hejdánek, who suggested that an independent peace movement, outside Charter 77, be formed.

56. Charter document, no. 13, 25 April 1986, with two supplements; in English, *East European Reporter*, 2, no. 1 (Spring 1986), pp. 23–7. For the longer statement, see *Infoch*, 1986, no. 6. Luboš Kohout and Petr Uhl, who signed, also issued separate statements.

57. For text of joint statement, see *Infoch*, extraordinary number, November 1986; see also *ibid.*, 1986, no. 7, p. 17; *ibid.*, 1986, no. 9, pp. 19–21. English text in *East European Reporter*, 2, no. 2 (1986), pp. 52–60.

58. Charter 77 document no. 2, 1 January 1985.

59. Citations in this and the following paragraph from *ibid.*

60. *The Times* (London), 25 June 1985. See also H. Gordon Skilling, 'Charter 77 – The International Impact', in Prečan, ed., *Ten Years*, pp. 32–51.

61. Prečan, *Vývoj Charty*, p. 18.

62. Document no. 2, 6 January 1987. English text in *RFE Research*, 12, no. 3 (23 January 1987), pt. 1, pp. 9–19.

63. Document no. 3, 6 January 1987. For other appraisals of the ten years of Charter 77, see V. Havel, 'The Meaning of Charter 77,' in Prečan, ed., *Ten Years*, pp. 7–31; an interview with seven Charter activists, 'The Growth of Independent Activity', *Labour Focus on Eastern Europe*, 9, no. 2 (July–October 1987), pp. 39–43. For discussion of Document no. 3, see Ivan Dejmal; letter of forty signatories; Martin Palouš; Luboš Vydra (*Infoch*, no. 6, 10, 11, 12, 1987 respectively).

4 Other Independent Currents

This, and the preceding chapter, were based on my 'Independent Currents in Czechoslovakia,' cited at the beginning of Chapter 3 above.

1. Charter document, no. 2, 1985.

2. For Havel's use of this phrase, see above, Chapter 3, n. 1.

3. For details, see H. Gordon Skilling, *Charter 77 and Human Rights in Czechoslovakia* (London, 1981), pp. 110–17, and Chapters 1 and 2 above. See also Zdena Tomin, 'The Typewriters hold the fort', *Index on Censorship*, 12, no. 2 (April 1983), pp. 28–30; Jan Vladislav, 'All you need is a typewriter', *ibid.*, pp. 33–5.

4. Charter document no. 17, 11 October 1984.

5. For religious *samizdat*, see the collections at Keston College, Keston,

Kent, England; for Petlice and Charter 77 materials, the collections in the Thomas Fisher Rare Books Library, University of Toronto. The richest archive of independent literature, built up by Dr. Vilém Prečan, is housed in the Documentation Centre for the Promotion of Independent Czechoslovak Literature in Scheinfeld, West Germany.

6. See Chapter 1, pp. 9–11; 2, pp. 35–7 above.
7. Ludvík Vaculík, *Český snář* (Czech Dreambook) (Toronto, 1983).
8. Vladislav, 'All you need is a typewriter', pp. 34–5. See also V. Prečan, 'Tajný čtenár, tajný kritik, tajný vydavatel' (Secret reader, secret critic, and secret publisher), in Jan Vladislav, *Male morálity* (Small moralities) (Munich, 1984), pp. 146–7.
9. Ivan Klima, 'Variations on eternal themes', *Listy*, XII, no. 3–4 (July 1982), pp. 30–1.
10. Miroslav Červinka, "Two Observations on Samizdat', *Kritický sborník*, 1985, no. 4, pp. 1–12.
11. *Ibid.*
12. 'A forgotten question-mark on unpublished (ineditní) literature', signed *p.f.*, *ibid.*, 1983, no. 2, pp. 94–7; The author refers to an earlier article, signed *n*, 'Question-marks on unpublished (ineditní) literature', *ibid.*, 1982, no. 4. pp. 29–36. Both articles are given in English in *Acta*, 1, no. 1 (Spring 1987), pp. 20–8 (published by Documentation Centre, fn. 5).
13. Ladislav Hejdánek, 'Offering a variety of views', *Index on Censorship*, 15, no. 3 (March 1986) pp. 25–6; Kathleen Wilkes, 'Unofficial Education in Czechoslovakia', *Government and Opposition*, 16, no. 2 (Spring 1981), pp. 167–84. See also Skilling, *Charter 77*, pp. 114–15.
14. Karel Kyncl, 'A Censored Life', *Index on Censorship*, 14, no. 1 (February 1985), pp. 137–42.
15. Jindřich Chalupecký, 'The Lessons of Prague', *Cross Currents*, IV (1985), pp. 323–34.
16. Skilling, *Charter 77*, Chapter 1.
17. Document no. 13, 1977, text given in *ibid.*, pp. 252–6; document no. 31, 1983, summarised fully in *Západ* (Ottawa), 5, no. 6 (December 1983), pp. 1–4.
18. Eighty-five young people in Moravia demanded the release of Jirous and others in a letter of 31 August 1983 (*Infoch*, August 1983, pp. 3–4).
19. For an explanation of the procedures for licensing rock bands and a classification of official and unofficial musical groups, see Mikoláš Chadima, *Od Rekvalifikace k 'Nová vlně se starým obsahem'* (From Relicensing to the 'New Wave with old content') *samizdat*, 1984–85, p. 727. See also his anonymous *samizdat* essay, *Česká Neoficielní rock ová scéna* (The Czech Unofficial Rock Scene) (Prague, January 1986). See below (Chapter 7) for Chadima's severe critique of Ivan Jirous' theory of the 'underground.'
20. Recordings were produced and distributed abroad by Boži mlýn, Toronto, Canada, and by Šafrán, in Frankfurt am M., Germany. For the Plastic People and the underground culture, see 'Banned in Bohemia', containing an interview with V. Brabenec and an article by Ivan Jirous, *Index on Censorship*, 12, no. 1 (February 1983), pp. 30–4.

21. For the following, see Charter document no. 31, 1983, and a report by the Jazz Section (see below), in *Západ* (Ottawa), 5, no. 4 (August 1983), pp. 16–21, under the name of Mary Novák, and later articles by Vladimir Burke, *ibid.*, 5, nos 5 and 6 (October and December 1983): 6, no. 5 (October 1984). For a detailed analysis of the Jazz Section, see Josef Škvorecký, 'Hipness at Noon', *The New Republic*, no. 3648, 17 December 1984, pp. 27–35; also Škvorecký, 'Hipness at Dusk,' *Cross Currents*, 6, (1987), pp. 53–62. For a full summary of JS activity and the result of an enquiry among its members as to their attitudes to it and to music in general, see *Jaci jsme* (Who Are We?), published on the 15th anniversary of its founding in 1986, *Edice Dokumenty* no. 4.

22. Škvorecký, 'Hipness at Noon', p. 28.

23. An archive of the Jazz Section, including most of its publications, is deposited in the Fisher Rare Book Library, University of Toronto.

24. Jan Krýzl, '"New" Wave with old content', *Tribuna*, no. 12, 23 March 1983 (also in *Západ*, October 1983, pp. 1–2); Z. Bakešová, *Rudé právo*, 30 March 1983.

25. *Edice Dokumenty*; text given also in *Západ*, October 1983, pp. 2–6.

26. *Západ*, December 1983, p. 4.

27. 43/10/88, December 1985. For the contents of the bulletin, see *Summary of Available Documents* (Palach Press Ltd., London) no. 26, May 1986, pp. 45–7. See also Michael T. Kaufman, *The New York Times*, 5 March 1986; *Infoch*, nos 4, 5, and 6, 1986.

28. *Infoch*, nos 2 and 3, 1986.

29. The concert was in December 1984; the trial in December 1985. The second trial was held in April 1986. See VONS no. 509, 21 March 1986, and no. 523, 12 May 1986 (*Listy*, xvi, no. 4 [July 1986], pp. 36, 38–9). For a description of an 'independent evening' of music and verse in a country inn, see NM, 'Underground? Druhá kultura?' *Listy*, xv, no. 4 (July 1985), pp. 27–30.

30. Vaclav Havel, *Dálkový vyslech* (Cross-examination from Afar), *samizdat*, Prague, 1985–6, p. 156.

31. See the joint statement by Charter 77 and VONS (no. 24, 1986) and the VONS communiqués (nos 467, 508, 559, 607); also Burke, *Západ*, no. 6 (December 1986); *Jaci jsme*, pp. 48–51. For the verdicts, see *The New York Times*, 13 March 1987.

32. Jiří Lederer, 'Charta 77 a Křestané' (Charter 77 and Christians), *Studie* (Rome), vi, (no. 84) (1982), pp. 581–86; in English, *Religion in Communist Dominated Areas* (henceforth RCDA)' xxi, nos. 7, 8, 9 (1983), pp. 104–7. See also Pedro Ramet, 'Religious Ferment in Eastern Europe', *Survey*, 28, no. 4 (Winter 1984), pp. 93–7; Alexander Tomsky, 'Modus Moriendi of the Catholic Church in Czechoslovakia', *Religion in Communist Lands*, 10, no. 1 (Spring 1982), pp. 23–54, with appendices; Mary Hrabik-Samal, 'Religion in Central Europe', *Cross Currents*, v (1986), pp. 46–51.

33. Josef Rabas, 'K církevnímu vývoji v Československu' (On Church developments in Czechoslovakia), *Studie*, iii–iv (nos 93–4), (1984), pp. 217–31.

34. Anon., 'The Church at the Crossroads', *Religion in Communist Lands*, 13, no. 3 (Winter 1985), pp. 250–60.
35. See the revealing speech, part of which was published in *Informaci o církvi*, 1985, no. 9, pp. 10–13, by Karel Hrůza, former head of the Secretariat for Church Affairs in the government.
36. Lederer, 'Charta 77 a Křestané', pp. 585–6.
37. See the letter of 23 April 1983, signed by 3397 Catholics and Protestants to Cardinal Tomásek protesting the country-wide harassment by the police of members of the orders in March 1983. See Charter documents, no. 8, 3 March 1982, on the limitation of freedom of conviction, including religious faith; no. 11, 10 March 1982, on the persecution of priests, believers, and others; no. 22, 8 July 1982, on the use of article 178 of the criminal code for the prosecution of clergymen; no. 21, 12 December 1984, on the situation of the religious orders. For detailed documentation of Catholics and Protestants and Charter 77, see V. Prečan, *Křestané a Charta '77* (Christians and Charter 77) (Cologne, 1980); also Skilling, *Charter 77*, pp. 50, 108, 287–88 on Protestants; pp. 55–56, 107–08, 288–90, on Catholics. See also Ann Ward, 'New Wave of Religious Persecution in Czechoslovakia', *Eastern European Reporter*, 1, no. 4 (Winter 1986) (*sic*, 1985), pp. 41–2. On the illegal church, see Tomsky, 'Modus Moriendi' p. 36, and appendices, pp. 40–42.
38. Detailed reports of the trial on 28 May 1986 in *Informace o církvi*, no. 6, 1986, pp. 8–18, and supplement, 16 pp. ; VONS communiqués, no. 522 and 530.
39. Interviews with Cardinal Tomásek, by Bradley Graham, *Washington Post National Weekly Edition*, 28 May 1984, p. 17, and by James M. Markham, *The New York Times*, 5 April 1984.
40. See Alexander Tomsky, '"Pacem in Terris" Between Church and State in Czechoslovakia', *Religion in Communist Lands*, 10, no. 3 (Winter 1982), pp. 274–82. For the two earlier letters, see Tomsky, 'Modus Moriendi,' pp. 39–40, 43. The Cardinal's letters were not published but were circulated in *samizdat*, for instance in *Informace o církvi*. For his letter on Pacem in Terris, see *Infoch*, October 1982, pp. 3–4; also *RCDA*, XXI, nos. 10, 11, and 12 (1982), p. 172. The letters of 1985 were given in *Informace o církvi*, No. 1, 1985. The 1986 memorandum was published only more than a year later in *Informace o Chartě*, 8, 1987, pp. 26–7.
41. English translation in *Czechoslovak Newsletter* (Washington, DC), VIII, no. 7/8 (82/83) (July–August 1983). The speech was surprisingly given in full text in *Katolické noviny*, 24 July 1983.
42. Prečan, *Křesťané*, J. Zveřina *et al.*, pp. 102 *passim*; Skilling. *Charter 77*, pp. 49–51, 108.
43. For the Velehrad events, see *Die Presse* (Vienna), 8 July 1985; *Informace o církvi*, 1985, no. 8; V. Benda, 'Znovu křesťanství a politika: jak dál po Velehradě?' (Once Again Christianity and Politics; What Next after Velehrad?) (typescripts, July–September 1985).
44. For the Protestants, see Skilling, *Charter 77*, pp. 50, 108, 287–88; Prečan, *Křesťané*, especially letter of criticism of regime measures by thirty-one Evangelicals, 7 May 1977, pp. 118–40; letter of criticism of the synod by

B. Komárková, 26 July 1977, pp. 152–61. See also *Radio Free Europe Research* 11, no. 29 (18 July 1986), pt 1. Two private communications from former pastors were also available as sources.

45. *Infoch*, 1985, no. 12, p. 36. See the criticism of the missile resolution by M. Rejchrt, in November 1983, *Summary of Available Documents*, no. 24 (July 1984), pp. 67–8.

46. On Dus, see VONS communiqué, nos. 541, 515, 527; *Infoch*, 1986, no. 9, pp. 12–13; on Keller, VONS communiqué, no. 541.

47. Skilling, *Charter 77*, pp. 54–8. See M. Kusý, 'Slovenský Fenomén', *Obsah*, June 1985 (*Listy*, xv, no. 5 [October 1985] pp. 28–36).

48. See below, Chapter 7.

49. *Informace o církvi*, 1986, no. 6, p. 17 (no date).

50. *Ibid.*, 1986, no. 5, pp. 6–8; *Infoch*, 1986, no. 12, p. 20; *Radio Free Europe Research*, 11, no. 32 (8 August 1986), pt 2.

51. Copies were sent to the Secretary General of the United Nations, the Pope, and other public and church personages in Czechoslovakia.

52. See Charter 77 document, no. 37, 28 December 1982; VONS communiqués, nos 317, 327, and 375; *Infoch*, July–August 1984, pp. 23–5; *ibid.*, 1985, no. 11, p. 21; documents nos 24, 25 (*Infoch*, no. 5, 1987). See also *ibid.*, no. 6, pp. 8–10.

53. Kusý, 'Neslovenský fenomén' (Non-Slovak phenomena), *samizdat*, n.d.

54. For a detailed analysis of the results of the poll, see Zdeněk Strmiska, 'Výsledky nezávislého průzkumu současného smýšlení v Československu' (Results of an independent survey of contemporary thinking in Czechoslovakia), *Svědectví*, xx, no. 78 (1986), pp. 265–334, to which is attached a list of all questions. For a good summary, see *Radio Free Europe Research*, 11, no. 32 (8 August 1986), pt 2.

55. Strmiska, 'Výsledky', p. 334. This was calculated on the basis of answers to questions 21–7.

56. Document no. 2, 1985.

57. Prečan, *Vývoj Charty, Záznam z konference ve Franken* (The Charter's Progress: Record of a Conference in Franken) (Cologne, Index, 1981) p. 27.

58. Václav Havel, 'Acceptance Speech', Stichting Praemium Erasmianum, (Amsterdam, 1986).

5 Independent Historiography Reborn

Published originally under the title 'The Muse of History – History, Historians and Politics in Communist Czechoslovakia', in *Cross Currents: A Yearbook of Central European Culture* (Ann Arbor, Mich, 1984), III, pp. 29–47. This article was published in Polish translation, in *samizdat*, in *Czas* (Poznan), 1985, nos 4–5, pp. 7–16 ('Muza historii 1984'); also in Czech, shortened, in *150,000 slov, Texty Odjinud*, IV, no. 10 (1985), pp. 24–31.

1. *Listy*, v, no. 5 (July 1975), pp. 32–43; in English, *Survey*, 21, no. 3 (Summer 1975), pp. 167–90; also in *Encounter* September 1975, pp. 14–29. Citations from *Survey*, pp. 183–4.

2. Miroslav Kusý, 'Slovak som a Slovak budem . . .' (I am and shall remain a Slovak), typescript, n.d. (*Listy*, xii, no. 6 (December 1982), pp. 46–49).

3. Milan Šimečka, 'Naš soudruh, Winston Smith' (Our Comrade, Winston Smith), afterword to George Orwell, *1984* (typescript), 1981–3; Orwell, *1984* (Cologne, Index, 1984), in Czech. References are to the latter, and to Orwell, *Nineteen Eighty-Four* (London, 1954).

4. Andrew Rossos, 'Czech Historiography', in two parts, *Canadian Slavonic Papers*, xxiv, no. 3 (September 1982), pp. 245–60; xxiv, no. 4 (December 1982), pp. 359–85. Citations from pp. 369, 379.

5. Masaryk, as President, wrote an article critical of Pekař under a pseudonym, 'Č.P.' (Československý President), which was published in *Česka mysl*, Spring 1932.

6. For the above, see Vilém Prečan, *Acta Creationis, Independent Historiography in Czechoslovakia 1969–1980; Unabhängige Geschichtsschreibung in der Tschechoslowakei 1969–1980*, published by V. Prečan (Hannover, 1981), foreword by Prečan, in German. English translation of foreword was published separately in Hannover, 1981. See especially pp. xiii–xvi (German). See the detailed analysis of the politicisation of history in Peter Heumos, 'Geschichtswissenschaft und Politik in der Tschechoslowakei', *Jahrbücher für Geschichte Osteuropas*, 26, no. 4 (1978), pp. 541–76.

7. Rossos, 'Czech Historiography,' pt ii, p. 384.

8. Vladimir Kusin, *The Intellectual Origins of the Prague Spring: The Development of Reformist Ideas in Czechoslovakia* (Cambridge, 1971), pp. 76–81, especially pp. 78–9.

9. Stanley Z. Pech, 'Ferment in Czechoslovak Marxist Historiography', *Canadian Slavonic Papers*, x, no. 4 (Winter 1968), p. 502.

10. The phrase is from Rossos, 'Czech Historiography', pt ii, p. 385. For a full treatment of the renascence, see Pech, 'Ferment', pp. 502–22. See also H. Gordon Skilling, *Czechoslovakia's Interrupted Revolution* (Princeton, NJ, 1979), pp. 102–6; Kusin, *Intellectual Origins*, pp. 76–81; Karel Bartošek, 'Czechoslovakia: The State of Historiography', *Journal of Contemporary History*, ii, no. 1 (1967), pp. 143–55.

11. Kusin, *Intellectual Origins*, p. 76.

12. Pech, 'Ferment', pp. 512–13.

13. *Ibid.*, pp. 516–17; Skilling, *Czechoslovakia's Interrupted Revolution*, p. 106.

14. For fuller details, see Pech, 'Ferment', and Skilling, *Czechoslovakia's Interrupted Revolution*; Kusin, *Intellectual Origins*; and Bartošek, 'Czechoslovakia: The State of Historiography'. See also Heumos, 'Geschichtswissenschaft und Politik', pp. 557*ff*.

15. Prečan, *Acta Creationis*, p. xix (German).

16. Z. A. B. Zeman, *Prague Spring: A Report on Czechoslovakia* (Harmondsworth, UK, 1968), p. 129.

17. Pech, 'Ferment', p. 522.

18. *Sedm pražských dnů, 21–27. srpen 1968, Dokumentace* (Prague: Czechoslovak Academy of Sciences, Historical Institute, 1968). It was later

published in several foreign languages, including English: Robert Littell, ed., *The Czech Black Book* (New York, 1969).

19. For a description of the preparation of the book, see an interview with Prečan and Otáhal (*Reportér*, 3, 23 January 1969), and Prečan's letter to Gustáv Husák (24 August 1971), given in Vilém Prečan, *Die Sieben Jahre von Prag, 1969–1976* (Frankfurt, 1978). For the subsequent indictment and Soviet intervention, *ibid.*, pp. 21, 55–6, 67–70.

20. *Acta Persecutionis, A Document from Czechoslovakia; Ein Dokument aus der Tschechoslowakei* (San Francisco, 1975). This was a biographical directory in English and German of dismissed historians.

Prečan's personal appeal to the world congress reinforced the impact of *Acta Persecutionis*. In a letter to his fellow historians he eloquently described the conditions under which he and his colleagues suffered and explained why he had decided to try to emigrate after six years of enforced scholarly idleness. In words which well expressed the attitude of those he later had to leave, he wrote: 'I wanted to remain an historian, convinced . . . that an historian must remain loyal to his duties and responsibilities under all circumstances. That he must go on working whatever the circumstances prevailing. This conviction is based on the justified belief that an historian is irreplaceable and indispensable' (typescript, Prague, July 1975). The full text is given in *Listy*, v, no. 7 (December 1975), pp. 31–4; English text in *Index on Censorship*, 4, no. 4 (Winter 1975), pp. 253–7; German text in Prečan, *Sieben Jahre*, pp. 214–22.

For a detailed discussion of the fate of the social sciences, including history, under normalisation, see Vratislav Prošek and Jiří Žemla (pseudonym for V. Prečan), 'Společenské vědy ve svěraku "konsolidace"' (Social Sciences in the Straitjacket of 'Consolidation'), *Listy*, IV (August 1974), pp. 24–8; (October 1974), pp. 39–44; (December 1974), pp. 34–7; v (February 1975), pp. 38–42; 'Společenské vědy v udobí 1948–68', *Svědectví*, XIII, no. 52 (1976), pp. 654–60. These articles appeared first in *samizdat*. See also Vilém Prečan, 'Pogrom of historians', *Index on Censorship*, 15, no. 4 (April 1986), pp. 24–8.

21. Jaroslav Purš, 'Historiographie čelem k budoucnosti' (Historiography Faces the Future), *Tvorba*, no. 39, 26 September 1979, p. 11.

22. J. Haubelt, *Československý časopis historický*, XXVIII, 6 (1979), pp. 907–915. This was a review of Kutnar, *Přehledné dějiny českého a slovenského dějepisectví* (A Survey History of Czech and Slovak Historiography), 2 vols (Prague, 1973, 1977).

23. These included V. Prečan, Karel Kapan, and Michael Reiman, and later Jan Tesař, Karel Durman, Jan Mlynárik, and Karel Bartošek.

24. Václav Havel, *O svobodě a moci* (On Freedom and Power), typescript, Prague, 1979, later published in English, V. Havel, *et al.*, *The Power of the Powerless*, edited by John Keane (London and Armonk, NY, 1985), p. 39 *passim*.

25. Šimečka, 'Naš soudruh, Winston Smith', p. 282 (Orwell, *Nineteen Eighty-Four*, p. 26).

26. Prečan, *Acta Creationis*, pp. 2–3.

27. The two preceding paragraphs are from my article, 'Independent

Historiography in Czechoslovakia', *Canadian Slavonic Papers*, xxv, no. 4 (December 1983), pp. 522–3. References are to Prečan, *Acta Creationis*, German version.

28. For my review article of the first eight issues of the historical journal (each had a different title), see *ibid*., pp. 518–39. This article later appeared in Czech translation in *samizdat: Kritický sborník*, 1985, no. 1.
29. J. Křen and H. Mejdrová, 'Současná československá historická literatura o Mnichovu' (Contemporary Czechoslovak Historical Literature on Munich), *Historické a sociologické studie, Sborník*, typescript, January 1982.
30. For these and the following articles, see Skilling, 'The Muse of History', cited above, p. 255, nn. 29–33.
31. J. Jablonický, 'Povstanie v Trnave' (The Uprising in Trnava) (January 1982), pp. 44–79. Jablonický was dismissed from the Slovak Historical Institute in 1973, and ultimately charged under the criminal code for writings harmful to the interests of the state. For his case see an essay by Prečan, in German and English, in Prečan, *Acta Creationis*, pp. 221–37.
32. J. César and Z. Snítil, *Československá revoluce 1944–1948* (The Czechoslovak Revolution 1944–8) (Prague, 1979), citations from pp. 161, 168. Review by J. Borovanský, *Studie československých dějin, Sborník* (December 1980), typescript. See also my review article, 'Independent Historiography,' pp. 33–4.
33. See table, pp. 110–11, for full list of titles of journals and other *sborníky*.
34. *Sborník ke dvoustému výročí tolerančního patentu*, edited by Milan Machovec (1981). Citations from Machovec, pp. 382, 385.
35. Milan Machovec, Petr Pithart, and Josef Dubska, eds, *T. G. Masaryk a naše současnost* (typescript, 1980), pp. 759. For my review article, see *Cross Currents*, II (1983), pp. 87–113. For English summaries of the symposium, see V. Prečan, *T. G. Masaryk and Our Times* (Hannover, 1986).
36. Otáhal, 'Význam bojů o Rukopisy' (The Significance of the Manuscript Struggles), *Současnost*, pp. 66–99. The text in English is given in *Cross Currents*, V (1986), pp. 247–77, under the title 'The Manuscript Controversy in the Czech National Revival'. See also the detailed work by Jaroslav Opat, *T. G. Masaryk v Čechách v letech osmdesátých/1882–1891/Příspěvek k životopisu* (T. G. Masaryk in Bohemia in the Eighties (1882–1891) A contribution to a Biography) (*samizdat*, 1985) 425 pp. published later abroad by Index under the title *Filozof a Politik – T. G. Masaryk 1882–1893* (Cologne, 1987).
37. Printed in Berlin, 1985; place of publication or names of editors not given. Karel Bartošek wrote an introductory essay, 'Historians making history', vol. 1, pp. 1–10. For a letter to Stuttgart written by twenty-six exiled historians (names not given), see *Listy*, xv, no. 5 (October 1985), pp. 56–7.
38. For the above and the following paragraph, see the introduction to the special issue of *Kosmas*, 'Real Socialism in Czechoslovakia and the Search for Historical Truth', by H. Gordon Skilling and Vilém Prečan, eds, *Kosmas*, 3, no. 2, and 4, no. 1 (Winter 1984/Summer 1985).

Abbreviated text in *Index on Censorship*, 15, no. 4 (April 1986), p. 25.

39. Anon., *Osmašedesátý: pokus o kritické porozumění historickým souvislostem* (Sixty-Eight: An Attempt at a Critical Understanding in a Historical Context), typescript, Prague, June 1977–August 1978. Later published abroad with the same title under the pseudonym, J. Sladeček (Index, Cologne, 1980); second edition under the author's real name, Petr Pithart (Rozmluvy, London, 1987).

40. See H. Gordon Skilling, 'Sixty-eight in Historical Perspective', *International Journal*, XXXIII, no. 4 (Autumn 1978), pp. 678–701.

41. Jan Příbram, 'Příbeh s nedobrým koncem' (An Event with a Not So Good Ending), *Svědectví*, XIV, no. 55 (1978), pp. 371–95. See response by Václav Šikl, *ibid.*, no. 56 (1978). See also an article by Petr Pithart (*ibid.*, no. 59) and subsequent controversy (*ibid.*, nos. 60, 61).

42. *Osmašedesátý*. See my review, on which the following paragraphs are based, in *Slavic Review*, 38, no. 4 (December 1979), pp. 663–6.

43. Jiří Hájek, *Dix ans après, Prague 1968–1978* (Paris, 1978).

44. Vladimir Kadlec, *Dubček – 1968: Československá specifická cesta k socializmu* (Dubček – 1968: A Czechoslovak Specific Path to Socialism), *samizdat*, April 1985; in shorter form, *Dubček – 1968* (Knižnice Listů, Cologne, 1986).

45. Zdeněk Jičinský, 'Poznámky na okraj některých hodnocení Pražského jara 1968 a k aktuálním problémům s tím spojeným' (Marginal notes on some evaluations of the Prague Spring of 1968), *Ze zásuvky i z bloku*, VII, n.d.; also in *Diskuse*, no. 38 (May 1986). See also Zdeněk Jičinský, *Vznik české národní rady v době Pražského jara 1968 a její pusobení do podzimu 1969* (The Rise of the Czech National Council at the time of the Prague Spring 1968 and its Operations to the Fall of 1969) (Prague, 1983–4), 181 pp.

46. Luboš Kohout, *Kritické poznámky k literatuře v roce 1968 v Československu* (Critical remarks on the literature dealing with the year 1968 in Czechoslovakia) (Prague, 1985), 273 pp.

47. The replies were published by Charter 77 in June 1986 under the title *O odpovědnost v politice a za politiku* (On Responsibility in politics and for politics). See below, Chapter 6 for further discussion. Šabata's reply was entitled 'On sixty-eight and eighty-six' and was dated June 1986.

48. Danubius, 'Tézy o vysídlení československých Němcov' (Theses on the Re-Settlement of the Czechoslovak Germans), typescript, December 1977, published later in shorter form in *Svědectví*, XV, no. 57 (1978), pp. 105–122.

49. Jan Mlynárik, 'List kolegovi historikovi' (Letter to a Colleague Historian), *Svědectví*, XVII, no. 68 (1983), pp. 699–704, especially pp. 703–4; his letter in the same issue, *ibid.*, pp. 838–40; Mlynárik, 'Danubius je črné svědomí národa' (Danubius is the Black Conscience of the Nation), *Národní politika*, Munich, March 1983. Mlynárik denied that he was a 'Czechophobe' and claimed that he wrote out of love for the Czech nation.

50. For this controversy, see successive issues of *Svědectví*, XV, nos. 58 and 59 (1979); no. 60 (1980); XVI, no. 61 (1980). For the debate in the ranks of exiled social democracy, see *Právo lidu*, Zürich, 83, nos 1 and 3

(1980). Two collections of essays, one for and one against the transfer, were issued in *samizdat*: *K dějinám českoněmeckých vztahů* (On the History of Czech–German Relations), 1980, 212 pp.; issued also in German in *samizdat*, *Zur Geschichte der deutsch–tschechischen Beziehungen*. *Sammelschrift* (Prague, 1980); *O odsunu Němců z Československa* (On the Transfer of Germans from Czechoslovakia), typescript, 1981, 370 pp. For a detailed analysis of the entire controversy, including its historical background, and the texts of the Bohemus article and the Mlynárik Theses in German, see Leopold Grünwald, ed., *Wir haben uns selbst aus Europa vertrieben, Tschechische Selbstkritik an der Vertreibung der Sudentendeutschen, Eine Dokumentation* (Munich, 1985), 160 pp.; Leopold Grünwald, ed., *Sudetendeutsche – Opfer und Tater* (Vienna, 1983), pp. 89–110. For other sources on the controversy, see my article in its original form, cited on p. 255, above.

51. Individual contributions to the debate included the following: Milan Hübl, 'Glosy k Danubiovým tézím o vysídlení Němců' (Some Glosses on the Danubius Theses on the Resettlement of the Germans), typescript, 2 April 1979 (shortened, *Svědectví*, xv, no. 58 (1979), pp. 387–96); Luboš Kohout, 'Kritické poznámky k tézím "Danubia"' (Critical Observations on the Danubius Theses), typescript, 8 March 1979 (*ibid.*, no. 59, pp. 565–69). For later essays, see Milan Hübl, 'Dodatečné glosy k Danubiovi' (Additional Glosses on Danubius), typescript, 3 July 1979; Milan Hübl, 'Nad dosavadním průběhem diskuse o odsunu čs. Němců' (On the Further Course of the Discussion on the Transfer of the Czech Germans), typescript, April 1980; Luboš Kohout, 'K "dopisu přiteli"', dopis no. 4/44, Dr. Hejdánek' (On a 'Letter to a Friend'), typescript, n.d.; 'Kritické poznámky k stanoviskům O. Filipa' (Critical Observations on O. Filip's Standpoint), n.d. (*Svědectví*, xvi, no. 61 (1980), pp. 179–82); Bohemus, 'Slovo k odsunu' (A Word on the Transfer), *Pravo lidu*, no. 1, 1980; Hejdánek, 'Dopis přiteli' (Letter to a Friend), no. 4/44, 10 March 1979 (typescript).

52. Hübl, 'Glosy k Danubiovým tézím,' *Svědectví*, pp. 387, 389–92.

53. Kohout, 'Kritické poznámky', *ibid.*, pp. 566–8.

54. Statement by L. Hejdánek and J. Hájek, 26 May 1979, *Informace o Charte 77*, 8 (1979), p. 15; statement by P. Uhl, 29 March 1979, *ibid.*, 4 (1979), p. 12 (also in *Svědectví*, no. 58, pp. 405–6).

55. For the above, see Mlynárik, 'List kolegovi historikovi', pp. 703–4. For a later account of the episode, see Mlynárik, 'K osudu Tézi o výsídlení československých Němců' (On the fate of the Thesis on the resettlement of the Czechoslovak Germans), *Svědectví*, xix, no. 75 (1985), pp. 685–711.

56. For earlier relevant documents, see above, Chapter 3, n. 17. The debate included contributions from professional historians M. Hübl, L. Kohout, J. Křen, J. Mezník, R. Malý, and two historians in exile, J. Tesař and J. Mlynárik, as well as others, Petr Uhl, J. Šabata, J. Jehlička, and P. Pithart. Their essays circulated in *samizdat*, and were given in full or in part in *Infoch*, July–August 1984 to no. 7, 11 May–3 June 1985. Some were published in the journal *Střední evropa*, from no. 1 on, and in two volumes edited by Milan Hübl, *Hlasy k českým dějinám* (Voices on

Czech history), i–ii (Prague, 1984–5). See also *Svědectví*, xix, no. 75 (1985), pp. 593–609. For a brief sketch of the controversy, see Zdenek Kavan, *East European Observer*, 1, no. 2 (Summer 1985), pp. 39–41; for the Charter document and some of the contributions to the debate, see *Summary of Available Documents* (Palach Press, London), no. 24 (July 1984), pp. 41–3; no. 25 (January 1985), pp. 13–26; no. 26 (May 1986), pp. 7–18.

57. For instance, J. Křen, 24 March 1985; the 'four', 27 March 1985 (typescript), and Charter document no. 15, 1985. See especially P. Pithart, 'Smlčeti zlato' (Silence is Golden), *Kritický sborník*, 1985, no. 2, pp. 91–99. See also Pithart's earlier essay, 'Šetřme své dějiny!' translated into English as 'Let Us Be Gentle to Our History', *Kosmas*, 3, no. 2/IV, no. 1 pp. 7–22. In the latter essay, Pithart called for 'a calmer and wiser attitude' and the seeking out of 'a shared historical consciousness'. He expressed similar views in his 'History, campaigns and national self-consciousness', n.d., published in *Pojetí českých dějin* (see n. 58).

58. See, for instance, *Pojětí českých dějin, sborník* (Concepts of Czech History, A Collection), Vol. i (Brno, January 1986). The volume contains interpretative historical essays by Erazim Kohák, Petr Pithart, Jaroslav Mezník, Milan Otáhal, and others.

59. Šimečka, 'Naš soudruh, Winston Smith', p. 301.

60. *Ibid.*, p. 282 (cited from Orwell, *Nineteen Eighty-Four*, p. 26). *Cf.* his essay 'Black Holes, Concerning the Metamorphoses of Historical Memory', *Kosmas*, special issue, 3, no. 2, and 4, no. 1 (Winter 1984/Summer 1985), where he refers to 'historians eliminating the black holes, that is, segments of history cloaked in total darkness, devoid of life, of persons, of ideas' and finding in these holes 'a meaningful heritage for the future and the present' (pp. 24–5).

61. Kusý, 'O čistote historického remesla', written for Josef Jablonický's fiftieth birthday, Bratislava, typescript, 1 March 1983, pp. 15, 18, and 21; in English, 'On the Purity of the Historian's Craft', *Kosmas*, special issue 3, no. 2, and 4, no. 1 (Winter 1984/Summer 1985), pp. 29–38. See also Kusý, 'Mravný zmysel historickej pravdy' (The Moral Sense of Historical Truth), typescript, n.d.

62. Havel's Letter to Husák, *Survey*, pp. 185–9.

6 Parallel Politics

1. Václav Havel, 'The power of the powerless', in John Keane, ed., *The Power of the Powerless, Citizens Against the State in Central–Eastern Europe*, by Václav Havel *et al.* (London, 1985; Armonk, N.Y., 1985) p. 49.; in Czech, *O svobodě a moci* (Cologne, 1980), p. 37. Translations have been modified according to the Czech original. For more on this book, see below, no. 9.

2. *Ibid.*, pp. 49, 79 (English); pp. 37, 66 (Czech).

3. The following two paragraphs were taken from H. Gordon Skilling and

Vilém Prečan, *Parallel Politics: Essays from Czech and Slovak Samizdat* (henceforth *Parallel Politics*), published as a special issue, *International Journal of Politics*, XI, no. 1 (Spring 1981), introduction, pp. 4–5.

4. H. Gordon Skilling, *Charter 77 and Human Rights in Czechoslovakia* (London, 1981), pp. 43–9.

5. Skilling and Prečan, *Parallel Politics* (n. 3) contained six essays from *samizdat*. The authors were Jan Patočka, Milan Šimečka, Miroslav Kusý, Rudolf Battěk, and Jan Tesař.

6. Skilling, *Charter 77*, p. 106. The following two paragraphs were taken from Skilling and Prečan, *Parallel Politics*, pp. 7–8.

7. Skilling, *Charter 77*, pp. 172–3.

8. Comment by Z. Bujak, cited by S. Lukes, in Keane, ed., *Power of the Powerless*, pp. 12–13.

9. In *samizdat* the book had a sub-title, *An International Collection of Essays on the Meaning of Independent Civic Initiatives in the Countries of the Eastern Bloc*, and was described as Part I, by Czech and Slovak contributors. It was published abroad in Czech under the same main title, (Cologne, Index, 1980) and was still identified as Part I. This edition included all the contributors to the *samizdat* volume, including Zdenek Mlynář, in exile after 1977, and also an earlier essay by Václav Benda, 'Paralelní polis'. The original *samizdat* manuscript was used by the present author in preparing his book, *Charter 77*. This important volume was not published in any foreign language (except Swedish, 1981) until 1985 when it finally appeared in English in book form (Keane, ed., *Power of the Powerless*), and simultaneously in *International Journal of Politics*, XV, nos 3–4 (1985). The English version included only ten of the original essays and omitted those by J. Dienstbier, L. Dobrovský, Z. Mlynář, J. Němec, Petr Pithart, J. S. Trojan, and Z. Vokatý. Havel's introductory essay was published earlier in French and Italian (1979), German (1980), Swedish (1981), and in Polish *samizdat*, *Krytyka*, 1980, no. 5 (also in *Krytyka* (London), 1982, no. 5).

10. *O odpovědnost v politice a za politiku* (June 1986). Included were responses by V. Benda, K. Čejka, J. Dienstbier, V. Havel, E. Kantůrková, R. Palouš, Z. Pokorný, J. Šabata, J. Šimsa, P. Uhl, and J. Vydráŕ; also the letter of the young Christians. Text of the latter also given in *Svědectví*, XX, 77 (1986) pp. 30–32.

11. The publication of the collected works of Patočka in *samizdat* and abroad in Czech is under way in Prague and in Vienna. Coordination and publication of these works is in the hands of the Documentation Centre for the Promotion of Independent Czechoslovak Literature, in Scheinfeld, West Germany. Eleven volumes are now planned; many of them are already edited and ready for printing. These will include Patočka's works on art, culture, ancient philosophy, phenomenology, philosophy of history, Czech history, Comenius, T. G. Masaryk, etc. Selected works in German and English are also contemplated and under way. For a full description of the Patočka project, see *Acta* published by the Documentation Centre for the Promotion of Independent Czechoslovak Literature (Scheinfeld, 1987), 1, no. 1 (Spring 1987). For Patočka's life and an obituary, see Skilling, *Charter 77*, pp. 20–3, 235–44.

12. Václav Havel, *Dálkový výslech* (see n. 20 below), pp. 114–15. Patočka's reluctance was not due to personal considerations, but to his belief that Professor V. Černý should be chosen.
13. 'What Charter 77 Is and What It Is Not', 7 January 1977 (Skilling, *Charter 77*, pp. 217–19) citations on pp. 218–19; 'What Can We Expect of Charter 77?,' 8 March 1977 (*ibid.*, p. 222).
14. Patočka, *Kacířské eseje o filozofii dějin* (Heretical Essays on the Philosophy of History) (Petlice, 1975); also Arkýř, Munich, 1980. The final chapter was published in Czech in *Svědectví*, XIII, no. 51 (1976) pp. 435–48; in English, trans. by Karel Kovanda, 'Wars of the Twentieth Century and the Twentieth Century as War', *Telos*, no. 30 (Winter 1976–7). References are to the English version.
15. 'Heroes of Our Times' (1986), republished in *Dialogy* 1, no. 3. 1979; English text, translated by Paul Wilson, *Parallel Politics*, pp. 10–15. For the meaning of the Czech words, 'otřesaní' and 'otřesení', from which the English word, 'shattered', is derived, see n. 3 and *passim*.
16. 'Pokus o českém národní filozofii a jeho nezdar', in Patočka, *Dvě studie o Masarykovi* (Petlice, 1977, 227 pp.). The first study is given in English translation by Mark Suino, in Milič Čapek and Karel Hrubý, eds, *T. G. Masaryk in Perspective* (1981), pp. 1–22. References in this and the following are to the translation, modified by the author.
17. Patočka, 'České myšlení v meziválečném období', (1976), given in Milan Machovec, Petr Pithart, and Josef Dubský, eds, *T. G. Masaryk a naše současnost* (T. G. Masaryk and Our Times), *samizdat*, 1980.
18. *Výslech*, pp. 9, 171.
19. Interview with J. Lederer in 1975, *O lidskou identitu*, p. 241; also in Lederer, *České rozhovory* (Cologne, 1979).
20. For a complete collection of Havel's writings between 1969 and 1979, together with a chronology of his life and bibliography of his plays, see Vilém Prečan and Alexander Tomský, eds, *Václav Havel, O lidskou identitu* (Rozmluvy, London, 1984). See also Havel's long interview with Karel Hvížďala, conducted by letter and tape between Bonn and Prague, *Dálkový výslech* (Cross Examination from Afar), Edice, no. 233 (Bonn–Prague, 1986), 175 pp.; also his interview, 'Doing Without Utopias', *Times Literary Supplement*, (23 January 1987), pp. 81–3. For Havel's political writings and essays about him, see Jan Vladislav, ed., *Václav Havel or Living in Truth* (London, 1986). See also the collection of his writings since 1983, edited by Vilém Prečan, *Václav Havel: Do různých stran. Sborník esejů, článků a rozhovorů z let 1983–87* (forthcoming, Cologne, 1988).
21. *Survey*, 21, no. 3 (Summer 1975), pp. 167–90; Skilling, *Charter 77*, p. 54; Havel, interview with Lederer in *O lidskou identitu*, pp. 223–37; text of letter, *ibid.*, pp. 19–49.
22. 'Last Conversation', 1 May 1977, Skilling, *Charter 77*, pp. 242–4.
23. *O lidskou identitu*, p. 237; *Výslech*, p. 166.
24. *Ibid.*, p. 126; Havel, *Dopisy Olze* (Letters to Olga) (Toronto, 1985), pp. 342 (English edition forthcoming 1988). For a fresh and original treatment of his prison experience, totalitarianism, and non-political politics, see Havel, 'Doing without Utopias', pp. 81–2.

25. *Power of the Powerless*, pp. 22–96, citation on p. 39.
26. For more on this theme, see Chapter 8 and 9 below.
27. Dated February 1984; in Czech, 'Politika a svědomí', *Listy*, XIV, no. 4 (July 1984), pp. 44–51; in English, 'In Search of Central Europe: Politics and Conscience', *The Salisbury Review*, 3, no. 2 (January 1985), pp. 31–8, citation on p. 35.
28. In Czech, 'Anatomie jedné zdrženlivosti', *Svedĕctví*, XIX, no. 75, 1985, pp. 569–91; *Listy*, XV, 2, 1985, supplement, pp. *iii–xii*; in English, 'An Anatomy of Reticence', *Cross Currents*, 5, 1986, pp. 1–23.
29. Havel's 'Reply to Young Christians', dated 12 November 1985, was published in *Obsah* (Prague), January 1986; also in *Odpovĕdnost* (see n. 10), pp. 56–61; also *Výslech*, pp. 16, 82–86.
30. *Příbeh a totalita*, typescript, n.d.; also in *Svĕdectví*, XXI, no. 81, 1987, pp. 21–43.
31. His earlier books were *Sociálne utópie a utopisti* (Social utopia and the utopians) (Bratislava, 1963) and *Krize utopizmu: O kontinuite a vyústení utopickych názorov* (The Crisis of Utopianism: The continuity and climax of utopian opinions) (Bratislava, 1967). For his life and thoughts from 1969 on, see his correspondence with Vilém Prečan, in Prečan (ed.), *Die Sieben Jahre von Prag, 1969–1976* (Frankfurt am Main, 1978).
32. It appeared in Czech under this title, with a subtitle, used in the original *samizdat: A contribution to the typology of real socialism* (Cologne, 1979). It also came out in French, Italian, and German, and in Polish *samizdat*, and finally, seven years later, in English, *The Restoration of Order, The Normalization of Czechoslovakia, 1969–1976* (London, 1984), trans. A. G. Brain. See also Skilling, *Charter 77*, pp. 53, 56, 112–13. For a full bibliography of his *samizdat* writings and their foreign translations up to 1984, see a second Czech edition (Rozmluvy, London, 1984), pp. 219–21. Šimečka was an author of many feuilletons, some of which, written in 1984, were collected in *Kruhová obrana* (All-round defence) (Cologne, 1985).
33. *Společenství strachu*, dated April 1979, published abroad in Czech, and in French, German, Italian, and English, the last-named in Skilling and Prečan, *Parallel Politics* (see n. 3 above), pp. 16–38. *Cf.* Skilling, *Charter 77*, p. 54.
34. *Naš soudruh, Winston Smith* (Our Comrade Winston Smith) in *samizdat*; published as an epilogue to George Orwell, *1984* (Cologne, 1984), pp. 257–324; in German, in Norbert Leser, ed., *Macht und Gewalt in der Politik und Literatur des 20. Jahrhundert* (Wien, 1985), pp. 292–362.
35. This essay, 'Svĕt s utopiemi nebo bez nich?' (A World With Utopias or Without Them?), dated October 1982, was published in Peter Alexander and Roger Gill, eds, *Utopias* (London, 1984), Chapter 14, pp. 169–77. It also appeared in the *samizdat* journal, *Kritický sborník*, I, 1984. *Cf.* Havel, 'Doing without Utopias', p. 82.
36. For fuller treatment, see Orwell, *1984* (Czech), Chapter 10, pp. 321–3.
37. *Ztráta skutečnosti* (Loss of Reality), originally circulated in *samizdat*, was included in the typewritten work by Kusý and Šimečka and later published abroad, see n. 43 below.

38. See also Kusý's essay, written for Šimečka's 50th birthday, 'On Civic Courage', *Parallel Politics*, pp. 39–51.
39. *Power of the Powerless*, pp. 152–77. Text in Slovak, 'Charta 77 a reálny socialismus', *Svědectví*, XVI, no. 59, pp. 423–43. See also S. Lukes, *Power of the Powerless*, pp. 16–17; Skilling, *Charter 77*, pp. 178–82.
40. 'On being a Marxist in Czechoslovakia', also in *Obsah*, January–February, 1985; *Listy*, XVI, no. 2 (April 1986), pp. 18–20.
41. *Obsah*, September 1984.
42. Dated the end of May 1983, with a supplement on June 15; *Listy*, XIV, no. 1 (February 1984), pp. 28–34. This essay was included in the Kusý–Šimečka book (discussed below, as published abroad, in n. 43).
43. The original *samizdat* version appeared in Bratislava in the Spring of 1980. It was later published abroad under the title, *Európska skúsenosť s reálnym socializmom* (The European Experience with Real Socialism) (Naše Snahy, Toronto, 1984). An Italian publication, *Il Grande Fratello e la Grande Sorella, ovvero la società della paura* (Bologna, 1982) contained an essay by Kusý under the same title as the book, and the two essays on fear and civic courage cited above (notes 33, 38). For the dialogue, in English, *Cross Currents* (Ann Arbor, Mich.), VI, 1987, pp. 249–74.
44. *Európska skúsenost*, pp. 85–100.
45. For these, see Skilling, *Charter 77*, p. 38, n. 14. For a criticism of his role after 1948, see the journal of the Social Democratic Party, *Právo lidu* (Wuppertal, West Germany) no. 1, 1985; for a defence of his present role by Chartists, see *ibid.*, no. 2, 1986.
46. *Dix ans après, Prague 1968–1978* (Paris, 1978); see also above, Chapter 5.
47. For his career and his role in Charter 77, see Skilling, *Charter 77*, pp. 26–8, and *passim*.
48. For text of his 'Human Rights, Peaceful Co-existence and Socialism' (17 February 1977), see Skilling, *Charter 77*, pp. 223–29; for his essay, 'The human rights movement and social progress'. *Power of the Powerless*, pp. 134–40. See also 'Lidská právo jako podstatná součást míru' (Human Rights as an Essential Component of Peace), published in German, in *Osteuropa, Die Achtung der Menschenrechte als Bestandteil einer Friedenspolitik*, 32, no. 3 (March 1982), pp. 177–87; 'Lidská právo a mírové soužití' (Human Rights and peaceful coexistence) (typescript) March 1977.
49. 'Několik poznámek ke Shromaždění END v Amsterdam, 1986' (Some Remarks for the END Assembly in Amsterdam in 1986), *Komentáře*, Summer 1985, pp. 1–4.
50. See the booklet published in three languages by the Czechoslovak Social Democratic Party, *The 'case' – Le 'cas' – Der 'Fall', Rudolf Battěk, Documents and comments* (Zürich, 1981).
51. 7 April 1978, text in Skilling, *Charter 77*, pp. 290–2; also letter to Socialist International, 1 July 1978, *ibid.* pp. 292–4.
52. Rudolf Battěk, *Politologické teze*, typescript, 21 March 1978.
53. 'O principu politické plurality' (On the Principle of Political Plurality), *Dialogy*, II, no. 8–9, 1978; in English, *Parallel Politics*, pp. 75–84.

54. 'Duchovní hodnoty, nezávislá aktivita a politika' (Spiritual values, independent initiatives, and politics), April 1979, given in English, in *Power of the Powerless*, pp. 97–109.
55. Battěk, *Eseje z ostrova* (1977); Battěk, *Strast z nekonečna* (Anxiety over the Infinite) (1983–5).
56. Battěk, *John Baker, Civilian Evangelist or Satirical Preacher* (1983–5). See also Karel Kyncl, 'John Baker, The Evangelist', *Index on Censorship*, 15, no. 1 (January 1986), pp. 17–20; *Listy*, xv, no. 6 (December 1985), pp. 41–3.
57. *Le Socialisme emprisonné, Une alternative socialiste à la normalisation* (Paris, 1980); *Die Herausforderung, eine sozialistische Alternative zur 'Normalisierung' in der CSSR* (Frankfurt, 1981); *Program společenské samosprávy* (Programme of social self-management) (Cologne, 1982). The essay, *Czechoslovakia and Socialism*, was given in full in the Czech version and in abbreviated form in the German and French editions. For Uhl's career, see *Herausforderung*, a foreword by Jean-Yves Touvais and his interview with Uhl, pp. 11–33; for Uhl's response to the young Christians, see n. 59 below; Skilling, *Charter 77*, p. 49 *passim*.
58. *Power of the Powerless*, pp. 188–97.
59. *Samizdat*, dated 1985, revised 1986. Text in *Diskuse*, no. 37, April 1986; also in *Odpovědnost* (n. 10), pp. 115–33.
60. English text given in *Labour Focus on Eastern Europe*, 9, no. 7. For a full description of the system and its development from 1948 to the present, see *Herausforderung*, pp. 65–126; *Program*, pp. 33–57, 58–75. See the ten point description of the system in *Czechoslovakia and Socialism*, in *Program*, pp. 207–9.
61. *Herausforderung*, pp. 128–47; *Program*, pp. 85–90. In the latter part of 'The Alternative Community', Uhl expands on the role of parallel communities (see Chapter 9).
62. *Herausforderung*, pp. 149–215; *Program*, pp. 99–73.
63. For the text of *Paralelní polis* (dated 17 May 1978) see V. Prečan, *Křesťané a Charta '77* (Christians and Charter '77) (Cologne, 1980), pp. 68–76; also *O svobodě a moci* (see n. 1) pp. 101–7. See Skilling, *Charter 77*, pp. 75–6, 183–4; also Chapter 9 below.
64. 'Katolicismus a politika – kořeny a perspektivy dnešní situace' (Catholicism and Politics) (dated January 1979), *Power of the Powerless*, pp. 110–24.
65. 'Papež Karol Wojtyla, Katolická Církev a Svět' (Pope Karol Wojtyla, the Catholic Church and the World), in *samizdat*, *Čtverec*, no. 1, 1979; also in *Studie* (Rome), 1, no. 67, 1980, pp. 1–10.
66. 'Znovu křesťanství a politika; jak dál po Velehradě' (Christianity and Politics Once More; After Velehrad What?) *samizdat*, July–September 1985; also in *Střední evropa*, iv, November 1985. Benda had written an earlier essay on this theme which had been seized by the police. See above, Chapter 4.
67. *Odpovědnost* (n. 10 above) pp. 15–28. Benda, in an essay, 'O problémech nejen morálních' (On problems that are not just moral), presented his views on contraception, divorce, and abortion, strongly opposing all

three, but admitting the right of the state to forbid only abortion. (Easter, 1985); also *Kritický sborník*, no. 2, 1985.

68. *Dopisy příteli* (*Petlice*, 1977, 1978 and 1979); also published in a single volume for all three years, (1980?) which contains a complete listing of the letters at the end. For a full text of a letter dealing with Charter 77 (no. 20, 18 May 1977), Skilling, *Charter 77*, pp. 229–33; see also *ibid.*, p. 121, n. 3, for a list of some of his letters. A German edition of his letters, *Briefe an einem Freund* was to appear in 1987 (Munich).

69. 'Perspectivy demokracie a socialismu ve východní Evropě' (Prospects for democracy and socialism in Eastern Europe), in English, *Power of the Powerless*, pp. 141–51. On socialism, see *Dopisy*, no. 4, 3 March 1977; no. 13 (34), 10 August 1978.

70. On socialism and Christianity, *Dopisy*, no. 17 (39), 2 November 1978.

71. *Power of the Powerless*, p. 149.

72. 'Socialismus včera, dnes and zítra' (Democracy Yesterday Today and Tomorrow), dated 1982, *Kritický sborník*, no. 3. 1983.

73. For the following, see *Dopisy*, no. 6, 19 March 1977; no. 3 (24), 2 February 1978; also no. 7 (28), 6 April 1978; no. 15 (36), 21 September 1978. For more abstract discussion of politics and its relationship to philosophy, see his essay, in a dialogue with R. Battěk, under the title, 'O souvislost filosofie a politiky' (On the connections between philosophy and politics), *Dialogy*, I, no. 2, 1977; and an essay dedicated to Karel Kosík on his fiftieth birthday, 'Reflexe v politice a otázka politického subjektu/O místo filosofie v politickém životě' (Reflection in politics and the political subject, On the place of philosophy in political life), n.d. *samizdat*. See also letters no. 14 (35), 31 August 1978, and no. 15 (36), 21 September 1978. For discussion of religion in politics, see *Křestanství v dnesním světě* (Christianity in the Modern World), *Dialogy*, no. 6–7, June–September 1978, with Miloš Rejchrt and Rudolf Battěk. See also *Dopisy*, nos 10 and 15, 1977.

74. Hejdánek discussed the concept of 'non-political politics' also in letter no. 5 (45), 29 March 1978, dealing with morality and politics and in no. 6 (46), 19 April 1979, with the citizen's participation in politics. On independent activities, see *Dopisy*, no. 4, 16 February 1978 and no. 5, 2 March 1978. See also Skilling, *Charter 77*, pp. 70, 71.

75. E.g., under the pseudonym, J. Sladeček, (Charta 77; Síla slabých' (Charter 77; Power of the Weak), 25 June 1977, published in shorter form under the title 'Nečekání na Godota' (Not to wait for Godot), *Svědectví*, XIV, no. 54, 1977, pp. 193–207; 'Diza-rizika' (Dissi-Risks), 28 February 1979, *O svobodě a moci*, pp. 269–86. For his book on 1968 and for his historical essays, see Chapter 5 above, note 39.

76. See Chapter 3, pp. 31–33; Dienstbier, *Snění o Evropě* (Dreaming of Europe), n.d., 1986?

77. For earlier writings, see *Profily/Jaroslav Šabata* (1980). For his articles on Charter 77 and its reform, see Skilling, *Charter 77*, *passim*; on the Prague Appeal, see Chapter 3 above, pp. 63–5 and n. 50. For his reply to the young Christians, see Chapter 5 above, p. 116 and n. 47.

78. 'Misto "dissidentů" na politické mapě dneška' (The Place of 'Dissidents' on Today's Political Map), 28 February 1979, *O svobodé a moci*, pp. 227–

56. See also his earlier study of the Prague Spring, *Československý pokus o reformu 1968* (The Czechoslovak Attempt at Reform in 1968) (Cologne 1975) and his book published in exile, *Mráz přichází z Kremlu* (Frost Comes from the Kremlin) (Cologne 1978); in English *Night Frost in Prague, The End of Humane Socialism* (New York 1980).

79. 'Nové šance svobody', in *O svobodě a moci*, pp. 257–68; also *Dopisy z Ruzyně* (Letters from Ruzyně, (Prague, 1980).

80. *Obrana politiky* (n.d. 1978?), which also appeared in *Dialogy*, II, nos 8–9, (1978); in English, trans. Paul Wilson, in *Parallel Politics*, pp. 52–74. See also his 'Svoboda a důstojnost člověka' (Freedom and Dignity of Man), March 1978, *O svobodě a moci*, pp. 307–318. Both essays were included in Trojan, *Studie 1975–1978* (*samizdat*, Prague, 1979).

81. These paragraphs are taken from *Parallel Politics* (pp. 52–74).

7 A Second Society: A Theoretical Framework

1. For a full analysis of the concept 'totalitarianism', as developed in Eastern Europe before and after 1968, see Jacques Rupnik, 'Le Totalitarisme vu de l'Est', in G. Hermet, ed., *Totalitarismes* (Paris, 1984), pp. 43–71.

2. Aleksander Smolar, 'Le Monde Soviétique: Transformation ou décadence?' in Hermet, ed., *Totalitarismes*, pp. 43–71.

3. John Keane, ed., *Civil Society and the State, New European Perspectives* (London and New York, 1988), which includes Keane, 'Despotism and Democracy: The Origins and Development of the Distinction Between Civil Society and the State, 1750–1850'.

4. Jacques Rupnik, 'Dissent in Poland, 1968–78', in Rudolf Tökes, ed., *Opposition in Eastern Europe* (London, 1979), Chapter 6, p. 60.

5. Z. A. Pelczynski, 'Solidarity and the Re-Birth of Civil Society in Poland 1976–1981', in Keane, ed., *Civil Society and the State*.

6. Andrew Arato, 'Civil Society Against the State: Poland, 1980–81', *Telos*, no. 47 (Spring 1981), pp. 23–48.

7. Andrew Arato, 'Empire vs. Civil Society: Poland, 1981–82', *Telos*, no. 50 (Winter 1981–2), pp. 19–48, especially pp. 22–6. Arato's articles, although scholarly studies, are marred by the use of sometimes obscure theoretical models and by his own advocacy of the theories and courses which ought to have been adopted by the Poles. Curiously, too, he cited none of the Czech or Slovak dissidents (but only the exiled Pelikan) and missed the entire Czechoslovak discussion of an independent or parallel society, in particular the analysis of civil society by Jan Tesař. See below, n. 9.

8. Kasimierz Wojcicki, 'The Reconstruction of Society', *Telos*, no. 47 (Spring 1981), pp. 98–104, citation from p. 103.

9. Jan Tesař, 'Totalitarian Dictatorships as a Phenomenon of the Twentieth Century and the Possibilities of Overcoming Them', typescript, 1977; English version, translated by Paul Wilson, in H. Gordon Skilling and Vilém Prečan, eds, *Parallel Politics: Essays from Czech and Slovak Samizdat, International Journal of Politics*, XL, no. 1 (Spring 1981), pp. 85–100.

10. Elemér Hankiss, 'The "Second Society": The Reduplication of the Social Paradigm in Contemporary Societies: The Case of Hungary', typescript (Budapest, 1986); revised as 'The "Second Society": Is there a Second Special Paradigm Working in Contemporary Hungary?' (Budapest, 1986); the latter was published in Hungarian, under the title 'A masodik, (A társadalmi paradigma megkettözödeséről) (The Second Society. Informal mechanisms and networks in contemporary Hungary), in Hankiss, *Diagnozisok 2* (Diagnosis 2) (Budapest, 1986). The new version retained the general framework of the original but modified the analysis substantially and drew quite different conclusions. Although some phrases of the original (I) are cited, citations are mainly to the revised English edition.

11. See Gregory Grossman, 'The "Second Economy" of the USSR', *Problems of Communism*, xxvi, no. 1 (January–February 1977), pp. 25–40. Other terms include a 'counter-economy', 'unofficial economy', 'parallel market', private enterprise and 'shadow economy'.

12. Hankiss, *Second Society*, pp. 5, 5a (Table I). *Cf.* the definition by another Hungarian economist, I. R. Gábor, 'The Second (Secondary) Economy', *Acta Oekonomika*, 22 (3–4), 1979, pp. 291–311.

13. István Kemény, 'The Unregistered Economy in Hungary', *Soviet Studies*, xxxiv, no. 3 (July 1982) pp. 349–66. See also Grossman, 'The "Second Economy",' and Gábor, 'The Second (Secondary) Economy', for detailed analysis of the components of this 'hidden' economy. See also the studies of the Hungarian and Polish cases: Iivàn Volgyes, 'Social Deviance in Hungary: The Case of the Private Economy', and Andrzej Korbonski, 'Social Deviance in Poland: The Case of the Private Sector', in Ivan Volgyes, ed., *Social Deviance in Eastern Europe* (Boulder, Colo., 1978), Chapters 4 and 5.

14. Steven Sampson, 'The Informal Sector in Eastern Europe', *Telos*, no. 66 (Winter 1985–6), pp. 44–66.

15. János Kenédi, *Do It Yourself: Hungary's Hidden Economy* (London, 1981).

16. Ivan Volgyes and John G. Peters, 'Social Deviance in Hungary: The Case of Prostitution'; J. L. Kerr, 'Social Deviance in Eastern Europe: The Case of Alcoholism', Chapters 3 and 7 respectively of Volgyes, ed., *Social Deviance*.

17. Walter D. Connor, *Deviance in Soviet Society: Crime, Delinquency, and Alcoholism* (New York, 1972), citation from pp. 2–3. *Cf.* a similar reference to R. K. Merton, in Volgyes, ed., *Social Deviance*, pp. 4–5, 14–15.

18. Connor, *Deviance*, pp. 255–6. *Cf.* also Walter D. Connor, 'Deviance, Stress and Modernization in Eastern Europe', in Mark G. Field, ed., *Social Consequences of Modernization in Eastern Europe* (Baltimore, 1976), Chapter 8.

19. Alfred G. Meyer, 'Political Change through Civil Disobedience in the USSR and Eastern Europe', in J. Roland Pennock and John W. Chapman, eds., *Political and Legal Obligation* (New York, 1970), Chapter 17; citation from p. 432.

20. Hankiss, *Second Society*, i, pp. 25–30.

21. For this, see Walter D. Connor and Zvi Gitelman, eds, *Public Opinion in European Socialist Systems* (New York, 1977).
22. Response by George Moldau (pseudonym) to a questionnaire (*anketa*) distributed among Czech and Slovak intellectuals by this author, to be discussed more fully in Chapter 9.
23. Csaba Gombár, cited by Hankiss, n. 7.
24. Jiřína Šiklová, 'Mládeže v CSSR a nábozenství' (Youth in Czechoslovakia and religion), *Svědectví*, xx, no. 79 (1986), pp. 513–21.
25. Hankiss, *Second Society*, pp. 31–2.
26. Pedro Ramet, 'Rock Counter Culture in Eastern Europe and the Soviet Union', *Survey*, 29, no. 2 (125) (Summer 1985), pp. 149–71, citation from p. 151.
27. I. Jirous (pseudonym Jan Houška), 'Report on the Czech underground musical revival', dated February 1975, published under another pseudonym, Jan Kobala, in *Svědectví*, xiii, no. 51 (1976); in English in *The Merry Ghetto*, booklet published with a recording, 'Egon Bondy's Happy Hearts Club Banned', by the Plastic People of the Universe (London, 1978). See also H. Gordon Skilling, *Charter 77 and Human Rights in Czechoslovakia* (London, 1981), pp. 116, 346. This was quoted extensively by Zdeněk Vokaty, *Sen o kole* (Dream of a Wheel), in *O svobodě a moci* (Cologne, 1980); in English in John Keane ed., *The Power of the Powerless* (London and New York, 1985).

    Jirous later claimed, with justice, that he had been the first to use the terms 'underground' and 'second culture', but that he had not created this phenomenon; he was merely designating something which already existed. See interview with I. Jirous, by P. Šustrová, *samizdat*, published in *Svědectví*, xx, no. 77 (1986), pp. 128–30. See also V. Havel, 'Dálkový výslech' (Cross Examination from Afar) (1986), pp. 129–30 (*samizdat*). As Havel explained, Jirous was then using the concept 'second culture' in the narrow sense of the nonconformist musical groups; only later was this interpreted more broadly to refer to the whole realm of independent culture (Keane *Power of the Powerless*, p. 78).
28. Magor, 'Nebyla nikdy v troskách' (It was never in ruins), *Svědectví*, xvi, no. 62 (1980), pp. 251–61.
29. Mikoláš Chadima, *Od Rekvalifikace k 'Nové vlně se starým obsahem'* (From Relicensing to the 'New Wave with the Old Content'), *samizdat*, 1984–5. See also his anonymous article cited above, Chapter 4, n. 19.
30. Ramet, 'Rock Counter Culture', pp. 158 *passim*.
31. For a full history of jazz in the Soviet Union and of changing official attitudes, see S. Frederick Starr, *Red and Hot: The Fate of Jazz in the Soviet Union, 1917–1980* (New York and Oxford, 1983). On rock, see Chapter 13; quotation is from p. 294.
32. Ramet, 'Rock Counter Culture', p. 159.
33. *Ibid.*, p. 170.
34. *Ibid.*, p. 155.
35. The joys, difficulties, and official harassment of several of these communes is described in Vokatý, *Sen o kole*.
36. Zsolt Krokovay, 'Politics and Punk', *Index on Censorship*, 14, no. 2 (April 1985), pp. 17–21.

37. Anna Pomian, 'Polish Punks and Pop Festivals', *Radio Free Europe, Research*, 11, no. 43 (24 October 1986), pt. 1; ibid., 12, no. 33 (21 August 1987), pt. 2; J. Tagliabue, *The New York Times*, 11 October 1987.

38. Krokovay, 'Politics and Punk', p. 17.

39. Cologne 1986. For an excerpt, and a commentary by Pavel Tigrid, see Jan Pelc, 'It's gonna get worse', *Index on Censorship*, 15, no. 6 (June 1986), pp. 27–30.

40. Starr, *Red and Hot*, *passim*, especially pp. 295–98, 303–304. See also Michael T. Kaufman, *The New York Times*, 4 January 1987, and Bill Keller, *The New York Times*, 9 January 1987.

41. *RFE*, 11, no. 38 (19 September 1986), pt 2.

42. Václav Havel, 'Power of the Powerless', pp. 67–8.

43. Other Czechs also shunned the notion of 'politics' in the normal sense and used the term 'non-political politics' to describe their activities. For example, see Hejdánek, in *ibid.*, pp. 44–45. The exiled writer, Antonin J. Liehm, proposed the term 'parallel polity', in Jane L. Curry, ed., *Dissent in Eastern Europe* (New York, 1983), pp. 175–81.

44. Antipolitics (San Diego, 1984), pp. 44, 92, 227–30; on moral opposition, pp. 126–27, 119–20.

45. *Cf.* Zvi Gitelman, 'Working the Soviet System', in Henry W. Morton and Robert C. Stuart, eds, *The Contemporary Soviet City* (Armonk, NY, 1984), p. 241.

46. Robert Sharlet sketched out a useful analysis of what he calls the 'contra-system', comprising most of the components which we have discussed above, from a second economy to a dissident movement. Although noting the different degree to which these parts were linked in the individual countries of Eastern Europe, he failed to make clear that this 'contra-system' existed only in certain countries and was least developed in the USSR (in spite of the title of his article). See his 'Dissent and the "Contra-System" in the Soviet Union', in Erik P. Hoffman, ed., *The Soviet Union in the 1980s*, Proceedings of the Academy of Political Science, 35, no. 3 (New York, 1984), pp. 135–46. See also his chapter, 'Varieties of Dissent and Regularities of Repression in the European Communist States: An Overview', in Curry, ed., *Dissent in Eastern Europe*, pp. 1–19.

8 A Second Polity: Contrasting Patterns of Reality

1. For accounts of dissent and opposition in Eastern Europe as a whole, see Jane L. Curry, ed., *Dissent in Eastern Europe* (New York, 1983); Rudolf L. Tökés, ed., *Opposition in Eastern Europe* (London, 1979). See also the series, *Violations of the Helsinki Accords: A Report prepared for the Helsinki Review Conference, Vienna, November 1986*, each dealing with a single country, published by the US Helsinki Watch Committee (New York, 1986), (henceforth cited as Helsinki Watch,

Violations, with the name of the country following). See also Laurie S. Wiseberg, ed., *Human Rights Internet Directory: Eastern Europe & the USSR* (Cambridge, Mass., 1987).

2. For fuller treatment see Skilling, *Charter 77*, index under 'civic initatives'; for the documents, *ibid.*, pp. 261–4, 265–7.
3. *Ibid.*, pp. 278–9.
4. *O svobodě a moci*, *samizdat*, published in English as *The Power of the Powerless, Václav Havel et al.* (London and Armonk, NY, 1985), citations on pp. 39–40, 64–67. For further information on this book and Havel's essay, see above, Chapter 6, n. 9.
5. Skilling, *Charter 77*, pp. 68–77, 83–84. See also essays in *The Power of the Powerless*, especially those by V. Hejdánek and Petr Uhl, and others which were included only in the *samizdat* edition, by J. Dienstbier, Z. Mlynář, and Petr Pithart.
6. Havel, *The Power of the Powerless*, pp. 78–9, 84–6, 93–5.
7. Adam Michnik, 'A New Evolutionism', in Michnik, *Letters from Prison and Other Essays* (Berkeley, Calif., 1985), pp. 135–48; also in French, 'Une stratégie pour l'opposition polonaise', in A. Erard and G. M. Zygier, eds., *La Pologne: une société en dissidence* (Paris, 1978), pp. 99–136.
8. Jacques Rupnik, 'Dissent in Poland', in Tökés, ed., *Opposition in Eastern Europe*, pp. 61, 92, 100, 102–103. See also Curry, ed., *Dissent in Eastern Europe*, pp. 158–61.
9. Rupnik, 'Dissent in Poland', pp. 79–80. For a full history of KOR, see Jan Józef Lipski, *KOR: Workers' Defense Committee in Poland* (Berkeley, Calif., 1983). This includes several key documents of KOR and the Initiative Committee for a Free Trade Union, and describes in some detail the free press and the *ROPCiO* movement (see below).
10. For text of the latter, see Peter Raina, *Political Opposition in Poland, 1954–1977* (London, 1978), pp. 468–84.
11. Declaration of October 1977, in *ibid.*, p. 453.
12. 'A Programme of Action', *Labour Focus on Eastern Europe* (hereafter cited as *LFEE*), 2, no. 6 (January–February 1979), pp. 11–14; also in Lipski, *KOR*, pp. 474–9.
13. Michnik, in a lecture given in November 1980, 'What We Want and What We Can Do', *Telos*, no. 47, pp. 66–77, citation from p. 71.
14. Lipski, *KOR* pp. 44–5, 62–71.
15. *Dissent in Poland, December 1975–July 1977* (London, 1977), pp. 79–82; also Raina, *Political Opposition*, pp. 485–88.
16. On ROPCiO, see Lipski, *KOR*, pp. 116–24, 194–203, 321–2, 392–5.
17. For the text of the latter, see Raina, *Political Opposition*, pp. 468–84. See also Curry, ed., *Dissent in Eastern Europe*, pp. 161–3.
18. 'Pour une plate-forme unique de l'opposition', *La Pologne*, pp. 113–36.
19. *Le Monde*, 29 January 1977, in *Dissent in Poland*, pp. 170–6.
20. Jacek Kuroń, 'The Situation in the Country and the Programme of the Opposition – Some Notes', (no date, June 1979?), *LFEE*, 3, no. 3 (July–August 1979), pp. 12–14.
21. Michnik and Lipski, 'Some Remarks on the Opposition and the General

Situation in Poland, 1979', dated September–October 1979, in Michnik, *Letters from Prison*, pp. 149–54.

22. For this paragraph, see Michnik, 'What We Want', *Telos*, p. 74; Michnik, *Letters from Prison*, pp. 101–31 (articles from the Solidarity period); Jacek Kuroń, 'What Next in Poland?' *Dissent*, 28 (Winter 1981), pp. 34–39; Kuroń, interview (1980), in *Telos*, no. 47 (Spring 1981), pp. 93–97.

23. Mihály Vajda, *The State and Socialism* (London, 1981), pp. 126–7.

24. 'Hungarian Profiles – An Interview with Milos Haraszti', *LFEE*, 2, no. 6 (January–February 1979), p. 17.

25. G. Schöpflin, in Tökés, ed., *Opposition in Eastern Europe*, pp. 142, 180; Schöpflin, in Curry, ed., *Dissent in Eastern Europe*, p. 75.

26. Konrád, *Antipolitics* (San Diego, Calif., 1984), p. 231.

27. Kivül Alló (pseudonym), from *Beszélö*, 1983, No. 4, in *LFEE*, 6, no. 1–2 (Summer 1983), pp. 32–3.

28. János Kis, 'The End of the Post-Stalin Epoch', *LFEE*, 5, no. 5–6 (Winter 1982–3), 12–17, especially pp. 16–17.

29. *Ibid.* See also János Kis and György Bence, 'On Being a Marxist: A Hungarian View', *Socialist Register*, 1980.

30. Mihály Vajda, 'On the "end of reformism"', published in Czech, in *Informační materiály*, no. 32 (May 1979), pp. 16–19; also Vajda, *State and Socialism*, pp. 128–31. On Marxist dissent see Schöpflin, in Tökés, ed., *Opposition in Eastern Europe*, pp. 149ff; Szelényi, *ibid.*, pp. 143, 182, n. 16.

31. Vajda, *State and Socialism*, pp. 130–31, 141.

32. György Bence, private communication, 23 August 1986; also his interview during a visit to Prague, in *Informace o Chartě 77* (1980), pp. 20–1. See his study, 'Censored and Alternative Modes of Cultural Expression in Hungary', *A Report from Helsinki Watch* (October 1985), unpaginated.

33. For the development of the Hungarian opposition, George Schöpflin, 'Opposition and Para-Opposition: Critical Currents in Hungary, 1968–78', in Tökés, ed., *Opposition in Eastern Europe*, Chapter 5; also Schöpflin, 'Opposition in Hungary: 1956 and Beyond', in Curry, ed., *Dissent in Eastern Europe*, Chapter 5; Helsinki Watch, *Violations: Hungary* (New York, 1986). See Bence, 'Censored and Alternative Modes'; interview with Demszky, in Polish *samizdat*, *Radio Free Europe Research*, 11, no. 15 (11 April 1986), pt 2; Bill Lomax, 'The Rise of the Democratic Opposition' (Hungary, 1977–82), *LFEE*, 5, no. 3–4 (Summer 1982), pp. 2–7; *Human Rights Directory*, Chapter 10. See also above, Chapter 2.

34. Kis, 'The End of the Post-Stalin Epoch', p. 15.

35. Konrád, *Antipolitics*, pp. 118–19; on circles, pp. 146–7, 177, 197–8; on the élite, pp. 216–18, 224.

36. András Hegedüs, 'Democracy and socialism in East and West', in Ken Coates and Fred Singleton, eds, *The Just Society* (Nottingham, 1977), pp. 162–83, especially pp. 165–6, 179, 181; interview with András Hegedüs, *Telos*, no. 47 (Spring 1981), pp. 132–7.

37. For this and the following, see articles on the peace movement by Bill Lomax in *Labour Focus on Eastern Europe*, 5, nos 3–4 (Summer 1982), pp. 31–2; no. 5–6 (Winter 1982–3), pp. 35–6; 7, no. 1 (Winter 1984),

pp. 23–26; and Milos Haraszti, 'The Hungarian Peace Movement', *Telos*, no. 61 (Fall 1984), pp. 134–44. See also *From Below: Independent Peace and Environmental Movements in Eastern Europe and the USSR* (Helsinki Watch, New York, 1987), Chapter 3.

38. For the following, see Gyula Dénes, 'The Politics of Environmental Protection', *East European Reporter*, 2, no. 2 (1986), pp. 4–7; *RFE Research*, 11, no. 29 (18 July 1986), pt 2, pp. 1–4; *LFEE*, 9. no. 2 (July–October 1987), pp. 47, 38. See also *From Below*, Chapter 3.

39. See above, Chapter 3. For the document to the Cultural Forum, see *Index on Censorship*, 15, no. 1 (January 1986), pp. 51–4.

40. For a full report on the Monor conference, see Steven Koppany, *RFE Research*, 11, no. 8 (21 February 1986), pt 1. See also *LFEE*, 8, no. 2 (May 1986), pp. 30–1. For further discussion of the idea of an open and courageous, but pro-Kádár opposition, see *Beszélő*, no. 17 (June 1986), given in English, 'Is dialogue possible? The case for a pro-government opposition', *East European Reporter*, 2, no. 2 (1986), pp. 8–10.

41. *RFE Research*, 12, no. 8 (27 February 1986), pt 1, pp. 9–27; *The New York Times*, 16 March 1986; Helsinki Watch, *Violations: Hungary*, pp. 21–3.

42. *RFE Research*, 12, no. 29 (24 July 1987) pt 2; *ibid.*, 12, no. 34 (28 August 1987) pt 1; *ibid.*, 12, no. 40 (9 October 1987) pt 1.; Henry Kamm, *The New York Times*, 25 October, 1987; Charles Gati, 'Gorbachev and Eastern Europe', *Foreign Affairs*, 65, no. 5 (Summer 1987), pp. 966–7; *East European Reporter*, 3, no. 1 (1987), pp. 54–60.

43. Pedro Ramet, 'Disaffection and Dissent in East Germany', *World Politics*, 37, no. 1 (October 1984), pp. 85–111.

44. Christiane Lemke, 'New Issues in the Politics of the German Democratic Republic: A Question of Political Culture?' *The Journal of Communist Studies*, 2, no. 4 (December 1986), pp. 341–58.

45. For the following, see, in addition to Ramet and Lemke, Michael J. Sodaro, 'Limits to Dissent in the GDR: Fragmentation, Cooptation, and Repression', in Curry, ed., *Dissent in Eastern Europe*, Chapter 6; Werner Volkmer, 'East Germany: Dissenting Views during the Last Decade', in Tökés, ed., *Opposition in Eastern Europe*, Chapter 4; Wolfgang Mleczkowski, 'In Search of the Forbidden Nation: Opposition by the Young in the GDR', *Government and Opposition*, 18, no. 2 (Spring 1983), pp. 175–93; Roger Woods, 'East German Intellectuals in Opposition', *Survey*, 28, no. 3 (122) (Autumn 1984), pp. 111–23. See also *Human Rights Directory*, Chapter 11. For a full study, with documents, see Roger Woods, *Opposition in the GDR under Honecker, 1971–85* (London, 1986).

46. Sodaro, 'Limits to Dissent', pp. 103, 105; Woods, 'East German Intellectuals', pp. 112–23.

47. Sodaro, 'Limits to Dissent', pp. 83–4, 86–89, 108–110; Woods, 'East German Intellectuals', pp. 11–22; Helsinki Watch, *Violations: East Germany*, pp. 11–22; *RFE Research*, 12, no. 1, pt 1 (4 January 1987); *East European Reporter*, 2, no. 3 (1987), p. 50.

48. Mleczkowski, 'In Search of the Forbidden Nation', pp. 182–83; Ramet, 'Disaffection and Dissent', pp. 96–97, 110–11; *LFEE*, 7, no. 1 (Winter

1984), p. 21; Joan DeBardeleben, *The Environment and Marxism–Leninism: The Soviet and East German Experience* (Boulder, Colo., 1985).

49. On the peace movement, see Ronald Asmus, 'Is there a peace movement in the GDR?' *Orbis*, 27, no. 2 (Summer 1983), pp. 301–41; Pedro Ramet, 'Church and Peace in the GDR', *Problems of Communism*, 33, no. 4 (July–August 1984), pp. 44–57; Gus Fagan, 'The Peace Movement enters its second year', *LFEE*, 6, no. 1–2 (Summer 1983), pp. 21–4, with other articles and documents, *ibid.*, pp. 24–28; Günter Minnerup, 'Hard Times Ahead for Peace Movement', *ibid.*, 7, no. 1 (Winter 1984), pp. 18–20, with other articles, *ibid.*, pp. 20–3; Helsinki Watch, *Violations: East Germany*, pp. 31–8. See also Ramet, 'Dissaffection and Dissent', pp. 93–6; Mleczkowski, 'In Search of the Forbidden Nation', pp. 184–91; Sodaro, 'Limits to Dissent', pp. 106–8. For documents on the peace movement, see Wolfgang Büscher, *et al.*, *Friedensbewegung in der DDR, Texte 1978–1982* (Hattingen, 1982); Klaus Ehring and Martin Dallwitz, *Schwerter zu Pflugscharen, Friedensbewegung in der DDR* (Reinbek, 1982). See also John Sandford, *The Sword and the Ploughshare: Autonomous Peace Initiatives in East Germany* (London, 1983); *From Below*, Chapter 2.

50. The following is based largely on Ramet, 'Church and Peace', especially pp. 51, 52. See also Ramet, 'Disaffection and Dissent', pp. 96–101; Meczkowski, 'In Search of the Forbidden Nation', p. 187.

51. *RFE Research*, 12, no. 27 (10 July 1987), pt 2; *ibid.*, 12, no. 39 (2 October 1987) pt 1.

52. Ramet, 'Dissafection and Dissent', p. 94; Fagan 'The Peace Movement', p. 19; *RFE Research*, 12, no. 28 (17 July 1987), pt 1.

53. Helsinki Watch, *Violations: East Germany*, pp. 39–41; *LFEE*, 8, no. 2 (May 1986), pp. 17–18; *ibid.*, 9, no. 1 (March–June 1987), pp. 30–2.

54. The main sources for this section were Emil Freund, 'Nascent dissent in Romania', in Curry, ed., *Dissent in Eastern Europe*, Chapter 4; Vlad Georgescu, 'Romanian Dissent: Its Ideas', in *ibid.*, Chapter 11; *Romania: Human Rights in a 'Most Favored Nation'* (New York, 1983); *Human Rights in Romania: A Report Prepared for the Most Favored Nation Hearings in the US Congress* (New York, 1984); *Violations: Romania* (New York, 1986). The last three were prepared by the US Helsinki Watch Committee, New York.

55. Georgescu, 'Romanian Dissent', pp. 191, 189–91; Helsinki Watch, *Violations: Romania*, p. 7. See Michael Shafir's analysis of 'acquiescence' or 'compliance' as a dominant feature of the political subculture of Romanian intellectuals ('Political Culture, Intellectual Dissent, and Intellectual Consent: The Case of Romania', *Orbis*, 27, no. 2 (Summer 1983), pp. 393–420).

56. Freund, 'Nascent Dissent', pp. 63–4; Georgescu, 'Romanian Dissent', p. 187, and n. 2.

57. *RFE Research*, 12, no. 5 (6 February 1987), pt 3, pp. 23–6; *ibid.*, 12, no. 22 (5 June 1987), pt 4, pp. 1–7, *ibid.*, 12, no. 38 (25 September 1987), pt 1; *ibid*, 12, no. 45 (23 October 1987), pt 1.

58. *Ibid.*, 11, no. 41 (10 October 1986), pt 4, pp. 33–36; *ibid.*, 11, no. 7 (14

February 1986), pt 1, pp. 9–13; Helsinki Watch, *Violations: Romania*, pp. 31–4.

59. Georgescu, 'Romanian Dissent', p. 188; Freund, 'Nascent Dissent', pp. 64–5; Helsinki Watch, *Violations: Romania*, pp. 23–8.

60. Freund, 'Nascent Dissent', p. 65; Georgescu, 'Romanian Dissent', p. 189; Helsinki Watch, *Violations: Romania* (1983), pp. 34–35; *RFE Research,* (17 July 1986), pt 2, pp. 35–7.

61. Georgescu, 'Romanian Dissent', pp. 187–8 and n. 24; Freund, 'Nascent Dissent', pp. 61–2; Helsinki Watch, *Human Rights* (1984), pp. 36–7; *LFEE*, 2, no. 1 (March–April 1978), pp. 12–13; *ibid.*, 3, no. 1 (March–April 1979), pp. 12–13, which contains the full text of the original SLOMR declaration.

62. *RFE Research*, 12, no. 5 (6 February 1987), pp. 7–10.

63. Freund, 'Nascent Dissent', p. 66; Helsinki Watch, *Human Rights*, pp. 44–7; Helsinki Watch, *Violations: Romania*, pp. 15, 40–1; *RFE Research*, 12, no. 9 (6 March 1987), pp. 17–20; ibid., 12, no. 26 (3 July 1987), pt 3, pp. 7–11.

64. Georgescu, 'Rumanian Dissent', pp. 182–94; *RFE Research* 12, no. 9 (6 March 1987), pt 1, pp. 13–6; *ibid*, 12, no. 26 (3 July 1987), pt 3, pp. 7–11.

65. See Michael Costello, 'Bulgaria', in Adam Bromke and Teresa Rakowska-Harmstone, eds, *The Communist States in Disarray, 1965–1971* (Minneapolis, Minn., 1972), pp. 150–1; Marin V. Pundeff, 'Bulgaria under Zhivkov', in Peter A. Toma, ed., *The Changing Face of Communism in Eastern Europe* (Tucson, Ariz., 1970), pp. 110–18.

66. Stephen Ashley, *RFE Research*, 12, no. 6 (13 February 1987), pt 2, pp. 21–6; Ashley, *ibid.*, 11, no. 29 (18 July 1986), pt 1, pp. 23–6.

67. Ashley, *ibid.*, pp. 26–8; Ashley, *ibid.*, 11, no. 23 (6 June 1986), pp. 33–8; Ashley, *ibid.*, pp. 3–7; Helsinki Watch, *Violations: Bulgaria* (New York, 1986), pp. 25, 29–32; *RFE Research*, 12, no. 20 (22 May 1987), pt 2, pp. 29–32.

68. *Violations: Bulgaria*, pp. 1–11.

69. Sharon Zukin, 'Sources of Dissent and Nondissent in Yugoslavia', in Curry, ed., *Dissent in Eastern Europe*, Chapter 7, especially pp. 119–22.

70. For a full history of *Praxis* and an analysis of its contents, see Gerson S. Sher, *Praxis: Marxist Criticism and Dissent in Socialist Yugoslavia* (Bloomington, In., 1977), pp. xvii, xix, 53, 67.

71. Zukin, 'Sources of Dissent', pp. 119, 129.

72. Sher, *Praxis*, pp. 197–241.

73. *Human Rights Directory*, Chapter 14.

74. Pedro Ramet, *Yugoslavia in the 1980s* (Boulder, Colo., and London, 1985), especially his introduction, pp. 3–26; citation on p. 5.

75. See *ibid.*, conclusions by George Schöpflin and Pedro Ramet, Chapters 13 and 14.

76. Helsinki Watch, *Violations: Yugoslavia* (November 1986), pp. 7–13, 19–23.

77. *RFE Research*, 11, no. 8 (21 February 1986), pt 1, pp. 7–9; *ibid.*, 11, no. 14 (4 April 1986), pt 2, pp. 1–3, 13–14; Helsinki Watch, *Violations:*

Yugoslavia, pp. 16–17; *Bulletin, Committee to Aid Democratic Dissidents in Yugoslavia* (New York), no. 37 (1986), pp. 7–8; *From Below*, Chapter 6.

78. *RFE Research*, 11, no. 14 (4 April 1986), pp. 11–13; *ibid.*, 11, no. 48 (28 November 1986), pt 2, pp. 7–11.

79. Helsinki Watch, *Violations: Yugoslavia*, pp. 15–17; *Bulletin*, no. 38, pp. 1–2, 6–7; no. 39 (1986), pp. 1–4. For an earlier statement in 1975 by the Praxis group, see 'The Meaning of the Struggle for Civil and Human Rights', *Telos*, no. 35 (Spring 1978), pp. 187–91. See also Oskar Gruenwald and Karen Rosenblum-Cale, *Human Rights in Yugoslavia* (New York, 1986), not available to the author.

80. Erica Blair conducted the interview with P. Gantar, of the University of Ljubljana; S. Lev, a regular contributor to journals; T. Mastnak, of the Institute of Marxist Studies, and S. Mežnarić, of the Slovenian Academy of Sciences. See *East European Reporter*, 2, no. 2 (1986); also in *Bulletin*, no. 39, pp. 11–13. See also *The New York Times*, 17 June 1987.

81. *Eastern Europe, Newsletter* (London), 1, no. 8 (16 September 1987); no. 9 (30 September 1987); David Binder, *The New York Times*, November 1 and 10, 1987.

82. Ludmilla Alexeyeva, *Soviet Dissent; Contemporary Movements for National, Religious and Human Rights* (Middletown, Ct, 1985), citations on pp. 269, 3; Peter Reddaway, *Uncensored Russia: The Human Rights Movement in the Soviet Union* (London, 1972), pp. 15–16.

83. Amalrik, quoted by Alexeyeva, *Soviet Dissent*, p. 268; Boris Shragin, quoted by Alexeyeva, *ibid.*, pp. 450, 451–2.

84. Peter Reddaway, 'Can the dissidents survive?' *Index on Censorship*, 9, no. 4 (August 1980), p. 33. See also Theodore Friedgut, 'The Democratic Movement: Dimensions and Perspectives', in Rudolf L. Tökés, ed., *Dissent in the USSR: Politics, Ideology and People* (Baltimore and London, 1985), Chapter 3, p. 123.

85. Friedgut, 'The Democratic Movement', p. 120; Mikhail Heller and Aleksandr Nekrich, *Utopia in Power* (New York, 1986), pp. 628–29.

86. For a comparative analysis of nineteenth-century Russian and contemporary Soviet dissent, see Marshall S. Shatz, *Soviet Dissent in Historical Perspective* (Cambridge, 1981), especially Chapter 7.

87. For a full discussion of the (Estonian) Democratic Movement and its programme, see F. J. M. Feldbrugge, *Samizdat and Political Dissent in the Soviet Union* (Leyden, 1975), especially p. 112–15, 135–50; for an earlier treatment, Reddaway, *Uncensored Russia*, pp. 171–83. This human rights group was not mentioned by Alexeyeva, and was not listed in the *Human Rights Directory*. The charges were laid against the five as members of the Estonian Democratic Movement (EDM) but Soldatov identified himself as the 'secretary and ideologist' of the EDM, 'a section of the Democratic Movement of the Soviet Union'. For the trial, see Andres Küng, *A Dream of Freedom* (Cardiff, 1980), Chapter 1, pp. 1–14; also *Sobranie dokumentov samizdata* (Samizdat Archive, Munich), 30 (1978).

88. For the groups, see Alexeyeva, *Soviet Dissent, passim*; *Sobranie dokumentov samizdata* (Samizdat Archive, Munich), 30 (1978) (henceforth

Sds), *passim.*; *Human Rights Directory*, *passim*. For the free trade unions, see Viktor and Olga Semyonova, *Workers Against the Gulag* (London, 1979); also Alexeyeva, *Dissent*, pp. 406–13. For dissent in the Baltic states, see Romuald J. Misiunas and Rein Taagepera, *The Baltic States: Years of Dependence, 1940–1980* (Berkeley, Calif., 1983), Chapter 5. For Ukrainian dissent and the human rights movement, see *Nonconformity and Dissent in the Ukrainian SSR, 1955–1975: An Annotated Bibliography* (Cambridge, Mass., n.d.); L. Verba and B. Yasen, eds, *The Human Rights Movement in the Ukraine: Documents of the Ukrainian Helsinki Group 1976–1980* (Baltimore, 1980).

89. Küng, *A Dream*, pp. 210–11.

90. See Chapter 1, above, for full discussion of Russian *samizdat*. For dissident journals, see Reddaway, 'Can the Soviet dissidents survive', pp. 30–32; *Human Rights Directory*, pp. 16–50, *passim*.

91. Michael Bourdeaux, *Land of Crosses* (Chumleigh, 1979), pp. 253–56, 264–92. This records the close cooperation of the Lithuanian *Chronicle* with the Moscow *Chronicle* and the admiration of the editors for Sakharov and Solzhenitsyn. See also *RFE Research*, 12, no. 18 (8 May 1987), pt 4.

92. For a full history of *The Chronicle*, see Mark Hopkins, *Russia's Underground Press: The Chronicle of Current Events* (New York, 1983); on *The Chronicle* as a unifying force, *ibid.*, pp. viii–ix, pp. 162–4; also Peter Reddaway, 'Notes from underground', *Times Literary Supplement*, 16 June 1978; for the mistrust of certain circles, see Friedgut, 'The Democratic Movement', pp. 122, 136. For an earlier treatment of *The Chronicle*, see Reddaway, *Uncensored Russia*.

93. See *The Moscow Helsinki Group – Ten Years*, a report from the International Helsinki Federation for Human Rights (Vienna, 1986). For the documents of the Committee see *Sds*, *passim.*, in many volumes.

94. For the spectrum of opinion, see Feldbrugge, *Samizdat*; Tökés, ed., *Dissent*; M. Meerson-Aksenov and Boris Shragin, eds, *The Political, Social, and Religious Thought of Russian 'Samizdat': An Anthology* (Belmont, Mass., 1977); also Donald S. Kelley, *The Solzhenitsyn–Sakharov Dialogue: Politics, Society, and the Future* (Westport, Ct, 1982); Shatz, *Soviet Dissent*, pp. 158–83; Reddaway, *Uncensored Russia*, pp. 20–2, 37–8. For the Russian nationalist movement and the nationalist journal *Pamyat* (Memory), see Alexander Yanov, *The Russian New Right: Right-wing Ideologies in the Contemporary USSR* (Berkeley, Calif., 1978); Alexeyeva, *Soviet Dissent*, pp. 431–56; *The New York Times*, 24 May 1987.

95. Reddaway, personal communication, 17 April 1986; Friedgut, 'The Democratic Movement', p. 117.

96. Pyotr Abovin-Egides and Pinkhos Podrabinek, 'The Democratic Movement in Perspective', *LFEE*, 3, no. 5 (November 1979–January 1980), pp. 16–21; 'The Democratic Movement, Workers and Party Reformers', *ibid.*, 3, no. 6 (February–March 1980), pp. 11–12.

97. *Ibid.*, pp. 16–17; Alexeyeva, *Soviet Dissent*, pp. 269–70, 355–60, 390–93. For guitar music, see G. S. Smith, *Songs for Seven Strings:*

Russian Guitar Poetry and Soviet 'Mass Song' (Bloomington, In., 1984).

98. For this see the unpublished paper by Jim Riordan, 'Soviet Youth Culture: "We don't want no educashun"', presented at the annual conference of the National Association of Soviet and East European Studies, Cambridge, 28–30 March 1987; also his 'Growing Pains of Soviet Youth', *Journal of Communist Studies*, 2, no. 2 (June 1986), pp. 145–67. See also *The New York Times*, 16 February and 7 March 1987.

99. Personal communication with Theodore Friedgut, March 1987. Scientific papers were published in *The Annals of the New York Academy of Sciences*; historical papers in *Journal* of *Academic Proceedings of Soviet Jewry*. Its first issue (1, no. 1, London, 1986) contained a bibliography of the Holocaust in German-occupied regions of Soviet Russia, as well as abstracts of scientific articles.

100. Ludmilla Alexeyeva, 'Dissent in the 1980s', *Human Rights Directory*, pp. 11–15.

101. Adam Michnik, *Letters from Prison*, dated August 1981, p. 124; 1985, pp. 77, 79, 85–86, 93, 98.

102. On the debate, see Andrzej Tymowski, 'The Underground Debate on Strategy and Tactics', *Poland Watch*, no. 1 (Fall 1982), pp. 75–87; 'Solidarity or a Political Program?' *ibid.*, no. 2 (Spring–Summer 1983), pp. 95–108; also Tymowski, ed., *Solidarity under Siege* (New Haven, Ct, 1982). For statements by J. Kuroń, Z. Bujak, W. Kulerski, and Z. Romaszewski, see Roman Stefanowski, ed., *Poland Under Martial Law: A Selection of Documents December 1981–December 1982*, *RFE Research* (March 1984), pp. 161–75, 187–200. For post-1981 Solidarity and other organizations and publications, see *Human Rights Directory*, pp. 130–57.

103. The Programmatic Declaration, 28 July 1982, Stefanowski, ed., *Poland Under Martial Law*, pp. 206–9; Declaration of Solidarity, 12 December 1982, *ibid.*, pp. 315–17.

104. Tymowski, 'Solidarity or a Political Program?', pp. 102–103; David Ost, 'November 1982: Opposition at a Turning Point', *Poland Watch*, no. 2 (Winter 1982–3), pp. 70–84. For the January programme, see *ibid.*, pp. 127–32.

105. Michnik, *Letters from Prison*, May 1982, pp. 41–63; 1985, pp. 80–1, 95; Michnik, 'From a Polish Prison', [?] June 1983, *Encounter* (December 1983), pp. 87–94. See also David Warszawski, 'An Independent Society', *Survey*, 26, no. 4 (117) (Autumn 1982), pp. 83–5.

106. For the above, and the following, see Chris Pszenicki, 'Solidarity Emerges Overground', *East European Reporter*, 2, no. 3 (1987), pp. 24–8, and article by Henryk Wujec, 22 October 1986, *ibid.*, pp. 28–9.

107. Texts given in *NEWS, Solidarność* (Brussels), 30 June, 16 and 31 July 1986.

108. Text, *ibid.*, 31 August 1986.

109. For the above and relevant documents see Pszenicki, 'Solidarity', pp. 26–8; *RFE Research*, 11, no. 47 (21 November 1986), pt 2, pp. 9–24; *ibid.*, 11, no. 48 (28 November 1986), pp. 3–9; *Committee in Support*

of Solidarity, REPORTS New York), no. 45, 17 October; no. 46, 10 November 1986; *NEWS, Solidarność,* 30 September and 31 October 1986.

110. *NEWS, Solidarność,* 30 November 1986; 30 June 1987; on the Pope's visit in 1987, *The New York Times,* 4 June to 14 June, 1987.
111. *NEWS, Solidarność,* 31 August 1987; 15 September 1987.
112. *East European Reporter,* 2, no. 3 (n.d.), 1987, pp. 30–33; *RFE Research,* 11, no. 39 (26 September 1986), pt 3, pp. 9–13; *ibid.,* 12, no. 6 (February 1987), pt 1, pp. 13–18.
113. For a summary of the work of three of the commissions, see the report prepared for a conference in Turin, Italy, in January 1985, in *East European Reporter,* 1, no. 2 (Summer 1985), pp. 12–14. See also *Reinventing Civil Society, Poland's Quiet Revolution, 1981–1986,* report of the Helsinki Watch Commission (New York, 1986).
114. W. K. Kulerski, *RFE Research,* 11, no. 3 (2 July 1986), pt 1, pp. 3–6.
115. See F. Michels, in *Studium, PAPERS* (Ann Arbor, Mich.), 10, no. 2 (April 1986), pp. 57–61.
116. *Solidarity REPORTS,* no. 44 (7 September 1986); *Infoch,* no. 9 (1986), pp. 6–11.
117. *Reinventing Civil Society,* pp. 99–100. The Committee's reports were usually published abroad by the Helsinki Watch Committee in New York or the Committee for the Support of Solidarity. For its memorandum to the UN Commission on Human Rights (March 1984), see *Poland Watch,* no. 6 (n.d., 1984?), pp. 137–69; for its report to the CSCE Helsinki conference in 1985, see *Solidarity, REPORTS,* no. 35 (31 August 1985), pp. 16–19. For KOPPs see *Poland Watch,* no. 7 (n.d., March 1985?), pp. 47–54; for the Intervention Bureau, *RFE Research,* 12, no. 6 (13 February 1986). pp. 7–12.
118. *Reinventing Civil Society,* pp. 43 *passim;* Committee in Support of Solidarity, report on the situation in Poland (November 1984), pp. 4–5; *REPORTS,* no. 38 (31 December 1985); *ibid.,* no. 49 (23 February 1987), pp. 21–26; *RFE Research,* 12, no. 4 (30 January 1987), pp. 3–6; *ibid.,* 12, no. 8 (27 February 1987), pt 2, pp. 13–15.
119. *Solidarity, REPORTS,* no. 38 (31 December 1985), pp. 23–5; *ibid.,* no. 49 (23 February 1987), pp. 27–31; *RFE Research,* 12, no. 37 (18 September 1987), pt. 2.
120. See *RFE Research,* 12, no. 15 (16 April 1987), pt 1, pp. 1–29; text of the Cracow declaration is given on pp. 11–12. The WiP programme is given in *East European Reporter,* 2, no. 1 (Spring 1986), pp. 44–7. It was also published in full in *Informace o Chartě,* no. 4 (1986), pp. 11–14. See also *From Below,* Chapter 4. On the Western peace movements see *RFE Research,* 12, no. 19 (15 May 1987), pt 1, pp. 17–20; for earlier distrust of Western movements, see Andrzej Tymowski, 'Underground Solidarity and the Western Peace Movements', *Poland Watch,* no. 5 (n.d., April 1984?), pp. 114–30.
121. *RFE Research,* 11, no. 45 (7 November 1986), pt 2, pp. 15–19; *The New York Times,* 18 April 1986.
122. *RFE Research* 12, no. 28 (24 July 1987), pt 3.

123. Gus Fagan, 'Political Groups in the Polish Underground', *LFEE*, 8, no. 2 (May 1986), pp. 26–8; also Chapter 2 above.

124. The following draws heavily on Adam Michnik's *Letters from Prison*, with page references given in text. For the period after martial law, see Vincent C. Chrypinski, 'Church and State in Poland After Solidarity', in J. L. Black and J. W. Strong, eds, *Sisyphus and Poland: Reflections on Martial Law* (Winnipeg, 1986) pp. 145–58; Tadeusz Kaminski, 'Poland's Catholic Church and Solidarity: A Parting of Ways?' *Poland Watch*, no. 6 (n.d., 1984), pp. 73–86; David Warszawski, 'The Price of Concessions', ibid., pp. 87–91.

125. Kulerski, 'The Underground Should Exist', *Solidarity, REPORTS*, no. 45 (17 October 1986) pp. 3–6.

126. A. Lawina, M. Poleski, and M. Zalewski, ibid., no. 50 (31 March 1987), pp. 14–17.

127. Flora Lewis, *The New York Times*, 3 December 1986.

128. Lawina *et al.*, *Solidarity, REPORTS*, no. 50 (31 March 1987), pp. 3–6.

129. For the above, see Arthur R. Rachwald, 'The Polish Road to the Abyss', *Current History*, 86, no. 523 (November 1987), pp. 369–72, 384–5; oral presentations by Krzysztof Jasiewicz and by Alexander Smolar at the American Association for the Advancement of Slavic Studies, Boston, 6 November 1987.

130. See the comments of Bujak, W. Frasyniuk, W. Romaszewski, and others, *Solidarity, REPORTS*, no. 48 (23 January 1987), pp. 1–18; *ibid.*, no. 50 (31 March 1987) pp. 5–17; Abraham Brumberg, 'A New Deal in Poland?' *New York Review of Books*, January 1987, pp. 32ff.

131. *NSZZ 'Solidarność' on Reforming the Polish Economy* (Brussels, August 1987); *NEWS, Solidarność*, 16–30 October 1987.

9 Towards an Independent Society?

1. References are to essays in *O svobodě a moci* (Cologne, 1980), pp. 103, 83, 237, 330–31. The essays by Havel and Uhl are included in John Keane, ed., *The Power of the Powerless, Václav Havel et al.* (London and New York, 1985), citations on pp. 79, 197.

2. The word used in Czech is invariably *nezavislý*, which means literally 'not dependent'. Almost synonymous is the word *samostátný*, literally 'standing on one's own' or 'self-supporting', but this is rarely used in this connection. We may compare the dictionary meaning of the English word 'independent' – according to Oxford, simply, as 'not dependent on authority'; or, in the several Webster renderings, free from control or determination of another; controlling or governing oneself; relying on oneself or one's own judgement; not receiving financial support from others; independent in thinking or actions. All of these seem applicable to the concept of an independent society.

3. In English the term 'parallel' suggests things that are closely similar or corresponding, and show similarity or likeness, or alternatively, in a mathematical sense, as things extending in the same direction, but apart at every point, so as never to meet (Webster). *Cf.* Benda, below.

4. The words *společnost*, which is normally used in this connection, and *společenství* (community or communities) are virtually synonymous. If there is a subtle difference, the word *společenství* refers to a narrower community or association, as opposed to the broader reference of *společnost* to the whole of society. *Cf.* the term *obec*, fn. 8 below.

5. In Czech, *samospráva* (self-government, autonomy, self-rule).

6. See above, Chapter 6, p. 148, and 8, pp. 177–8; on Hankiss, pp. 160ff.

7. Benda's original *samizdat* essay was published in *O svobodě a moci*, pp. 101–110. It was not included in Keane, ed., *Power of the Powerless*, but see comment on it by S. Lukes, p. 12. For discussion of the parallel *polis* by L. Hejdánek and P. Uhl, *ibid.*, pp. 141–51, 188–97. For the entire debate see H. Gordon Skilling, *Charter 77 and Human Rights in Czechoslovakia* (London, 1981), pp. 75–6, 183–4, *passim*. See also Jan Vladislav, 'La culture parallèle en Tchécoslovaquie', *L'Alternative*, no. 27–28 (May–August 1984), pp. 37–9; Antonin Liehm, 'The New Social Contract and the Parallel Polity', Chapter 10 in Jane L. Curry, ed., *Dissent in Eastern Europe* (New York, 1983); Miroslav Novák, 'Paralelní struktury a reformní komunismus', *Svědectví*. XVII, no. 68 (1983), pp. 691–97.

8. Benda used the Greek term *polis* more or less as an equivalent of the Czech word *obec*, which, among its many meanings, connotes 'community'. He also used more or less interchangeably the word *společenství* (community). Perhaps worthy of note is the fact that the word *občanský* (civic or civil) is derived from *obec*.

9. The responses were usually without title and addressed to H. Gordon Skilling for use in the writing of this book. Each, of course, was separately paginated so that exact references cannot be made. Only one has so far been published in Czech, namely, Eva Kantůrková, *Informace o Chartě 77* no. 8 (1986), pp. 8–13; also *Listy*, XVII, no. 1 (February 1987), pp. 45–7. Selected essays will be published in English in a forthcoming issue of *Social Research* (New York). In most cases references are made to the respondents in the text.

10. *Cf.* my conclusions, Chapter 3 above, pp. 69–72. See also the poll on the influence of *samizdat* publications and on the extent of independent activities (Chapter 4, pp. 92–7). On the international impact of Charter 77, see Skilling, in V. Prečan, ed., *Ten Years of Charter 77* (Hannover, 1987), pp. 32–51.

11. Alexander Babyonyshev, ed., *On Sakharov* (New York, 1982), p. 246.

12. *RFE Research*, 11, no. 39. pt 2 (26 September 1986), pp. 19–25; Adam Short, *East European Reporter*, 1, no. 4 (Winter 1986), pp. 24–5; M. T. Kaufman, *The New York Times*, 4 January 1987. See also Liehm, 'The New Social Contract', pp. 177–9.

13. See above Chapters 3, 4, and 8. Text of the 1956 anniversary statement in *New York Review of Books*, 15 January 1987; interviews with Köszeg and Haraszti, *East European Reporter*, 2, no. 3. pp. 41–3. See also *Infoch*, no. 11, 1987, pp. 11–13.

14. For such criticism, see in particular Petr Pithart, 'On the Shoulders of Some' (31 December 1978), in Skilling, *Charter 77*, p. 78; his 'Dizi-Rizika' (Dissi-Risks), *O svobodě a moci*, pp. 269–86; also his response

to the *anketa* and on conversations with the author in Prague.

15. For these discussions, see Skilling, *Charter 77*, pp. 51–3, 74–80; for the document, above, Chapter 3.
16. See Rio Preisner, 'O tzv. paralelní kultuře – take v Cechách' (London), no. 1 (1983), pp. 10–44; Benda, 'On the ethics of polemics and the necessary measure of tolerance', *samizdat* (January–February 1984), published abroad in *Paternoster* (Vienna), no. 4 (1983) and no. 5 (1984), pp. 2–17.
17. 'Underground Society 1987', published in *Kultura Niezalezna* (Warsaw) and republished in *Committee in Support of Solidarity, Special Reports*, no. 1 (July 1987), pp. 1–6.
18. Interview with Elemér Hankiss, by Suzanne Klausen, *East European Reporter*, 3, no. 1 (November 1987), pp. 63–7.
19. Sara M. Evans and Harry C. Boyte, *Free Space, The Sources of Democratic Change in America* (New York, 1986), pp. 3–4.
20. William H. Luers notes that *glasnost* is closer in meaning to publicity than to openness. See Luers, 'The U.S. and Eastern Europe', *Foreign Affairs*, 65, no. 5 (Summer 1987), p. 976.
21. Alexezeva, 'Dissent in the 1980s', in Laurie S. Wiseberg, ed., *Human Rights Internet Directory, Eastern Europe and the USSR* (Cambridge, Mass., 1987), pp. 11–15.
22. Charles Gati, 'Gorbachev and Eastern Europe', *Foreign Affairs* (Summer 1987), pp. 158–75.
23. Michnik, 'The Great Counter-Reformer', *Labour Focus on Eastern Europe*, 9, no. 2 (July–October 1987), pp. 22–3.
24. The first issues were published abroad under the same title, *Glasnost*, in full English translation (Centre for Democracy, New York, 1987).
25. Bill Keller, *The New York Times*, 19 October and 18 November, 1987. For details, see *From Below, Independent Peace and Environmental Movements in Eastern Europe & the USSR* (Helsinki Watch, New York, 1987, Chapter 5).
26. *Glasnost*, no. 5, October 1987.
27. *Labour Focus on Eastern Europe*, 9, no. 3 (November 1987–February 1988).
28. *The New York Times*, 27 and 28 December, 1987, 3 and 7 January, 1988.
29. Full report and text of Hejdánek's speech, *Infoch*, no. 12, 1987. See also Charter document no. 52 on the fiftieth anniversary of Masaryk's death, and no. 62 on the seventieth anniversary of Czechoslovak independence (*ibid.*, no. 12 and 13).
30. This was reported briefly in *Rudé právo*, 7 May, 1987, with all the above passages omitted. For the full text, *Listy* (Rome), XVII, no. 4 (August 1987), pp. 5–8.
31. Szelényi, in Rudolf L. Tökés, ed., *Opposition in Eastern Europe* (London, 1979), pp. 204–5.
32. Petr Pithart, response to *anketa*, 1987.
33. Richard Day, 'The Rule of Law, Democratic Control, and Scientific Stalinism:Thoughts on the Future of Socialism', to be published in R. Day and J. Masciulle, ed, *Democratic Theory and Technological Society*.

Index